Food, Animals, and the Environment

Food, Animals, and the Environment: An Ethical Approach examines some of the main impacts that agriculture has on humans, nonhumans, and the environment, as well as some of the main questions that these impacts raise for the ethics of food production, consumption, and activism. Agriculture is having a lasting effect on this planet. Some forms of agriculture are especially harmful. For example, industrial animal agriculture kills 100+ billion animals per year; consumes vast amounts of land, water, and energy; and produces vast amounts of waste, pollution, and greenhouse gas emissions. Other forms, such as local, organic, and plant-based food, have many benefits, but they also have costs, especially at scale. These impacts raise difficult ethical questions. What do we owe animals, plants, species, and ecosystems? What do we owe people in other nations and future generations? What are the ethics of risk, uncertainty, and collective harm? What is the meaning and value of natural food in a world reshaped by human activity? What are the ethics of supporting harmful industries when less harmful alternatives are available? What are the ethics of resisting harmful industries through activism, advocacy, and philanthropy? The discussion ranges over cutting-edge topics such as effective altruism, abolition and regulation, revolution and reform, individual and structural change, single-issue and multi-issue activism, and legal and illegal activism. This unique and accessible text is ideal for teachers, students, and anyone else interested in serious examination of one of the most complex and important moral problems of our time.

Christopher Schlottmann is Clinical Professor, Associate Chair, and Director of Undergraduate Studies in the Department of Environmental Studies at New York University, USA. He works on the ethical and social dimensions of environmental change.

Jeff Sebo is Clinical Assistant Professor of Environmental Studies, Affiliated Professor of Bioethics, Medical Ethics, and Philosophy, and Director of the Animal Studies M.A. Program at New York University, USA. He works primarily in bioethics, animal ethics, and environmental ethics.

Food, Animals, and the Environment
An Ethical Approach

Christopher Schlottmann and
Jeff Sebo

LONDON AND NEW YORK

First published 2019
by Routledge
2 Park Square, Milton Park, Abingdon, Oxon OX14 4RN

and by Routledge
711 Third Avenue, New York, NY 10017

Routledge is an imprint of the Taylor & Francis Group, an informa business

British Library Cataloguing-in-Publication Data
A catalogue record for this book is available from the British Library

Library of Congress Cataloging-in-Publication Data
A catalog record has been requested for this book

ISBN: 978-1-138-80111-0 (hbk)
ISBN: 978-1-138-80112-7 (pbk)
ISBN: 978-1-315-75511-3 (ebk)

Typeset in Goudy
by Swales & Willis Ltd, Exeter, Devon, UK

Contents

1 Introduction

1.1 What this book is about

At least since Upton Sinclair published *The Jungle* in 1906, people have been raising awareness about the public health and environmental risks of food production. Ruth Harrison's *Animal Machines* in 1964 and Peter Singer's *Animal Liberation* in 1975 built on this foundation by drawing attention to the animal welfare impacts as well.[1] At that point many people still saw animal and environmental issues as separate, in part because the animal and environmental movements were still focusing on relatively separate issues. However, since then, people have started to see animal and environmental issues as connected, in part because these movements have started to develop a shared interest in animal agriculture. In 2006 the Food and Agriculture Organization of the United Nations (UN FAO) published *Livestock's Long Shadow*, the first major report on the environmental impacts of animal agriculture. Over the past decade, the idea that animal agriculture harms animals and the environment alike has received increasingly widespread acceptance.

This book is set at the intersection of food, animals, and the environment. We will examine the impacts of industrial animal agriculture—as well as of alternative food systems—for humans, nonhumans, and the environment. We will also examine the questions that these impacts raise for the ethics of food production, consumption, activism, and advocacy.

There are many reasons why we are focusing on the intersection of food, animals, and the environment. These include but are not limited to the following:

→ The number of terrestrial animals used for animal agriculture is staggering: There are about 1.5 billion cows, hundreds of millions of sheep and goats, hundreds of millions of pigs, and 50–60 billion individuals of other species, most of whom are poultry. The annual number of aquatic animals used for food is at least in the hundreds of billions, and probably in the trillions. All in all, we use and kill an estimated 100+ billion domesticated animals annually for food.[2]

→ Animal agriculture contributes to local waste and pollution. Animals on industrial farms produce too much waste to be disposed of properly, and deregulation makes improper disposal easy. As a result, animal waste seeps into the land and water of surrounding communities. We selected the cover art for this book in part because it captures the scale and local impact of animal agriculture—in this case a waste lagoon on a feedlot.

➔ About 70% of the world's freshwater[3] and 80–90%[4] of the U.S.'s consumed water use is for agriculture, especially for farmed animals,[5] making it a much larger user of water than industry and end-consumers (those who use water at home) combined.

➔ Of land used for agriculture, 75% is used for raising animals.[6] Because we produce so much food to feed to humans and nonhumans, it requires over a third of all land.[7] (By contrast, urban settlements make up only about 4% of global arable land.[8]) On a global scale, about 60% of crops are used to feed humans directly; one third is fed to nonhumans.[9] Grazing land accounts for a large percentage of global land use,[10] and the clearing of land for grazing emits significant CO_2 and—when land is cleared by burning—black soot and other particulate matter pollution. Because so much land is used for animal agriculture and feed production, "plant-based agriculture grows 512% more pounds of food than animal-based agriculture on 69% of the mass of land that animal-based agriculture uses."[11]

➔ Farmed animals who eat feed (accounting for the vast majority of farmed animals in industrialized countries) convert these calories inefficiently. It takes 4,000 calories of fossil fuel to eventually produce 1,000 calories of protein in a chicken raised for human consumption.[12] In part due to conversion, "ruminant meat has impacts ~100 times those of plant-based foods."[13]

➔ A large percentage of global arable land is also used to grow crops that are used for feed. This further contributes to CO_2 and nitrous oxide emissions.

➔ Animal agriculture is responsible for an estimated 14.5% of all anthropogenic greenhouse gas (GHG) emissions on a 100-year time scale. This percentage increases substantially on a 20-year time scale, since methane (CH_4) and nitrous oxide (N_2O) proportionately trap much more heat on a 20-year time scale.[14]

   ◆ Animal agriculture is responsible for an estimated 9% of global carbon emissions.[15]

   ◆ When ruminant animals (mammals who can ferment plants in specialized digestive systems) digest, enteric fermentation occurs—resulting in methane emissions. All in all, animal agriculture is responsible for an estimated 37% of all anthropogenic (human-induced) methane, and methane traps heat an estimated 23 times as effectively as carbon dioxide over 100 years.[16]

   ◆ The management of manure emits nitrous oxide and methane. All in all, animal agriculture is responsible for an estimated 65% of all anthropogenic nitrous oxide, and nitrous oxide traps heat an estimated 296 times as effectively as carbon dioxide over 100 years.[17]

→ If we want to increase our chances of meeting the greenhouse gas targets from Paris' COP21 conference, animal product consumption needs to be considered, as just the projected increase in animal product consumption could account for much or all of the "carbon budget" keeping the increase in global temperature to 2 degrees Celsius (about 3.6 degrees Fahrenheit).[18]

Animals are also central to the framing of this book because the impact that modern agriculture has on them is morally important in and of itself. Most of the 100+ billion domesticated animals killed annually for food live very short lives relative to how long they could live otherwise. In industrialized settings, they are subject to inhumane conditions that lead to disease, suffering, and eventually slaughter. In non-industrialized settings, they still live short lives, but often have more freedom and space, and lower rates of diseases.

Agriculture also impacts animals not raised for food. When we clear land, we alter or destroy animal habitats. When we create grazing land we threaten animals such as prairie dogs and coyotes.[19] When we harvest wheat with combines we kill mice, and when we spray (organic and synthetic) pesticides on crops we kill insects. Our industrial practice of extracting aquatic animals from their habitats (in addition to farming aquatic animals) captures billions of animals who are not intended to be eaten. These animals are subsequently thrown back into the ocean, often no longer alive. Many industrial fishing practices, such as bottom trawling, destroy habitat for aquatic animals.

Numerous ethical questions arise in light of this situation. How do we feed people while minimizing animal and environmental harms? Should cultural values override animal welfare and environmental impacts? Is it better for animals on free-range farms to live short lives they otherwise would not have lived, or to never have existed in the first place? How much should individuals shoulder these dilemmas, given that large companies and governments control how food is produced? As the human population rises and food production industrializes, these questions are more urgent than ever.

These ethical questions do not have easy answers. All agriculture harms animals and the environment at least to a degree. As we transform nature, we change habitats, convert energy, release pollution, and otherwise alter the environment. In an industrialized world of over 7 billion people, we cannot help but transform nature radically in food production. However, there are more and less harmful ways to transform nature, and determining which food systems are best, and which ways of bringing these food systems about are best, is a necessarily messy, complex, and multifaceted matter.

1.2 How this book is organized

Food, Animals, and the Environment: An Ethical Approach introduces readers to the major concepts and values at the intersection of food and the environment, emphasizing the unique place of animals. We will proceed as follows.

In Chapter 2, we will discuss key concepts related to food, animals, and the environment, including the distinction between—and relationships among—descriptive concepts (concerning facts) and prescriptive concepts (concerning values).

In Chapter 3, we will discuss key concepts related to moral theory. This will include discussion of moral methodology as well as of some of the main moral theories that people accept, and how these theories relate to each other both in theory and in practice.

In Chapter 4, we will discuss key concepts related to moral status. This will include discussion of the moral value of humans, nonhumans, plants, species, and ecosystems. We will also discuss collective responsibility and duties to people in other nations and future generations.

In Chapter 5, we will discuss the empirical dimensions of food, animals, and the environment that apply to all agriculture, including a discussion of the scale of animal, environmental, and human impacts.

In Chapter 6, we will discuss the empirical dimensions of food, animals, and the environment that apply to industrial agriculture, including a brief history and the modern impacts of industrial practices.

In Chapter 7, we will discuss the empirical dimensions of food, animals, and the environment, focusing on alternatives to industrial agriculture, specifically alternative animal agriculture, local food, organic food, and agriculture without animals (including plant-based agriculture, plant-based meat, and cultured meat).

In Chapter 8, we will discuss the implications of these impacts for the ethics of food production. What are the ethics of working in industrial animal agriculture, and what are the ethics of alternatives? Here we will consider free-range animal agriculture, hunting, plant-based agriculture, and plant-based and cultured meat.

In Chapter 9, we will discuss the implications of these impacts for the ethics of food consumption. What are the ethics of supporting harmful industries when other, less harmful options are available? Is ethical consumption futile, and too demanding? We will consider costs and benefits from many perspectives.

In Chapter 10, we will discuss the implications of these impacts for the ethics of legal food activism. Do we have a moral obligation to participate in food activism? Either way, how should food activists think about debates between moderate and radical approaches to food activism, in theory and in practice?

In Chapter 11, we will discuss the implications of these impacts for the ethics of illegal food activism. Are we ever morally permitted (or maybe even required) to break the law? Either way, how should food activists think about tactics such as civil disobedience, property destruction, and violence, in theory and in practice?

Finally, in Chapter 12, we will close with a brief discussion of the ethics of hope, and of future directions for discussions about the ethics of food, animals, and the environment.

1.3 How this book is written

We designed this book to provide readers with both the critical thinking tools and basic concepts and information necessary to analyze the many challenges and values concerning food, animals, and the environment. This includes explaining how to make clear and consistent arguments, how to assess the relationship between facts and values, how to assess the relationship between theory and practice, and how to think rigorously and systematically about the empirical impacts of food systems and the ethical questions that these impacts raise.

Food ethics is a vast area, and we will not be able to give equal attention to everything that merits attention. In the empirical realm, we will not discuss in detail fiber, biomass, forestry, gardening, biofuels, industrial products, flowers, alcohol, non-food animals, bait fishes, pets, or grass. In the ethical realm, we will not discuss in detail the legal and political status of animals and the environment, public policy regarding food production or consumption, or treatment of animals within particular cultures or religions. With that said, at multiple points we will reference these topics and emphasize their importance, as well as their connections with the topics that we do make a central focus.

Even within the topic of food, animals, and the environment, we will not be able to give equal attention to everything that merits attention. For example, the empirical chapters will focus more on the environmental impacts of animal agriculture than on the animal welfare impacts, not because the former impacts are more important, but rather because the former impacts are covered less extensively elsewhere. Similarly, the ethical chapters will focus more on animal ethics than on environmental ethics, not because the former topic is more important, but because animal use in agriculture is central to many of the impacts of agriculture for humans, nonhumans, and the environment alike.

Finally, even with respect to the topics that we do focus on, we do not discuss these topics in as much detail as we might like. Our interest is in showing how a wide range of complex empirical and ethical issues interact with each other, rather than in providing a complete explanation of any particular empirical or ethical issue. We also aim to write clearly and succinctly, so that the overall book can be short enough to be read closely in an academic semester and comprehensive enough so that readers can see the many links across issues. Our hope is that readers will experience this book as an invitation to delve more deeply into the topics we discuss, rather than as the final word on any particular topic.

We took a modular approach to writing this book. Our chapters are all interconnected, so that people who read all of them can benefit from the connections drawn across them. However, our chapters are also intended to be useful as standalone readings. For example, Chapters 2, 3, and 4 can serve as an introduction to moral theory and moral status. Chapters 5, 6, and 7 can serve as an introduction to industrial and non-industrial food systems. Chapters 8 and 9 can serve as an introduction to the ethics of supporting harmful industries. And, Chapters 10 and 11 can serve as an introduction to the ethics of resisting harmful industries. We hope that different people will find different parts of this book useful for different purposes.

Given that our aim is to facilitate thinking and discussion about these topics, we will explore this material from multiple perspectives rather than only our own. With that said, we do not think that complete neutrality is possible or desirable for a book like this. Thus, we will attempt to strike a balance in our discussion here. In particular, with respect to questions about which reasonable people can disagree, we will leave these questions open (e.g., we will treat it as an open question whether use, captivity, and death are intrinsically harmful for animals). But with respect to questions about which reasonable people tend to agree, we will not (e.g., we will not treat it as an open question whether animal agriculture contributes to animal suffering or climate change).

This point extends to our use of terminology. This book draws from many disciplines, some of which use certain kinds of terminology differently. For example, some people use "it" to refer to nonhuman animals, and other people use "he," "she," or "they." Similarly, some people use "livestock" to refer to nonhuman animals raised for food, and other people use "farmed animals." As before, we think that full neutrality is neither possible nor desirable, and so we will not attempt that here. For example, we will for the most part use "they" to refer to individual nonhuman animals, and "farmed animals" to refer to animals raised for food. However, we will do our best to write in accurate and useful terms, and to note terminological disagreements (as well as the deeper normative disagreements that underlie them) where they arise.

More generally, since we want this book to be as accessible as possible, we will use plain language and minimize technical and specialized terms wherever we can. For those interested in more detail, we will provide extensive references that offer opportunities for deeper dives into various subjects. In all cases where we think that technical and specialized terms are useful, we place them in boldface and define them.

Any generalization about a vast, complex topic such as food, animals, and the environment must be qualified. If we refer to environmental statistics, we are using a global scale unless otherwise noted. By virtue of where we teach and research, there is unavoidably a United States bias in many of the examples and case studies we use. However, as we will emphasize repeatedly, this does not diminish the importance of other countries. Indeed, the international and intergenerational impacts of industrial animal agriculture will shape much of our discussion throughout the book.

1.4 Acknowledgments

This book originated in a class on Food, Animals, and the Environment that Chris developed at New York University in 2009, and that Chris and Jeff have since taught at multiple institutions. We started work on this book in spring 2014 and completed work in spring 2018. We divided the labor as follows: Chris is the author of Chapters 2, 5, 6, 7; Jeff is the author of Chapters 3, 4, 8, 9, 10, 11; and Chris and Jeff are co-authors of Chapters 1 and 12. With that said, we developed the structure of the book together and provided each other with detailed feedback on all chapters. The result is, we hope, a book with enough continuity to facilitate sustained examination of these issues, and enough discontinuity to reflect our individual interests and approaches, where appropriate.

We never could have written this book without support from many people in our lives. It would be impossible for us to list them all here, but we do want to list some of them.

For feedback and/or discussion on various aspects of this project, we would like to thank: Carol Adams, Yanoula Athanassakis, Anne Barnhill, Andrew Bell, Brookes Brown, Mark Budolfson, Una Chaudhuri, Eileen Crist, Nicolas Delon, Tyler Doggett, Sue Donaldson, Andy Egan, Bob Fischer, Jonathan Foley, David Frank, Becca Franks, Lauren Gazzola, Dan Honig, Ramona Ilea, Jennifer Jacquet, Colin Jerolmack, David Kanter, Syl Ko, Will Kymlicka, Mia Macdonald, Barry Maguire, Sonali McDermid, James McWilliams, Graham Meriwether, Marion Nestle, Kate Nolfi, Timothy Pachirat, Will Potter, Jacy Reese, Nick Riggle, Martin Rowe, Jay Shooster, Peter Singer, Kim Smith, Kim Stallwood, Nandini Thiyagarajan, Erin Thompson, Tyler Volk, Rich Wallace, Eve Wetlaufer, Kelly Witwicki, David Wolfson, and our students in Food, Animals, and the Environment and other classes.

Additionally, we would like to thank Helen Bell, Khanam Virjee, Leila Walker, Kelly Watkins, and the rest of the team at Routledge/Earthscan, as well as Adam Bell, Rachel Carter, and the rest of the team at Swales & Willis, for their consistent support with this project.

Four people deserve special thanks from both of us. First, thanks to Lori Gruen and Dale Jamieson for teaching us so much of what we know and for supporting us as much as you have. Your friendship and mentorship mean the world to us. Second, thanks to Sofia Davis-Fogel and Tyler John for serving as research assistants, for providing extensive and excellent feedback on the penultimate draft, and for substantially improving the entire book as a result (our only reason for not mentioning particular contributions in endnotes is that it would quickly eat up our word count). You are amazing and we are deeply grateful for you.

Jeff would also like to thank: Maryse Mitchell-Brody and Smoky Sebellody for your love and support (as well as, Maryse, for teaching me so much of what I know about social justice); Sheryl, Eric, and Marc Sebo for the same; my former colleagues at the Department of Bioethics at the National Institutes of Health (especially David DeGrazia) and at the Department of Philosophy at the University of North Carolina at Chapel Hill (especially Matthew Kotzen) for supporting my research; and, finally, my colleagues at Animal Charity Evaluators, the Animals & Society Institute, and Minding Animals International for helping to broaden my understanding of these issues.

Thanks to Faunalytics and the Food and Climate Research Network (FCRN) at the University of Oxford for invaluable research resources.

Thanks to Randall Munroe, xkcd.com, for permission to use his image of the weight of land mammals on page 71.

Cover art courtesy of Mishka Henner and Bruce Silverstein Gallery, New York. The image title is: Mishka Henner, Coronado Feeders, Dalhart, Texas (detail), 2012.

All proceeds from this book will be used to support educational initiatives related to food, animals, and the environment (give or take a few vegan dinners that we might treat ourselves to).

This book is dedicated to the hundreds of billions of individuals impacted annually by animal agriculture, as well as to the increasingly many individuals willing to do something about it.

Notes

1 Upton Sinclair, *The Jungle* (Doubleday, Jabber & Company, 1906).
   Ruth Harrison, *Animal Machines* (Ballantine Books, 1964).
   Peter Singer, *Animal Liberation* (Random House, 1975).
2 We came to this number by calculating the aggregate of land animals slaughtered using the sources below. Some are a few years old, many have ranges, and all are estimates. We agreed upon 70 billion as an approximate total.
   "FLEISCHATLAS: Daten und Fakten über Tiere als Nahrungsmittel," Heinrich Böll Stiftung, 2014, www.boell.de/sites/default/files/fleischatlas2014_vi.pdf#page=19 (~65 billion in 2011).
   "Visualize Data," Livestock Primary, Food and Agriculture Organization of the United Nations, www.fao.org/faostat/en/#data/QL/visualize. (60–75 billion in 2016).
   "Strategic Plan 2013–2017," Compassion in World Farming, www.ciwf.org.uk/media/3640540/ciwf_strategic_plan_20132017.pdf.
   Che Green, "Animal Advocacy by Numbers," Faunalytics, published July 15, 2016, https://faunalytics.org/animal-advocacy-by-numbers/.
   "Worldwide Animal Slaughter Statistics," Faunalytics, published August 12, 2008, https://faunalytics.org/worldwide-animal-slaughter-statistics/ (54 billion in 2004).
3 "Water Withdrawal by Sector, around 2007," Aquastat, Food and Agriculture Organization, last updated September 2014, www.globalagriculture.org/fileadmin/files/weltagrarbericht/AquastatWithdrawal2014.pdf.
   "In 2000, agriculture accounted for 70 percent of water use and 93 percent of water depletion worldwide . . . (Turner et al., 2004)."
   Henning Steinfeld et al., "Livestock's Long Shadow," Food and Agriculture Organization of the United Nations, published 2006, www.europarl.europa.eu/climatechange/doc/FAO%20report%20executive%20summary.pdf. 26.
4 Glenn Schaible and Marcel Aillery, "Overview," U.S. Department of Agriculture Economic Research Service, last updated April 28, 2017, www.ers.usda.gov/topics/farm-practices-management/irrigation-water-use.aspx.
5 David Pimentel and Marcia Pimentel, "Sustainability of Meat-based and Plant-based Diets and the Environment," *American Journal of Clinical Nutrition* 78, no. 3 (September 2003): 660S–663S.
6 Globally, only 62% of crop production (on a mass basis) is allocated to human food, versus 35% to animal feed (which produces human food indirectly, and much less efficiently, as meat and dairy products) and 3% for bioenergy, seed and other industrial products . . . As we face the twin challenges of feeding a growing world while charting a more environmentally sustainable path, the amount of land (and other resources) devoted to animal-based agriculture merits critical evaluation. For example, adding croplands devoted to animal feed (about 350 million hectares) to pasture and grazing lands (3.38 billion hectares), we find the land devoted to raising animals totals 3.73 billion hectares—an astonishing 75% of the world's agricultural land. We further note that meat and dairy production can either add to or subtract from the world's food supply. Grazing systems, especially on pastures unsuitable for other food production,

and mixed crop–livestock systems can add calories and protein to the world and improve economic conditions and food security in many regions. However, using highly productive croplands to produce animal feed, no matter how efficiently, represents a net drain on the world's potential food supply.

Jonathan A. Foley et al., "Solutions for a Cultivated Planet," *Nature* 478 (October 2011): 337–342.

7 David Tilman et al., "Forecasting Agriculturally Driven Global Environmental Change," *Science* 292, no. 5515 (April 2001): 281–284.

8 This surpasses human habitat by many orders of magnitude: Settlement and infrastructure makes up 360 million hectares (MHa) or 1.4 million square miles, whereas agriculture makes up 5,600 MHa, about 20 times more space. Uwe R. Fritsche et al., "Urban Food Systems and Global Sustainable Land Use," Globalands, draft published April 2015, www.iinas.org/tl_files/iinas/downloads/land/IINAS_2015_Urban_Food_Issue_Paper.pdf.

9   Globally, only 62% of crop production (on a mass basis) is allocated to human food, versus 35% to animal feed (which produces human food indirectly, and much less efficiently, as meat and dairy products) and 3% for bioenergy, seed and other industrial products.

Jonathan A. Foley et al., "Solutions for a Cultivated Planet," *Nature* 478, (October 2011): 337–342.

10 Vaclav Smil, *The Earth's Biosphere: Evolution, Dynamics, and Change* (Cambridge: MIT Press, 2003).

11 Jorge Sigler, James Videle, Catherine Perry, and Amanda Gray, "Animal-based Agriculture Vs. Plant-based Agriculture: A Multi-product Data Comparison," The Humane Party, published March 22, 2017, https://humaneherald.files.wordpress.com/2017/12/animal-vs-plant-based-agriculture.pdf.

12 I. Veermäe et al., "Energy Consumption in Animal Production," Estonian University of Life Sciences, http://enpos.weebly.com/uploads/3/6/7/2/3672459/energy_consumption_in_animal_production.pdf. Using Pimentel's calculations.

13 Michael Clark and David Tilman, "Comparative Analysis of Environmental Impacts of Agricultural Production Systems, Agricultural Input Efficiency, and Food Choice," *Environmental Research Letters* 12, no. 6 (June 2017).

14 "Key Facts and Findings," Food and Agriculture Organization of the United Nations, www.fao.org/news/story/en/item/197623/icode/.

15 Christopher Matthews, "Livestock a Major Threat to Environment," FAO Newsroom, published November 29, 2006, www.fao.org/newsroom/en/news/2006/1000448/index.html.

16 P. Forster et al., "Changes in Atmospheric Constituents and in Radiative Forcing," in "Climate Change 2007: The Physical Science Basis," Intergovernmental Panel on Climate Change, published 2007, www.ipcc.ch/pdf/assessment-report/ar4/wg1/ar4-wg1-chapter2.pdf.

17 "Key Facts and Findings," Food and Agriculture Organization of the United Nations, www.fao.org/news/story/en/item/197623/icode/.

18 Bojana Bajželj et al., "Importance of Food-demand Management for Climate Mitigation," *Nature Climate Change* 4 (2014): 924–929.

19 Coyotes are often predatory toward grazing animals, and prairie dog burrows can be dangerous for cows and other large animals who might step in the holes and break their legs or otherwise harm themselves. Gaverick Matheny, "Least Harm: A Defense of Vegetarianism from Steven Davis's Omnivorous Proposal," *Journal of Agricultural and Environmental Ethics* 16, no. 5 (September 2003): 505–511.

2 Facts, values, and naturalness

2.1 Introduction

We hear claims about our food on a daily basis. "Natural food is good for the planet." "Organic food is good for human health." "Free-range meat supports happy animals." Claims like this are common, and stem from concepts as well as values—some of which are unclear or in conflict. How can we advance our understanding of these claims in a domain as complicated as that of food, animals, and the environment? In this chapter we will introduce and explain basic terms, concepts, and arguments used throughout the rest of the book that will help us to answer this question. We will also explain how different types of value are relevant to different aspects of agriculture, raising a host of questions about the relationships between facts and values that we will explore in the following 11 chapters. We will then describe and analyze naturalness, a concept that pervades much thinking and writing in this area. We will conclude by exploring values that arise when discussing food, animals, and the environment. While some empirical content is included in this chapter, we will discuss such content in much more detail in Chapters 5, 6, and 7.

2.2 Description and prescription

When making decisions about food, we might select for attributes we value, and these attributes are often based on claims about facts as well as values. For example, when discussing organic food, we might note that organic apples are grown with minimal synthetic pesticides and fertilizers, and that, as a result, organic apple production involves less reliance on industrial pesticide production. These are **descriptive** claims. They concern facts about characteristics of organic food and the consequences of organic food production. We might also say that people should eat organic food rather than non-organic food, all else equal, since eating food that involves less reliance on industrial pesticide and fertilizer production is better for us, as well as for other humans, nonhumans, and the environment, than eating food that involves more reliance on industrial food production. These are **prescriptive** claims. They concern values that we hold, and the implications of those values for how we ought to behave.

As these examples show, there can be different kinds of facts as well as different kinds of values. For example, the claim that organic apples are grown with minimal synthetic pesticides and fertilizers involves a **definitional fact**: This is a fact about how the term "organic food" is defined. In contrast, the claim that organic apple production involves less reliance on industrial pesticide production involves an **empirical fact**: This is a fact about the consequences of organic food production, given this definition. Likewise, the claim that we ought to eat organic apples because doing so is better for us involves **prudential value**: This is a prescriptive claim about what we ought to do for *our own* sake. In contrast, the claim that we ought to eat organic apples because doing so is better for other humans, nonhumans, and the environment involves **moral value**: This is a prescriptive claim about what we ought to do for the sake of *others*. (We will discuss the nature of morality, as well as the relationship between morality and prudence, at length in this book.)

Many of our judgments about food involve descriptive as well as prescriptive claims, often in ways that are difficult to tease apart. For example, the idea that we ought to eat a locally grown apple might be combining the idea that eating this apple supports the local economy (a descriptive claim) with the idea that supporting the local economy is a good thing (a prescriptive claim). Similarly, the idea that we ought to eat free-range meat might be combining the idea that eating this meat supports a certain kind of animal agriculture (a descriptive claim) and the idea that supporting a certain kind of animal agriculture is a good thing (a prescriptive claim, concerning the ethics of food consumption). In general, then, seemingly simple statements about food can involve a complicated set of interconnected facts and values.

In light of this interconnectedness, no way of describing food production, consumption, activism, and advocacy is fully neutral. For example, if you refer to a nonhuman animal as "it," that makes you more likely to see nonhuman animals in general as objects, and therefore as okay to eat. Whereas if you refer to a nonhuman animal as "he, she, or they," that makes you more likely to see nonhuman animals in general as subjects, and therefore as not okay to eat. We will consider these issues in the context of activism in Chapters 8–11.

Accurate descriptions and justified prescriptions advance our understanding of complex issues and help us make better ethical decisions. A change in landscape might come with both benefits (the creation of habitat for one animal) and harms (the destruction of habitat for another animal). Such changes require an evaluative component in order to be assessed as good or bad. We now turn to discussing this point in connection with the idea of naturalness.

2.3 Naturalness

The concept of **naturalness** is central in popular and scholarly literature on food, animals, and the environment, and it implicitly and explicitly guides many of our ideas in this arena. People use this concept both descriptively—to assert that a product was grown without synthetic chemicals—and prescriptively—to assert that a natural product is preferable to a "conventional" or "artificial" one. It carries powerful meaning for many people, and is commonly used in food marketing, writing, and conversation.

Many characteristics of a crop can be described as natural: its ability to absorb water through its roots, to photosynthesize, and to use nitrogen from the soil, for example. Many characteristics of an animal can be described as natural as well: freedom to engage in species-typical behaviors (e.g., pecking by a chicken), the exclusion of certain synthetic chemicals such as antibiotics from their bodies, or the possession of genes that have not been altered through human-directed breeding. However, the naturalness of a plant or animal does not necessarily correlate with goodness or badness of the plant, the animal, or anyone who consumes them. For example, carbon dioxide, methane, and nitrous oxide are all natural gases, but they act and react in ways that trap heat in the atmosphere, so the presence of significant amounts of them results in climate change. The naturalness of the molecule does not have a bearing on its impact—regardless of whether that impact is positive or negative.

There are two main concerns with the concept of naturalness: its descriptive meaning, and its prescriptive utility. The philosopher John Stuart Mill addressed both of these concerns in his essay "On Nature" in the late 1800s. Mill starts by noting an ambiguity in our use of naturalness as a descriptive concept. On one hand, sometimes we use this concept in a *wide* sense: to refer to anything that occurs in the natural world. On this conception of naturalness, everything that humans do is natural, since humans are naturally occurring in the natural world and therefore everything that they do is, by extension, part of it.[1] On the other hand, sometimes we use this concept in a *narrow* sense: to refer to anything that occurs in the natural world without interaction from human beings. On this conception of naturalness, everything that humans do is unnatural, since everything that humans do is a product of human activity. Thus, for example, in the wide sense of the term, domesticated corn is natural—since it is part of the natural world. Yet in the narrow sense of the term, domesticated corn is unnatural—since it is a product of selective breeding by humans.

Mill also critically evaluates our use of naturalness as a prescriptive concept. Here there are two related issues. The first issue is that in both the wide and narrow sense of naturalness, it is not a particularly useful guide for action. On one hand, if we accept the wide conception of naturalness (according to which it refers to everything in the natural world), we have no reason to try to favor natural things over unnatural things, because everything we do is natural no matter what (because the distinction does not even exist). On the other hand, if we accept the narrow conception of naturalness (according to which it refers to everything in the natural world, absent human interference), we have no models for constructive interaction, because everything we do is unnatural no matter what.

The second issue is that even if we solve this problem, we still face another— we do not have reason to expect that natural things are always good or that unnatural things are always bad. On one hand, many natural things—such as disease, injury, and early death—are bad. On the other hand, many unnatural things—such as medicine, surgery, and sanitation systems—are good. So, if we want to determine whether a particular food system is good or bad, we need to do more than observe that this food system is natural or unnatural. We also need to articulate a moral theory that explains what makes things good or bad, and then evaluate this food system according to that standard. Indeed, philosophers have a name for the type of fallacy that involves deriving an "ought" from the fact that something has a natural property without justification: **the naturalistic fallacy.** Recognizing the distinction between facts and values is essential in order to avoid this fallacy.

In spite of these critiques, the idea that natural things are better than unnatural things—without additional justification—lives on. For example, Michael Pollan writes that the "natural order has its own rules,"[2] implying that these are rules that one should follow. And, since one "rule" of the natural order is that animals eat other animals, one implication of this idea is that humans should eat other animals as well (as this is a kind of predation). This claim derives an *ought* (we should eat animals) from an *is* (the natural order includes eating animals).

Likewise, many people support certain food systems over others on the grounds that they are more natural than others. Local and organic food are often described as "all natural," and free-range farmed animal products are often described as "naturally raised." As we discussed above, these labels are combining a descriptive claim (that local, organic, and free-range food systems cohere more with the "natural order" than other food systems) with a prescriptive claim (that food systems that cohere with the "natural order" are better than food systems that do not).

Some people also place negative value on the loss of naturalness, such as the cutting down of a forest. Indeed, some early environmentalists valued naturalness to such a degree that they claimed that domesticated animals, having lost their wildness, are now value-free artifacts.[3] Similarly, both Prince Charles and the Union of Concerned Scientists opposed genetically engineered crops on the grounds that these crops are not natural.[4] As development of plant-based meat and cultured meat continues, some people oppose these products on similar grounds.

However, unless there is independent justification for them, each and every one of these prescriptive claims is a product of the naturalistic fallacy. On this point historical and contemporary philosophers are in agreement. For example, John Stuart Mill[5] writes that "[e]ither it is right that we should kill because nature kills; torture because nature tortures; ruin and devastate because nature does the like; or we ought not to consider at all what nature does, but what it is good to do."[6] Similarly, Lori Gruen writes, "[t]he moral permissibility of exercising a particular capacity, or engaging in a particular action, is not determined by the evolutionary history or the success of the use of the capacity."[7] After all, if we treated the evolution of a behavior as justification for that behavior, then anything from our evolutionary past—including torture and murder—would automatically be morally permissible. Thus, many philosophers agree that even if we have a clear definition of naturalness, nothing follows ethically from this definition.[8]

Certain views take naturalness as a morally positive feature. One example of such a view is reflected in Pollan's requoting of Sir Albert Howard saying that "mother nature never attempts to farm without livestock."[9] Pollan is describing a non-industrial farm that uses animal manure for fertilizer (thus cycling nutrients in a small area), in addition to other practices that "mimic nature." However, there are some concerns with this view. Insofar as these views make moral claims, they are subject to the same criticisms that Mill, Gruen, and others have made.

First, natural systems are often defined as being untouched by humans, and yet farming is almost by definition disruptive of at least some natural process.[10] When we farm, crops and animals are bred, our landscapes are changed, the plant cover of an area is manipulated (which can change water cycles, cloud cover, surface temperature, and wind patterns), and water, carbon, and nutrient cycles are altered. This is true of both organic and non-organic agriculture, with the very rare exceptions of harvesting non-bred fruits, vegetables, and grains, or hunting wild animals (though these practices often use technology as well, and they remove energy and nutrients from systems).[11] Agriculture is almost universally a process of manipulating nature, and the fact that human intervention is required is reflected in the words we use to describe the practice (cultivate, manage, raise, etc.).

Another concern with using the concept of naturalness to guide ethical decision making is that it might not apply to a modern world defined by global transportation, nearly instant communication, and advanced technology. Author and activist Bill McKibben argues in *The End of Nature*[12] that nonhuman nature has disappeared due to anthropogenic climate change. If we accept this claim, it poses a challenge for guiding our actions and values. If nonhuman nature has already disappeared, what value does the remaining nature have? The answer to this, and the question of how we value nature, is central to the utility of the term naturalness in understanding agriculture. Agricultural models based on naturalness might have served as a guide in a pre-industrial world with fewer than 1 billion humans, but are they able to play this role well in an industrial world with over 7 billion humans (to say nothing of everyone else in the world)? In these cases, the concept of nature is used in a form that fails to integrate human activity fully, leaving us without a complete model of interaction with natural systems.[13]

One version of this debate has played out in the American context, where purportedly untouched nature—"wilderness"—was considered valuable and therefore important to preserve in an untouched state. Nature that was influenced directly by humans—such as agricultural landscapes and urban developments— was considered of less natural value; its preservation was secondary if considered at all. In response to this view, agrarian proponent Wendell Berry calls for an *interactive* model of valuing nature: "The question isn't to use it or not use it, but *how* to use it."[14] Such a proposal shifts a conversation away from a focus on naturalness or preservation to one of interaction with the land. This proposal is complex and often contested, and rests on assumptions, evidence, arguments, and theories about what is valuable. If, for example, nature is *more* valuable when *least* touched by human action, then the resulting environmental ethic might propose forms of agriculture that minimize such interaction.

People who use naturalness as a guide might claim that they do indeed have independent justification for doing so. Natural systems evolved over many millennia to work the way that they do, and when we alter them without fully understanding them, we can often do more harm than good. It is true that using naturalness as a guide might encourage caution, humility, and a respect for the messiness and complexity of nature. If people are using naturalness as a guide for this kind of reason, then they are not necessarily committing the naturalistic fallacy. However, this would be an *indirect* reason to care about naturalness, not a *direct* reason to care about it. The idea here is that we should care about naturalness not because naturalness is valuable in and of itself, but rather because naturalness tracks other values, such as well-being for human or nonhuman animals. Insofar as it can do this, we are justified in caring about it. Insofar as it cannot, we are not.

Human activity has a global effect on natural processes, including nitrogen, water, and carbon cycles. As a result, many scholars believe that we are now living in a new era. Some call this new era the **Anthropocene**, since they see human activity as the dominant influence on the environment. Others call this new era the **Capitalocene**, since they see capitalism as the dominant influence on the environment.[15] Both further complicate our ideas about the meaning and value of naturalness. The Anthropocene collapses the distinction between human-dependent and human-independent systems directly (since humans are responsible for environmental change on this view) and the Capitalocene collapses this distinction indirectly (since humans are responsible for capitalism and capitalism is responsible for environmental change on this view). As the "baseline" against which we compare our actions changes, our evaluation of our actions changes as well. Moreover, note that while the ideas of the Anthropocene and Capitalocene are descriptive (since they posit a new dominant force on the planet), they are sometimes used prescriptively as well (when they are used to argue that such kinds of domination are undesirable).

There are a range of climate change interventions that are considered possible in the Anthropocene or Capitalocene, and these are informed by a variety of descriptive and prescriptive assessments. Our response to the Anthropocene or Capitalocene might be to mitigate further influence on the planet as much as possible, or to actively manage Earth's systems using technology. If human activity is the dominant driver of many formerly independent cycles (such as the carbon, nitrogen, and water cycles), then we might think that we should intentionally manipulate these cycles to achieve positive outcomes, rather than avoiding intervention.

Whether or not we choose to actively manage Earth's systems on a global scale, we are already actively managing many components of those systems— such as genes and ecosystems—on a local scale. Consider several examples. First, **domestication** is the manipulation and selection of genetic material to favor desired traits. In plants, this includes breeding for fruit size, color, flavor, sugar content, resistance to "pests," and drought or salt tolerance, among other features. In farmed animals, it includes breeding for size, growth rate, docility, and tissue composition, among other features. It is important to note that domestication refers to these changes as they occur over the long term in populations, rather than as they occur in the short term in individuals, as with taming or training. Very few land animals who are eaten by humans are not domesticated.

The ability to alter genes has increased dramatically with industrialization, but altering genes is as old as civilization. People bred corn from teosinte—a grass with very little edible material—over thousands of years. Indeed, both plant and animal domestication began about 11,000 years ago. According to marine scientist Carlos Duarte: "[A]n estimated 90% of the species presently cultivated on land had already been domesticated 2000 years ago. The increase in the number of domesticated [terrestrial] plant and animal species [since then] has been [~3%]."[16] Aquatic animals are an exception to this, as much of their domestication has occurred since the beginning of industrialization.[17] In both cases, fewer than 1% of the land and marine plants and animals in existence have been domesticated for agricultural use.[18]

Importantly, the domestication process often makes the plant or animal reliant upon controlled environments and inputs, resulting in their inability to survive in their wild habitat unaided any longer. This creates special kinds of vulnerabilities and dependencies that arguably raise special kinds of moral obligations, such as what kind of existence we owe them.

Similarly, **genetic engineering**—also referred to by the term "genetic modification"—is a process that involves attempting to share particular genes across species, with the aim of passing the desired traits along to the next generation. Commercially available examples include the gene for *Bacillus thuringiensis* (*Bt*), an insecticide, in corn or cotton. These crops express *Bt* in the field without the need to spray insecticides. Other forms of genetic engineering include Enviropig (pigs who are genetically engineered to reduce the amount of phosphorus in their manure), AquAdvantage (a type of salmon who grow more rapidly than normal), and Roundup Ready crops such as soybeans and cotton (which are tolerant to the herbicide glyphosate—brand name Roundup—allowing the crops to be sprayed with this at lower risk to the plant). These solutions would reduce some of the effects of industrial agriculture without requiring us to move to a less industrialized or plant-based agricultural system. (Of course, others argue that this would only serve to legitimize a seriously harmful agricultural system, and that we should instead aim to abolish this system. We discuss these issues at greater length in Chapter 10.)

As domestication and genetic engineering have important implications for species and biodiversity, it is worth introducing these concepts as well. First, the term **species** refers to the classification of groups of organisms, most commonly as members of a group that can reproduce with one another. However, species are not stable categories with essential features. There is variation within species, overlap across species, and change within and across species over time. These changes can result from evolution across long time scales, and from technology across short time scales.

Second, the term **biodiversity** refers to a certain kind of species variety and interaction—the genetic, functional, taxonomic, and ecological variety of life. Agriculture impacts biodiversity by changing environments, which results in the increase or decrease in plant and animal life, increase or decrease in nutrients and resources, and disruption of food chains. Agricultural landscapes can also both create and destroy habitat for wild animals, with many species-specific costs and benefits.

As we will see in Chapter 4, some moral philosophers hold that species and ecosystems have direct moral status, which means that they are morally valuable in and of themselves. Others hold that they have only indirect moral status, meaning that they are morally valuable only to the degree that they benefit particular human or nonhuman animals. We will now consider the relationship between direct and indirect value, as well as other kinds of relationships that values can have, in more detail.

2.4 Assessing multiple values

Many decisions and assessments involve multiple values and considerations. The decision to eat a hamburger involves culture, religion, accessibility, aesthetic preferences, animal ethics, environmental ethics, labor ethics, and more. Some people decide not to eat a hamburger based on animal or environmental ethics, while others might decide to eat it based on taste, culture, or religion. Decisions about food and agriculture almost always involve many values, and these values might or might not be directly or easily comparable, depending on the context and on which moral theory we accept.

2.4.1 Conflicting and converging values

Many values conflict at the intersection of food, animals, and the environment. Eating some animals carries a higher cost for animal welfare but a lower cost for climate change. Eating other animals has the opposite effect. Meanwhile, many people have cultural, religious, or taste preferences for eating farmed animals, or feel that they benefit nutritionally or economically from doing so. Navigating these conflicts in a principled way requires rigorous, systematic, moral inquiry, and is a central theme that we will be discussing in this book.[19]

Some moral philosophers believe that all values are comparable, at least in theory. For example, some moral philosophers think that everything that we care about—culture, religion, accessibility, affordability, and so on—is valuable insofar as, and only insofar as, it contributes to the well-being of human or nonhuman animals. (We will define and discuss well-being in more detail in Chapter 8.) On this view, we can resolve apparent conflicts of value through **cost–benefit analysis**, which adds up all the positive and negative impacts of each course of action and generates a comprehensive assessment about which course of action will do the most good overall. Thus, for example, if eating a hamburger has positive impacts aesthetically, culturally, and religiously, and if it has negative impacts by supporting a food system that harms humans, nonhumans, and the environment, then we can add up all these impacts in order to generate a comprehensive assessment of whether eating the hamburger will do more good or harm overall. In practice, such calculations might be complicated (it can be challenging to compare the pleasure of two different subjective experiences, for example). However, they are possible in theory, and at least in many cases they are possible in practice as well.

Other moral philosophers do not believe that all values are comparable in the same kind of way. For example, some philosophers believe that certain values or rights morally **override** certain other values or rights, which means that any amount of the former morally outweighs any amount of the latter. A typical example is the idea that some rights (such as the right to life, liberty, or property) are absolute—and so we are never morally permitted to violate these rights no matter how much good we can achieve by doing so. Indeed, some people even think that some choice situations are tragic, in that every possible course of action is morally wrong, and so no possible course of action is morally permissible. Other philosophers believe that certain values or rights are **incomparable**, which means that they cannot be compared at all. A typical example of is the idea that some goods, such as liberty, equality, security, and so on, are *directly* valuable. That is, these goods are valuable in and of themselves, not merely because they contribute to other goods such as well-being. On this view, it might not be possible to compare these goods at all. After all, how can you compare the intrinsic value of liberty, equality, or security with the intrinsic value of enjoying an evening with friends?

Needless to say, a major source of disagreement within food ethics is about whether or not certain kinds of values are comparable, and about which values, if any, override others if they are. For example, Michael Pollan argues that the importance of "table fellowship"—accepting what your host offers, out of tradition and respect—overrides the importance of avoiding industrialized animal products.[20] Others argue the reverse—that refusing to support an industry that harms humans, nonhumans, and the environment alike outweighs or overrides the importance of accepting what your host offers.[21] Moreover, as we have seen, no food system is perfect. Every food system alters nature, benefits some individuals, and harms other individuals as a result. Thus, for many people, which food system is preferable is partly a function of which individuals we should prioritize. For example, if you care more about humans than nonhumans, then you might care more about the human impacts of different food systems (e.g., regarding labor, public health, and the environment) than about the nonhuman impacts. In contrast, if you care about humans and nonhumans equally, then you will care about all of these impacts, as well as how they relate to each other. We will explore these and other examples of conflicting values in more detail in Chapters 3–4 and 8–11.

Many values also converge at the intersection of food, animals, and the environment. Indeed, many of the values that people accept arguably converge more than they diverge in this area, even if we discuss divergence more because it raises more challenging ethical questions. For example, as we will see, industrial animal agriculture causes severe and unnecessary harm for humans, nonhumans, plants, species, and ecosystems. As a result, this industry is morally problematic no matter which of these individuals or groups we take to be morally valuable. Similarly, many moral theories imply that we should never harm others unnecessarily, and that we should at least sometimes help others as well. Granted, the details are different from case to case, and these differences matter in practice. But this similarity matters in practice too. As we will see in Chapters 8–11, we can look to these areas of convergence to identify practical moral principles that can be accepted from a variety of moral perspectives.

2.4.2 Direct and indirect values

As we have discussed (and will discuss more in future chapters), moral philosophers disagree about which beings have direct value and which beings have merely indirect value.

When it comes to who has moral status (i.e., which individuals or groups are morally valuable for their own sake), some people think that all and only humans have moral status. Some people think that all and only rational agents (i.e., beings capable of pursuing goals) have moral status. Some people think that all and only sentient beings (i.e., beings capable of consciously experiencing pleasure and pain) have moral status. Some people think that all and only living beings have moral status. Some people think that species and ecosystems have moral status. And some people accept still more complex views. (We will consider these views more in Chapter 4.) When it comes to which things are good or bad for these individuals and groups, some people think that pleasure and the absence of pain, or desire-satisfaction and the absence of desire-frustration, are the only intrinsically good things. In contrast, other people think that goods such as liberty, equality, and security are intrinsically good as well. (We will consider these views more in Chapter 8.)

However, even if moral philosophers disagree about these issues in theory, they can still agree about many issues in practice. For example, even if you think that all and only humans have direct (or *intrinsic*) value, you might still think that other kinds of beings have indirect (or *extrinsic*) value. After all, humans care about animals and the environment, and we also depend on them in many ways. So even on this very narrow view about moral status, we will still have reason to care about animals and the environment in practice. Similarly, even if you think that pleasure and the absence of pain are the only directly or intrinsically good things for human or nonhuman animals, you might still think that other kinds of goods, such as liberty, equality, and security, are indirectly or extrinsically good for them. After all, we need a certain amount of liberty, equality, and security to stand a reasonable chance of pursuing our interests, thereby securing pleasure or desire-satisfaction for ourselves. So even on this very narrow view about well-being, we will still have reason to care about many different (sometimes conflicting and sometimes converging) goods in practice.

It is important to note that valuing something directly does not necessarily mean valuing it strongly. Similarly, valuing something only indirectly does not necessarily mean valuing it weakly. On most accounts, a glass of water does not have direct value, as it is not capable of experiencing pain or desire-frustration or flourishing in any other way. But the only glass of water available to a dehydrated hiker is of tremendous indirect value, as it contributes to their continued existence. Plants and ecosystems might be valued in this form—indirectly, but very strongly, as their contribution to the well-being of humans or nonhumans is substantial.

Thus, when we explore convergences and divergences across moral theories in future chapters, part of what we will be tracking is where they agree and disagree in theory (taking into account only what they directly value), and part of what we will be tracking is where they agree and disagree in practice (taking into account what they indirectly value as well). When we do this, we will find that while there are many disagreements in theory, and while there are some disagreements in practice, there is much more agreement in practice than in theory. That will once again give us opportunity to find common ground across theoretical disagreement.

2.4.3 Behavior, context, and values

There are behavioral and strategic dimensions to navigating decisions involving multiple values. Calculating every decision is demanding, and requires substantial time and cognitive resources. Adopting a set of rules or habits avoids the demandingness of calculating everyday decisions while allowing one to (hopefully) pursue a morally preferable path.[22] For instance, instead of analyzing each decision, we might think that we should follow a maxim (rule) that prohibits dishonesty—not because honesty is best in literally every case, but rather because a policy of honesty is (relatively) easy to follow and generates good outcomes much more often than not. Similarly, in the domain of food, some people believe that we should follow a maxim that prohibits eating animals—not because eating plants is best in literally every case, but rather because a policy of veganism is (relatively) easy to follow and generates good outcomes more often than not.[23] Other people accept similar views regarding local food and organic food.[24]

The value and disvalue of an activity is often contingent upon the context within which it occurs. In the case of food, animals, and the environment, this could include assessing the personal costs and benefits of producing or consuming particular food products in particular contexts. Some food is considered "subsistence food," meaning that it is either directly consumed in order to survive (with few alternatives) or that the sale of it allows the producer to pass a minimum financial threshold for affording basic necessities. Similarly, aspirational veganism and contextual vegetarianism[25] hold that whether or not one should avoid animal products in a particular situation depends on many factors, including health needs, economic needs, indirect effects of consumption or abstention, and more.[26] Another relevant contextual factor is the set of broader political costs and benefits of particular acts of food production or consumption. To the degree that these acts have social or economic impacts, we should arguably take those impacts into account. And, to the degree that these acts have greater social or economic impacts in some contexts than in others, we should arguably take those contextual factors into account as well. We will discuss these issues in detail in Chapters 8 and 9.

As with consideration of direct and indirect values, consideration of behavior, context, and values reveals that moral theories agree in practice more than they do in theory. For example, as we will see, some moral theories hold that there are simple, general, moral principles that apply in all contexts. Other moral theories hold that there are not. However, even if one holds that there is a simple, general, moral principle that applies in all contexts, one might still need to apply this principle differently in different contexts. For example, a principle according to which we should maximize pleasure in the world might have very different implications in cases where avoiding meat has many personal costs and few political benefits and in cases where it has few personal costs and many political benefits.

2.4.4 Real and apparent values

As we discussed above, there is no fully neutral way to talk about moral questions related to food, animals, and the environment. The terminology that we use shapes how people think, feel, and behave regarding different issues. As a result, different people frame the moral questions that we will be discussing in this book in quite different ways, which raises questions about how we can find common ground in spite of such different framings.

These questions are especially pressing for food activists, because food activists are advocating for a better food system in a social, political, and economic context that frames our current food systems as standard and good, and that frames alternative food systems as deviant and bad. Likewise, they are advocating for a better food system in a social, political, and economic context that frames adherence to the status quo as natural and good, and that frames deviation from the status quo as unnatural and bad. This places food activists at a disadvantage, since people will often see them as making a different and more radical claim than they actually are—or as making this claim in a different and more confrontational manner than they actually are.

To make matters even more complex, many other sources of bias can distort conversations about food ethics as well. For example, we are all susceptible to status quo bias (which leads us to favor current systems over different systems), sunk cost reasoning (which leads us to favor practices that we have already committed resources to), confirmation bias (which leads us to interpret new information in ways that confirm our existing beliefs) as well as to the tendency to be epistemically unjust (which leads us to see individuals with privilege as having more epistemic authority than individuals without privilege, all else being held equal).[27]

As we will see, this distinction between real and apparent values often places food activists in a double bind. When society frames activists as more radical or confrontational than they actually are, they can either continue to take this stigmatized approach—in which case they will alienate many people—or they can take a different, less stigmatized approach—in which case they will be allowing the opposition to set the terms of debate. There is rarely an easy solution to this problem, though understanding the nature of the problem is a good first step. (We will discuss real and apparent values, and resulting double binds, in more detail in Chapters 10 and 11.)

2.4.5 Understanding the nature of the problem

As Garrett Hardin writes in his canonical paper on the "tragedy of the commons," there can be technical and non-technical solutions to certain problems.[28] **Technical solutions** are ones that require a change in scientific knowledge, management practice, or technique to resolve. Examples include genetically engineering crops to increase yield to lessen famine, or developing plant-based or cultured animal products to reduce the impacts of industrial animal agriculture. **Non-technical solutions**, on the other hand, require a change in values or social ordering. Hardin writes that "[t]he population problem has no technical solution; it requires a fundamental extension in morality."[29] By this he means that solving the population problem requires a shift in values. Examples of non-technical solutions include reducing meat consumption for ethical reasons and engaging in civic activities to prevent environmental harms (e.g., organizing a protest). In cases where both technical and non-technical solutions are possible, they both have costs and benefits. On one hand, technical approaches are often less demanding for individual members of society, as they do not require a change in lifestyle or the slow, challenging process of moral introspection. On the other hand, technical solutions are not always sufficient to bring about needed change, might not have lasting effects, and do not always address the root cause of the problem (in this case, our broken relationships with nonhuman animals and the environment).

The tragedy of the commons is what is considered a **collective action problem**. Collective action problems arise when many people act in a way that does more good than harm for each of them individually, but that does more harm than good for all of them collectively. Hardin's example involves individual herders grazing their animals in a common field. Each individual herder has a personal incentive to add another animal to the field, as that means they will have an additional animal to sell. However, if *every* individual herder acts in self-interest by adding one additional animal, the common field gets overgrazed and is therefore ruined for everyone—resulting in a "tragedy of the commons." Of course, this example assumes that each herder is reasoning only prudentially and seeking only to maximize their own profit and/or well-being, rather than reasoning at least partly morally and seeking at least partly to maximize profit and/or well-being for all. As a result, Hardin proposes a solution in which everyone agrees to create a coercive power that can constrain their herding practices, a system he refers to as "mutual coercion mutually agreed upon."[30] If everyone agrees to cap the number of animals grazing, then no individual herder suffers disproportionately. The common field is preserved, creating a long-term benefit for all.

Some collective action problems are unsurprising, given their scale. Climate change is perhaps the best example of a collective action problem at a very large (global and intergenerational) scale. Few if any individuals contribute significantly to climate change on their own, and therefore few if any individuals have a narrowly self-interested reason to stop contributing to it. Yet if everyone keeps contributing to climate change, it will get much worse, and everyone will suffer as a result.[31]

Animal and environmental ethicists wrestle with cases like global climate change, where a collective problem caused by many individuals contributes incrementally to an aggregate problem that has moral consequences. As we will see, while some of the morally important consequences of individual food choices are direct and measurable—such as inflicting suffering, confinement, and premature death on 100+ billion domesticated animals annually—others are not. Rather, they contribute in an indirect, long-term, and diffuse manner to problems such as scarce natural resource consumption, waste and pollution, and greenhouse gas emissions.

2.4.6 Positive values and agriculture

Throughout this book we will be describing many animal and environmental impacts that are often harmful to humans, nonhumans, and the environment alike. However, agricultural practices influence all of these communities in different and complex ways, including by creating positive values. The first and most obvious benefit from agriculture is providing food for humans. Some other benefits include:

→ Farmlands sometimes create habitat for nonhuman animals.
→ Some studies suggest that mixed grazing systems increase biodiversity.[32]
→ Certain forms of coffee plantations that provide sufficient shade can become habitat for birds.
→ Natural perennial grasses have the potential to sequester (fix) significant amounts of carbon[33] (as does properly managed soil[34]—both are promising areas for climate mitigation research).
→ "Carbon farming," in the form of grasslands restoration or regenerative agriculture, could occur on some of the hundreds of millions of hectares of abandoned farmland, avoiding the clearing of new land.[35]
→ Restorative and regenerative agriculture aims to renew and add environmental services to a landscape by using cover crops, minimizing tillage and synthetic chemicals, and rotation crops (such techniques are proven to increase carbon stores, but are also often labor intensive).[36]

2.5 Conclusion

In this chapter, we discussed basic concepts and schools of thought for understanding food, animals, and the environment, including the concept of naturalness and how this idea affects descriptions and moral claims, and how values interact in social contexts. On the whole, the concepts and arguments overviewed in this chapter will help to advance our understanding of the empirical and ethical dimensions of agriculture.

In the next chapters, we will discuss fundamental theories on ethics that advance our understanding of what is valuable, and what actions might be more or less ethically warranted.

Notes

1 If we take the example of organic corn and genetically engineered corn, we can say that both are the result of a corn plant absorbing nutrients, photosynthesizing, and replicating plant cells—all characteristics that one can think of as being either natural or unnatural. But in Mill's words, "the same laws of vegetation" grow domesticated corn and wild roses. So depending on the characteristic we emphasize, genetically engineered corn and robots could be considered equally natural (in that they follow the natural laws of gravity, for example) and organic apples could be considered unnatural (we have intervened to keep insects from eating them, which could be considered unnatural intervention). "The corn which men raise for food grows and produces its grain by the same laws of vegetation by which the wild rose and the mountain strawberry bring forth their flowers and fruit."

   John Stuart Mill, "On Nature" in *The Utility of Religion and Theism* (London: Watts & Co., 1904): 9.

2 Michael Pollan, *The Omnivore's Dilemma* (New York: Penguin, 2006): 328.

3   One of the more distressing aspects of the animal liberation movement is the failure of almost all its exponents to draw a sharp distinction between the very different plights (and rights) of wild and domestic animals. But this distinction lies at the very center of the land ethic. Domestic animals are creations of man. They are living artifacts, but artifacts nevertheless, and they constitute yet another mode of extension of the works of man into the ecosystem. From the perspective of the land ethic a herd of cattle, sheep, or pigs is as much or more a ruinous blight on the landscape as a fleet of four-wheel drive off-road vehicles. There is thus something profoundly incoherent (and insensitive as well) in the complaint of some animal liberationists that the 'natural behavior' of chickens and bobby calves is cruelly frustrated on factory farms. It would make almost as much sense to speak of the natural behavior of tables and chairs.

   J. Baird Callicott, "Animal Liberation: A Triangular Affair," *Environmental Ethics* 2, no. 4 (1980): 311–338.

4 "I have always believed that agriculture should proceed in harmony with nature, recognizing there are natural limits to our ambition."

   Prince Charles, quoted in Mark Sagoff, "Nature and Human Nature," in Harold W. Baillie and Timothy K. Casey, eds., *Is Human Nature Obsolete? Genetics, Bioengineering, and the Future of the Human Condition* (Cambridge: MIT Press, 2005): 88.

   "This unprecedented ability to shuffle genes means that genetic engineers can concoct gene combinations that would never be found in nature."

   "What Is Genetic Engineering?" Union of Concerned Scientists, https://web.archive.org/web/20150205093201/http://www.ucsusa.org/food_and_agriculture/our-failing-food-system/genetic-engineering/what-is-genetic-engineering.html from June 3, 2016.

5   Conformity to nature has no connection whatever with right and wrong. The idea can never be fitly introduced into ethical discussions at all, except, occasionally

and partially, into the question of degrees of culpability . . . There is hardly a bad action ever perpetrated which is not perfectly natural, and the motives to which are not perfectly natural feelings. In the eye of reason, therefore, this is no excuse, but it is quite 'natural' that it should be so in the eyes of the multitude; because the meaning of the expression is, that they have a fellow feeling with the offender.

John Stuart Mill, "On Nature" in *The Utility of Religion and Theism* (Watts & Co., 1904): 31–32.

6 John Stuart Mill, "On Nature" in *The Utility of Religion and Theism* (Watts & Co., 1904): 18.

7 Lori Gruen, *Ethics and Animals: An Introduction* (Boston, MA: Cambridge University Press, 2011): 52.

8   [E]ven if we can agree that some things are natural and some are not, what follows from this? The answer is: nothing. There is no factual reason to suppose that what is natural is good (or at least better) and what is unnatural is bad (or at least worse).

Julian Baggini, *Making Sense: Philosophy behind the Headlines* (Oxford: Oxford University Press, 2004): 181–182.

9 Sir Albert Howard quoted in Michael Pollan, *The Omnivore's Dilemma* (New York: Penguin, 2006): 149.

10 "Farming of any sort interrupts nature."
      James E. McWilliams, *Just Food: Where Locavores Get It Wrong and How We Can Truly Eat Responsibly* (New York: Hachette Book Group, 2010): 166.

11 Others, like William Cronon, have noted that our concepts of nature in the U.S. often lack human interaction. If we envision a pristine national park unaltered by human activity, we might ignore the role that human habitants have played in shaping the part.

      Think of the beautiful Mediterranean Sea coast with blue-green water and grassy hillsides grazed by goats tended by herders. As beautiful as that may be, it is anything but "natural" . . . By 2,000 years ago, that part of the world had been heavily transformed by humans, and nature was no longer in control of the landscape. Nor was it in control of the atmospheric CO_2 trend. Humans had taken control.

William F. Ruddiman, *Plows, Plagues and Petroleum: How Humans Took Control of Climate* (Princeton, NJ: Princeton University Press, 2005): 94.
      William Cronon, *Changes in the Land* (New York: Hill & Wang, 1983).

12 Bill McKibben, *The End of Nature* (Anchor Books, 1989).

13 Others, like environmental historian William Cronon, have noted that our concepts of nature in the U.S. often lack human interaction. If we envision a pristine national park unaltered by human activity, we might ignore the role that human habitants have played in shaping the part. For example, see quotation by William Ruddiman in note 11 above.

14 Wendell Berry, *The Unsettling of America: Culture and Agriculture* (Berkeley: Counterpoint Press, 2015): 29.

15 For more on the Anthropocene and Capitalocene, see:
      Jason Moore, ed., *Anthropocene or Capitalocene? Nature, History, and the Crisis of Capitalism* (Oakland: PM Press, 2016).

16 Carlos M. Duarte, Nùria Marbá, and Marianne Holmer, "Rapid Domestication of Marine Species," *Science* 316, no. 5823 (2007): 382.

17 "About 430 (97%) of the aquatic species presently in culture have been domesticated since the start of the 20th century, and an estimated 106 aquatic species have been domesticated over the past decade."

Carlos M. Duarte, Nùria Marbá, and Marianne Holmer, "Rapid Domestication of Marine Species," *Science* 316, no. 5823 (2007): 382.

18 "0.08% of known land plant species and 0.0002% of known land animal species have been domesticated (7), compared with 0.17% of known marine plant species and 0.13% of known marine animal species."

Brian Groombridge and Martin Jenkins, eds., *World Atlas of Biodiversity: Earth's Living Resources in the 21st Century* (Oakland: University of California Press, 2002) cited in Carlos M. Duarte, Nùria Marbá, and Marianne Holmer, "Rapid Domestication of Marine Species," *Science* 316, no. 5823 (2007): 382.

19 Elin Röös, Lena Ekelund, and Heléne Tjärnemo, "Communicating the Environmental Impact of Meat Production: Challenges in the Development of a Swedish Meat Guide," *Journal of Cleaner Production* 73 (June 2014): 154–164.

20 Michael Pollan, *The Omnivore's Dilemma* (New York: Penguin, 2006): 314.

21 Jonathan Safran Foer, *Eating Animals* (New York: Hachette Book Group, 2010): 55–56.

22 Richard Mervyn Hare, *Moral Thinking: Its Levels, Method, and Point* (Oxford: Oxford University Press, 1981).

23 Peter Singer, *Animal Liberation* (New York: Random House, 1975).

24 Wendell Berry, *The Unsettling of America: Culture and Agriculture* (Berkeley: Counterpoint Press, 2015).

25 This term was first coined by Deane Curtin and was then popularized by Lori Gruen.

Deane Curtin, "Toward an Ecological Ethic of Care," *Hypathia* 6, no. 1 (Spring 1991): 68–71.

Lori Gruen, *Ethics and Animals* (New York: Cambridge University Press, 2012).

26 Katarina Bälter et al., "Is a Diet Low in Greenhouse Gas Emissions a Nutritious Diet?—Analyses of Self-selected Diets in the LifeGene Study," *Archives of Public Health* 75, no. 17 (April 2017).

27 For more on epistemic injustice, see:

Miranda Fricker, *Epistemic Injustice: Power and the Ethics of Knowing* (Oxford: Clarendon Press, 2007).

Kristie Dotson, "Tracking Epistemic Violence, Tracking Practices of Silencing," *Hypatia* 26, no. 2 (2011): 236–257.

28 Garrett Hardin, "The Tragedy of the Commons," *Science* 162, no. 3859 (December 1968): 1243–1248.

29 Garrett Hardin, "The Tragedy of the Commons," *Science* 162, no. 3859 (December 1968): 1243–1248.

30 Garrett Hardin, "The Tragedy of the Commons," *Science* 162, no. 3859 (December 1968): 1247.

31 For a detailed analysis of why global climate change is an especially challenging problem to conceive of and respond to, see:

Stephen M. Gardiner, *A Perfect Moral Storm: The Ethical Tragedy of Climate Change* (Oxford: Oxford University Press, 2011).

32 Mariecia D. Fraser, Jon M. Moorby, James E. Vale, and Darren M. Evans, "Mixed Grazing Systems Benefit Both Upland Biodiversity and Livestock Production," *PLoS One* 9, no. 2 (February 2014), doi: 10.1371/journal.pone.0089054.

33 I. Mathew, H. Shimelis, M. Mutema, and V. Chaplot, "What Crop Type for Atmospheric Carbon Sequestration: Results from a Global Data Analysis," *Agriculture, Ecosystems & Environment* 243 (June 2017): 34–46.

34 K. Paustian et al., "Climate-Smart Soils," *Nature* 532, no. 7597 (April 2016): 49–57.

35 J. Elliott Campbell, David B. Lobell, Robert C. Genova, and Christopher B. Field, "The Global Potential of Bioenergy on Abandoned Agriculture Lands," *Environmental Science & Technology* 42, no. 15 (June 2008): 5791–5794.

36 Beth Gardiner, "A Boon for Soil, and for the Environment," *The New York Times*, May 17, 2016.

3   Moral theory

3.1 Introduction

This chapter will introduce key concepts in moral theory that will be relevant to our discussion of food ethics in this book. We will start by examining the nature of morality. What is the basis of morality, and how can we discuss morality with each other in a productive way? We will then consider some of the main moral theories that people accept, and some of the main arguments for and against these theories.

While these topics are abstract and complex, they are an essential part of any serious discussion about food ethics. The fact that something as concrete, personal, and meaningful as food is a site where so many theoretical issues intersect is part of what makes this topic so challenging—as well as so important to think about rigorously and systematically.

3.2 What is morality?

We argue about morality all the time. We argue about how we should act individually (e.g., in discussions about whether or not euthanasia is morally permissible) as well as about how we should act collectively (e.g., in discussions about whether or not euthanasia should be legal). These conversations take place across families, cultures, nations, and generations. Indeed, two people could come from entirely different parts of the world—with different belief and value systems, different social and political roles, and so on—yet if they met in person (or, more realistically, on Facebook or Twitter), they could easily find themselves in a long debate about, say, whether or not the state can permissibly tax some people to help others. Such is the power that morality has in our lives: It commands our attention and respect, with the result that we often feel compelled to morally justify our behavior, and to ask that others do the same.

It is important to note that, when we have these debates with each other, we are not simply talking about how people happen to act. (After all, if we were, we would not be debating each other at all. Instead each of us would simply be saying, "This is how I do things," and we would then all go our separate ways.) Instead, we are talking about how people *ought* to act, whether or not they currently act that way. Of course, we might think that how people act is *relevant* to how people ought to act. For example, driving on the right side of the road is right if and only if driving on the right side of the road is the norm in this area. But this does not mean that how people act *determines* how people ought to act. For example, torturing innocent children for fun is wrong even if torturing innocent children for fun is the norm in this area.

When we stop and think about this, it might seem puzzling. What determines how people ought to act? Most people spend decades debating morality without ever pausing to ask this question. Moreover, many people who do ask this question find that they disagree with each other about the answer. We will not be able to get to the bottom of this issue here (nor will we need to, for our purposes). However, we will start with a brief discussion of this issue to make a simple point that will be useful in our discussion about food ethics. This point is that even if we disagree about what the basis of morality is, we can still benefit from discussing morality with each other—since we can still use a shared method for asking and answering moral questions together.

With that in mind, consider three different theories about the basis of morality that one might accept.[1] First, **moral realists** think that morality exists independently of our beliefs and values in roughly the same kind of way that many people think that math does. Compare: Many people think that $2 + 2 = 4$ is true regardless of what people happen to believe about math. On this view, even if everybody denied that $2 + 2 = 4$ (or even if nobody existed to think about math in the first place), $2 + 2$ would still equal 4. In the same kind of way, moral realists believe, torturing innocent children for fun is wrong regardless of what people happen to believe about morality. On this view, even if everybody denied that torturing innocent children for fun is wrong (or even if nobody existed to think about morality in the first place), torturing innocent children for fun would still be wrong. For a realist, then, the point of talking about morality is to try to figure out which moral principles are objectively true or false in this sense.[2]

Second, **moral antirealists** think that morality depends essentially on our beliefs and values roughly the same kind of way that many people think that etiquette does. Compare: Many people think that eating with your elbows on the table is rude if and only if our beliefs and values entail that it is. On this view, if nobody held beliefs or values that entail that eating with your elbows on the table is rude, then eating with your elbows on the table would not be rude. In the same kind of way, moral antirealists believe, torturing innocent children for fun is wrong if and only if our beliefs and values entail that it is. On this view, if nobody held beliefs or values that entail that torturing innocent children for fun is wrong, then torturing innocent children for fun would not be wrong. (Fortunately, most if not all of us do hold beliefs and values that entail that torturing innocent children for fun is wrong.) For an antirealist, then, the point of talking about morality is to try to figure out which moral principles best reflect our own most deeply held beliefs and values so that we can live an examined, autonomous, and authentic life.[3]

Third, **divine command theorists** think that morality is related to divine commands; that is, they think that an action is right or wrong if and only if God says so (or, if and only if Gods say so). This view has been popular for thousands of years. However, as philosophers as far back as Plato have noted, it invites the following question: Are actions right *because* God *says so*, or does God say actions are right *because they are*?[4] If we take the first option, that means that God is the basis of morality, but it also means that God has no basis for telling us what to do. God simply issues commands that we should follow even though they are not based on anything at all. In contrast, if we take the second option, it means that God does have a basis for telling us what to do, but it also means that God is not the basis of morality. As a result, we still have to ask what the basis for morality is, and we still have the same options as before: realism or antirealism (or, perhaps, the denial of moral truth altogether).[5]

There are multiple varieties of realism, antirealism, and divine command theory, and there are other theories about the basis of morality (including the denial of moral truth altogether—though even on this view, one still needs a basis for deciding what to do, and one must still ask many of the same questions that we will be asking here, even if these questions are not framed in terms of morality). Given such widespread disagreement, we might wonder why people even bother trying to debate moral questions at all. For example, if, say, 40 students are taking a food ethics class, and if everyone in this class has a different perspective not only on what morality requires but also on what the basis of morality is, then what good could it possibly do for them to debate the ethics of food production, consumption, activism, or advocacy? They might think that there would be no shared basis for a conversation, and that they would be better off simply thinking about these issues from their own perspectives.

These concerns are understandable. But the good news is that, even if different people have different views about the basis of morality, most if not all of us still have at least three things in common—and this common ground makes it not only useful but essential that we talk through ethical issues together.

The first thing that we have in common is that we have values that we live by. It is difficult, if not impossible, for a person to never think about how they should act (assuming that they have the ability to do so). Of course, you might not be fully aware of what your values are—you might have only a vague sense of what kinds of principles govern your behavior. But you likely still have values: Every time you make a decision about what to do (rather than simply acting on instinct), you are acting on a principle or set of principles. The task of moral theory is to make these principles explicit, to critically and constructively assess them, and to revise or replace them as necessary until we reach a coherent and stable set of principles that we can endorse after sustained reflection.[6]

The second thing that we have in common is that we have an interest assessing the values that we live by. For example, if you are a moral realist, then you will want to figure out which moral principles are objectively true or false. If you are a moral antirealist, then you will want to figure out which moral principles are subjectively true or false. If you are a divine command theorist, then you will want to figure out which moral principles are divine commands, which will mean using your own best judgment about which scripture is correct and which interpretation of that scripture is correct. (After all, it is unlikely that everything your parents raised you to believe is exactly right, without any revision needed at all.) So most if not all of us have values that we live by as well as an interest in assessing these values critically and constructively.

The third thing that we have in common is that, no matter what we think about the basis of morality, we can benefit from using roughly the same procedure to assess the values that we live by. To see what that procedure is like, consider an analogy with the **scientific method**. Very roughly speaking, we can engage in the scientific method as follows:

1   *Ask a question.* We start by asking a question that we want to answer.
2   *Create a hypothesis.* We then make a guess about what the answer to our question is. In many cases, this means identifying a scientific principle that we think might explain the relevant phenomena, and then using this scientific principle to inform our guesswork.
3   *Test our hypothesis.* We then collect data so that we can test our hypothesis. This means performing experiments, collecting evidence, and then comparing that evidence with our guesses to see if our guesses were correct.
4   *Draw a conclusion.* We then draw a conclusion based on our evidence. If our evidence confirms our hypothesis, we can increase our confidence in our hypothesis. However, if our evidence disconfirms our hypothesis, we should decrease our confidence in our hypothesis (or find a reason to reject our evidence, for example by identifying a flaw in our experiment that might have affected the outcome).

For a simple example of how the scientific method works in practice, suppose that you live in 1604 and want to learn more about planetary motion. You start by asking a question: Why do planets orbit the sun the way they do? You then create a hypothesis: You guess that planets orbit the sun the way they do because every celestial object moves in a circle. You then test your hypothesis: You study the planets through a telescope, and you mark the paths that they take on a map. You then draw a conclusion: To your surprise and dismay, it turns out that the planets move in ellipses, not circles. At first you try to reject the evidence: Maybe was there a smudge on the microscope that distorted your data? But eventually, upon further reflection, you accept the truth: You need to find a different principle of planetary motion, perhaps one involving gravity.[7]

As we saw in Chapter 2, there are many differences between facts and values, and therefore between science (which concerns facts) and morality (which concerns values) that we need to keep in mind. Yet in spite of these differences, we can still use a **moral method** that works in roughly the same way as the scientific method does.[8] Specifically, we can:

1   *Ask a question.* As before, we start by asking a question that we want to answer. The only difference is that instead of asking a question about how things *are*, we ask a question about how things *ought to be*, for example a question about what a person should do in a particular situation.

2   *Create a hypothesis.* As before, we then make a guess about what the answer to our question is. And, as before, this means identifying a principle that we think might explain the relevant phenomena, and then using this moral principle to inform our guesswork. But in this case we are not looking for a principle that tells us how things *are* but, rather, we are looking for a principle that tells us how things *ought to be.*

3   *Test our hypothesis.* As before, we then collect data so that we can test our hypothesis. And, as before, this means performing experiments, collecting evidence, and then comparing that evidence with our guesses to see if our guesses were correct. But in this case we are not performing experiments in the world but, rather, we are performing **thought experiments** in our minds, by considering situations in which people face moral problems, and then thinking about which solutions are intuitively plausible in those cases.

4   *Draw a conclusion.* We then draw a conclusion based on our evidence. As before, if our evidence confirms our hypothesis, we can increase our confidence in our hypothesis. However, if our evidence disconfirms our hypothesis, we should decrease our confidence in our hypothesis (or find a reason to reject our evidence, for example by identifying a cognitive bias in our moral reasoning that might have affected the outcome).

To see how this moral method works in practice, consider one of the most famous thought experiments in moral philosophy, developed by Philippa Foot[9] and expanded by Judith Jarvis Thomson[10] and many others: **the trolley problem**. This thought experiment is designed to help us to clarify our thinking about the ethics of killing and letting die. We might start out with a certain hypothesis about this topic—for example, we might think that killing is always wrong, or that killing is right if it serves the greater good. Either way, we can test these hypotheses by considering the following (somewhat modified) pair of cases.

First, imagine that you are the only person on a runaway train. Everyone else, including the conductor, is unconscious and you have no way to wake them up. The train is speeding down the track and, if it continues on its current path, it will run over five innocent children who are stuck on the track. You have two options. First, you can do nothing and allow the train to kill these children. Second, you can do something: You can push a button that will switch the train onto a separate track, where it will run over only one innocent child. For the sake of simplicity, we can assume that these are your only options. We can also assume that your action will have no consequences beyond the ones that we are considering here. The question is: What should you do? Should you allow five children to die? Or should you kill one child to save five? (Keep in mind that refusing to answer this question amounts to picking the first answer.)

Now consider a different case. You are standing on a bridge, and you see a runaway train on the tracks below. Everyone on the train, including the conductor, is unconscious. The train is speeding down the track and, if it continues on its current path, it will run over five innocent children who are stuck on the track. You have two options. First, you can do nothing and allow the train to kill these children. Second, you can do something: There is an innocent child wearing a very heavy coat standing next to you on the bridge. If you push this child off the bridge, they will fall onto the track below and the train will kill them, grinding to a halt before it reaches the other five. We can once again assume that these are your only options, and that your action will have no consequences beyond the ones that we are considering here. The question is once again: What should you do? Should you allow the five children to die? Or should you kill one child in order to save five? (Keep in mind once again that refusing to answer this question amounts to picking the first answer.)

Some people find that they have the same intuition about both of these cases. For example, some people have the intuition that you should allow five to die in both cases. Other people have the intuition that you should kill one to save five in both cases. If either of these describes you, then that might tell you something about what moral theory you accept (at least for now; as we will see, it takes a lot more than consideration of a couple of cases to justify accepting a moral theory). In particular, if you think that you should allow five to die in both cases, then that suggests that you accept a **deontological** moral theory, according to which we should never harm or kill innocent people against their will, even if doing so would bring about the best consequences. In contrast, if you think that you should kill one to save five in both cases, then that suggests that you accept a **consequentialist** moral theory, according to which we should always try to bring about the best consequences, even if that means sometimes harming or killing innocent people against their will. (We will consider these theories in more detail below.)

However, most people find that they have different, seemingly conflicting intuitions about these cases: That is, they think that you should kill one to save five in the first case but not in the second. If this describes you, then you have at least three options for addressing this apparent conflict. First, you can reject your first intuition. It initially seemed like you should kill one to save five in the first case, but now that you see what that kind of reasoning commits you to in the second case, you think that you should let the five die instead. Second, you can reject your second intuition. It initially seemed like you should let the five die in the second case, but now that you see what that kind of reasoning commits you to in the first case, you think that you should kill one to save five instead.

Third, you can try to identify a *relevant difference* between these cases that justifies drawing different conclusions about them. For example, you might think that killing one as a *side-effect* of saving five (which is what happens in the first case) is permissible, but that killing one as a *means* to saving five (which is what happens in the second case) is impermissible. Or you might think that killing someone *impersonally* (which is what happens in the first case) is permissible, but that killing someone *personally* (which is what happens in the second case) is impermissible.[11] Or you might think that ethics is more *pluralistic, situational* and *structural* than this simple thought experiment suggests: Different features of each case are morally relevant, there is no general fact of the matter about how to assess their relevance, and ethics is not only about resolving conflicts as they arise but also about preventing them from arising in the first place. (We will consider examples of such theories, including virtue theory, care theory, and relational theory, below as well.)

This third option—identifying a relevant difference between these cases that justifies drawing different conclusions about them—might seem tempting. But keep in mind: If you take this option, then you are essentially proposing a new hypothesis (e.g., that the difference between killing someone as a *side-effect* and as a *means* is morally relevant, that the difference between killing someone *impersonally* and *personally* is morally relevant, or that there is no general fact of the matter about what to do in tough cases), and we can test this hypothesis with new thought experiments. If these new thought experiments confirm your hypothesis, great! You can increase your confidence that this hypothesis is correct. If not, you will have to decrease your confidence that this hypothesis is correct, and either search for a new relevant difference between these cases or decide that these cases are relevantly similar after all (and reject one of your intuitions about them accordingly).

Note that while this discussion might seem theoretical, it will have important practical implications throughout this book. For example, if you think that the difference between killing as a side-effect and as a means is morally relevant, then that might imply that killing farmed animals as a means to making animal products is impermissible, but that killing wild animals as a side-effect of making plant products is permissible. Similarly, if you think that the difference between killing impersonally and personally is morally relevant, then that might imply that killing an animal yourself is impermissible, but that paying others to do so for you is permissible. And, if you think that there is no general fact of the matter about what to do in tough cases, then that might imply that there is no need to try to treat like cases alike to begin with.

Since this moral method is easy to misunderstand, we should emphasize two further points about it here. The first is that, in both science and ethics, we cannot draw any hard and fast conclusions on the basis of one, or two, ten, or even 100 experiments. Science and ethics are holistic enterprises. To do them well, we need to ask a very wide range of questions about a very wide range of topics, and to consider how our answers to these questions fit together. We also need to keep in mind all our background knowledge in science and philosophy, so that we can interpret our findings in light of our background knowledge and interpret our background knowledge in light of our findings. This means that there is no shortcut to scientific or moral wisdom: The only path is years of rigorous, systematic, open-minded inquiry.

Second, and relatedly, we should not draw any hard and fast conclusions on the basis of any particular kind of experiment. For example, many scientists believe that if you want to really understand the world, then it helps to consider simple, artificial laboratory research *and* complex, realistic field research. Why? Because each approach has different costs and benefits: The benefit of laboratory research is that we can test a particular variable while holding everything else constant, yet the cost is that this research might not tell us much about what to expect in the real world. Meanwhile, field research has the opposite costs and benefits. The implication is that we should look to both kinds of research for information about how the world works and why: Otherwise, if all we do is laboratory research, our findings will be clear but often irrelevant, and if all we do is field research, our findings will be relevant but often unclear.

Similarly, many ethicists believe that if you really want to understand how to live, then it helps to consider simple, artificial thought experiments such as the trolley problem *and* complex, realistic thought experiments such as historical cases. Why? Because, once again, each approach has different costs and benefits. The benefit of simple, artificial cases is that we can test the moral relevance of a particular variable (e.g., the difference between killing and letting die) while holding everything else constant. Yet the cost is that our moral judgments about artificial cases might not tell us much about what to do in the real world (e.g., about whether or not we should have a policy of killing the few to save the many in everyday life). Meanwhile, complex, realistic thought experiments have the opposite costs and benefits. As before, the implication is that we should look to both kinds of research for information about what theory to accept and why: Otherwise, if all we consider are simple thought experiments, our findings will be clear but often irrelevant, and if all we consider are complex thought experiments, our findings will be relevant but often unclear.[12]

As we indicated above, this method can be a useful tool for assessing the values that we live by no matter what we think the basis for morality is. Granted, different people might have different interpretations of what makes this moral method useful. For example, a moral realist might see this method as revealing the objective moral truth. A moral antirealist might see this method as revealing the subjective moral truth. A divine command theorist might see this method as revealing divine commands (since, again, they need to use their own best judgment to determine which scripture is correct and which interpretation of that scripture is correct). And so on. But what matters for present purposes is that, in spite of these different interpretations, we can still benefit from talking about morality with each other. We all have an ethic, we all have an interest in assessing it, and we can all benefit from using the same method as part of doing so. Moreover, if we engage in this activity together, then we will make much more progress in the long run than if we think about these issues alone, since everyone can bring different experiences, arguments, and ideas to the table.[13]

This moral method might seem daunting. But if we keep at it, then we will slowly but surely make progress in our moral thinking. Of course, this process might take a long time, and we might find that our moral perspective changes a lot along the way. But this can be okay. After all, every previous generation made mistakes. Why should we think that our generation is any different? Using the same kind of method to think morally that we use to think scientifically is an opportunity to correct our mistakes sooner rather than later, so that we can make progress much more quickly than would otherwise be possible.

Although our focus in this book will be on food ethics, many other ethical issues will turn out to be relevant too: issues concerning duties to animals and the environment; duties to other nations and future generations; duties of social justice including anti-racism, anti-sexism, and anti-ableism; and more. We will not be able to fully cover all of these issues in this book, of course, but our hope is that we can at least point to some of the central ethical issues that arise in food ethics, some of the connections that these issues have with other issues, and some of the central ethical tools that we can use in order to think about them all.

3.3 What does morality require?

How should we treat each other? People have offered many different answers to this question. For our purposes it will be useful to canvas four of the most prominent approaches, along with attempts at combining them. The main difference between these approaches is what they choose to focus on. Should we focus on what we do, the consequences of what we do, the character traits that we have, or the caring relationships that we can develop?

Deontologists think that what primarily matters in morality is what we do. Deontologists disagree about which kinds of actions are right and wrong, but the most prominent kind of deontology, and the only kind that we will be considering here, is **Kantianism**. This moral theory, which is based on the work of 18th-century German philosopher Immanuel Kant, requires us to act on reason, and to do so by following two related principles: the universal law principle and the ends principle. (Kant discusses other principles as well, but these are the two that we will focus on here.)[14]

First, according to the **universal law principle**, we should do only what we can will as a universal law. That is, before you perform a certain action in a certain situation, you should ask, "What if everyone did that?" In particular, can you imagine a world in which everyone performed the same action in the same situation? And, are you okay with such a world? If the answer to both questions is yes, then you can proceed with your action. If not, then you need to find a different action to perform instead, since morality requires acting only on principles that we can treat as valid for everyone. Thus, for example, Kant thinks that lying fails the universal law test, since we cannot even *imagine* a world where everyone does this: After all, in a world where everyone lied, nobody would believe anyone, and so nobody would lie (since why would you bother lying if nobody would believe you?). Similarly, Kant thinks that refusing to help anyone fails the universal law test, since even if we can *imagine* a world where everyone does this, few of us would be *okay* with such a world. Instead, most of us prefer a world where people help each other at least sometimes.[15]

Second, and relatedly, according to the **ends principle**, we should always treat others as ends rather than merely as means. What does this mean? Roughly speaking, it means that you have a moral duty to pursue your goals in a way that allows everyone else to do the same, rather than in a way that treats anyone else as a mere object, or tool, or instrument. Kant thinks that this principle places strict constraints on our treatment of each other. For example, he thinks that if you lie, cheat, or steal, then you are treating others merely as means to your ends and therefore you are acting wrongly. Importantly, this is true even if your ends are altruistic. Thus, for instance, suppose that you can save someone from death by lying to someone else. Kant would say that you still have a moral duty not to tell a lie: Even if this action would save a life, you would still be treating someone merely as a means to this end, and therefore your action would still be morally wrong. (A brief terminological note: Kant calls this principle the "humanity formula" since he thinks that we have this duty to human beings. However, as we will discuss in the next chapter, some Kantians now reject this idea, and so we will use the "ends principle" instead.[16])

If you recall our discussion of overriding obligations in the last chapter, Kantians and other deontologists are the kinds of theorists who tend to think about morality in terms of overriding obligations: They tend to think that some kinds of actions, such as killing a person against their will as a means to your ends, are wrong no matter how much good you can do as a result. With that said, some deontologists allow for exceptions, for reasons that we will see later on.

Many people find Kantianism plausible. They like the idea that we should do only what we can will as a universal law, as well as the idea that we should treat others as ends rather than merely as means. However, other people have reservations about these ideas, or at least about the above interpretations of these ideas, since they seem to have implausible implications in some cases.

In particular, if we interpret Kantianism as people traditionally have, then it seems to forbid many actions that we would typically think are permissible or required, such as lying, cheating, or stealing in minor, harmless ways in order to save people from suffering or dying. Yes, lying, cheating, and stealing are wrong in standard situations, but are they really wrong in situations where they clearly do so little harm and so much good? Similarly, if we interpret Kantianism as people traditionally have, then it seems to forbid *every possible action* in certain tough cases. For example, suppose you make a promise to keep someone safe, and then you realize that the only way you can keep this promise is by lying to someone else. In this case Kantianism seems to forbid every possible action (since one possible action involves lying and the other involves promise-breaking). Yet you still need to decide what to do, and you might think that the correct moral theory should be able to provide guidance in this kind of case.

Kantians can respond to these objections in different ways. One option is to accept that Kantianism has these implications and insist that these implications are correct. Sure, it might seem plausible that lying and promise-breaking are sometimes permissible or that there should always be a right thing to do in tough cases. But the point of moral theory is not to vindicate all our current intuitions or satisfy all our current desires. Instead, the point of moral theory is to help us achieve moral wisdom. And while we might vindicate some of our current intuitions or satisfy some of our current desires along the way, we will inevitably have to revise some of our intuitions and frustrate some of our desires too. And for some Kantians, the idea that we should always follow the universal law principle and ends principle, as interpreted above, is more plausible than the idea that lying and promise-breaking are sometimes morally permissible. So if these ideas are in conflict, then some Kantians will insist that we should accept the former idea instead of the latter, no matter how implausible or confounding the implications might be in particular cases.

Another option for responding to these objections is to deny that Kantianism has these implications in the first place. For example, suppose we apply the universal law principle by asking, "What if everyone performed the same exact action in the same exact situation?" If this is the test, then we might decide that the universal law principle permits lying, cheating, or stealing in some cases after all. Why? Because even if we cannot imagine or endorse a world where everyone lies, cheats, or steals whenever they like, we might be able to imagine and endorse a world where everyone, e.g., lies, cheats, or steals when doing so is necessary to prevent suffering or death. Similarly, suppose we apply the ends principle by asking, "Is this action compatible with equal consideration for all?" If this is the test, then we might decide that the ends principle permits harming or killing people in some cases after all. Why? Because even if harming or killing people whenever we like is incompatible with equal consideration for all, harming or killing people when doing so is necessary to prevent an even greater amount of suffering or death might be compatible with equal consideration for all. On this interpretation, Kantianism might end up having characteristically *consequentialist* implications, as we will now explore.[17]

Consequentialists think that what primarily matter in morality are the consequences of what we do. Different consequentialists have different views about which consequences are good and bad (and so about which actions are right or wrong), but the most prominent kind of consequentialism, and the only kind that we will be considering here, is **utilitarianism**. This moral theory, which is based on the work of 18th-century English philosopher Jeremy Bentham, 19th-century English philosopher John Stuart Mill, and 19th-century English philosopher Henry Sidgwick, among others, requires us to maximize utility, usually understood in terms of pleasure and the absence of pain.[18]

Utilitarianism is an impartial and benevolent moral theory. It holds that our moral obligation is to maximize utility for everyone in the world, from now until the end of time. Moreover, our moral obligation is to secure this result by any means necessary. Sure, it might *often* be the case that telling the truth, keeping your promises, not harming or killing anybody, and so on will maximize utility. But if, in a particular case, your only options are to, say, kill one or let five die, then you should kill one, holding everything else fixed. Thus, utilitarians deny that certain kinds of actions, such as torture or murder, are always wrong: Instead, they think that such actions are *usually* wrong (because they *usually* do more harm than good) but not necessarily *always* wrong (because they will not necessarily *always* do more harm than good). Utilitarians also deny that there is a morally relevant difference between causing and allowing harm (e.g., between killing and letting die). Instead, they think that if we are in the position to determine whether someone lives or dies, what matters is that we secure the best outcome for that individual (and for everyone else), not how we do so.

If you recall our discussion of cost–benefit analysis in the last chapter, utilitarians and other consequentialists are the kinds of theorists who tend to think about morality in terms of cost–benefit analysis: At least in theory, they tend to think that we can determine which actions are right by adding up the expected costs and benefits of every possible action, and then selecting the actions with the best expected consequences overall. With that said, they do not always advise reasoning this way in practice, for reasons that we will see later on.

As with Kantianism, many people find utilitarianism plausible. They like the idea that morality requires us to bring about the greatest good for the greatest number. But also as with Kantianism, other people have reservations about this idea, not only because utilitarianism seems to have implausible implications in some cases (e.g., cases where it requires intuitively impermissible actions such as killing one to save five), but also because it seems to involve too much cluelessness and demandingness.

First, some critics worry that utilitarianism involves too much **cluelessness**. In particular, if our moral obligation is to maximize utility in the world, then we can never know for sure if we are acting rightly or wrongly, since the full consequences of our actions are never clear in advance. This raises at least two problems. First, if we actually attempted to think like utilitarians in everyday life, we might never make any decisions at all. Instead we might simply spend all our time wondering what socks to wear. (How can you possibly know whether wearing black, white, or owl socks will maximize utility for everyone from now until the end of time?[19]) Second, even if we manage to make decisions, we can never be sure that our decisions are the right ones. Thus, for example, suppose that two people buy a hamburger. In the first case nothing happens: The person has lunch and nothing else changes in the world. But in the second case a lot happens: This purchase causes the restaurant to order more patties, which causes more animal welfare, public health, and environmental harms in the world. In this case both people did the same thing with the same information, yet one action had good effects overall and the other had bad effects overall. Is it really fair for us to evaluate these people differently?[20]

Second, some critics also worry that utilitarianism involves too much **demandingness**. In particular, if our moral obligation is to maximize utility in the world, then we might have to sacrifice our own projects and relationships for the sake of the greater good. Sure, *if* it happens to be the case that having a fancy dinner tonight will maximize utility, *then* utilitarianism implies that you can (and should) do that. But how likely is that? On the face of it, it seems more likely that selfless activities will maximize utility on any given evening than that selfish activities will. And, of course, this point applies to much more than what you eat for dinner. It also applies to what you study in college, what you do for a living, whether or not you get married, whether or not you have kids (and, if you do, whether or not you have them biologically), and what you do in many other important respects. But is it really fair to hold you to such a high standard? Could it really be the case that everything that you might want to do in life is morally permissible if and only if it maximizes utility for everyone in the world, from now until the end of time? If so, then, needless to say, pretty much everyone will turn out to be acting wrongly pretty much all the time.[21]

Like Kantians, utilitarians can respond to these objections in different ways. One option is to accept that utilitarianism has these implications and insist that these implications are correct. Sure, it might seem plausible that we can know for sure if our actions are right or wrong, or that we can do what makes us happy whether or not doing so promotes the greater good. But remember that the world is a complicated and, for many, terrible place. It contains vast amounts of suffering, we might not always know how to reduce that suffering, and we might not always be able to promote our own happiness and reduce that suffering at the same time (indeed, in many cases promoting our own happiness might *promote* that suffering). So, yes, in a world like this one, morality involves a lot of cluelessness and demandingness. If you feel upset about that, then you should take it up with the world, not with the moral theory that tells you how to deal with the world.[22]

Another option for responding to these objections is to deny that utilitarianism has these implications in the first place. One way to do this is to argue as follows: Sure, morality might involve some cluelessness and demandingness. But it does not involve as much as critics worry, for at least two reasons. First, with respect to cluelessness, even if our moral evaluation of *actions* depends on *actual* consequences, our moral evaluation of *persons* depends on *foreseeable* consequences. So, you can still be a good person even if you unforeseeably cause harm, and vice versa. Second, with respect to demandingness, even if utilitarianism sets a very high standard, part of what we need to do to meet that standard is create a life in which altruism is sustainable for us. So, if the choice is between an unsustainable full-time altruism and a sustainable part-time altruism, utilitarianism might well require us to spend time hanging out with friends after all.[23]

Another way to deny that utilitarianism has these implications is to interpret it differently. In particular, instead of saying that we should perform *actions* that maximize utility (this interpretation is called **act utilitarianism**), we can say that we should follow *rules* that, if followed by everyone, would maximize utility (this interpretation is called **rule utilitarianism**). Some people find rule utilitarianism more plausible than act utilitarianism. For instance, even if a particular *act* of killing would maximize utility, a general *rule* of killing, if followed by everyone, might not. Thus, if our intuition is that killing one to save five is wrong, then we might find rule utilitarianism more plausible all else equal. We might also think that rule utilitarianism results in less cluelessness and demandingness, since rules are easier to evaluate and optimize than actions. On this interpretation, then, utilitarianism might end up having characteristically *deontological* implications.[24]

Third, **virtue theorists** think that what primarily matter in morality are the character traits that we have. For a virtue theorist, the question we should be asking ourselves is: What kinds of character traits would a good person have (these are then called **virtues**), and what kinds of character traits would a bad person have (these are then called **vices**)? Virtue theorists think we should try to condition ourselves to have virtues instead of vices in everyday life.

Aristotle, an early and influential virtue theorist, explains the theory this way. We all understand that things can have purposes, and that these purposes can inform what makes something a good or bad version of its kind. For example, since the purpose of a knife is to cut, a good knife is a knife that cuts well, and a bad knife is a knife that cuts poorly. As a result, a *virtue* for a knife is a feature that helps the knife to achieve its purpose (e.g., sharpness is a virtue for a knife), and a *vice* for a knife is a feature that does the opposite (e.g., dullness is a vice for a knife). Aristotle thinks that the same applies to us. In his view, our purpose is to flourish in life (by rationally pursuing our natural good), and therefore a good human is someone who flourishes in life, and a bad human is someone who does not. As a result, a *virtue* for a human is a character trait that helps us to rationally pursue our natural ends in life (e.g., confidence is a virtue), and a *vice* for a human is a character trait that does the opposite (e.g., rashness and timidity are vices).[25]

As this example suggests, Aristotle thinks of virtue primarily in terms of character, and he thinks that a virtue is the "golden mean" between two vices (e.g., confidence is the mean between rashness and timidity). These points are related. Aristotle thinks of virtue primarily in terms of character because he recognizes that most of our behavior results not from rational deliberation but rather from character and conditioned habit. As a result, if we want to live well, then we should focus not on acting rationally but rather on acting virtuously; that is, discovering and internalizing character traits and habits that will lead us to act well in everyday life. Relatedly, Aristotle thinks that a virtue is the golden mean between two vices because the only way to become virtuous is through experimentation and habituation: to try out different ways of life, discover our limits through trial and error, and then train ourselves to operate within those limits. Thus, for example, the best way to cultivate confidence is by learning about rashness and timidity the hard way, and attempting to navigate between these extremes in everyday situations.[26]

Contemporary virtue theorists preserve many of these ideas, but they update them to reflect contemporary worldviews. Thus, instead of talking about the *purpose* of a human life, a contemporary virtue theorist might talk about the *function* of human life.[27] But the overall idea is the same: A good person is someone who flourishes, a virtue is a trait that contributes to flourishing, and the best way to cultivate virtue is through experimentation and habituation. Some virtue theorists have also updated the list of virtues to reflect the kinds of traits that contribute to flourishing in contemporary societies. Some of these discussions focus on relatively universal virtues such as respect, sympathy, and admiration.[28] Others focus on relatively culturally specific virtues such as awesomeness, downness, and gameness.[29] Either way, the general project is the same as before: to discover and internalize the traits that will allow us to live well, given everything we know about our talents, interests, and other relevant features of our situation.

If you recall our discussion of incomparable values in the last chapter, virtue theorists sometimes but not always hold that values are incomparable in this sense. In particular, if you think that we have no way to compare virtues, then you might think that we have no way to compare the values that flow from different virtues either. (This would make virtue theory a kind of *pluralist* and *situational* moral theory, as we mentioned in our discussion of moral methodology.) However, if you think that we can compare virtues based on their contribution to flourishing, then you might think that we can compare the values that flow from different virtues in the same kind of way.

As we have indicated, a benefit of virtue theory is that it can explain why so many people feel drawn toward multiple ideals, such as deontological and consequentialist ideals. The reason is that a good person will have different virtues, some of which (such as respect) will resemble deontological ideals, some of which (such as sympathy) will resemble consequentialist ideals, and some of which (such as awesomeness) might resemble other ideals entirely. As a result, virtue theory plausibly honors the messiness and complexity of our moral experience better than other, simpler theories. After all, why try to reduce all of morality down to a single, unified ideal when we can instead allow multiple ideals to co-exist?

However, virtue theory has costs as well. One cost is that insofar as virtue theory implies that our purpose or function is to flourish in life, it might seem to permit too much selfishness in life, since, after all, our own flourishing seems to be an egoistic rather than altruistic ideal. Another cost is that insofar as virtue theory is pluralist and situational, it might seem to have trouble telling us what to do in tough cases. For example, in the case where you can kill one to save five, what should you do? A pluralist and situational virtue theory seems to have a hard time answering this question. Seemingly all it can say is that you would be expressing one virtue (sympathy) by saving lives, you would be expressing another virtue (respect) by refusing to kill, and these virtues can have different weights in different situations. However, as we have seen, we might have hoped for more from a moral theory than this: We might have hoped for moral guidance in tough cases, not mere confirmation that these cases are tough.

Like Kantians and utilitarians, virtue theorists can respond to these objections in different ways. One option is to accept that virtue theory has these implications and insist that these implications are correct. Sure, virtue theory might tell us to flourish in life, and sure, it might permit a certain degree of selfishness as a result. But so what? This is a natural and fulfilling way to live. And, sure, we might wish that we always knew what to do in tough cases. But, again, the point of moral theory is not to satisfy our desire for moral clarity. Instead, the point of a moral theory is to reveal the moral truth. And if the moral truth is that we should cultivate multiple virtues, that virtues sometimes conflict, and that nothing general can be said about how to resolve cases of conflict, then that (admittedly frustrating) result is all that we should expect from the correct moral theory.

Another option for responding to these objections is to deny that virtue theory has these implications in the first place. Sure, virtue theory might tell us to flourish in life, but as it happens, we will experience more flourishing in life if we work in service of others than if we do not. And, sure, sometimes different character traits (e.g. respect and sympathy) support performing different actions. However, we can still make a decision about what to do, because some character traits are more important in some situations than others (e.g., respect is more important than sympathy sometimes, and sympathy is more important than respect sometimes). Which character traits are most important in which situations? We might not be able to answer that question in the abstract. Still, if we can each discover this answer for ourselves through practical experience, then virtue theory can offer moral guidance in tough cases after all.

Finally, and relatedly, **care theorists** and **relational theorists** think that what primarily matter in morality are relationships of care that we can develop with others.[30] For a care or relational theorist, the question we should be asking is: How can we take a caring approach to all of our relationships, local as well as global, through personal as well as political action?[31]

Carol Gilligan, Nel Noddings, and others developed feminist care ethics in the 1980s as a corrective to biases that they perceived in moral philosophy at the time, and which many care theorists perceive to this day. In particular, many care theorists, like virtue theorists, believe that moral philosophy has a bias in favor of reason over emotion. It encourages us to use reason to overcome emotion rather than use both to decide what to do, and it distorts our moral thinking as a result. Second, many care theorists believe that moral philosophy has a bias in favor of abstract, general moral analysis framed legally (in terms of duties and rights) over concrete, situational moral analyses framed socially (in terms of relationships of care). As a result, it distorts our moral thinking by ignoring the messy, complex social realities in which most people face moral questions. Finally (though there are other examples too), many care theorists believe that moral philosophy has a bias in favor of some kinds of question, for example about whether or not to kill one to save five, over other kinds of question, for example about how to respond with respect and compassion to what others are going through. As a result, it distorts our moral thinking by leading us to see some issues as more deserving of moral reflection than others.[32]

According to many care theorists, these biases also reinforce sexism and misogyny, in the following sense.[33] As a result of traditional (binary, essentialist, oppressive) views about sex and gender, people associate rationality with masculinity and emotionality with femininity. So, if moral philosophy favors rationality over emotionality, it also favors conventionally masculine voices and perspectives over conventionally feminine voices and perspectives. This is bad theoretically as well as practically, since it limits the content as well as the demographics of moral philosophy. Intersectional theorists and other critical theorists extend this analysis to other oppressions as well, noting that people also tend to associate rationality disproportionately with cisgender people, straight people, white people, adult people, healthy people, non-disabled people, attractive people, wealthy people, educated people, English-speaking people, and more.[34] To the degree that one holds privilege in these ways, society will tend to see one as rational and treat one accordingly. Otherwise it will not—though, as intersectional theorists emphasize, a lot depends on how oppressions interact in particular cases.[35] So, if moral philosophy has a bias in favor of rationality, then it risks reinforcing not only sexism and misogyny but many other linked oppressions as well.

If this analysis is right, what should we do? There are at least two options to consider (options which, we should stress, are not mutually exclusive). The first is to challenge traditional assumptions about morality. Morality involves more than rational analysis of topics such as killing and letting die. It also involves emotional perception of the needs of others. The second option is to challenge traditional assumptions about social identities. The fact that someone happens to hold a particular identity in no way entails that they are more or less rational or emotional than someone else. Plausibly we should combine these options: We should at one and the same time challenge the idea that rationality is more important than emotionality and challenge the idea that a certain narrow group of humans are more rational than everyone else. As part of this, we should promote social justice with respect to these issues, so that a wider range of people can hold positions of power and authority in moral discussions. (We will return to these issues in the context of food activism later on, especially in Chapter 10.)[36]

What does moral theory look like when you pay more attention to emotionality and social contexts? It depends on who you ask (care theory and relational theory are distinct but overlapping moral frameworks), but, in general, you start asking more questions such as: How can I take a caring approach to resolving conflicts as they arise and to preventing conflicts before they arise? How can I honor my relationships with others locally as well as globally, in my personal life as well as in my political life, all at the same time? More concretely, you also start asking questions such as: How should I approach this holiday, in light of the fact that I love my family, yet I also think that some of the traditions that they participate in support violence and oppression? And, how can I work to reform some of these traditions over time, so that we can continue to celebrate our culture while resisting rather than supporting violence and oppression? Attending to all these issues holistically is difficult to do. But it is also, on this kind of approach, necessary to do if we want to live well.

Like virtue theorists, care theorists sometimes but not always hold that values are incomparable. In particular, if you think that we have no way to compare relationships, then you might think that we have no way to compare the values that flow from different relationships. (As with virtue theory, this would make care theory and relational theory a kind of *pluralist* and *situational* moral theory.) However, if you think that we can compare relationships based on their contribution to flourishing (or some other good), then you might think that you can compare the values that flow from different relationships in the same kind of way.

As with virtue theory, one benefit of care and relational theories is that they can explain why so many people feel drawn toward multiple moral ideals. In this case, the reason is that we all have different relationships of care, and each one might centrally involve some moral ideals more than others. But one cost of care and relational theories is that, insofar as they imply that our moral duties come from our emotions or social contexts, they might seem to permit too much partiality in life, since they might seem to support rather than challenge our personal biases. Another cost is that insofar as care and relational theories are pluralist and situational, they might seem to have trouble telling us what to do in tough cases.

For example, in the case where you have to kill one to save five, we might worry that all that a pluralist and situational care or relational theorist can say is that different features of this situation are relevant in different ways. And, as before, we might have hoped for more guidance than this.

As with other theories, care and relational theorists can respond to these objections in different ways. One option is to accept that their theory has these implications and insist that these implications are correct. Of course we have special moral obligations to our friends: We care about them, we have a history with them, and more. Similarly with our parents, children, cats, dogs, fishes, neighbors, colleagues, improv comedy teammates, and everyone else in our lives. Another option is to deny that their theory has these implications. Yes, in some respects we owe more to our friends than to complete strangers. But in other respects we owe more to complete strangers than to our friends. For example, if we benefit from a system of oppression that harms others, then we might have special obligations to these other people in light of our different positions within this system.[37]

As we discussed in the last chapter, when we think about all of these moral theories together, we might find that some of these moral theories *converge* more than they initially appear. For example, as we saw above, if someone interprets Kantianism as requiring us to follow specific rules in specific situations, and if they interpret utilitarianism as requiring us to do the same, then they might see Kantianism and utilitarianism as converging to a degree. Similarly, if someone thinks that one should cultivate different character traits for different relationships, then they might see virtue, care, and relational theory as converging to a degree. Indeed, some philosophers think that most if not all major moral theories will turn out to converge in some or all of these ways: As Derek Parfit puts this idea, people who accept different moral theories are not climbing different mountains but are rather climbing the same mountain from different sides.[38]

Moreover, even if we deny that these theories converge *in principle*, we might still find that some of them converge *in practice*. After all, these theories all have similar implications for what we should do much of the time (we should tell the truth, keep our promises, not kill people, and so on). And even if they disagree about which considerations matter *directly*, they might still agree about which considerations *matter*. For example, a Kantian or utilitarian might hold that we can treat others as ends or maximize utility more effectively if we cultivate different virtues in different relationships. If so, then they would endorse virtue, care, and relational theory in many cases in practice, for indirect reasons. Similarly, a virtue, care, or relational theorist might think that we can be better people in our relationships if we aim to treat others as ends or maximize utility in some cases. If so, then they would endorse Kantianism and utilitarianism in some cases in practice, for indirect reasons.[39]

Does this dissolve all the disagreement among these moral theories? Not necessarily. We might still think that these theories diverge in principle, as well as, in some cases, in practice. We will consider many such cases later on (and, when we do, we will focus on standard interpretations of these theories, according to which they diverge at least somewhat). However, it does show that a good moral theorist will do more than pick one theory and ignore the rest. No matter which theory we pick, our moral thinking will benefit from sustained, open-minded engagement with other theories.

3.4 Conclusion

We will further explore each of these theories throughout the book, seeing what they reveal about food ethics as well as what food ethics reveals about them. As we consider these issues, it will help for us to do two things. First, keep an open mind. This is a challenging subject. We have to consider these theories in many different cases before we can start to get a sense of which we think is most plausible overall. Second, keep in mind that the point of a moral theory is to be correct, not to be convenient for us. For example, yes, cluelessness and demandingness are real issues, and we will consider them in much more detail in later chapters. But ultimately what makes a moral theory succeed or fail is not whether or not it allows us to maintain the privileges that we currently enjoy, but rather whether or not it captures our considered judgments about how we should treat ourselves and each other. This is a difficult task. But if we approach it with patience, humility, and generosity, we can develop a set of beliefs, values, and practices that more fully reflects who we are and who we aspire to be. In our view, this is well worth the effort.

Notes

1 The branch of philosophy that studies the basis of morality is known as metaethics. For more on metaethics, including many references, see: Geoff Sayre-McCord, "Metaethics," *The Stanford Encyclopedia of Philosophy*, Edward N. Zalta ed., https://plato.stanford.edu/entries/metaethics/.

2 For more on moral realism, see:
Stephen Finlay, "Four Faces of Moral Realism," *Philosophy Compass* 2, no. 6 (2007): 820–849.
Geoff Sayre-McCord, "Moral Realism," *The Stanford Encyclopedia of Philosophy*, Edward N. Zalta ed., https://plato.stanford.edu/entries/moral-realism/.

3 For more on moral antirealism, see:
Richard Joyce, "Moral Anti-Realism," *The Stanford Encyclopedia of Philosophy*, Edward N. Zalta ed., https://plato.stanford.edu/entries/moral-anti-realism/.
Sharon Street, "What Is Constructivism in Ethics and Metaethics?" *Philosophy Compass* 5, no. 5 (May 2010): 363–384.

4 Plato, "Euthyphro," in George Maximilian Anthony Grube and John M. Cooper, *Five Dialogues: Euthyphro, Apology, Crito, Meno, Phaedo* (Indianapolis: Hackett Publishing, 1938).

5 For more on divine command theory, see:
Matthew C. Jordan, "Theism, Naturalism, and Meta-Ethics," *Philosophy Compass* 8, no. 4 (March 2013): 373–380.
Mark Murphy, "Theological Voluntarism," *The Stanford Encyclopedia of Philosophy*, Edward N. Zalta ed., https://plato.stanford.edu/entries/voluntarism-theological/.

6 For more on the idea that we all have a moral framework that we live by, see:
Dale Jamieson, *Ethics and the Environment: An Introduction* (New York: Cambridge University Press, 2008): Chapter 2.

7 For philosophical discussion about the scientific method, including about its basis and nature, see:
   Hanne Anderson and Brian Hepburn, "Scientific Method," *The Stanford Encyclopedia of Philosophy*, Edward N. Zalta ed., https://plato.stanford.edu/entries/scientific-method/.

8 The technical term for the moral method that we will be discussing here is "wide reflective equilibrium." For more on wide reflective equilibrium, see:
   Norman Daniels, "Reflective Equilibrium," *The Stanford Encyclopedia of Philosophy*, Edward N. Zalta ed., https://plato.stanford.edu/entries/reflective-equilibrium/.
   Nelson Goodman, *Fact, Fiction, and Forecast* (Boston: Harvard University Press, 1983).
   John Rawls, *A Theory of Justice: Revised Edition* (Boston: Harvard University Press, 2009).
   For more on moral reasoning in general (including other approaches to moral reasoning), see:
   Henry S. Richardson, "Moral Reasoning," *The Stanford Encyclopedia of Philosophy*, Edward N. Zalta ed., https://plato.stanford.edu/entries/reasoning-moral/.

9 Philippa Foot, "The Problem of Abortion and the Doctrine of Double Effect," in *Virtues and Vices and Other Essays in Moral Philosophy* (Oxford: Oxford University Press, 2002).

10 Judith Jarvis Thomson, "Killing, Letting Die, and the Trolley Problem," *The Monist* 59, no. 2 (April 1976): 204–217.

11 For a detailed examination of these and many other issues, see:
   Peter K. Unger, *Living High and Letting Die: Our Illusion of Innocence* (Oxford: Oxford University Press, 1996).
   Fiona Woollard and Frances Howard-Snyder, "Doing vs. Allowing Harm," *The Stanford Encyclopedia of Philosophy*, Edward N. Zalta ed., https://plato.stanford.edu/entries/doing-allowing/.

12 For a critique of simple thought experiments, please see Marti Kheel, "From Heroic to Holistic Ethics: The Ecofeminist Challenge," in Greta Gaard, ed., *Ecofeminism: Women, Animals, Nature* (Philadelphia: Temple University Press, 1993): 243–271.

13 For more on the epistemic and practical need to include many voices in philosophical conversations, see:
   Kristie Dotson, "Tracking Epistemic Violence, Tracking Practices of Silencing," *Hypatia* 26, no. 2 (March 2011): 236–257.
   Miranda Fricker, *Epistemic Injustice: Power and the Ethics of Knowing* (Oxford: Oxford University Press, 2007).
   Alvin Goldman and Thomas Blanchard, "Social Epistemology," *The Stanford Encyclopedia of Philosophy*, Edward N. Zalta ed., https://plato.stanford.edu/entries/epistemology-social/.

14 For more on Kantianism in particular, see:
   Robert Johnson and Adam Cureton, "Kant's Moral Philosophy," *The Stanford Encyclopedia of Philosophy*, Edward N. Zalta ed., https://plato.stanford.edu//entries/kant-moral/.
   Immanuel Kant, *Groundwork of the Metaphysics of Morals*, trans. Jens Timmermann and Mary J. Gregor (New York: Cambridge University Press, 2011).

15 For discussion of all of the principles and cases discussed in this section on Kantianism, see:
   Immanuel Kant, *Groundwork of the Metaphysics of Morals*, trans. Mary J. Gregor (New York: Cambridge University Press, 1998).

16 For an example of a Kantian who rejects the idea that we have this duty to all and only human beings, see:
   Christine Korsgaard, "A Kantian Case for Animal Rights," in Tatjana Višak and Robert Garner, eds., *The Ethics of Killing Animals* (Oxford: Oxford University Press, 2015): 154–177.

17 For more on this kind of interpretation of Kantianism, see:
   Richard Mervyn Hare, *Freedom and Reason* (Oxford: Oxford University Press, 1965).

J.L. Mackie, *Ethics: Inventing Right and Wrong* (New York: Penguin, 1990).
Derek Parfit, *On What Matters Vol. 1* (Oxford: Oxford University Press, 2011).
18 For more on utilitarianism in particular, see:
Jeremy Bentham, *Introduction to the Principles of Morals and Legislation* (Gloucestershire: Clarendon Press, 1907).
John Stuart Mill, *Utilitarianism* (London: Longman, 1901).
Henry Sidgwick, *The Methods of Ethics* (Indianapolis: Hackett Publishing, 1907).
For more on consequentialism in general, see:
Walter Sinnott-Armstrong, "Consequentialism," *The Stanford Encyclopedia of Philosophy*, Edward N. Zalta ed., https://plato.stanford.edu/entries/consequentialism/.
19 Actually this is a bad example, since owl socks clearly maximize utility. But you get the idea.
20 For more on the cluelessness objection, see:
James Lenman, "Consequentialism and Cluelessness," *Philosophy & Public Affairs* 29, no. 4 (January 2005): 342–370. For more on cases where rightness and wrongness seem to depend in part on luck, see:
Thomas Nagel, "Moral Luck," in *Mortal Questions* (New York: Cambridge University Press, 1979): 24–38.
21 For more on the demandingness objection, see:
Samuel Scheffler, *The Rejection of Consequentialism* (Oxford: Oxford University Press, 1982).
22 For more on this kind of response, see:
Shelly Kagan, *The Limits of Morality* (Oxford: Oxford University Press, 1989).
Peter Singer, "Famine, Affluence, and Morality," *Philosophy & Public Affairs* 1, no. 3 (Spring 1972): 229–243.
Peter Unger, *Living High and Letting Die* (New York: Oxford University Press, 1996).
23 For more on this kind of response, see:
Richard Mervyn Hare, *Moral Thinking: Its Method, Levels, and Point* (Gloucestershire: Clarendon Press, 1981).
Peter Railton, "Alienation, Consequentialism, and the Demands of Morality," *Philosophy & Public Affairs* 13, no. 2 (1984): 134–171.
Walter Sinnott-Armstrong, "You Ought to Be Ashamed of Yourself (When You Violate an Imperfect Moral Obligation)," *Philosophical Issues* 15, no. 1 (2005): 193–208.
24 For more on rule utilitarianism, see:
Brad Hooker, *Ideal Code, Real World* (Oxford: Oxford University Press, 2000).
25 For more on Aristotelian virtue theory, see:
Aristotle, *Nichomachean Ethics*, trans. Joe Sachs (Indianapolis: Hackett Publishing, 2011): Book I.
26 For more, see:
Aristotle, *Nichomachean Ethics*, trans. Joe Sachs (Indianapolis: Hackett Publishing, 2011): Book II.
27 For an example of a contemporary naturalist virtue theory, see:
Philippa Foot, *Natural Goodness* (Gloucestershire: Clarendon Press, 2003).
For more on virtue theory in general, see:
Rosalind Hursthouse and Glen Pettigrove, "Virtue Ethics," *The Stanford Encyclopedia of Philosophy*, Edward N. Zalta ed., https://plato.stanford.edu/entries/ethics-virtue/.
28 For example, see:
Elizabeth Anderson, "Animal Rights and the Values of Nonhuman Life," in Cass R. Sunstein and Martha C. Nussbaum, eds., *Animal Rights: Current Debates and New Directions* (Oxford: Oxford University Press, 2005): 277–298.
29 For example, see:
Nick Riggle, *On Being Awesome: A Unified Theory of How Not to Suck* (New York: Penguin, 2017).

30 Thanks to Carol Adams for helpful feedback on our material about care theory throughout this book.
31 For a general survey of care, relational, and contextual theories, see:
    Rosemarie Tong and Nancy Williams, "Feminist Ethics," *The Stanford Encyclopedia of Philosophy*, Edward N. Zalta ed., https://plato.stanford.edu/entries/feminism-ethics/.
    For different examples (all of which emphasize different considerations), see:
    Carol Adams and Lori Gruen, eds., *Ecofeminism: Feminist Intersections with Other Animals and the Earth* (New York: Bloomsbury, 2014).
    Josephine Donovan and Carol Adams, eds., *The Feminist Care Tradition in Animal Ethics* (New York: Columbia University Press, 2007).
    Carol Gilligan, *In a Different Voice* (Boston: Harvard University Press, 1982).
    Lori Gruen, *Entangled Empathy: An Alternative Ethic for our Relationships with Animals* (New York: Lantern Books, 2015).
    Virginia Held, *The Ethics of Care: Personal, Political, and Global* (Oxford: Oxford University Press, 2006).
    Nel Noddings, *Caring: A Relational Approach to Ethics and Moral Education* (Berkeley: University of California Press, 2013).
    Clare Palmer, *Animal Ethics in Context* (New York: Columbia University Press, 2010).
    Sara Ruddick, *Maternal Thinking: Toward a Politics of Peace* (Boston: Beacon Press, 1995).
32 For more on feminist correctives to biases in moral thinking, see:
    Alison M. Jaggar, "Feminist Ethics," in Hugh LaFollette and Ingmar Persson, eds., *The Blackwell Guide to Ethical Theory*, 2nd edn (Hoboken: Blackwell Publishing, 2013): 433–460.
33 For a philosophical account of misogyny, see:
    Kate Manne, *Down Girl: The Logic of Misogyny* (Oxford: Oxford University Press, 2017).
34 For discussion of some of these links across oppressions, see:
    Mel Y. Chen, *Animacies: Biopolitics, Racial Mattering, and Queer Affect* (Durham: Duke University Press, 2012).
    Aph Ko and Syl Ko, *Aphro-ism: Essays on Pop Culture, Feminism, and Black Veganism from Two Sisters* (New York: Lantern Books, 2017).
    Donna-Dale Marcano, "Particularity and Situated Universality: Problems for a Black Feminist Philosophy." *The Black Scholar* 43, no. 4 (November 2015): 139–145.
    Sunaura Taylor, *Beasts of Burden: Animal and Disability Liberation* (New York: The New Press, 2017).
35 For discussion of intersectionality, see:
    Kimberlé Williams Crenshaw, "Demarginalizing the Intersection of Race and Sex: A Black Feminist Critique of Antidiscrimination Doctrine, Feminist Theory and Antiracist Politics," *University of Chicago Legal Forum* 1989: 139–167.
    Kimberlé Williams Crenshaw, "Mapping the Margins: Intersectionality, Identity Politics, and Violence against Women of Color," *Stanford Law Review* 43, no. 6 (1991): 1241–1299.
    Patricia Hill Collins and Sirma Bilge, *Intersectionality* (Hoboken: John Wiley & Sons, 2016).
36 For a good discussion of these issues, see:
    Julia Driver, "Feminist Ethics," in *Ethics: The Fundamentals* (Hoboken: John Wiley & Sons, 2013).
37 For an example of this kind of argument, see:
    Clare Palmer, *Animal Ethics in Context* (New York: Columbia University Press, 2010).
38 Derek Parfit, *On What Matters Vol. 1* (New York: Columbia University Press, 2011).
39 For an example of a consequentialist who embraces this kind of approach, see:
    Dale Jamieson, "When Utilitarians Should Be Virtue Theorists," *Utilitas* 19, no. 2 (June 2007): 160–183.

4 Moral status

4.1 Introduction

In the last chapter we discussed moral methodology and different theories about what our moral duties are. We will now extend this discussion by asking who has moral status—in other words, who we have moral duties *to*. Do we have moral duties to all and only humans? If so, why? If not, why not, and who do we have moral duties to instead? For example, do we have moral duties to animals, plants, species, or ecosystems? We will then consider several further questions that will be relevant for the discussion in this book. For example, how should we decide what to do in cases involving risk and uncertainty? How should we assess questions about individual and collective responsibility, duties to people in other nations, and duties to people in future generations? These questions are abstract and complex. Yet as with the topics discussed in the last chapter, each one of these topics is also an essential part of any serious discussion about food ethics.

4.2 Moral status

As we will see, our food system impacts many different individuals and groups—including humans, nonhumans, species, and ecosystems. For this reason, one question that we need to ask is which of these individuals or groups have **moral status**? That is, to which of these individuals or groups do we have moral duties *for their own sake*?

Many of us think that all humans have moral status. That is, we think that we have moral duties to all humans for their own sake. In contrast, most of us think that objects such as toys do not have moral status. For example, we might have a moral duty to treat your teddy bear well, but this is not because we have moral duties *to your teddy bear*. Instead, it is because we have moral duties *to you*: we should treat your teddy bear well because you care about it.

The question is: What does it take to have moral status? In other words, what marks the difference between you and the teddy bear such that we have moral duties to you but not to your teddy bear? And, do animals, plants, species, and ecosystems have what it takes to merit this kind of moral consideration? Why or why not?

For most of human history, up to and including the present day, people have accepted narrow and exclusionary conceptions of moral status. People have been (and remain) racist, sexist, cissexist, heterosexist, ageist, ableist, classist, and much more. As a corrective to these views, many people have taken to saying that *all humans are equal*. What does this mean? As Peter Singer argues, it does not mean that all humans are *factually* equal; that is, it does not mean that all humans have the same capacities or relationships. For example, we know that different people have different talents and occupy different social and biological categories. Instead, Singer argues, what it means is that all humans are *morally* equal: All humans merit equal consideration independently of how talented they happen to be and independently of which social and biological categories they happen to occupy. To think otherwise is nothing more than unjustified prejudice.[1]

As a result, the idea that all humans are equal—independently of race, gender, disability status, and so on—is a big step in the right direction: Even if we still have a lot of work to do in these areas (as we surely do), the fact that many people now endorse the general ideal of human equality represents real progress. But the question that we then face is: *Why* are all humans equal? One answer that many people are drawn to is that humans are equal *because humans are human*. But even though the idea that *all* humans are equal is good as far as it goes, the idea that *only* humans are equal is problematic. After all, we normally think that membership in a particular social or biological category is not *in and of itself* morally relevant. For example, it would be wrong for us to think that some people have higher moral status than others solely on the basis of race, gender, or disability status. So why should we think that species is any different? Many philosophers think that it is not. Specifically, they think that we should reject what they call **speciesism** for the same kind of reason that we should reject racism, sexism, ableism, and other such oppressions. In each case we would be discriminating on the basis of membership in a particular social or biological category alone, rather than on the basis of individual capacities, relationships, or other such criteria.[2]

Consider the following thought experiment, developed by David DeGrazia, Dale Jamieson, and others: Imagine that evolution had gone differently. In particular, imagine that several hominin (human-like) species had survived to the present day. We all look the same, walk the same, talk the same, and so on. Moreover, we all live in the same societies: We go to the same schools, work in the same businesses, and vote in the same elections. Of course, each individual is different. But statistically speaking, there are no relevant differences across hominin species. Literally the only difference that species membership makes is that each species is reproductively isolated, and therefore we can reproduce only with other members of our own species. Now suppose that you discover that your best friend belongs to a different species than you. Nothing has changed about them: They still like to watch TV, play card games, go on hikes, and so on. But whereas you thought that you were both *Homo sapiens*, you now realize that only one of you is *Homo sapiens*. The question is: Would this take away your moral duties to your friend? For example, would you now be morally permitted to kill them and eat them if you wanted to? Intuitively the answer is no. Your friend is still the same person they have always been, and you still have moral duties to them regardless of how they happen to be classified in biology textbooks.[3]

In response to this argument, one might claim that our humanity gives us moral status in the following way: As humans, we have certain characteristics that other species lack, such as language and rationality. One might then claim that *if* members of other species had these characteristics, *then* they would have moral status too. But, as it happens, only humans have these characteristics, and therefore only humans have moral status.

In response to this argument, we can make two points. First, if you think these characteristics are the basis of moral status, then you do not endorse speciesism after all: Your view is that moral status depends on whether or not one has certain characteristics, not on whether or not one is a member of a certain species. Second, if you accept this kind of view, then it will be difficult for you to sustain the view that all and only humans have moral status. After all, no matter which characteristic you select, there will always be some humans who lack it and/or some nonhumans who have it. In particular, when we focus on characteristics that all nonhumans lack (such as rationality, understood as the capacity to act on judgments about reasons), we find that many humans lack them too, and that we all lack them during some parts of life. And, when we focus on characteristics that all humans have (such as rationality, understood as the capacity to pursue goals), we find that many nonhumans have them too. Either way, then, once we reject speciesism, we must also reject the idea that all and only humans have moral status.

So what theory of moral status should we accept instead? We will here consider five alternative theories: three that focus on capacities, and two that focus on other, more relational considerations.

First, **rationalists** hold that you have moral status if and only if you are *rational*. Historically most rationalists have accepted a *narrow* interpretation of this view, according to which you have moral status if and only if you can act on judgments about reasons. For example, Thomas Hobbes claimed that morality is a social contract created by and for rational agents, so that they can live and let live. You agree not to kill me and, in exchange, I agree not to kill you. On this picture of morality, it makes no sense to include "nonrational" beings, since they are not capable of agreeing to this kind of social contract.[4] For another example, Immanuel Kant claimed that morality is a requirement of rationality. In order for you to be a rational agent at all, you have to value rationality in yourself and others, and therefore you have to respect yourself and others as rational agents. On this picture of morality, you do not have to respect "nonrational" beings, since doing so is not a requirement of rationality.[5] Many people still accept narrow rationalism. However, fewer people accept it now than in the past, since, as we have seen, not only does it imply that all nonhumans lack moral status, but it also implies that some humans lack moral status (and that all humans lack moral status during some parts of life). Thus, it is fundamentally at odds with contemporary standards of human rights. As a result, many people now reject narrow rationalism in favor of either wide rationalism (according to which you have moral status if and only if you can pursue goals) or a different view entirely. Either way, the result is the same: Moral status is not exclusively human.[6]

Second, **sentientists** hold that you have moral status if and only if you are *sentient*; that is, if and only if you are capable of having positive and negative experiences. Why might one accept this view? Singer argues that it follows from the ideal of human equality that we already accept. As we have seen, he thinks that when we say that all humans are equal, what we mean is that we have a moral duty to equally consider the interests of all humans no matter how rational they happen to be and no matter what social or biological categories they happen to occupy. And if this is true, then it means that all it takes to have moral status is: *You have to have interests.* Why do I have moral duties to dogs for their own sake but not to trees for their own sake? Because dogs have mental lives full of positive and negative experiences, and therefore it matters to them what happens to them. Trees, on the other hand, do not seem to have mental lives at all, and therefore it does not seem to matter to them what happens to them. (We will discuss what to do if we feel uncertain whether a particular being is sentient below.) Singer concludes that sentientism is an inclusive and non-arbitrary theory of moral status: If interests are necessary and sufficient for moral status, and if sentience is necessary and sufficient for interests, then sentience is necessary and sufficient for moral status.[7] However, some critics claim that sentientism is *too* inclusive, since it implies that we have duties to many beings who have no duties to us.[8] Other critics claim that sentientism is not inclusive *enough*, since, as with rationalism, it once again defines moral status in terms of a capacity that species like ours happen to have and that other species happen to lack.[9]

Third, **biocentrists** hold that you have moral status if and only if you are *biologically alive*. Why might one accept this view? There are at least two reasons. First, one might deny that interests are necessary for moral status. Second, one might accept that interests are necessary for moral status, but deny that sentience is necessary for interests. For example, Kenneth Goodpaster argues that Singer is correct to say that interests are necessary for moral status but incorrect to say that sentience is necessary for interests, since, Goodpaster thinks, plants can have interests whether or not they can have positive or negative experiences. Why does he think this? Because it seems clear to him that sunlight, water, and other such things are *good for plants*, and that deprivation of sunlight, water, and other such things are *bad for them*. It also seems clear to him that if things can be good or bad for plants, then plants have *interest* in things that are good for them and against things that are bad for them. Goodpaster concludes that biocentrism is a better theory than sentientism: If interests are sufficient for moral status, and if life is sufficient for interests, then life is sufficient for moral status. However, some critics claim that this is a mistake, since it confuses metaphorical interests for literal interests. As Dale Jamieson puts it, we might find it useful to talk about the "interests" of plants in the same kind of way that we find it useful to talk about the "interests" of cars ("premium gas is good for my car"). But we should not make the mistake of taking this talk literally ("premium gas is good for my car, *and therefore my car has moral status*").[10] Other critics claim that biocentrism, sentientism, and rationalism are all making a more fundamental mistake, which we will now consider.

Thus far, all of the theories that we have considered are *individualist* and *capacities-based*. That is, they think that *individuals* rather than *groups* have moral status, and they also think that individuals have moral status in virtue of their *capacities* rather than in virtue of other, more *relational* factors. However, not all philosophers agree with these assumptions.

For example, **ecocentrists** reject this individualist, capacities-based approach to moral status. They think that species and ecosystems have moral status rather than individual animals and plants. Why might one accept this view? Look at it this way. Many people think that we have moral duties to *organisms as a whole*, not to *the cells that make them up*. We also think that if we can help an organism by killing some of its cells (e.g., by removing a cancerous tumor), then we should do it. In the same kind of way, some ecocentrists think that we have moral duties to *species and ecosystems as a whole*, not to *the organisms that make these species and ecosystems up*. And they think that if we can help species or ecosystems as a whole by killing some of the organisms that make them up (e.g., by hunting to cull the herd), then we should do so.[11] However, critics claim that this is a mistake, since it confuses direct and indirect moral status. (Recall our discussion of the difference between direct and indirect value in Chapter 2.) Yes, species and ecosystems have *indirect* value ("We should save the environment because human and nonhuman animals depend on the environment"), but they do not have *direct* value ("We should save the environment for its own sake"). Critics also claim that ecocentrism is difficult to act on, since species and ecosystems are difficult to tell apart (where does one ecosystem end and the next begin in space, and where does one ecosystem end and the next begin across time?), as well as difficult to tell how to benefit (if the nature of ecosystems is to change, then do we benefit an ecosystem by changing it, by keeping it the same, or by doing something else entirely?).[12]

Relatedly, many **virtue, care,** and **relational theorists** reject individualist, capacities-based approaches to moral status as well. As we saw in the previous chapter, these theorists claim that morality is a matter of cultivating character traits that contribute to flourishing (in the case of virtue theory), cultivating relationships of care with others (in the case of care and relational theory), and keeping in mind all relevant features of our social, political, economic, ecological, and historical contexts (in all cases). These theorists make similar claims about moral status, since, if your moral duties to me depend on these kinds of considerations, then my moral status relative to you must depend on these kinds of considerations as well. For example, on this kind of view, your friends have moral status relative to you *not* because they are rational, or sentient, or even alive, but *rather* because they either actually or potentially stand in certain kinds of relationships with you. The same is true of everyone else as well.[13] (Of course, our capacities might play a role in shaping our relationships, and might therefore play an *indirect* role in shaping our moral statuses on this kind of view, but our relationships are what directly shape our moral statuses on this kind of view.) However, as we saw in the last chapter, some critics worry that these theories have unfair implications, since if moral status depends on relational facts, then your friends could turn out to have higher moral status than strangers, relative to you. Critics also worry that these theories have trouble telling us what to do in tough cases. However, as we have seen, virtue, care, and relational theorists have replies to these objections, which we will explore in more detail in later chapters.

As with the moral theories that we discussed in the last chapter, when we think about these theories of moral status together, we might find that some of them *converge* more than they initially appear to. For example, if we think that all and only sentient beings are rational (perhaps because we interpret rationality as goal directedness and we think that all and only sentient beings are goal directed), then we will think that rationalism and sentientism converge. Similarly, if we think that all and only living beings are sentient (perhaps because we interpret sentience as detection of helpful and harmful stimuli and we think that all and only living beings detect helpful and harmful stimuli), then we will think that sentientism and biocentrism converge.

Moreover, even if we deny that these theories converge *in principle*, we might still find that some of them converge *in practice*. After all, they all imply that most humans have moral status most of the time, and all but narrow rationalism imply that all humans and many nonhumans have moral status. And even if they deny that certain individuals or groups have *direct* moral status, they might still agree that they have *indirect* moral status. For example, a rationalist can say that sentience matters indirectly, because it affects our activity as rational agents. Similarly, a sentientist can say that rationality matters indirectly, because it affects our interests and experiences as sentient beings. And, of course, both can say that life, species, ecosystems, characters, emotions, relationships, and contexts matter indirectly, because rational agents and sentient beings depend on them and care about them, and vice versa.

As before, this does not necessarily dissolve all disagreement among these theories. But it does show that we need to do more than simply pick one theory and ignore the rest. Regardless of which theory we pick, we can deepen our understanding of moral status by considering the many ways in which our goals, interests, experiences, drives, characters, emotions, relationships, and contexts all contribute to shaping what makes us merit moral consideration, directly and indirectly.

As a result of these kinds of overlap, some of the issues that we discuss in this book will not be particularly controversial. For example, as we will see, industrial animal agriculture causes unnecessary harm to humans, nonhumans, and the environment alike. So, our assessment of industrial animal agriculture will likely be similar no matter which theory of moral status we accept. However, not all of the issues that we discuss in this book are like this. For example, the ethics of free-range farming will depend in part on who has moral status. (If we accept narrow rationalism, we might think that killing nonhuman animals for food is morally permissible. Otherwise we might not.) Similarly, the ethics of hunting will depend in part on who has moral status. (If we accept wide rationalism, sentientism, or biocentrism, we might think that we should focus on impacts for individual animals. If we accept ecocentrism, we might think that we should focus on impacts for species or ecosystems.) So, we will need to keep these theories in mind as we evaluate these practical issues, and vice versa.

In any case, there is a further question that we have to ask no matter which theory of moral status we accept, which is how to treat others in cases of uncertainty about whether or not they meet our criteria for moral status. For example, suppose that we accept that all and only sentient beings have moral status. We now have to ask: Which beings are sentient? (Recall that we are interpreting sentience as the capacity to have positive or negative experiences.) We might feel relatively confident that, say, all vertebrates are sentient.[14] So far so good. But what about invertebrates? For example, what about lobsters? When people boil lobsters alive in order to eat them, do the lobsters experience pain? It seems hard to answer that question with complete confidence either way. On one hand, lobsters are behaviorally, physiologically, and evolutionarily continuous with other animals who experience pain in many ways (e.g., they have nociception-like pain receptors). On the other hand, lobsters are behaviorally, physiologically, and evolutionarily discontinuous with other animals who experience pain in many ways too (e.g., they lack a central nervous system).[15] So the evidence is mixed. And yet we still have to decide how to treat lobsters notwithstanding this mixed evidence. And to be clear, this problem is not unique to sentientism. Similar problems arise for other theories too.[16]

How should we decide what to do in such cases?[17] As a general matter, philosophers tend to favor either a precautionary principle or a cost–benefit principle in cases of risk or uncertainty. According to a **precautionary principle**, if you are uncertain whether or not a particular action will cause harm, you should err on the side of caution and not perform that action. An application of this is: If you are uncertain whether building a nuclear reactor will cause a meltdown, you should err on the side of caution and not build it. In contrast, according to a **cost–benefit principle**, if you are uncertain whether a particular action will cause harm, you should multiply (a) the probability that it will cause harm by (b) the level of harm that it would cause if it did, and then treat the product of that equation as the level of harm it will actually cause for all intents and purposes. An application of this principle is: If you are uncertain whether building a nuclear reactor will cause a meltdown, you should multiply the probability that it will (e.g., you might think there is a 1% chance that building the reactor will cause a meltdown) with the level of harm that it would cause if it did (e.g., you might think that building the reactor would harm 5,000 people in the event of a meltdown). And then you should treat the product of that equation—50 people harmed—as the level of harm that the nuclear reactor will cause for all intents and purposes. The question then becomes whether or not you are justified in harming 50 people as a side-effect of producing energy, and the answer to this question will, of course, depend on what your other options are, what the expected effects of those options will be, and which moral theory you accept.[18]

How do these principles apply to our present question? A precautionary principle would imply that, in cases of uncertainty about whether a particular individual is sentient, a sentientist should err on the side of caution and treat them as though they are. An application of this is: If you are uncertain whether boiling a lobster alive will cause them pain, you should err on the side of caution and not boil them alive. Whereas a cost–benefit principle would imply that, in cases of uncertainty about whether a particular individual is sentient, a sentientist should multiply the probability that they are by the amount of pain they would experience if they were, and then treat the product of that equation as the amount of pain they will actually experience for all intents and purposes. An application of this is: If you are uncertain whether boiling a lobster alive will cause them pain, you should multiply the probability that it will (e.g., you might think that there is a 10% chance boiling them alive will cause them pain) with the amount of pain it would cause if it did (e.g., you might think that boiling the lobster alive would cause them 5,000 units of pain in the event that they are sentient). And then you should treat the product of that equation (500 units of pain) as the level of harm that boiling the lobster alive will cause for all intents and purposes. The question then becomes whether or not you are justified in causing a lobster 500 units of pain as a means to preparing a meal, and the answer to this question, as before, will depend on what your other options are, what the expected effects of those options will be, and which moral theory you accept.

Which of these approaches to risk and uncertainty makes more sense? This is a tricky question. Generally speaking, cost–benefit principles work best when we have enough information about probability and level of harm to engage in cost–benefit analysis in a reliable way, whereas precautionary principles work best when we do not. So what kind of case is this? What makes this issue tricky is that it is hard to say. On one hand, it is difficult if not impossible to say how likely certain animals, such as lobsters, are to be sentient and, if they are, how much pain they are likely to be experiencing in a particular situation. That seems to suggest that a precautionary principle is best: Instead of engaging in cost–benefit analysis, we should simply err on the side of caution and treat lobsters as sentient for all intents and purposes. On the other hand, there might be at least some cases where rough guesses about probability and level of harm are good enough. For example, if a house is burning down and you have time to save only a lobster or a robot lobster, then perhaps you should save the being who appears more likely to be sentient given your evidence (i.e., the lobster) rather than simply flipping a coin.

As we have indicated, these questions about risk and uncertainty matter for other theories of moral status too. For example, they will inform whether or not a rationalist should care about certain robots or nonhuman animals for their own sake (are they rational?), whether or not a biocentrist should care about certain robots or viruses for their own sake (are they alive?), whether or not a care or relational theorist should care about certain robots or nonhuman animals for their own sake (can we have caring relationships with them?), and so on.[19] As with many of the questions that we will raise in this book, we will not be able to fully answer these questions here. But we can say at least this much. In the same kind of way that we can agree on certain things no matter what theory of moral status we accept—for example, that industrial animal agriculture is bad—we can also agree on certain things no matter what approach to risk and uncertainty we accept. For example, even though precautionary principles and cost–benefit principles diverge on many issues, they converge on this issue: In cases of uncertainty about whether or not a certain individual or group has moral status, we should *not* treat them as though they do not. We should instead *either* treat them as though they do *or* treat them as though they at least partially do. Either way, that will often be enough to make certain behaviors, for example boiling a lobster alive for lunch instead of making a peanut butter and jelly sandwich, morally wrong according to multiple moral theories.

Before we move on, we should emphasize one more point about the ethics of risk and uncertainty, as it relates to our ongoing conversation about convergence and divergence across moral theories. Recall that in previous chapters we claimed that some moral theorists, such as utilitarians, tend to think about morality in terms of cost–benefit analysis, at least in theory, and other moral theorists, such as Kantians, tend to think about morality in other ways. As a result of these differences, moral theorists such as utilitarians tend to have a general preference for cost–benefit principles in cases of risk and uncertainty, and moral theorists such as Kantians tend to have a general preference for precautionary principles. However, as we indicated in the last chapter and will discuss more in later chapters, this is not necessarily always the case. For example, in cases where we do not have enough information about probabilities and utilities to do cost–benefit analysis in a reliable way, utilitarians might decide to use a precautionary principle (at least in part). This would not mean that they have abandoned utilitarianism: instead, it might simply mean that they see a precautionary principle as conducive to good results in this kind of case. Conversely, in cases where we do have enough information about probabilities and utilities to do cost–benefit analysis in a reliable way, Kantians might decide to use a cost–benefit principle (at least in part). This would not mean that they have abandoned Kantianism: instead, it might simply mean that they think that the expected consequences of a particular action are part of what determines whether or not that action treats everybody as ends.

4.3 The future of morality

We have now considered different moral theories (i.e., what moral duties we have) as well as different theories of moral status (i.e., to whom we have these moral duties). In order to fully inform our approach to food ethics, then, we need to combine these theories together and see what the resulting picture looks like.

Historically, some combinations have been more popular than others. For example, in the past, most deontologists have been narrow rationalists, and most consequentialists have been sentientists. Meanwhile, as we have seen, virtue, care, and relational theorists have been pluralists. But some people now think that we should break free from these traditional combinations. For example, Tom Regan and Christine Korsgaard combine deontology with sentientism / wide rationalism: They think that we should treat all sentient, goal-pursuing beings as ends.[20] (We may interpret them as either sentientists or as wide rationalists. Either way the result is about the same.) Similarly, some environmental ethicists combine consequentialism or deontology with biocentrism or ecocentrism. Some of these combinations are easy to grasp: For example, the idea of promoting well-being for plants or of treating plants as ends is relatively easy to grasp, though perhaps harder to motivate. However, other combinations are harder to grasp. For example, is it possible to combine consequentialism or deontology with eco-centrism? That would require determining what it means to promote well-being for a species or ecosystem, or what it means to treat a species or ecosystem as an end, which is hard to do.[21] Of course, this does not necessarily mean we should reject that combination. Instead, it might only mean that moral theory is still a work in progress, and that some combinations are better developed than others. The challenge moving forward is to continue to try to think carefully through all the options, and to accept the option that we find most plausible overall.

As we have seen, we will not need to select a particular combination of theories in order to answer some of the moral questions that we will be asking in this book. For example, industrial animal agriculture will turn out to be bad on most moral theories and theories of moral status. However, this is not true about all of the questions that we will be asking. To see what we mean, consider two kinds of moral question that we will be asking in this book from the perspective of a sentientist / wide rationalist Kantian (i.e., treat all sentient / goal-pursuing beings as ends) and a sentientist / wide rationalist utilitarian (i.e., maximize utility for all sentient / goal-pursuing beings).

Free-range farming. Consider a pair of cases inspired by Alastair Norcross that will be relevant to our discussion about the ethics of food production and con-sumption in Chapters 8 and 9.[22] First, suppose that a man raises a small number of puppies in his backyard. He treats them well throughout their lives, giving them plenty of opportunity to socialize and play. He then slits their throats at age 3, and he sells their flesh at local markets. (We can assume that this practice is fully legal in this community.) What should we say about this kind of case? At least in cultures where people treat dogs as companions, many people have the intuition that this activity is wrong. Second, suppose that a man raises a small number of piglets in his backyard. He treats them well throughout their lives, giving them plenty of opportunity to socialize and play. He then slits their throats at age 3, and he sells their flesh at local markets. (As before, we can assume that this prac-tice is fully legal in this community.) What should we say about this kind of case? At least in cultures where people treat pigs as food (many of which are the same as cultures that treat dogs as companions), many people have the intuition that this activity is permissible. Yet seemingly the only difference about these cases is the species of animal in question. So, what should we say about these cases? Should we say that this activity is permissible in both cases, should we say that this activity is wrong in both cases, or should we look for a relevant difference that justifies making different judgments about them (e.g., that many people in this culture happen to care more about dogs than about pigs)?

Now consider, as an illustration of how moral theories can converge and diverge, how sentientist / wide rationalist Kantians and utilitarians would evaluate these cases. First, most Kantians would say that raising these animals for food is wrong. After all, we would never think that raising and killing humans for food treats them as ends, so why should we think that raising and killing nonhumans for food is any different, according to sentientism / wide rationalism?[23] (With that said, we will consider a possible objection to this claim when we discuss the harm of death in Chapter 8.) In contrast, utilitarians would say that it all depends on the expected consequences of this practice. If, as a matter of fact, this man can expect to do more good by raising these animals for food than by spending his time, energy, money in other ways, then he should do so; otherwise he should not. So what should we say about the expected consequences of this practice? This is a difficult question. In cultures where people treat pigs as food and dogs as companions, it might be tempting, when thinking about the pig case, to say that this practice is likely to do more good than harm. After all, one might think, this practice benefits everyone involved: The farmer gets to make money, his customers get to eat food they like, and the pigs get to live for a few years before they die.[24] However, it might also be tempting, when thinking about the dog case, to say that this practice is likely to do more harm than good. After all, the farmer can provide people with food for profit in other, less harmful ways. Moreover, even if this practice benefits dogs in some ways, it also harms them in some ways, in part by reinforcing the idea that dogs are commodities, which can cause further harms down the road. (We will consider the ethics of free-range farming and the interaction of moral and cultural values later on.)

Rescue. Now consider a pair of cases inspired by Peter Singer that will be relevant to our discussion of food activism and advocacy in Chapters 10 and 11.[25] First, suppose that you walk by a pond wearing a brand new $50 outfit, and you see a puppy drowning. Nobody else is around to help, so, if you do nothing, the puppy will drown. Are you morally required to save the puppy, even if doing so will ruin your brand new outfit? At least in cultures that treat dogs as companions, many people have the intuition that you are morally required to rescue the puppy. Second, suppose that you come home from school, and you find a letter from Animal Charity Evaluators.[26] This letter informs you that, every year, more than 100 billion chickens, cows, pigs, and fishes suffer and die in terrestrial and aquatic farms. However, if you send $50 to an effective animal advocacy organization such as the Humane League, you can save or spare more than *100 animals* from this horrific fate. Are you morally required to send them $50? At least in cultures where people treat chickens, cows, pigs, and fishes as food (many of which are the same as cultures that treat dogs as companions), many people have the intuition that you are not morally required to save or spare these farmed animals. Yet seemingly the only difference between these cases is that you can save more animals for less money! So, what should we say about these cases? Should we say that saving these animals is required in both cases, should we say that saving these animals is not required in both cases, or should we look for a relevant difference that justifies making different judgments about them (e.g., that many people in this culture happen to care more about some animals than about others)?

Now consider, once again, how sentientist / wide rationalist Kantians and utilitarians would evaluate these cases. First, many Kantians would say that you are not required to save these animals (including the puppy). After all, as we saw in the last chapter (including in our discussion of the trolley problem), many Kantians think that there is a moral difference between killing and letting die: If you kill someone, then you are morally responsible for their death, whereas if you merely let someone die, then you are not. Thus, many Kantians would say that you are morally *permitted* to save these animals (and, if you did, that would reflect well on your character) but you are not morally *required* to do so. (Granted, you might have a moral obligation to help others *sometimes* on this kind of view, but you can pick and choose when you do that.) In contrast, utilitarians would once again say that it all depends on the overall consequences of this activity. As we saw in the last chapter (including in our discussion of the trolley problem), utilitarians think that there is no moral difference between killing and letting die. If you are in the position to decide whether or not someone lives or dies, and you make the decision that results in their death, then you are morally responsible for their death. Thus, many utilitarians would say that you are morally required to save these animals if and only if saving them does more good overall than other things you could be doing with your time, energy, and money. For example, if all you could otherwise be doing is hanging out with your friends, then maybe you should save the animals instead (though if you were to spend *all* your time saving animals, then you might burn out, which could be harmful for animals in the long run). On the other hand, if you could otherwise be, say, giving a speech about animal rights at the United Nations, then *maybe* you should do that instead (provided, of course, that your speech might actually make a difference).

As these thought experiments demonstrate, sometimes Kantianism is more restrictive than utilitarianism (e.g., when it tells us that we are not morally permitted to painlessly kill moral subjects for food no matter what), and sometimes utilitarianism is more restrictive than Kantianism (e.g., when it tells us that we are not morally permitted to allow moral subjects to suffer or die, all else equal). It might be tempting to select the less restrictive moral theory overall. After all, who wants to feel morally complicit in the suffering and death of literally billions of human and nonhuman animals every time they, say, buy a new outfit, go out for dinner, and engage in other ordinary activities? But as we discussed in the previous chapter, this is not how moral theory works. The question is not what moral theory we personally benefit from accepting. The question is rather what moral theory best reflects the moral judgments that we take to be correct in a wide range of cases. We must therefore follow the best arguments where they lead, rather than assess arguments based on where we want them to take us. With that said, it is a complicated question exactly how restrictive each of these theories will turn out to be in practice, since, as we have indicated, different theories tend to be restrictive in different ways, and some of them also have different implications in theory and in practice (e.g., utilitarianism allows us to hang out with friends sometimes in practice, since doing so is an important part of sustainable altruism in the real world). To be clear, in a world that contains as much suffering and death as ours, most if not all plausible moral theories will probably be at least somewhat restrictive (though utilitarianism will probably be more so than others). Then again, no one ever said that ethics is easy.[27]

These thought experiments also demonstrate the role that bias can play in our moral thinking: We have many of the intuitions that we have not only because our moral intuitions are linked with moral truths but also because our moral intuitions reflect bias and prejudice. This is a complex matter. On one hand, the fact that bias is possible means that we should always be prepared to discount our moral intuitions accordingly. On the other hand, the fact that bias is possible does not mean that the views that our biases support are always wrong. The challenge, then, is to allow our moral intuitions to guide our moral thinking, while also cultivating a healthy skepticism toward our moral intuitions and working to discount them in cases where bias is likely to be playing a role. Of course, this is easier said than done in practice. For example, if you have a stronger aversion to killing dogs than pigs, or to letting a dog die right in front of you than to letting a dog die far away from you, are these intuitions tracking morally important facts and/or are they reflecting morally irrelevant biases (such as speciesism or proximity bias)? The only way to answer this question with any confidence is by considering these issues from as many perspectives as possible (and in as many cases as possible, both simple and complex), and by always being prepared to change your mind if a new, revisionary moral theory starts to seem more plausible than your current, conventional moral theory, all things considered.[28]

With that in mind, consider now two other, related moral questions that will be relevant to our discussion in later chapters. First, our traditional understanding of **moral responsibility** evaluates individuals in light of the individual, direct harms they cause rather than the collective, indirect harms they participate in causing. For example, here is a paradigmatic case where we can all agree that you are morally responsible for a particular harm: you punch me in the face. All else equal, if you do that, then you wrong me, and you are blameworthy (i.e., you merit blame) for doing so. And, 10,000 years ago, when we lived in small, self-contained villages, this approach to thinking about morality might have been enough. But now that we live in a global village, things are very different. More and more, we are harming each other not only through our individual behavior but also through our collective behavior. Moreover, we are harming each other not only directly but also indirectly, through complicated causal chains that extend across national and generational boundaries. This raises the question: How should we morally assess the harms that we cause collectively? Moreover, how should we morally assess the harms that we cause indirectly, across nations and generations? As we will see, these questions are central to the ethics of food, since the harms that we collectively and indirectly cause to other nations and generations through our food system are massive. (Indeed, the contribution that our food system makes to climate change alone is arguably among the most pressing moral issues of our time.) So, it will be useful for us to close this chapter with a brief discussion of collective morality as well as international and intergenerational ethics.[29]

First, consider the relationship between individual and collective harms. Suppose that Tom lives in a small community (population: 1,000 people) where everyone depends on a lake at the center of town—they drink from it, water their crops with it, and more. Now suppose that Tom has 1,000 gallons of chemical waste that he needs to get rid of, and it would be very costly for him to dispose of this waste in an ecologically responsible way. So, one night, Tom sneaks down to the lake and dumps all 1,000 gallons of chemical waste into the water. Unfortunately, this is more than enough to contaminate the lake—and sure enough, within weeks many of the people in this town start to get sick. Most of us would say that Tom has acted wrongly in this case, and he deserves blame for what he did. But now imagine a different case. Suppose that everyone in a small community (population: 1,000 people) depends on a lake at the center of town. Now suppose that everyone has one gallon of chemical waste that they need to get rid of, and it would be costly for them to dispose of this waste in an ecologically responsible way. So, one by one, they each sneak down to the lake and dump their gallon of chemical waste into the water. Fortunately (we can suppose), one gallon of chemical waste is not enough to do any harm—it will dissipate in the water and everything will be fine. But 1,000 gallons is more than enough to contaminate the lake—and sure enough, within weeks many people in this town start to get sick. So, what should we say about this case?

What makes this case difficult to assess is that it has the structure of a collective action problem (recall that we discussed collective action problems such as the tragedy of the commons in Chapter 2).[30] Each person can think, "If I dump my gallon of chemical waste in the lake, then I will save a lot of money. Meanwhile, one gallon of chemical waste will not, in and of itself, cause any harm. So I should dump it in the lake." Yet if everyone thinks this way, then everyone will dump their gallon of chemical waste in the lake, and they will collectively contaminate the lake.

There are three approaches that one can take to thinking about this kind of problem. The first is to say that the people in this community are *collectively* responsible for contaminating the lake, but that nobody is *individually* responsible for anything bad. After all, one might think, if my individual action did not, in and of itself, cause any harm, then why should I merit blame for performing it? And why should I have a moral duty to act differently in the future? If you take this approach, then you might think that the solution is collective reform, not individual reform. The people in this community should advocate for legal changes that would require, or at least motivate, everyone to act differently. But while they wait for these changes to occur, they might as well continue to pour their chemical waste into the lake (since, they might think, disposing of their waste in a more ecologically responsible manner would still be worse for them and no better for the community in and of itself). Walter Sinnott-Armstrong expresses this idea in the context of climate change as follows:

[G]lobal warming is such a large problem that it is not individuals who cause it or need to fix it. Instead, governments need to fix it, and quickly. . . . Environmentalists should focus their efforts on those who are not doing their job rather than on those who take Sunday afternoon drives just for fun.[31]

The second approach is to say that the people in this community are collectively *and* individually responsible for contaminating the lake. In particular, they are collectively responsible for contaminating the lake, and they are individually responsible for their participation in this activity (whether or not they individually make a difference in the outcome). After all, one might think, how can we be completely blameless for knowingly and willingly participating in an activity that causes so much harm? If you take this approach, then you might think that the solution is collective reform *and* individual reform. The people in this community should advocate for legal changes that would require, or at least motivate, everyone to act differently. And while they wait for these legal changes to occur, each individual should take it upon themselves to dispose of their chemical waste in an ecologically responsible way (even though it will be costly for them to do so, and will not do any good for the community in and of itself). Christopher Kutz argues that this kind of approach is necessary if we want to preserve individual accountability in the modern world:

> The most important and far-reaching harms and wrongs of contemporary life are the products of collective actions, mediated by social and institutional structures. . . . So long as individuals are only responsible for the effects they produce, then the result of this disparity between collective harm and individual effect is the disappearance of individual accountability.[32]

The final approach is to deny that the original description of the case is accurate. Drawing from Shelly Kagan, we can say that if 1,000 gallons of chemical waste contaminates the lake, then *it cannot possibly be true* that nobody, by pouring one gallon of chemical waste into the lake, causes any harm.[33] That harm has to occur at some point, right? And that can only happen in one of two ways. First, it could happen gradually. Each gallon causes $\frac{1}{1000}$ of the contamination, and therefore each person is morally responsible for $\frac{1}{1000}$ of the contamination. Second, there could be a tipping point. Maybe a certain number of people cause no harm when they pour their waste into the lake. But then the next person causes the amount of waste in the lake to pass a threshold, and causes all the harm at once. In this scenario, each person stands a $\frac{1}{1000}$ chance of causing 1,000 units of harm, and therefore each person should expect that their action will cause one unit of harm. (As we saw above, this is how cost–benefit analysis works in cases of risk and uncertainty: You multiply the probability of harm by the level of harm and treat the product as the expected amount of harm your action will cause.) Either way, then, the people in this town should not think of their individual actions as harmless. Instead, they should think of their individual actions as causing a small, but real, amount of harm, and therefore they should, as with the second approach, try to solve this problem through collective as well as individual reform: They should advocate for legal changes that would require, or at least motivate, everyone to act differently. And while they wait for these legal changes to occur, each individual should take it upon themselves to dispose of their chemical waste in an ecologically responsible way, since, while it might be costly for them to do so, it is also, on expectation, beneficial for the community (and, as a result, for them as a community member) for them to do so.

Now consider **international** and **intergenerational morality**. Suppose that community 1 and community 2 are near each other, and connected by a river. Now suppose that everyone in community 1 has one gallon of chemical waste that they need to get rid of, and it would be costly for them to dispose of this waste in an ecologically responsible way. So, one by one, they sneak down to the river and dump their gallon of chemical waste into the water. The waste then travels to community 2, contaminating their water supply and causing many of the members of community 2 to get sick. Most of us would say that the people in community 1 collectively (as well as, perhaps, individually) acted wrongly in harming the people in community 2 in this kind of way. But now consider two variations on this case. In one variation, everything about the case is the same, except community 2 is much farther away. When the people in community 1 pour their chemical waste into the water, they know that the waste will harm people in community 2, but they also know that the waste will travel, say, 1,000 miles rather than, say, one mile before it does so. In the other variation, everything about the case is the same, except community 2 exists in the future rather than in the present. When the people in community 1 pour their chemical waste into the water, they know that the waste will harm people in community 2, but they also know that, say, 100 years rather than, say, one day will pass before it does so. What should we say about these variations?

The question that we are trying to get at here is: Does distance in space and time matter morally in and of itself? If we harm or kill someone who lives on the other side of the planet, or in the next generation, is our action less wrong (or blameworthy) because the harm is so far away from us? We might feel less uneasy at the thought of harming or killing people so far away from us: It is much easier, psychologically, to kill someone by ordering a drone strike than to kill someone by plunging a knife into their chest. But does this difference matter morally, all else equal? Some philosophers think that the answer is yes: The farther away someone is from you in space and time, the less wrong it is for you to harm or kill them, all else equal. Some people find this view plausible because, if we reject it, then we might find that our duties to people in other nations and future generations overwhelm our duties to people in our own nation and generation (since, after all, there are *so many more people* in other nations and future generations, and many of them are *so much worse off* than people here and now, especially if we live in a nation with a developed industrial economy at the start of the twenty-first century). Other philosophers think that the answer is no: If you know that your action will harm or kill someone, then who cares how far away they are? If knowingly and willingly killing someone one mile away from you is wrong, then knowingly and willingly killing someone 10 miles, or 100 miles, or 1,000 miles away from you is equally wrong, all else equal. And if knowingly and willingly killing someone one day from now is wrong, then knowingly and willingly killing someone one year, 10 years, or 100 years from now is equally wrong, all else equal.

Of course, even if distance in space and time is irrelevant *in principle*, it might still be relevant *in practice*. This might be true for several reasons. First, it might be true for *practical* reasons: For example, the farther away we are from people in space and time, the fewer things we can do to help them. Thus, maybe we should place more weight on our duties to people nearby in practice, since we are in a better position to do things that will help them. Second, this might be true for *epistemic* reasons: For example, the farther away we are from people in space and time, the less we know about how our actions will affect them. Thus, perhaps we should place more weight on our duties to people nearby in practice, since we are in a better position to know all the relevant facts. Third, this might be true for *moral* reasons: For example, we have closer relationships with many people in our own community than with many people in other communities, and therefore we might think that we have certain special obligations to many people in our own community that do not extend to many people in other communities, especially on virtue, care, and relational theories. Moreover, it is sometimes useful to commit to a moral division of labor, where we all focus on taking care of the members of our own community, and that way people in every community get taken care of in an efficient way.[34] Finally, and relatedly, sometimes the best way to help others is to help yourself. For example, Wilfred Beckerman argues that, if we want to help future generations, then we should focus on creating a just and decent society for them to inherit rather than try to anticipate and meet their needs directly. Why? For all the reasons listed above: We are practically, epistemically, and morally better equipped to work on the former task than the latter task. And if we work on the former task, then future generations will be better equipped to identify and meet their own needs than they would otherwise be.[35]

However, there are other considerations that push in the opposite direction. First, as we have indicated, there are expected to be many more people in need in other nations and generations than in our own nation and generation (especially if we live in a nation with a developed industrial economy at the start of the twenty-first century). So if, as many people believe, we should either do the most good overall or the most good for the least well off members of society, then we might think that we should prioritize people in other nations and future generations, all else equal. Also, some of our activities harm people in other communities more than they harm people in our own community, and therefore we might think that we have stronger special obligations of reparation to people in other communities than to people in our own community, relative to these activities. Moreover, if everyone adopts a "moral division of labor" that leads each community to focus on itself, then they could contribute to *global* collective action problems. For example, each community might decide to stimulate the local economy in order to help people locally rather than build stable international institutions in order to help people globally. If so, then they would be doing more good than harm for themselves, but they would also be doing more harm than good for the world. Finally, while we might not be able to anticipate or meet every need that people will have in other nations or future generations, we can anticipate and meet at least some of the most pressing, such as the need to not live in a world reshaped by global catastrophe.[36] At the very least, then, practical considerations cut both ways, and at least some support placing more, not less, emphasis on our moral duties to those who live far away from us in space and time.[37]

When we put all these considerations together, we see what makes our present topic so morally complex. Sure, many food systems cause individual, local harms that are easy to measure and evaluate. For example, when an individual farmer generates enough waste to contaminate local air, water, and soil, it is easy to explain why they are acting wrongly. But increasingly (and more importantly), our food systems are causing collective, distant harms as well, and these harms are much harder to measure or evaluate. For instance, as we will see, the vast majority of our food now comes from multinational corporations with a wide and diffuse network of employees and an even wider and more diffuse network of consumers. Additionally, while our food system does indeed impact people locally, it disproportionately impacts people in other species, other nations, and other generations. So if we want to develop a complete picture of food ethics, we will have to consider the individual, local dimension as well as the collective, global dimension.

4.4 Conclusion

We have considered many complicated ethical questions in this chapter—questions about moral status as well as about collective, international, and intergenerational ethics. If you feel confused about some of these issues, this is good. Ethics is an incredibly messy, complex, and difficult subject, and no one can reasonably expect to have everything figured out right away. So, rather than try to resolve any confusion that you might be feeling as quickly as possible, we hope that you can accept this confusion for what it is, and try to resolve it gradually over time by thinking about an increasingly wide range of moral issues and constructing an increasingly coherent and stable moral theory that addresses them all. In what follows, we will illustrate this process by discussing the impacts of industrial and non-industrial food systems as well as the moral questions that these impacts raise for food production, consumption, activism, and advocacy.

Notes

1 Peter Singer, *Animal Liberation* (New York: Random House, 1975): Chapter 1.
2 The term "speciesism" was coined by Richard Ryder and popularized by Peter Singer in *Animal Liberation*.

3 David DeGrazia, "Human-animal Chimeras: Human Dignity, Moral Status, and Species Prejudice," *Metaphilosophy* 38, no. 2–3 (February 2007): 309–329.

Dale Jamieson, *Ethics and the Environment* (New York: Cambridge University Press, 2012): Chapter 5.

4 Thomas Hobbes, *Leviathan* (New York: Penguin, 1982).

5 Immanuel Kant, *Groundwork of the Metaphysics of Morals*, trans. Mary J. Gregor (New York: Cambridge University Press, 1998).

6 For work that discusses nonhuman animal agency and its implications for moral status, see:

Christine Korsgaard, "Interacting with Animals: A Kantian Account," in Tom L. Beauchamp and R.G. Frey, eds., *The Oxford Handbook of Animal Ethics* (Oxford: Oxford University Press, 2011): 91–118.

Jeff Sebo, "Agency and Moral Status," *Journal of Moral Philosophy* 14, no. 1 (2017): 1–22.

7 Peter Singer, *Animal Liberation* (New York: Random House, 1975): Chapter 1.

8 For an argument that sentientism is too inclusive, see:

Peter Carruthers, *The Animals Issue: Moral Theory in Practice* (New York: Cambridge University Press, 1992): Chapter 5.

9 For an argument that sentientism is not inclusive enough, see:

Kenneth Goodpaster, "On Being Morally Considerable," *Journal of Philosophy* 75, no. 6 (June 1978): 308–325.

10 For an argument that plants have interests only in a metaphorical sense, see:

Dale Jamieson, *Ethics and the Environment* (New York: Cambridge University Press, 2014): 147–149.

11 For an argument that species are individuals, see:

David Hull, "A Matter of Individuality," *Philosophy of Science* 45, no. 3 (September 1978): 335–360.

For other kinds of arguments for ecocentrism, see:

Aldo Leopold, *A Sand County Almanac* (New York: Ballantine Books, 1986).

Freya Matthews, *The Ecological Self* (New York: Routledge, 2006).

Arne Næss, "The Shallow and the Deep, Long-range Ecology Movement. A Summary," *Inquiry* 16, no. 1–4 (1973): 95–100.

Holmes Rolston III, *Environmental Ethics: Duties to and Values in the Natural World* (Philadelphia: Temple University Press, 1989).

12 For more on these critiques of ecocentrism, see:

Dale Jamieson, *Ethics and the Environment* (New York: Cambridge University Press, 2014): 149–153.

For more on the moral value of species, see:

Ronald L. Sandler, *The Ethics of Species: An Introduction* (New York: Cambridge University Press, 2012).

13 For examples of this kind of argument, see:

Elizabeth Anderson, "Animal Rights and the Values of Nonhuman Life," in Cass R. Sunstein and Martha Craven Nussbaum, eds., *Animal Rights: Current Debates and New Directions* (Oxford: Oxford University Press, 2004): 277–298.

Cora Diamond, "Eating Meat and Eating People," *Philosophy* 53, no. 206 (October 1978): 465–479.

14 Even this claim is controversial, since some people deny that nonhuman animals are sentient, and some people assert that plants are sentient. We can set these views aside for present purposes.

15 For more on continuities and discontinuities between human and nonhuman animals, see:

David DeGrazia, *Animal Rights: A Very Short Introduction* (Oxford: Oxford University Press, 2002): Chapter 3.

16 For more on the science and philosophy of animal minds, see:

Kristin Andrews, *The Animal Mind: An Introduction to the Philosophy of Animal Cognition* (New York: Routledge, 2014).

Marc Bekoff, *The Emotional Lives of Animals: A Leading Scientist Explores Animal Joy, Sorrow, and Empathy—and Why They Matter* (Novato: New World Library, 2008).

Sara J. Shettleworth, *Cognition, Evolution, and Behavior*, 2nd edn (Oxford: Oxford University Press, 2010).

Clive D.L. Wynne, *Animal Cognition: The Mental Lives of Animals* (Basingstoke: Macmillan, 2001).

17   For more on how to treat animals in cases of uncertainty about whether they experience pain, see:

Alexander Guerrero, "Don't Know, Don't Kill: Moral Ignorance, Culpability, and Caution," *Philosophical Studies* 136, no. 1 (October 2007): 59–97.

Jeff Sebo, "The Moral Problem of Other Minds," *The Harvard Review of Philosophy*. Published online May 23, 2018. DOI: 10.5840/harvardreview20185913

David Foster Wallace, "Consider the Lobster," *The New York Times*, March 12, 2006.

The next four paragraphs will draw from Jeff Sebo, "The Moral Problem of Other Minds."

18   Some people think that we should discount very unlikely benefits or harms. For discussion of this and other complications, see:

Johann Frick, "Contractualism and Social Risk," *Philosophy & Public Affairs* 43, no. 3 (November 2015): 175–223.

19   To see why this kind of question is more complicated than you might expect, see:

Fred Feldman, *Confrontations with the Reaper: A Philosophical Study of the Nature and Value of Death* (Oxford: Oxford University Press, 1994).

20   Christine Korsgaard, "A Kantian Case for Animal Rights," *Philosophy and Public Affairs* 43, no. 3 (Summer 2015): 175–223.

Tom Regan, *The Case for Animal Rights* (Berkeley: University of California Press, 2004).

21   In part for this reason, Holmes Rolston III argues that we need new frameworks for thinking about our moral duties to species and ecosystems. For more, see:

Holmes Rolston III, "Biodiversity," in Dale Jamieson, ed., *A Companion to Environmental Philosophy* (Hoboken: Blackwell Publishers, 2001): 402–415.

22   Alastair Norcross, "Puppies, Pigs, and People: Eating Meat and Marginal Cases," *Philosophical Perspectives* 18, no. 1 (November 2004): 229–245.

23   Tom Regan makes similar arguments in:

Tom Regan, *Animal Rights, Human Wrongs: An Introduction to Moral Philosophy* (New York: Rowman & Littlefield, 2003): Chapter 7.

24   For discussion of this kind of consideration, see:

Michael Pollan, *The Omnivore's Dilemma* (New York: Penguin, 2006): Chapter 17.

25   Peter Singer, "Famine, Affluence, and Morality," *Philosophy & Public Affairs* 1, no. 3 (Spring 1972): 229–243.

26   Disclosure: Jeff Sebo is on the board of directors at Animal Charity Evaluators.

27   Thank you to Richard Galvin for saying this many, many, many times when Jeff Sebo was in college.

28   For discussion of how cognitive biases affect human reasoning, see:

Daniel Kahneman, *Thinking, Fast and Slow* (Basingstoke: Macmillan, 2011).

For discussion of these issues in the context of moral reasoning in particular, see:

Regina Rini, "Morality and Cognitive Science," *The Internet Encyclopedia of Philosophy*, www.iep.utm.edu/m-cog-sc/.

Cass R. Sunstein, "Moral Heuristics," *Behavioral and Brain Sciences* 28, no. 4 (2005): 531–541.

29   For an argument that we need a new moral framework for this new stage in human history, see:

Dale Jamieson, *Reason in a Dark Time: Why the Struggle Against Climate Change Failed—and What it Means for our Future* (Oxford: Oxford University Press, 2014): Chapter 5.

30 For discussion of the tragedy of the commons, see:
  Garrett Hardin, "The Tragedy of the Commons," *Journal of Natural Resources Policy Research* 1, no. 3 (2009): 243–253.
31 Walter Sinnott-Armstrong, "It's Not My Fault: Global Warming and Individual Moral Obligations," in *Perspectives on Climate Change: Science, Economics, Politics, Ethics* (Bingley: Emerald Group Publishing Ltd, 2005): 293–315, 312.
32 Christopher Kutz, *Complicity: Ethics and Law for a Collective Age* (New York: Cambridge University Press, 2007).
33 Shelly Kagan, "Do I Make a Difference?" *Philosophy & Public Affairs* 39, no. 2 (July 2011): 105–141.
34 For discussion of this kind of consideration, see:
  Robert Goodin, "What Is So Special about Our Fellow Countrymen?" *Ethics* 98, no. 4 (July 1988): 663–686.
35 Wilfred Beckerman, "Sustainable Development and Our Obligations to Future Generations," in Andrew Dobson, ed., *Fairness and Futurity: Essays on Environmental Sustainability and Social Justice* (Oxford: Oxford University Press, 1999): 71–92.
36 For more, see:
  Nick Bostrom and Milan M. Cirkovic, eds., *Global Catastrophic Risks* (Oxford: Oxford University Press, 2011).
37 For discussion of climate change as an international, intergenerational collective action problem, see:
  Stephen M. Gardiner, *A Perfect Moral Storm: The Ethical Tragedy of Climate Change* (Oxford: Oxford University Press, 2011).
  For a practical argument against pure time discounting, see:
  Toby Ord and Robert Wiblin, "Should We Discount Future Health Benefits When Considering Cost-effectiveness?" *Giving What We Can Research*, www.givingwhatwecan.org/sites/givingwhatwecan.org/files/attachments/discounting-health2.pdf.

5 Agriculture and the environment

5.1 Introduction

This chapter will examine the empirical dimensions of food, animals, and the environment that apply to all agriculture—including a discussion of the scale of animal, environmental, and human impacts. This helps us to understand the impacts of agriculture: what kinds of harm it causes and in what proportions. The next two chapters will then describe industrialized and non-industrialized forms of agriculture, respectively, in greater depth.

Before we begin, we should note that while we will be providing a broad overview of food, animals, and the environment, we cannot offer one that is comprehensive. We should also note that, while this chapter will have separate sections on animals, the environment, and humans, these categories interact in many important ways. Food agriculture involves clearing land; using pesticides, herbicides, and fungicides; changing carbon, nitrogen, and water cycles; and adding and removing nutrients from the soil. This affects humans, nonhumans, and the environment alike. Some sectors, such as transportation, impact all three areas as well. For example, transportation affects farmed animals when they are moved, affects wild animals through infrastructure, pollution, and carbon emissions, and affects humans through air pollution and carbon emissions as well. We will also discuss how disadvantaged groups often suffer these impacts disproportionately.

5.2 The big picture

The first "big picture" concept at the center of food, animals, and environment is **scale**. The scale of agriculture is immense, and difficult to fully appreciate. Few human activities have impacted land use, water cycles, nutrient cycles, human habitation, and nonhuman animal habitat as dramatically as agriculture has. In addition to the fact that agriculture employs over one billion workers,[1] human populations have grown exponentially due to agricultural technologies such as synthetic nitrogen—fundamentally changing global trends.

Grazing land covers a quarter of global land, and crops fed to nonhuman animals cover one third.[2] Ecologist Jonathan Foley and his colleagues write that "croplands and pastures have become one of the largest terrestrial biomes[3] on the planet, rivaling forest cover in extent."[4] According to the United

Nations Food and Agriculture Organization (UN FAO), "[three quarters] of the world's food is generated from only 12 plants and five animal species."[5] Humans are changing the environment dramatically, and are doing so in a form that comes with substantial negative impacts for themselves, nonhuman animals, and the environment.

The number of terrestrial animals used for animal agriculture is staggering: There are about 1.5 billion cows (whose combined weight is much more than the combined weight of all humans),[6] hundreds of millions of sheep and goats, hundreds of millions of pigs, and 50–60 billion individuals of other species, most of whom are poultry.[7] Estimates put the number of terrestrial animals slaughtered in agriculture annually at around 70 billion.[8]

Many of the significant claims about the harm of animal agriculture are best understood in terms of scale—these claims invoke the number of large animals who exist and how many resources (including land) they use. In the U.S., farmed animals produce 130 times as much waste as humans do.[9] Something as seemingly innocuous as cow burps can actually add up to substantial heat-trapping methane emissions, when you recognize that these burps are multiplied by 1.5 billion animals who weigh over a thousand pounds each (or in some cases, more than twice that much). Figure 5.1 powerfully illustrates the immense scale of Earth's farmed mammals.

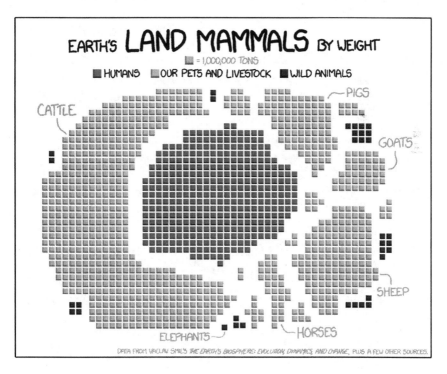

Figure 5.1 Earth's land mammals by weight, using data from environmental scientist Vaclav Smil[10]

The second "big picture" concept at the center of food, animals, and environment is **conversion**. In the conversion process, an animal eats a plant or another animal, and much of the energy from this food is used to maintain the animal who consumed it. This animal grows tissue, respires, moves, and otherwise uses energy. For this reason, only a small percentage of the original energy from the plant or animal product ends up in the final animal product. When we multiply the efficiency of feed conversion by the billions of animals consuming these grains,[11] the scale of environmental impact becomes apparent.

The transfer of energy from plant to animal can be more or less efficient, so we use the concept of **conversion efficiency** to talk about the percentage of energy that transfers between orders. The ordering of food describes the transfer of energy within ecological systems.

First order foods are ones at the first trophic level. A **trophic level** is a category in an ecosystem where organisms get energy from similar sources. Organisms at the first trophic level are plants—they are called **primary producers**, and can convert inorganic materials such as water and sunlight into biomass. This biomass can be nutritionally valuable, such as carbohydrates in the case of plants. When humans eat first order food directly, all of the energy in that food is used by the human.

Second order foods are ones that have been converted once, putting them at the second trophic level. For example, the same corn that ended up on your dinner plate as first order food can also be eaten by a cow, who in turn is eaten as a steak. In this case some but not all of the energy from the corn will be present in the steak.

Third order foods are ones that have been converted twice, putting them at the third trophic level. For example, one animal might eat first order matter (e.g., a krill eats phytoplankton), another animal might then eat that animal (e.g., a fish eats the krill), and a human might then eat this last animal (e.g., a human eats the fish).

In ecology, there are higher orders in the food chain that include apex predators and carnivores, but they are less common in human food systems. Humans who only eat plant-based foods occupy the second trophic level, and those who also eat nonhuman animals occupy the third trophic level.

As we have indicated, delivering energy from the primary level to humans entails a loss of energy. The efficiency of this transition can be a rough proxy for the environmental impact of a food, but only in cases where the first order food is edible and nutritious for humans (e.g., soybeans but not grass).[12] In cases where animal feed is edible and nutritious for humans, the environmental impact of the feed is a fraction of the environmental impact of the animal product. For instance, pigs have a feed conversion ratio of about 3:1.[13] So, if a farmer feeds soybeans to a pig and then sells the pig for food, we would want to include the environmental impact of three pounds of soybean production in our assessment of the impact of one pound of pig meat production (in addition to the other environmental impacts of farmed animal production, detailed later). In this way, the production of one pound of meat can require 3–10 pounds of grain[14]—and according to one estimate, animal food systems consume roughly 67% of total crops (in terms of net calories), in exchange for providing about 13% of our net calories.[15] So, when we feed first order food to nonhuman animals and then eat those animals, we are feeding food to "food," and a large percentage of energy is lost in the process.

Insects (along with other cold-blooded animals like most fishes) have a relatively high conversion efficiency—which is part of why some people see them as a promising source of environmentally efficient animal protein.[16] As a solution to the loss of biodiversity, for example, some scholars propose that humans could eat at a lower trophic level. This would mean eating "down the food web," for instance by eating smaller fishes who convert energy more efficiently.[17] Such proposals are based solely on assessing the efficiency of conversion of biomass, and are not based on considerations of animal welfare. (However, given how many insects and fishes would have to be consumed to provide the same calories as larger animals, the animal welfare impacts of this shift in consumer behavior have the potential to be immense.)

Environmental scientist David Pimentel calculates how many calories of fossil-fuel energy are used to produce feed for farmed animals.[18] He shares, for example, that "broiler-chicken [young chickens raised for meat] production was the most energy efficient, with 1 kcal of broiler protein produced with an input of 4 kcal of fossil energy."[19] This means that it takes 4,000 calories of fossil fuel to eventually produce 1,000 calories of protein in a broiler chicken. Additionally, environmental scientists Michael Clark and David Tilman estimate that "ruminant meat has impacts ~100 times those of plant-based foods."[20]

In some calculations, these estimations restrict inputs to on-farm fossil-fuel energy such as heating and cooling buildings. In others, they include transportation and supermarket heating and cooling as well. In still others, they include at-home energy use in the kitchen. Because of the variation across these inclusions and exclusions, assessments of environmental impact vary considerably.

In the next sections we discuss the animal, environmental, and human impacts of agriculture at this scale and with these degrees of conversion.

5.3 Animals

As mentioned earlier, there are tens of billions of terrestrial animals bred and raised for food—roughly 70 billion slaughtered every year.[21] We also kill hundreds of billions of aquatic animals annually, primarily for the purposes of eating them, feeding them to terrestrial and aquatic animals (using them as "fish meal"), and converting them to products such as fish oil. A large percentage of these animals is also wasted.

While some animal agricultural systems treat animals better than others, they all involve impacts that raise moral questions. We will discuss the animal welfare impacts of industrial animal agriculture in detail in Chapter 6 and the animal welfare impacts of non-industrial animal agriculture in detail in Chapter 7. We will also, in Chapter 8, discuss the ethics of such treatment in industrial as well as non-industrial settings. Animal welfare impacts are not limited to domesticated animals, however. Land use, water use, waste, pollution, and other impacts of animal agriculture affect liminal[22] and wild animals too. We will here focus on these latter impacts.

5.3.1 Biodiversity

Many scholars consider animal agriculture to be the single biggest driver of bio-diversity loss,[23] largely due to the clearing of land, the use of pesticides (often synthetic), and the prevalence of **monocultures** (the widespread cultivation of a single crop).[24] Changing a landscape from a forest or grassland to a farm alters its suitability as a habitat for nonhuman animals. Unless nearby habitat is available for those who are displaced, they will die—leading to a net loss of biodiversity. Journalist Richard Manning claims that "the transformation of the American plains for food production wiped out 99% of the grasslands biome along with the great diversity of plants, animals, and other organisms that constituted it."[25]

The UN FAO study mentioned earlier further supports the conclusion that animal agriculture leads to biodiversity loss: Some 306 of the 825 terrestrial ecoregions identified by the World Wide Fund for Nature (WWF)—ranging across all biomes and biogeographical realms—report animal farming as a threat.[26] Other studies support this conclusion as well.[27] At a more regional level, tens of thousands of acres in the midwestern U.S. have been converted from grasslands to corn and soy crops, and large swaths of the western U.S. have been significantly altered by the grazing activities of introduced cows. Environmental scientists estimate that:

> Across the [Western Corn Belt], more than 99% of presettlement tallgrass prairie has been converted to other land covers, mostly agricultural, with losses in Iowa approaching 99.9% of an original 12-million ha of tallgrass prairie . . . Potential expansion of corn and soybean cultivation into remaining fragments of tallgrass prairie in the WCB presents a critical ecosystem conservation issue.[28]

The grazing of cows in the western U.S. dramatically changes soil chemistry, plant ecology, and riparian zones (the areas alongside a river or stream). Managed grazing also often involves the killing of prairie dogs and coyotes in the U.S., as well as the killing of kangaroos in Australia. This information raises questions about whether killing domesticated animals for food is morally relevantly different from killing liminal and wild animals in the course of creating food, which we will discuss in more detail in Chapter 8.

Domesticated animals constitute a large percentage of animals used for food. We breed a small subset of all animals, and the genetic diversity of terrestrial animals raised for meat, milk, and eggs is modest. Older breeds (including those bred by Indigenous communities) are often endangered, as commodity breeds have become more prevalent. The FAO estimates that 20% of "livestock breeds" are at risk of extinction.[29] Traits such as resilience to climate stresses or drought might be lost, further increasing the risk that animals will die as a result of environmental changes. Some groups—such as the organization Slow Food—are attempting to preserve heritage or heirloom breeds, but doing so often requires a market for animal products that might not exist at scale due to the expense of raising these breeds and the aesthetic and economic preferences of consumers.

5.3.2 Aquaculture and fishing

Many of the calories consumed by humans and nonhuman animals are aquatic, not terrestrial. We farm fishes in **aquaculture** (controlled settings designed for raising sea animals) and catch them in wild settings. Fishes make up about 20% of animal protein intake globally,[30] and aquatic animals constitute a large and increasing percentage of food production. In fact, the scale is so large that some people describe them collectively (as "seafood") and measure them by weight, rather than by number of individuals. The extraction of animals from the oceans and inland aquatic systems can be done both industrially and non-industrially, with wide variation in environmental and social impacts.

We extract about 109 million metric tons of fishes from the oceans per year,[31] who are caught using a variety of tools (e.g., longlines[32] and purse seines[33]) that often have their own environmental impacts. We also raise fishes with high trophic levels—such as tunas and salmons—in ocean pens, in addition to raising the majority of farmed fishes in inland fish farms. These fishes are fed fishmeal made primarily from wild caught fishes. About one third of captured fishes are used as feed for other animals, both terrestrial and aquatic.[34]

While the amount of wild caught fishes has remained steady since around 1985, aquaculture has increased. This is largely due to the challenge of fishing from increasingly depleted fish stocks.[35] Estimates from 2010 indicate that 37 billion–120 billion fishes are farmed annually, but the number has increased since then,[36] with China producing the majority of the world's farmed fishes, mostly for domestic consumption. As in other food sectors, a large percentage of fishes are not consumed either directly or indirectly, and they are therefore wasted.[37]

Overfishing and intensive fishing practices greatly reduce biodiversity. Since the animals we take from the oceans are mostly wild (unlike the terrestrial animals we consume), the impact on aquatic biodiversity is more direct and dramatic than the impact on terrestrial biodiversity. This loss is further increased by those intensive fishing practices, such as trawling, that destroy coral and other aquatic animal habitats and catch vast amounts of fishes who are thrown back into the ocean ("bycatch").

5.4 Environment

As we have indicated, plant and animal agricultural practices are varied— they can use industrial and non-industrial tools and practices, occur in varying ecosystems and climates, and exist at a range of scales. Because of these characteristics, assessing and modeling environmental impacts can be difficult, and there is uncertainty about the precise environmental and climate impact of agriculture. Still, due to the large scale of agriculture, its environmental impacts are certainly substantial.

Environmental change is a disturbance in the environment, usually understood to be human-caused. Environmental change impacts animal habitats, ecosystem characteristics, and resources such as air, water, and climate capacity.[38] Agriculture—both industrial and non-industrial—is a key driver of environmental change.[39] According to ecologist David Tilman,

> agriculture affects ecosystems by the use and release of limiting resources that influence ecosystem functioning (specifically nitrogen, phosphorus, and water), release of pesticides, and conversion of natural ecosystems . . . [t]hese sources of global change may rival climate change in environmental and societal impacts.[40]

The environmental impacts of food are caused by land clearing (e.g., deforestation), land use (e.g., tilling soil), processing, transportation, storage, and preparation. Of these activities, the production of food (what happens in the field or animal feeding facility, including irrigating and fertilizers, for instance) is often the primary driver of greenhouse gas emissions and other environmental impacts.[41] Within food production, animal agriculture uses substantially more nitrogen,[42] water,[43] land,[44] and phosphorus[45] than other forms of agriculture.

In addition to the existing environmental impacts of food agriculture, most projections indicate increased stresses on environmental systems as the world population grows and more people consume animal products.

5.4.1 Waste

Much of the food that humans eat requires significantly more energy in its production than comparably nutritious food that is consumed less frequently. In a sense, this excess energy is wasted, as it could have been used to produce more nutrients for humans. The many forms of waste in food systems (both industrial and non-industrial) include:

→ Conversion of feed to animal-based products or biofuels (up to 90% of calories can be lost in the conversion of "food that we feed to food")
→ Crops left in the field or damaged by insects or weather
→ Food that perishes on the way to processing or market or that is purchased but never eaten
→ Food disposed of for aesthetic or regulatory reasons (e.g., fruits or vegetables with bruises on them, or foods no longer free of bacterial contamination—up to 50% in industrialized countries)[46]
→ Bycatch of aquatic animals (up to 90% for certain animals such as shrimps).

These forms of waste are significant: Only 62% of our crops go toward food we actually eat. About 35% goes to farmed animal feed and about 3% goes to biofuel, fiber, or seed production.[47] About 50% of farmed and wild caught fishes in the U.S. are discarded.[48]

5.4.2 Genetic modification

Humans have modified the genes of plants and nonhuman animals for thousands of years. Early farmers would save seeds from plants that had desirable qualities (such as size or insect resistance). Over generations of planting, those traits became more prevalent.

Genetically modified organisms (GMOs) are plants, fungi, yeasts, and nonhuman animals engineered to include specific genes from donor species not normally found in the host. Genetic modification typically focuses on one or a small number of specific genes. This can take the form of using CRISPR, a technology allowing targeted altering of a genome, to "knock out" a susceptibility gene—thereby creating resistance to certain microorganisms.

Traditional plant breeding consists of breeding two genetically similar plants with desirable traits (such as sugar content or resistance to "pests") with the aim of creating new plants that express the desired traits. In contrast, genetic engineering consists of precise, transgenic breeding; that is, of inserting genes from one organism into another, unrelated organism.

Genetically engineered organisms are engineered to express certain traits—mainly insect resistance, herbicide resistance, and nutrient profile. Crops engineered for nutrients include canola, soybean, and corn—these are often altered in order to change the oil or protein content. Crops engineered for herbicide resistance reduce the need for labor pulling weeds in fields, reduce the need for tillage (which keeps more carbon in the soil), and allow larger areas of monocultures to be grown. Crops engineered for insecticide resistance reduce the need for insecticide use. As mentioned in Chapter 2, *Bacillus thuringiensis* (Bt), a bacterium that kills certain insects, is expressed in Bt crops such as Bt cotton and Bt corn, thereby providing internal protection against insects. Crops can also be engineered to resist fungi and diseases such as viruses (papaya is one such crop). When successful, such engineering increases yield, allows an industry to survive, and/or decreases use of fungicides and pesticides.

The most common genetically engineered crops are commodity crops—such as corn, cotton, canola, potato, tobacco, soybeans, and alfalfa. These crops are grown in the U.S., Brazil, China, India, and Canada, and are often used as animal feed and fuel, rather than being fed to humans directly: According to the Institute for Agricultural and Trade Policy, "[a]round 60 percent of corn and 47 percent of soy produced in the United States is used in domestic livestock production for feed."[49] Eighty percent of soy grown in the Amazon is used for animal feed.[50]

The debates over regulation of genetically engineered crops touch on a number of issues, including ownership of the seeds, performance of crops, resistance to herbicides,[51] promotion of monocultures, and the fact that there is a need to use patented herbicides, such as glyphosate (Roundup). Despite safety concerns on the part of the public, a number of scientific and regulatory agencies have concluded that genetically engineered foods are safe for human consumption.[52]

5.4.3 Transportation

The long-distance transportation of food expands markets and allows more foods to be accessible in many locations. However, many people see long-distance transportation as undesirable. While food transportation accounts for a relatively low percentage of the total climate impact of food—estimated at less than 10% of total greenhouse gases[53]—most food transportation occurs via trucks or ships powered by diesel engines, which contribute significantly to particulate matter pollution and ozone depletion. This also changes the economic characteristics of food production, distributing profits across a broader area. In response to these issues, many people are promoting a shift toward more local and seasonal food production, which includes farmers' markets. We will discuss these and other alternatives in greater depth in Chapter 7.

5.4.4 Land use

Changing landscapes and land use has significant environmental impacts: Clearing a forest, grassland, or wetland alters habitats of nonhuman animals, alters water retention, releases carbon dioxide into the atmosphere, and increases soil erosion (by removing the roots and vegetation that keep soil in place).

The clearing of land (mostly forest) for agricultural use makes up almost half of total anthropogenic land use.[54] Given this fact, agriculture—inclusive of grazing and feed crops—is the leading driver of deforestation globally. The UN FAO estimates that "grazing occupies 26 percent of the Earth's terrestrial surface, while feed crop production requires about a third of all arable land."[55]

Forests, in addition to plants and soil (discussed later in this chapter) are **carbon sinks**,[56] meaning that they sequester carbon.[57] Rainforest and mangrove conversion is particularly impactful, as they store significant amounts of carbon. (Mangroves also provide habitat for aquatic animals.) One recent study calculated that the clearing of mangroves for a single shrimp and beef meal releases an amount of carbon dioxide equivalent to what would be released driving a fuel-efficient car from New York to Los Angeles.[58]

Clearing can be done with machinery or via slash-and-burn, where forest or field is cut down and then burned. This creates erosion, air pollution (including black carbon and other particulate matter pollution), and the rapid depletion of soil nutrients, leaving less carbon in the soil. Alternatives include slash-and-char, which leaves more carbon in the soil, and alley cropping, which involves planting trees that either provide shade or fix nitrogen (a process discussed later on in this chapter; also called sequestration). These practices partially mitigate some of the damages of slash-and-burn. When a plot of land is depleted of sufficient nutrients to grow crops, as is often the case after slash-and-burn, new land needs to be cleared—releasing carbon and causing more environmental harm. In addition to these impacts, clearing and changing land alters its **albedo** (reflectivity) and surface roughness. This changes local climate conditions and local water conditions.

But while the environmental impacts of clearing land can include many harms, they can also include some benefits. For example, they can create new habitats and fix carbon.

The range of activities that impact the release and storage of carbon dioxide are called **land use, land-use change, and forestry (LULUCF)** activities. LULUCF activities have environmental costs as well as benefits. Examples include (but are not limited to):

→ The conversion of mangroves to land releases large amounts of carbon
→ The burning of tropical peatland for palm plantation releases large amounts of carbon as well[59]
→ Plants grow roots, which reduce the rate of erosion
→ Nutrients from crops can be returned to the soil to increase organic matter, nitrogen, and minerals
→ Grazing can distribute nitrogen-rich manure across pastures, thereby reducing the need for feed crops.[60]

When we are talking about land use and land-use change concern, we are often talking about animal agriculture. Of land used for agriculture, 75% is used for raising farmed animals.[61] This includes land used for grazing as well as for production of animal feed such as soybeans and corn. In contrast, fruits and vegetables cover ~5% of U.S. cropland.[62] Corn is used primarily for fuel and feed, with less than 20% of the crop going directly toward food products.[63] On a global scale, about 60% of crops are used to feed humans directly; one third is fed to nonhuman animals.[64]

Since land-use change is such a significant environmental impact, the intensification of production on existing land can in some senses be preferable (even if it causes other environmental harms) to clearing new land. There are different forms of intensification (more or less monocultured, more or less fertilized), and possible functions of the land. A given plot could be used for conservation ("land sparing"); a mix of agriculture, habitat and ecosystem services ("land sharing"); or simply intensive agriculture without environmental benefits.

The environmental impacts of land use and land-use change are distributed unevenly across the world. Industrialized countries that import many goods and adopt environmental regulation have seen a drop in agricultural land use, in part because land is seen as more valuable for real estate than for agriculture. Industrializing countries are seeing an increase in land clearing for agricultural use.

As we will see, such land-use choices have both positive and negative impacts on food production, biodiversity, climate change, and agricultural economies. We should note that difficult trade-offs are often unavoidable. A recent analysis discusses meeting UN Sustainable Development Goals and notes that "[s]imultaneous achievement of multiple targets is rare owing to the complexity of sustainability target implementation and the pervasive trade-offs in resource-constrained land systems."[65] Others identify this trade-off when comparing land use for bioenergy and food.[66] In other words, if you care about food production, biodiversity, climate change, erosion and agricultural economies, it might be quite difficult to optimize in each of these domains.

5.4.5 Trade-offs in food production

Trade-offs can arise when comparing agricultural systems. An intensive agricultural area, such as corn-growing regions in the midwestern U.S., produces a large yield per acre. By some calculations, what is produced in these areas might be the maximum yield possible with given crops and technology. The intensive production often requires specialized crops, high inputs of fertilizers, and aggressive management of species considered to be "pests." All of these attributes contribute to environmental impacts—nitrogen pollution, significant pesticide and herbicide use, and destruction of habitat. At the same time, these practices produce a lot of corn. Herein lies a deep tension in agricultural practices: Intensive practices use more resources for a given area of land, but also produce more food for a given area of land.

This tension poses a conflict. Often, we can either extract a maximum amount of a crop from a given piece of land (thereby using more energy on these crops), or we can produce fewer crops on a larger piece of land (thereby clearing more land for these crops).[67] Depending on the environmental impact of the LULUC (here we exclude forestry and focus on land use directly related to food agriculture), each choice might be better in some contexts. Some people also argue that this trade-off is exaggerated, and that the appropriate emphasis should be on *sustainable intensification*, which preserves the strengths of each form of land use.[68] Some forms of sustainable intensification might lower greenhouse gas emissions as well if they require no additional land use.[69]

Different landscapes support different agricultural functions. Some are suitable for grazing but not for crops, and others are suitable for some crops but not for others. Lands that are not suitable for crops but are sometimes suitable for grazing are called **marginal lands**. Land used for grazing and animal feed cannot *all* be converted to non-feed cropland.[70] Finally, we should note that assessments of land use contain multiple facets, including the opportunity costs of using land for one purpose (such as feed crops) rather than for another (for instance, carbon sequestering grasslands).

Any projection of land-use needs based on existing trends should be qualified accordingly. We will need significantly more land to feed a growing population *if* they consume higher order foods. Diets can change, however, and any change in diets can change projections dramatically. A host of recent studies emphasize this variability by finding that meat-heavy diets harm the environment much more than alternatives.[71]

5.4.6 Soil

Soil is a fundamental part of most agricultural systems. "Healthy" soil needs soil organic matter (SOM), organisms (especially nitrogen-fixing ones), characteristics such as permeability and density, and nutrients such as nitrogen, phosphorus, potassium, carbon, and minerals. Both industrial and non-industrial practices can affect soil dramatically. Land management practices such as rotational grazing, crop rotations, conservation agriculture, cover cropping, monocultures, and intensive management can extract nutrients, add nutrients, and yield agricultural products in different proportions. The practice of crop rotation and planting cover crops (plants like rye and vetch that fix nitrogen, decrease erosion, and add organic matter to soil) can balance nitrogen and residues for protection from the elements. Allowing land time to be fallow can restore fertility.

Erosion is a form of soil degradation where soil is displaced, resulting in the loss of nutrients. This can happen both naturally and anthropogenically, but agriculture is the largest cause of erosion globally.[72] Because of the scale of agriculture, agricultural practices such as deforestation, monocropping, terracing, grazing, plowing, and tilling[73] have a significant effect on erosion. Some causes of erosion (e.g., mechanized plowing) are due to industrialization, while others (such as slash-and-burn) exist in both industrial and non-industrial forms.

Nitrogen is a macronutrient that is essential for leaf and plant growth, because it is needed for chlorophyll and protein development. Atmospheric nitrogen needs to be in a form that is usable to (non-leguminous) plants, meaning that it has to be "fixed" by other elements to convert it to ammonia and make it chemically available to the plant. This can be done industrially or via microorganisms. We will use the term "nitrogen" in a wide sense that refers to any form that can be available to plants, rather than in a narrow sense that refers to a particular chemical element.

Plants can get nitrogen from the atmosphere, SOM, animal manure, plant matter (created from plants plowed back into the soil as "green manure"), or synthetic fertilizers (created via industrial fixation, called the Haber-Bosch process). Some plants, such as soy, alfalfa, and peanuts, are hospitable to microbes that fix nitrogen, and therefore require less nitrogen input from fertilizer and can be used to replenish soils.

Nitrogen that is not used by plants is often released into the air or water. Especially in intensive agricultural settings, this creates nutrient fluxes, which result in the overgrowth of algae, blocking of sunlight to plants beneath the algae, decomposition of those plants, decreases in the dissolved oxygen content of the water, and subsequent diminishing of fishes and plant life. This can create "dead zones" that kill fishes due to oxygen depletion. As of 2017, the dead zone in the Gulf of Mexico is the largest recorded, at almost 9,000 square miles.[74] Animal agriculture contributes to these issues both directly (by producing massive amounts of manure) and indirectly (by using fertilizers in the growth of farmed animal feed that contribute to runoff).

In addition to nitrogen, potassium and phosphorus are the other two elements needed for plants to grow. **Potassium** (K) is derived from ashes or mined from deposits. Mined potassium is finite with unclear industrial substitutions, and is concentrated in a small number of countries.[75] **Phosphorus** (P) is derived from rock phosphate. It is unevenly distributed, with over 70% occurring in Morocco.[76] In the 1800s, phosphorus was also sourced from guano (droppings from bats and seabirds).

Current rates of phosphorus use are unsustainable. Some estimate that we will run out of it in 50–100 years[77] and that we have now reached "peak phosphorus,"[78] meaning that we are using phosphorus at higher rates than we can extract it. Such estimates depend on a number of variables, making the exact date of the peak difficult to calculate.[79]

Animal agriculture has a disproportionate impact on phosphorus use. According to a study in *Environmental Research Letters*:

> Meat consumption was the most important factor affecting P footprints; it accounted for 72% of the global average P footprint. Our results show that dietary shifts are an important component of the human amplification of the global P cycle.[80]

As with other finite resources, these predictions about phosphorus raise concerns about geopolitical tensions[81] as well as about potential substitutes.[82]

While insufficient nutrients lead to low plant growth and impaired photosynthesis, excess nutrients can harm plants (e.g., with fertilizer burn) and ecosystems. Growing crops intensively can deplete soils of secondary nutrients and micronutrients if they are not replenished.

5.4.7 Soil carbon

Soil is one of the major stores of carbon. This means that soil management is not only affected by climate change, but also affects climate change in turn. Because grasslands, forests, and other types of land store carbon, the conversion of these lands for agriculture often results in the release of carbon and reduction of carbon entering the soil due to lost vegetation. Soils that are disrupted regularly, for example by tillage during field agriculture, generally have lower amounts of carbon in them.[83] Reducing tillage can reduce the release of carbon from soils, but since tillage is a form of weed control, this reduction often requires the introduction of herbicides. The bulk of U.S. farmland is losing soil through erosion at six times the sustainable rate.[84]

Soil ecologist Richard Bardgett describes the basic relationship between soil and carbon:

> The amount of carbon in soil is determined by how much goes in from plants and how much goes out through decomposition of organic matter, burning, and soil erosion. To increase soil carbon content you therefore need to put

more carbon into the soil and at the same time reduce how much comes out. Many of the world's soils are depleted in carbon as a result of the burden of decades of heavy cultivation and overgrazing.[85]

The relationship between climate change and soil carbon is not linear, as it is part of a complex ecological system. Increased temperature can make more nitrogen available to trees (or the opposite, depending on the region), increasing their carbon sequestration. Droughts can kill trees, releasing carbon as they decompose. Temperature changes impact soil moisture, which in turn impacts microbial activity and erosion. Lastly, variations in grazing animals—both wild and domesticated—can also influence soil carbon: Depending on what the animals eat, the vegetation will change to be more or less dominant, influencing soil carbon, erosion, soil temperature, and nitrogen cycling.[86]

The amount of carbon cycling through the soil-plant-atmosphere system allows for many interventions that could potentially store significant amounts of carbon. There are some practices that generally lead to an increase in carbon storage. According to the Intergovernmental Panel on Climate Change (IPCC):

> Soil carbon content can be protected and even increased through alteration of tillage practices, crop rotations, residue management, reduction of soil erosion, improvement of irrigation and nutrient management, and other changes in forestland and cropland management.[87]

These practices have side benefits such as decreases in erosion and the building of SOM as well. As a large-scale mitigation effort, it is difficult to generalize about their efficacy. Climate, moisture, crops, grazing animals, and interactions between carbon, nitrogen, microbes, and plant matter are all relationships that vary across regions and agricultural practices.

Given the massive scale of the amount of carbon coming in and out of soils, any seemingly small changes can have big impacts. Bardgett writes:

> Although scientists are divided on the benefits of soil carbon sequestration for combating climate change, it has been proposed that by changing the way we manage the world's agricultural and degraded soils, we could boost soil carbon pools by 0.4 to 1.2 billion tonnes per year, which is equivalent to 5 to 15 percent of the global fossil-fuel emissions.

Recent estimates indicate that climate change will substantially increase carbon release from soils, making up 12–17% of total anthropogenic emissions by 2050.[88] A recent French government proposal calculated that carbon neutrality was possible with proper soil management.[89] However, one critique calculates that in order for soils to sequester that much additional carbon, a significant amount of nitrogen fertilizers would have to be used—offsetting the carbon sequestration.[90] While sequestering carbon in soil has great potential, there is substantial uncertainty about the degree of regional variability, the likelihood of achieving a net improvement through this methodology, and the best ways to accurately measure the amount of carbon sequestered.

5.4.8 Water

Industrial agriculture gets and distributes water through natural irrigation (snow-melt, rainfall, and flooding) and artificial irrigation (canals, artifical flooding, and redirecting water from wells). The scale of industrial agriculture and the advanced technology for finding groundwater, pumping water, and building tunnels has allowed for increased sourcing of water. Many modes of getting groundwater and surface water to crops and animals are pre-modern, including channels, tunnels, wells, aqueducts, and remarkably sophisticated long-distance transport and storage systems.

Groundwater (water that we get from below the surface) and surface water is called "blue water," rain is called "green water," and water with only trace amounts of salt is called "freshwater."[91] Depending on the crop, water in the same region might be sufficient in certain times of year such as the early spring, but not in the summer. In areas where arable land is not being used for agriculture, water needs might be insufficient or excessively expensive for growing food.[92] The impact of water use depends on the season, crop, and end use of the water (e.g., water crops or providing water to farmed animals). A crop that can be irrigated in the spring, for instance, might have similar water use to one that must be irrigated in the summer, but cause more of a strain on water reserves due to less available water in the summer. Similarly, blue water suitable for human consumption is not required for many crops, and so it draws from different sources.

Agriculture is the most significant user of freshwater in the world, comprising 70% of freshwater consumed in the world[93] and 80–90%[94] of freshwater consumed in the U.S.[95] This makes it a much larger user of water than industry and end-consumers (those who use water at home) combined. Experts estimate that "[o]nly about 17% of the world's cropland is irrigated, but this irrigated land produces 40% of the world's food."[96]

The amount of water required for different food products varies greatly, from 2,000 liters/kilogram (240 gallons/pound) for soybeans to 51,000 liters/kilogram (~6,123 gallons/pound) for sheep.[97] Since farmed animals raised for food consume land as well as crops that require irrigation, their water "footprint" (the amount of water used toward the final food product, such as a hamburger) tends to be very high. Larger animals eating forage and feed use a disproportionate amount of water. Scholars write that

> [t]he production of animal protein requires significantly more water than the production of plant protein . . . Although U.S. livestock directly uses [by drinking] only 2% of the total water used in agriculture . . . the indirect water inputs for livestock production are substantial because of the water required for forage and grain crops.[98]

Water use in agriculture is part of a complex ecological system. As with pesticides and fertilizers, a large percentage of agricultural water does not reach the intended plants or animals—instead evaporating, leaking, or running off. In the case of crops, land is irrigated for the entire growing season, and water often evaporates either in channels on the way to the field or during the process of being sprayed over the crops. This water loss occurs over many weeks, adding up significantly. In some cases, simple technical solutions exist, and just need to be adopted. These include using drip irrigation, using dryland farming techniques, and planting drought-resistant crops.

After being harvested or slaughtered, the processing of crops and animals requires even more water as they are cleaned, frozen, prepared, and/or packaged. The amount of water needed for these tasks is significantly more than daily showers or faucet use. By one estimate, "people consume 30–300 litres [~8–80 gallons] per person a day for domestic purposes, while 3,000 litres [~793 gallons] per day are needed to grow their daily food (Turner et al., 2004)."[99] As with animal use and land use, the key to understanding water use in agriculture is understanding the massive scale at which it operates.

Groundwater is becoming depleted, primarily due to irrigation[100] and is distributed asymmetrically, meaning that only three countries use the majority of groundwater linked to international food trade. California, a historically dry area, produces the majority of the fruits, vegetables, and nuts in the U.S. It only recently benefited from canals and pipelines moving water from the wetter north to the drier south. If snowpack in the Sierra continues to diminish, as it is projected to due to climate change, a significant amount of water for agricultural use would no longer flow into aquifers supplying agricultural land.

Overall, water use far exceeds long-term availability in several areas of agricultural significance: According to environmental scientists, "humans are overexploiting groundwater in many large aquifers that are critical to agriculture, especially in Asia and North America."[101] If we continue current trends in water use without efficiency improvements, we will outstrip available supplies by 40% by 2030.[102]

5.4.9 Climate

Agriculture accounts for about a third—with cows in particular producing about a tenth—of anthropogenic greenhouse gas emissions.[103] Certain land-use practices are also especially intensive in their emissions of greenhouse gases (such as burning palm plantations in Indonesia).

Carbon dioxide (CO_2) is the main greenhouse gas, and it is emitted by deforestation and land-use change, soils, and the burning of fossil fuels by farm equipment. It is relatively stable in the atmosphere, meaning that it continues to trap heat for many decades.

The IPCC describes many kinds of changes in carbon stocks due to land-use change, including conversion of natural ecosystems to permanent croplands or pasture, shifting of cultivation, and abandonment of croplands or pastures.[104] Each of these has complicated impacts on carbon stocks. For example, the clearing of land releases carbon dioxide from the soil and, if trees are burned, from combustion.

Methane (CH_4) is created in anaerobic environments (environments with little or no available oxygen). In agriculture, the main sources of methane are rice paddies (which are flooded, creating an anaerobic environment), the digestion of ruminant animals such as cows (whose stomachs are anaerobic environments), and animal waste (due to the anaerobic decomposition). As the IPCC notes, "[r]ice cultivation and livestock (enteric fermentation) have been estimated to be the two primary sources of CH_4 . . . Alteration of rice cultivation practices, livestock feed, and fertilizer use are potential management practices that could reduce CH_4 and N_2O sources."[105]

Rice production already has a significant climate impact, which is getting worse due to decreased yield resulting from climate change.[106] Rice paddies are responsible for 20–100 megatons of methane per year.[107] Meanwhile, farmed animals are responsible for 85–130 megatons of methane per year because of digestion and waste. In the U.S., the Environmental Protection Agency (EPA) estimates that methane emissions from cows comprise 25% of all methane emissions.[108] This is approximately the same as (and might be higher than) methane emissions from the energy sector.[109] Methane emissions due to animal waste are greater in industrialized settings, as the anaerobic environment created by waste lagoons and piles creates the anaerobic conditions necessary for methane production. Methane emissions have been increasing at a more rapid rate in the last 20 years, with agriculture thought to be the main contributor to this increase.[110]

Nitrous oxide (N_2O) is created when synthetic and manure fertilizers are applied to fields, and also occurs naturally in soils. In addition to trapping heat in the atmosphere, nitrous oxide depletes the ozone layer and pollutes waterways and groundwater. Unlike carbon and methane, it does not have a major natural sink, meaning that the earth does not reabsorb much of it.[111] Nitrogen pollution, such as nitrites in drinking water, is a significant health problem in some agricultural areas.

The IPCC notes that "[t]he primary sources of N_2O are denitrification and nitrification processes in soils. Emissions of N_2O are estimated to have increased significantly as a result of changes in fertilizer use and animal waste."[112] Since there are no substitutes for nitrogen (it is an essential nutrient for plant growth), mitigation pathways for nitrogen pollution are different from those for carbon dioxide and methane.[113]

Carbon dioxide, methane, and nitrous oxide are all released when synthetic fertilizer is manufactured. Agriculture differs from the energy and transportation sectors in that CO_2 is not the dominant greenhouse gas. According to one landmark study, farmed animals account for 9% of anthropogenic CO_2, 37% of anthropogenic methane, and 65% of anthropogenic nitrous oxide, totaling 80% of all agricultural emissions.[114] Other greenhouses gases—such as chlorofluorocarbons, which include refrigerants—are used when transporting and storing food.

Of the greenhouse gas impact of animal agriculture, 35% is due to deforestation and desertification,[115] 30% is manure management (direct and indirect),[116] and 25% is enteric fermentation.[117] Note that these categories apply in cases of both industrial and non-industrial animal agriculture.

Given the tremendous percentage of land use caused by agriculture, this adds up to a large percentage of overall greenhouse gases. About one-third of total greenhouse gas emissions are attributed to agriculture and land-use change (especially deforestation), though this number does not account for the sequestering of carbon in ecosystems.[118]

Life cycle assessments—which quantify the impacts of a product from production to consumption—vary based on a number of factors. One factor is the classification of impacts. For example, the environmental impacts of transportation of agricultural products can be categorized as transportation impacts or as agricultural impacts. But they cannot be accurately categorized as both, since that would involve double counting. Thus, how we classify such impacts will play a significant role in shaping our assessments of each sector.

Another factor affecting variation across estimates is how different variables are weighed. For example, the amount of heat that each gas traps is a function of the time period we are measuring. Carbon dioxide stays in the atmosphere for much more time than methane and nitrous oxide do. However, methane and nitrous oxide trap heat more effectively while in the atmosphere than carbon dioxide does. This means that if we look at the environmental impacts of agriculture on, say, a 100-year timescale, this will amplify the role of carbon in the climate impacts, whereas if we look at the environmental impacts of agriculture on, say, a 20-year timescale, this will amplify the roles of methane and nitrous oxide in the climate impacts.

This has policy implications, as agriculture accounts for "52% and 84% of global anthropogenic methane and nitrous oxide emissions."[119] If we are concerned about limiting temperature increase in the long run, then carbon dioxide becomes the dominant concern. If we are concerned about limiting temperature increase in the short term, then methane and nitrous oxide become the dominant concern. In particular, some note that if we want to address climate change in the near future, then we should target cow production, as cows live short lives and contribute methane to the atmosphere.[120]

These impacts raise questions about how we incentivize and practice diets. Many studies show that reductions in meat consumption lead to reductions in dietary greenhouse gas emissions.[121] For example, one study shows that dietary greenhouse gas emissions in self-selected meat-eaters are approximately twice as high as those in vegans.[122] As a result, many people now believe that if we want to meet greenhouse gas targets, then we need to address consumption of animal products.[123] The projected increase in consumption of animal products alone could account for much or all of the "carbon budget," which keeps the increase in global temperature to 2 degrees Celsius (about 3.6 degrees Fahrenheit).[124] Environmental scientists Pelletier and Tyedmers write that:

> To meet sustainability boundary conditions whilst maintaining year 2000 proportional contributions to total anthropogenic impacts for GHG emissions, biomass appropriation, and reactive nitrogen mobilization may require reductions in anticipated per capita consumption in 2050 to the order of 19%, 42%, and 21% of projected levels, respectively.[125]

5.5 Humans

Agriculture is fundamental to human civilization and values—it provides food for the world's population and underlies dozens of cultural and religious practices. Agriculture impacts trade, cultural exchange, and settlement patterns. The human dimension of agriculture takes myriad forms, which we will discuss briefly in this chapter before detailing them in their industrial and non-industrial contexts in Chapters 6 and 7, respectively.

5.5.1 Labor

Over one billion people—over one third of the available workforce—are employed in the global agricultural sector.[126] Agriculture constitutes approximately 70% of the global employment of children, and in many countries it employs the largest percentage of women of any sector.[127] Within agriculture, the livestock sector makes up 40% of agricultural economic product and produces one third of total protein intake.[128]

Agricultural workers are often expected to do demanding work for poor compensation and tend to be socially, politically, and economically vulnerable. Many have no alternative economic prospects, and their economic subsistence is heavily reliant upon market forces beyond their control. In industrialized countries, the labor required for farm work (including harvest) is often done by migrant workers. Farm labor is excluded from many U.S. legal protections, and workers without immigration documentation are often highly vulnerable. Since agricultural practices vary tremendously, agricultural labor can range from automated and well compensated (much less common) to exceptionally demanding and poorly compensated (much more common). This applies in industrialized as well as non-industrialized agricultural settings. Fruit and vegetable pickers in the U.S., for example, are exempt from standard labor laws governing overtime compensation,[129] work grueling hours at tasks that are extremely taxing on their bodies, and are subjected to harmful environmental conditions such as pesticide and sun exposure.

Non-industrial labor practices might be preferable to those in industrial settings in that less dangerous machinery is involved and air pollution from synthetic fertilizers and pesticides is lower. In some cases, however—such as berry picking—the repetitive motion stresses and exposure to sun and the elements negatively impact laborers in both settings.

5.5.2 Population

Many ethical concerns about agriculture are based on projections of population growth and consumption growth and changes. There are currently more than 7 billion humans on the planet, and experts predict that this number will reach 9 or 10 billion by 2050 and 10 or 11 billion by 2100.[130] While many people accept these projections, many other people encourage us to challenge them: humanity is using the planet excessively both as a source (for land cultivation and grazing, freshwater, wild fishes, bushmeat, fossil fuels, wood products, and so on) and as a sink (an environment that absorbs wastes such as carbon dioxide, nitrogen, trash, pesticides, industrial chemicals, and farmed animal manure). Stabilizing and lowering our numbers globally—non-coercively, through the exercise of reproductive rights—is a strategy for scaling down consumption on all fronts.[131] This is a non-technical approach to addressing environmental problems, which complements technical as well as non-technical approaches to reducing consumption and emissions per capita.

5.5.3 Justice

Within any labor market, there are concerns about equity and rights. The unequal distribution of benefits and harms—and the exclusion of the individuals most impacted from the decision-making process—raises important moral and political questions. This includes questions about who owns land, crops, seeds, and equipment. It also includes questions about the affordability of supplies on the production side, and the affordability of culturally and nutritionally appropriate foods on the consumption side. The following movements encompass some of the main responses to injustices.

Food security is the provisioning of healthful, culturally appropriate foods to all people. This can take the form of local food production and distribution—as supply is no longer dependent upon outside actors—but it can also take the form of global food production and distribution, provided that food products reliably reach everyone who needs them. However, some have criticized the concept of food security for being inadequate to fully account for the complexity and ethical gravity of the problem of food access and agency.

Unfortunately, many parts of the world that rely on agriculture as a primary source of income have water shortages. The UN FAO notes that "[o]ne of the major challenges in agricultural development today is to maintain food security and alleviate poverty without further depleting water resources and damaging ecosystems."[132] Some of this is a function of local climate or historical overuse, and some is a function of lack of basic irrigation technology (one of the problems targeted in the Green Revolution, discussed in Chapter 6).

Food justice is the equitable access to food. A more encompassing view includes the equitable distribution of benefits and harms associated with agricultural production, as well as links with other, related social justice issues involving race, gender, health and disability status, and more.[133]

Food sovereignty is control over food production. It includes community decision making regarding food, and takes different forms in different cultural contexts. It is often positioned in opposition to globalized trade of commodity foods, as it emphasizes local autonomy and genetic diversity of foods, among other values.

There is a strong connection between poverty and the lack of access to land and water resources. Worldwide, many of the most economically disadvantaged people have the least access to land and water. They are locked in a poverty trap of small farms with low quality soils and high vulnerability to land degradation and uncertain weather. Technologies and farming systems within reach of economically disadvantaged people typically contribute to land degradation.[134]

Ownership of land impacts food security and farmer autonomy. As industrialized countries have used most of their arable land, they are acquiring land in more economically disadvantaged parts of the world.[135] This can undermine food security in these regions, as farmers might not have enough land to grow crops needed for subsistence, forcing them to purchase food at markets. This is more expensive, and, as a result, it maintains the cycle of poverty.

We will discuss some of the human rights implications of industrial and non-industrial food systems in Chapters 6 and 7, and we will discuss some of the implications for the ethics of food production, consumption, and activism in Chapters 8, 9, and 10.

5.5.4 Public health

The public health impacts of waste and pollution in agriculture are extensive. Independent of whether or not the source of pollution is industrial, such harms impact local communities in multiple ways.

Agriculture is a main user and polluter of all water. Agriculture can drain aquifers[136] and rivers,[137] diverting water from other uses. Manure, pesticides, and synthetic nitrogen fertilizer all pollute water. This same water becomes drinking water and animal habitat. The pollution is both bacterial (from manure) and chemical (from an excess of nitrogen).[138]

Concentrations of pollutants are often worse in industrial agriculture. In some cases, such as **concentrated animal feeding operations** (CAFOs) and intensive industrial plant agriculture, nitrogen pollution is incredibly concentrated—resulting in more severe health consequences.[139] This pollution has direct health consequences for populations, especially historically and presently disenfranchised communities near agricultural land.

Agriculture also results in air pollution. One source is fertilizer (both synthetic and organic), which produces nitrous oxide. Another is farm machinery, which produces CO_2 and particulate matter pollution, and leads to respiratory diseases such as asthma. This once again disproportionately impacts disenfranchised communities near agricultural land and food distribution centers.

Other public health concerns include the use of antibiotics (and the development of antibiotic-resistant bacteria, including superbugs) and of pesticides—which are harmful to crops, insects, weeds, rodents, fishes, fungi, algae, and others. Antibiotics are used much more frequently in industrial animal agriculture, while pesticides, although more predominant in industrial settings, are used in both settings.

The health impacts of exposure to pesticides in or near agricultural fields are significant.[140] This includes associations with chronic disease and cancer.[141] The main impacts are on workers, children, wildlife, and pollinators.[142] We discuss this in more detail in Chapters 6 and 7.

5.5.5 Hunger

We produce enough food for everyone, and yet hundreds of millions of people across the globe live in hunger.[143] This is due to a combination of poverty, corruption, inefficient distribution of food, inefficient use of food, and food waste. We convert first order food like corn and soy into animal products, less nutritious non-perishable food products, and non-food products such as ethanol. We store food, distribute it to those with political power, and trade it on a global market for prices unaffordable to many. For those regions that provide sufficient food, it often comes at a significant environmental cost: recent research concludes that "no country meets basic needs for its citizens at a globally sustainable level of resource use."[144] Even in areas where we produce sufficient food, climate change threatens future production of food.[145]

Many people think that increasing food production will allow us to "feed the world." But if we already produce more calories than people need, then simply producing more food might be neither necessary nor sufficient for feeding the world. Instead, structural, social, political, and economic changes connected to food justice, food sovereignty, and plant-based agriculture might be necessary.

First, in addition to ensuring sufficient production, we need to ensure that food is accessible, affordable, culturally appropriate, and nutritious for everyone. Second, shifting just 16 major crops to first order food for humans can increase food calories *delivered* by 50% (1 billion tons).[146] The U.S. produces massive amounts of corn but does not feed much of it to humans. As Jonathan Foley writes, "the corn *crop* is highly productive, but the corn *system* is aligned to feed cars and animals instead of feeding people."[147] Similarly, soybeans in the Amazon are grown on cleared rainforest land and largely used as feed for farmed animals.

Some solutions include consuming first order food and decreasing problems in supply, transportation, and storage that inhibit food from reaching its targeted audience. Given that we currently use much of the food we grow to feed to farmed animals, decreasing this amount would ultimately yield more first order food. (Dietary shifts must also be culturally appropriate in order to be adopted.) The political, cultural, and market complexities of such a shift are hotly debated, however.[148] For example, eating less meat and more wheat could increase the price of wheat in more economically disadvantaged parts of the world, causing hardship.

5.6 Conclusion

As we have seen, many impacts of agriculture arise from both industrial and non-industrial forms. The scale of agriculture—specifically, the number of animals used, the amount of land use involved, and the conversion of energy—partially explains its significant impacts.

The next two chapters detail industrial agriculture and alternatives to industrial agriculture. We should note that this division is imperfect, as many practices resist this categorization—an organic farm might use non-synthetic pesticides and fertilizers, but might also use modern genetic varieties, mechanized farm equipment, and refrigerated storage facilities. Overall, however, this division will help us to see the distinctive impacts of industrial agriculture. They will also help us to see that while non-industrial food systems have many benefits, they have many costs as well.

Notes

1 PDF linked from "Fair Compensation for Farmworkers in Global Agricultural Supply Chains: Emerging Good Practices and Challenges," Fair Labor Association, published February 2017. Accessible from "World Food and Agriculture," FAO Statistical Yearbook 2012, published 2012, www.fao.org/docrep/015/i2490e/i2490e00.htm.

2 Elke Stehfest et al., "Climate benefits of changing diet," *Climatic Change* 95, no. 1–2 (April 2008): 83–102.

3 A biome is a large community of plants and animals adapted to their specific environment.

4 Jonathan A. Foley et al., "Global Consequences of Land Use," *Science* 309, no. 5734 (July 2005): 570–574.
   "Land Use," Food and Agriculture Organization of the United Nations, accessed February 16, 2018, www.fao.org/faostat/en/#data/EL.

5 "What Is Happening to Agrobiodiversity?" Food and Agriculture Organization of the United Nations, www.fao.org/docrep/007/y5609e/y5609e02.htm (cache).

6 Cows weigh 450 million tons and humans weigh 280 million tons.
   Vaclav Smil, *The Earth's Biosphere: Evolution, Dynamics, and Change* (Cambridge: MIT Press, 2003).

7 "Meat Production Continues to Rise," Worldwatch Institute, last updated March 17, 2018, www.worldwatch.org/node/5443.

8 We came to this number by calculating the aggregate of land animals slaughtered using the sources below. Some are a few years old, many have ranges, and all are estimates. We agreed upon 70 billion as an approximate total.
   "FLEISCHATLAS: Daten und Fakten über Tiere als Nahrungsmittel," Heinrich Böll Stiftung, 2014, www.boell.de/sites/default/files/fleischatlas2014_vi.pdf#page=19 (~65 billion in 2011).
   "Visualize Data," Livestock Primary, Food and Agriculture Organization of the United Nations, www.fao.org/faostat/en/#data/QL/visualize (60–75 billion in 2016).
   "Strategic Plan 2013–2017," Compassion in World Farming, www.ciwf.org.uk/media/3640540/ciwf_strategic_plan_20132017.pdf.
   Che Green, "Animal Advocacy by Numbers," Faunalytics, published July 15, 2016, https://faunalytics.org/animal-advocacy-by-numbers/.
   "Worldwide Animal Slaughter Statistics," Faunalytics, published August 12, 2008, https://faunalytics.org/worldwide-animal-slaughter-statistics/ (54 billion in 2004).

9 Jonathan Safran Foer, *Eating Animals* (New York: Hachette Book Group, 2010): 174.
   "Farms and Farmland," United States Department of Agriculture, published September 2014, www.agcensus.usda.gov/Publications/2012/Online_Resources/Highlights/Farms_and_Farmland/Highlights_Farms_and_Farmland.pdf.

10 Randall Munroe, "Land Mammals," *xkcd*, https://xkcd.com/1338/ using data from:
   Vaclav Smil, *The Earth's Biosphere: Evolution, Dynamics, and Change* (Cambridge: MIT Press, 2003).

11 "Livestock and Landscapes," Food and Agriculture Organization of the United Nations, www.fao.org/docrep/018/ar591e/ar591e.pdf.

12 Energy is lost in the conversion when animals eat first order food unsuitable for human consumption, as in the case of a grazing sheep eating alfalfa. But since the first order food—the alfalfa—is not edible to humans, it is not the case that we are feeding food to food. As such, the environmental story differs from the grain-fed case.

13 L. Brown, R. Hindmarsh, and R. Mcgregor, *Dynamic Agriculture Book Three*. 2nd edition (Sydney: McGraw-Hill Book Company, 2001).

14 David Tilman et al., "Agricultural Sustainability and Intensive Production Practices," *Nature* 418 (August 2002): 671–677.

15 Stefan Wirsenius, "The Biomass Metabolism of the Food System: A Model-Based Survey of the Global and Regional Turnover of Food Biomass," *Journal of Industrial Ecology* 7, no. 1 (February 2008): 47–80.

16 For example, see:
   Arnold van Huis, *Edible Insects: Future Prospects for Food and Feed Security* (Food and Agriculture Organization of the United Nations, 2013).

17 Daniel Pauly et al., "Fishing Down Marine Food Webs," *Science* 279, no. 5352 (February 1998): 860–863.

18 David Pimentel, "Livestock Production and Energy Use," in *Encyclopedia of Energy*, vol. 3 (Basingstoke: Macmillan, 2000).

19 I. Veermäe, J. Frorip, E. Kokin, J. Praks, V. Poikalainen, A. Ruus, L. Lepasalu, "Energy Consumption in Animal Production," Estonian University of Life Sciences, http://enpos.weebly.com/uploads/3/6/7/2/3672459/energy_consumption_in_animal_production.pdf.

20 Michael Clark and David Tilman, "Comparative Analysis of Environmental Impacts of Agricultural Production Systems, Agricultural Input Efficiency, and Food Choice," *Environmental Research Letters* 12 (June 2017).

21 We came to this number by calculating the aggregate of land animals slaughtered using the sources below. Some are a few years old, many have ranges, and all are estimates. We agreed upon 70 billion as an approximate total.
   "FLEISCHATLAS: Daten und Fakten über Tiere als Nahrungsmittel," Heinrich Böll Stiftung, 2014, www.boell.de/sites/default/files/fleischatlas2014_vi.pdf#page=19 (~65 billion in 2011).
   "Visualize Data," Livestock Primary, Food and Agriculture Organization of the United Nations, www.fao.org/faostat/en/#data/QL/visualize (60–75 billion in 2016).
   "Strategic Plan 2013–2017," Compassion in World Farming, www.ciwf.org.uk/media/3640540/ciwf_strategic_plan_20132017.pdf.
   Che Green, "Animal Advocacy by Numbers," Faunalytics, published July 15, 2016, https://faunalytics.org/animal-advocacy-by-numbers/.
   "Worldwide Animal Slaughter Statistics," Faunalytics, published August 12, 2008, https://faunalytics.org/worldwide-animal-slaughter-statistics/ (54 billion in 2004).

22 Liminal animals are animals who occupy a middle ground between domesticated and wild, such as pigeons or rats who live in human communities or feral cats or dogs who live outside of human communities.

23 Bojana Bajželj et al., "Importance of Food-demand Management for Climate Mitigation," *Nature Climate Change* 4 (2014): 924–929.

24 "[H]alving of the number of plant species within a plot leads to a 10–20% loss of productivity."
    David Tilman, "Causes, Consequences and Ethics of Biodiversity," *Nature* 405 (May 2000): 208–211.
25 Richard Manning, *Grassland: The History, Biology, Politics and Promise of the American Prairie* (New York: Penguin, 1997) quoted in:
    Eileen Crist, Camilo Mora, and Robert Engelman, "The Interaction of Human Population, Food Production, and Biodiversity Protection," *Science* 356, no. 6335 (April 2017): 260–264.
26 Henning Steinfeld et al., "Livestock's Long Shadow," Food and Agriculture Organization of the United Nations, published 2006, http://www.europarl.europa.eu/climatechange/doc/FAO%20report%20executive%20summary.pdf. 26.
    Additionally, from the same source:

    Conservation International has identified 35 global hot spots for biodiversity, characterized by exceptional levels of plant endemism and serious levels of habitat loss. Of these, 23 are reported to be affected by livestock production. An analysis of the authoritative World Conservation Union Red List of Threatened Species shows that most of the world's threatened species are suffering habitat loss where livestock are a factor.

27 Ben ten Brink, "Rethinking Global Biodiversity Strategies," Netherlands Environmental Assessment Agency, published 2010, http://www.pbl.nl/en/publications/2010/Rethinking_Global_Biodiversity_Strategies. 81.
28 Christopher K. Wright and Michael C. Wimberly, "Recent Land Use Change in the Western Corn Belt Threatens Grasslands and Wetlands," *Proceedings of the National Academy of Sciences* 110, no. 10 (March 2013): 4134–4139.
29 "Animals," Biodiversity, Food and Agriculture Organization of the United Nations, www.fao.org/biodiversity/components/animals/en/.
30 Z. Shehadeh et al., "Review of the State of World Aquaculture," Food and Agriculture Organization of the United Nations Fisheries Circular No. 886, Food and Agriculture Organization of the United Nations Inland Water Resources and Aquaculture Service, Fishery Resources Division, 1997, www.fao.org/docrep/003/W7499E/W7499E00.HTM.
31 Daniel Pauly and Dirk Zeller, "Catch Reconstructions Reveal that Global Marine Fisheries Catches Are Higher Than Reported and Declining," *Nature Communications* 7, no. 10244 (January 2016).
32 "Fishing Gear Types: Drifting Longlines," Fisheries and Aquaculture Department, Food and Agriculture Organization of the United Nations, www.fao.org/fishery/geartype/233/en.
33 "Fishing Gear Types: Purse Seines," Fisheries and Aquaculture Department, Food and Agriculture Organization of the United Nations, www.fao.org/fishery/geartype/249/en.
34 Albert G.J. Tacon and Marc Metian, "Fishing for Feed or Fishing for Food: Increasing Global Competition for Small Pelagic Forage Fish," *AMBIO: A Journal of the Human Environment* 38, no. 6 (March 2009): 294–302.
35 "The State of World Fisheries and Aquaculture: Contributing to Food Security and Nutrition for All," Food and Agriculture Organization of the United Nations, published 2016, www.fao.org/3/a-i5555e.pdf.
36 "Fish Count Estimates," Fishcount, published 2014, http://fishcount.org.uk/fishcount-estimates#farmedestimate.
37 Dana Gunders, "Wasted: How America Is Losing Up to 40 Percent of Its Food from Farm to Fork to Landfill," National Resources Defense Council, published August 2012, www.nrdc.org/sites/default/files/wasted-food-IP.pdf.

38 "Global Environmental Change," Climate Change and Human Health, World Health Organization, www.who.int/globalchange/environment/en/.
39 William F. Ruddiman, *Plows, Plagues and Petroleum: How Humans Took Control of Climate* (Princeton: Princeton University Press, 2010).

Even in preindustrial times, the environmental impact of agriculture was far-reaching. Early rice farming might have released enough methane to contribute to climate change.
40 David Tilman et al. "Forecasting Agriculturally Driven Global Environmental Change," *Science* 292, no. 5515 (2001): 281–284.
41 "Agricultural production, including indirect emissions associated with land-cover change, contributes 80%–86% of total food system emissions, with significant regional variation."

Sonja J. Vermeulen et al. "Climate Change and Food Systems," *Annual Review of Environment and Resources* 37, no. 1 (2012): 195–222.
42 P. Gerbens-Leenes and S. Nonhebel, "Consumption Patterns and Their Effects on Land Required for Food," *Ecological Economics* 42 (March 200): 185–199.
43 Mesfin M. Mekonnen and Arjen Y. Hoekstra, "A Global Assessment of Water Footprint of Farm Animal Products," *Ecosystems* 15, no. 3 (January 2012): 401–415.
44 Thomas Kastner, Maria Jose Ibarrola Rivas, Wolfgang Koch, and Sanderine Nonhebel, "Global Changes in Diets and the Consequences for Land Requirements for Food," *Proceedings of the National Academy of Sciences* 109, no. 18 (March 2008): 6868–6872.
45   Dietary choices have played an important role in the increased demand for mineral P fertilizer over the past 50 years. The global P footprint increased between 1961 and 2007, but the magnitude and direction of these changes varied among countries. Furthermore, there is a positive correlation between [2007 Human Development Index (HDI) value] and national per capita food P footprints, likely because increases in HDI are associated with a more meat intensive diet. Because meat consumption is the biggest diet contributor to P footprints, future meat consumption may play an important role in the demand for P resources. Decreasing meat consumption in already high P footprint countries could play an important role in sustainable P management strategies, and in synergies with other health and environmental sustainability priorities.

Geneviève S. Metson, Elena M. Bennett, and James J. Elser, "The Role of Diet in Phosphorus Demand," *Environmental Research Letters* 7 (December 2012).
46 For one example from the U.K., see:
"Wasted Milk Is a Drain on Resources," University of Edinburgh, published April 13, 2016, www.ed.ac.uk/news/all-news/140512-climate.
47   Globally, only 62% of crop production (on a mass basis) is allocated to human food, versus 35% to animal feed (which produces human food indirectly, and much less efficiently, as meat and dairy products) and 3% for bioenergy, seed and other industrial products . . . As we face the twin challenges of feeding a growing world while charting a more environmentally sustainable path, the amount of land (and other resources) devoted to animal-based agriculture merits critical evaluation. For example, adding croplands devoted to animal feed (about 350 million hectares) to pasture and grazing lands (3.38 billion hectares), we find the land devoted to raising animals totals 3.73 billion hectares—an astonishing 75% of the world's agricultural land. We further note that meat and dairy production can either add to or subtract from the world's food supply. Grazing systems, especially on pastures unsuitable for other food production, and mixed crop–livestock systems can add calories and protein to the world and improve economic conditions and food security in many regions. However, using highly

productive croplands to produce animal feed, no matter how efficiently, represents a net drain on the world's potential food supply.

Jonathan A. Foley et al., "Solutions for a Cultivated Planet," *Nature* 478 (October 2011): 337–342.
    Ruben N. Lubowski et al., "Major Uses of Land in The United States, 2002," Economic Information Bulletin Number 14, Economic Research Service, United States Department of Agriculture, May 2006, www.ers.usda.gov/webdocs/publications/43967/13011_eib14_1_.pdf?v=42061.

> [D]ue to cumulative losses, the proportion of global agricultural dry biomass consumed as food is just 6% (9.0% for energy and 7.6% for protein), and 24.8% of harvest biomass (31.9% for energy and 27.8% for protein). The highest rates of loss are associated with livestock production, although the largest absolute losses of biomass occur prior to harvest. Losses of harvested crops were also found to be substantial, with 44.0% of crop dry matter (36.9% of energy and 50.1% of protein) lost prior to human consumption. If human overconsumption, defined as food consumption in excess of nutritional requirements, is included as an additional inefficiency, 48.4% of harvested crops were found to be lost (53.2% of energy and 42.3% of protein).

Peter Alexander et al., "Losses, Inefficiencies and Waste in the Global Food System," *Agricultural Systems* 153 (May 2017): 190–200.
48 Dave C. Love, Jillian P. Fry, Michael C. Milli, and Roni A. Neff, "Wasted Seafood in the United States: Quantifying Loss from Production to Consumption and Moving toward Solutions," *Global Environmental Change* 35 (November 2015): 116–124.
49 "Below-Cost Feed Crops: An Indirect Subsidy for Industrial Animal Factories," Institute for Agricultural and Trade Policy, published June 2006, www.iatp.org/sites/default/files/258_2_88122_0.pdf.
50 "Soy Agriculture in the Amazon Basin," Yale School of Forestry and Environmental Studies, http://globalforestatlas.yale.edu/amazon/land-use/soy.
51 For example, "superweeds." See:
    Natasha Gilbert, "Case Studies: A Hard Look at GM Crops," *Nature* 497, no. 7447 (May 2013): 24–26.
52 "Safety of Genetically Engineered Foods: Approaches to Assessing Unintended Health Effects," The National Academies Press, published 2004, www.nap.edu/read/10977/chapter/1.
    Suzie Key, Julian K.-C. Ma, and Pascal M.W. Drake, "Genetically Modified Plants and Human Health," *Journal of the Royal Society of Medicine* 101, no. 6 (June 2008): 290–298.
    "A Decade of EU-funded GMO Research (2001–2010)," European Commission on Food, Agriculture & Fisheries & Biotechnology, 2010, https://ec.europa.eu/research/biosociety/pdf/a_decade_of_eu-funded_gmo_research.pdf.
    "Safety of Genetically Engineered Foods: Approaches to Assessing Unintended Health Effects," The National Academies Press, published 2004, www.nap.edu/read/10977/chapter/1.
    "The Impact of Genetically Engineered Crops on Farm Sustainability in the United States," Committee on the Impact of Biotechnology on Farm-Level Economics and Sustainability, Board on Agriculture and Natural Resources, National Research Council of the National Academies, 2010, www.nap.edu/read/12804/chapter/1#iii.
    Yanhui Lu et al., "Widespread Adoption of Bt Cotton and Insecticide Decrease Promotes Biocontrol Services," *Nature* 487 (July 2012): 362–365.
    Charles M. Benbrook, "Impacts of Genetically Engineered Crops on Pesticide Use in the U.S.—the First Sixteen Years," *Environmental Sciences Europe* 24, no. 24 (September 2012).

David G. Heckel, "Insecticide Resistance after Silent Spring," *Science* 337, no. 6102 (September 2012): 1612–1614.

Louis J. Guillette Jr. and Taisen Iguchi, "Life in a Contaminated World," *Science* 337, no. 6102 (September 2012): 1614–1615.

53 Christopher L. Weber and H. Scott Matthews, "Food-Miles and the Relative Climate Impacts of Food Choices in the United States," *Environmental Science & Technology* 42, no. 10 (May 2008): 3508–3513.

54 Jonathan A. Foley, "Can We Feed the World and Sustain the Planet?" *Scientific American*, November 2011, www.scientificamerican.com/article/can-we-feed-the-world/.

"Land Use," Food and Agriculture Organization of the United Nations, http://faostat3.fao.org/download/E/EL/E.

Jonathan A. Foley et al., "Global Consequences of Land Use," *Science* 309, no. 5734 (July 2005): 570–574.

55 "2015 International Year of Soils," Food and Agriculture Organization of the United Nations, published May 26, 2015, www.fao.org/soils-2015/news/news-detail/en/c/287299/.

Further,

> [e]xpansion of grazing land for livestock is a key factor in deforestation, especially in Latin America: some 70 percent of previously forested land in the Amazon is used as pasture, and feed crops cover a large part of the reminder. About 70 percent of all grazing land in dry areas is considered degraded, mostly because of overgrazing, compaction and erosion attributable to livestock activity.

56 Under the United Nations Framework Convention on Climate Change any process, activity or mechanism which removes a greenhouse gas from the atmosphere is referred to as a 'sink.' Human activities impact terrestrial sinks, through land use, land-use change and forestry (LULUCF) activities, consequently, the exchange of CO_2 (carbon cycle) between the terrestrial biosphere system and the atmosphere is altered.

"Land Use, Land-Use Change and Forestry (LULUCF)," United Nations, http://unfccc.int/land_use_and_climate_change/lulucf/items/1084.php.

57 This is the same as fixing carbon.

58 On the basis of measurements of ecosystem carbon stocks from 30 relatively undisturbed mangrove forests and 21 adjacent shrimp ponds or cattle pastures, we determined that mangrove conversion results in GHG emissions ranging between 1067 and 3003 megagrams of carbon dioxide equivalent (CO_2 e) per hectare. There is a land-use carbon footprint of 1440 kg [~3,175 pounds] CO_2 e for every kilogram of beef and 1603 kg [~3,534 pounds] CO_2 e for every kilogram of shrimps produced on lands formerly occupied by mangroves. A typical steak and shrimp cocktail dinner would burden the atmosphere with 816 kg [~1,799] CO_2 e. This is approximately the same quantity of GHGs produced by driving a fuel-efficient automobile from Los Angeles to New York City. Failure to include deforestation in life-cycle assessments greatly underestimates the GHG emission from food production.

Boone Kauffman et al., "The Jumbo Carbon Footprint of a Shrimp: Carbon Losses from Mangrove Deforestation," *Frontiers in Ecology and the Environment* 15, no. 4 (April 2017): 183–188.

59 Indonesia, despite having an economy 5% the size of the U.S.'s, emits more greenhouse gases. This is in large part due to burning peatlands, which has a "global warming [impact that] may be more than 200 times greater than fires on other lands."

Nancy Harris, Susan Minnemeyer, Fred Stolle, and Octavia Payne, "Indonesia's Fire Outbreaks Producing More Daily Emissions than Entire US Economy," World Resources Institute, published October 16, 2015, www.wri.org/blog/2015/10/

indonesia%E2%80%99s-fire-outbreaks-producing-more-daily-emissions-entire-us-economy.

60 Some claim that carefully managed forms of grazing mimic disruptions to the land that are beneficial to the local ecology (as discussed in Chapter 7).
   Nicolette Hahn Niman, *Defending Beef: The Case for Sustainable Meat Production* (White River Junction: Chelsea Green Publishing, 2014).

61 Jonathan A. Foley et al., "Global Consequences of Land Use," *Science* 309, no. 5734 (July 2005): 570–574.

62 "Farms and Farmland," United States Department of Agriculture, published September 2014, www.agcensus.usda.gov/Publications/2012/Online_Resources/Highlights/Farms_and_Farmland/Highlights_Farms_and_Farmland.pdf.

63 Jonathan Foley, "It's Time to Rethink America's Corn System," *Scientific American*, March 5, 2013, www.scientificamerican.com/article/time-to-rethink-corn/.

64   Globally, only 62% of crop production (on a mass basis) is allocated to human food, versus 35% to animal feed (which produces human food indirectly, and much less efficiently, as meat and dairy products) and 3% for bioenergy, seed and other industrial products.

   Jonathan A. Foley et al., "Solutions for a Cultivated Planet," *Nature* 478 (October 2011): 337–342.

65 Lei Gao and Brett A. Bryan, "Finding Pathways to National-scale Land-sector Sustainability," *Nature* 544 (April 2017): 217–222.

66 Lena R. Boysen, Wolfgang Lucht, and Dieter Gerten, "Trade-offs for Food Production, Nature Conservation and Climate Limit the Terrestrial Carbon Dioxide Removal Potential," *Global Change Biology* 23, no. 10 (October 2017): 4303–4317.

67 Nigel Dudley et al., "How Should Conservationists Respond to Pesticides as a Driver of Biodiversity Loss in Agroecosystems?" *Biological Conservation* 209 (May 2017): 449–453.

68 Elena M. Bennett, "Changing the Agriculture and Environment Conversation," *Nature Ecology & Evolution* 1, no. 18 (January 2017): 18.
   Nigel Dudley et al., "How Should Conservationists Respond to Pesticides as a Driver of Biodiversity Loss in Agroecosystems?" *Biological Conservation* 209 (May 2017): 449–453.

69 R. de Oliveira Silva et al., "Increasing Beef Production Could Lower Greenhouse Gas Emissions in Brazil if Decoupled from Deforestation," *Nature Climate Change* 6 (January 2016): 493–497.

70 At the same time, "marginal lands" is not a precise term, and how much of Earth's land is marginal is not agreed upon. It has been defined as "characterized by high erosion risk and vulnerability to drought," but this definition is inclusive of corn and soy (and presumably other plant) agriculture.
   Christopher K. Wright and Michael C. Wimberly, "Recent Land Use Change in the Western Corn Belt Threatens Grasslands and Wetlands," *Proceedings of the National Academy of Sciences* 110, no. 10 (March 2013): 4134–4139.

71 Hanna Treu et al., "Carbon Footprints and Land Use of Conventional and Organic Diets in Germany," *Journal of Cleaner Production* 161 (September 2017): 127–142.

72 Committee on 21st Century Systems Agriculture, *Toward Sustainable Agricultural Systems in the 21st Century* (Washington, D.C.: National Academies Press, 2010).

73   Cropland soils can lose carbon as a consequence of soil disturbance (e.g., tillage). Tillage increases aeration and soil temperatures (Tisdall and Oades, 1982; Elliott, 1986), making soil aggregates more susceptible to breakdown and physically protected organic material more available for decomposition (Elliott, 1986; Beare et al., 1994). In addition, erosion can significantly affect soil carbon stocks through the removal or deposition of soil particles and associated organic matter.

"Land-Use Management," Land Use, Land-Use Change, and Forestry, Intergovernmental Panel on Climate Change, www.ipcc.ch/ipccreports/sres/land_use/index. php?idp=34.

74 "Gulf of Mexico 'Dead Zone' Is the Largest Ever Measured," National Oceanic and Atmospheric Administration, published August 2, 2017, www.noaa.gov/media-release/gulf-of-mexico-dead-zone-is-largest-ever-measured.

75 Jeremy Grantham, "Be Persuasive. Be Brave. Be Arrested (if Necessary)," *Nature* 491, no. 7424 (November 2012): 303.

76 Arno Rosemarin, "Phosphorus a Limited Resource—Closing the Loop," Global Status of Phosphorus Conference, Malmö, Sweden, October 27–28, 2016, https://dakofa. com/fileadmin/user_upload/1600_Arno_Rosemarin_Stockholm_Environment_ Institute.pdf.

77 Dana Cordell, Jan-Olof Drangert, and Stuart White, "The Story of Phosphorus: Global Food Security and Food for Thought," *Global Environmental Change* 19, no. 2 (May 2009): 292–305.

78 James J. Elser, "Phosphorus: A Limiting Nutrient for Humanity?" *Current Opinion in Biotechnology* 6 (December 2012): 833–838.

James Elser and Stuart White, "Peak Phosphorous," *Foreign Policy*, April 20, 2010, www.foreignpolicy.com/articles/2010/04/20/peak_phosphorus.

Tina-Simone S. Neset and Dana Cordell, "Global Phosphorus Scarcity: Identifying Synergies for a Sustainable Future," *Journal of the Science of Food and Agriculture* 92, no. 1 (October 2011): 2–6.

79 A complete list of nutrient needs includes secondary nutrients such as calcium (Ca), magnesium (Mg), and sulfur (S), and micronutrients like iron (Fe), boron (B), copper (Cu), chlorine (Cl), manganese (Mn), molybdenum (Mo), zinc (Zn), cobalt (Co), and nickel (Ni). Some of these are industrially produced and some are animal products.

80 Geneviève S. Metson, Elena M. Bennett, and James J. Elser, "The Role of Diet in Phosphorus Demand," *Environmental Research Letters* 7, no. 4 (December 2012).

81 Jeremy Grantham, "Be Persuasive. Be Brave. Be Arrested (if Necessary)," *Nature* 491, no. 7424 (November 2012): 303.

82 Fred Pearce, "Phosphate: A Critical Resource Misused and Now Running Low," *Environment 360*, Yale School of Forestry and Environmental Studies, http://e360.yale. edu/feature/phosphate_a_critical_resource_misused_and_now_running_out/2423/.

83 Richard Bardgett, *Earth Matters: How Soil Underlies Civilization* (Oxford: Oxford University Press, 2016): 142.

84 David Pimentel and Marcia Pimentel, "Sustainability of Meat-based and Plant-based Diets and the Environment," *American Journal of Clinical Nutrition* 78 (2003): 660S–663S.

85 Richard Bardgett, *Earth Matters: How Soil Underlies Civilization*. (Oxford: Oxford University Press, 2016): 150–154.

Bardgett further writes,

> And many ways have been suggested to reverse this process by changing the way we grow crops or by slowing down the decomposition of dead plants matter in soil. These include the use of no tillage farming, which cuts out soil disturbance by tillage and the breakdown of crop residues, the conversion of arable land to perennial grasslands, which causes a build-up of organic matter at the soil surface because of increased root growth and the lack of tillage, and using cover crops in rotations, which increase the input of organic matter input to soil. Of course, taking land out of arable agriculture to lock up more carbon in soil, while good for combating climate change, works against another major global challenge: producing enough food to feed a growing population.

86 Richard Bardgett, *Earth Matters: How Soil Underlies Civilization* (Oxford: Oxford University Press, 2016): 150–154.

87 "Land-Use Management," Land Use, Land-Use Change, and Forestry, Intergovernmental Panel on Climate Change, www.ipcc.ch/ipccreports/sres/land_use/index.php?idp=34.

88 T.W. Crowther et al., "Quantifying Global Soil Carbon Losses in Response to Warming," *Nature* 540, no. 7 (December 2016): 104–108.

89 "Welcome to the '4 per 1000' Initiative," 4 Pour 1000, http://4p1000.org/.

90 Jan Willem van Groenigen et al., "Sequestering Soil Organic Carbon: A Nitrogen Dilemma," *Environmental Science and Technology* 51, no. 9 (April 2017): 4738–4739.

91 Specifically, freshwater has less than 1,000 ppm of sodium chloride (NaCl).

92 Emma Li Johansson, Marianela Fader, Jonathan W. Seaquist, and Kimberly A. Nicholas, "Green and Blue Water Demand from Large-scale Land Acquisitions in Africa," *Proceedings of the National Academy of Sciences* 113, no. 41 (October 2016): 11471–11476.

93 "Water Withdrawal by Sector, around 2007," Aquastat, Food and Agriculture Organization of the United Nations, last updated September 2014, www.globalagriculture.org/fileadmin/files/weltagrarbericht/AquastatWithdrawal2014.pdf.

"In 2000, agriculture accounted for 70 percent of water use and 93 percent of water depletion worldwide . . . (Turner et al., 2004)."

Henning Steinfeld et al., "Livestock's Long Shadow: Environmental Issues and Options," Food and Agriculture Organization of the United Nations, 2006, www.europarl.europa.eu/climatechange/doc/FAO%20report%20executive%20summary.pdf.

94 "Overview," United States Department of Agriculture, last updated April 28, 2017, www.ers.usda.gov/topics/farm-practices-management/irrigation-water-use.aspx.

95 David Pimentel and Marcia Pimentel, "Sustainability of Meat-based and Plant-based Diets and the Environment," *American Journal of Clinical Nutrition* 78 (2003): 660S–663S.

96 David Pimentel et al., "Water Resources: Agricultural and Environmental Issues," *BioScience* 54, no. 10 (October 2004): 909–918.

D. Molden, ed., *Water for Food, Water for Life: A Comprehensive Assessment of Water Management in Agriculture* (London: Earthscan International Water Management Institute, 2007).

Further, "Worldwide, the amount of irrigated land is slowly expanding, even though salinization, waterlogging, and siltation continue to decrease its productivity" (Gleick 2002).

97 David Pimentel et al., "Water Resources: Agricultural and Environmental Issues," *BioScience* 54, no. 10 (October 2004): 912.

98 David Pimentel et al., "Water Resources: Agricultural and Environmental Issues," *BioScience* 54, no. 10 (October 2004): 913.

99 Henning Steinfeld et al., "Livestock's Long Shadow: Environmental Issues and Options," Food and Agriculture Organization of the United Nations, 2006, www.europarl.europa.eu/climatechange/doc/FAO%20report%20executive%20summary.pdf.

100 Carole Dalin, Yoshihide Wada, Thomas Kastner, and Michael J. Puma, "Groundwater Depletion Embedded in International Food Trade," *Nature* 543 (March 2017): 700–704.

101   [H]umans are overexploiting groundwater in many large aquifers that are critical to agriculture, especially in Asia and North America. We estimate that the size of the global groundwater footprint is currently about 3.5 times the actual area of aquifers and that about 1.7 billion people live in areas where groundwater resources and/or groundwater-dependent ecosystems are under threat.

Tom Gleeson et al., "Water Balance of Global Aquifers Revealed by Groundwater Footprint," *Nature* 488 (August 2012): 197–200.

102 "Charting our Water Future," McKinsey & Company, published November 2009, www.mckinsey.com/business-functions/sustainability-and-resource-productivity/our-insights/charting-our-water-future.

103 Natasha Gilbert, "One-third of Our Greenhouse Gas Emissions Come from Agriculture," *Nature*, October 31, 2012, www.nature.com/news/one-third-of-our-greenhouse-gas-emissions-come-from-agriculture-1.11708.
   "Cattle (raised for both beef and milk, as well as for inedible outputs like manure and draft power) are the animal species responsible for the most emissions, representing about 65% of the livestock sector's emissions."
   "Total emissions from global livestock: 7.1 Gigatonnes of CO_2-equiv per year, representing 14.5 percent of all anthropogenic GHG emissions."
   "Key Facts and Findings," Food and Agriculture Organization of the United Nations, www.fao.org/news/story/en/item/197623/icode/.

104 "The Influence of Land Use on Greenhouse Gas Sources and Sinks," Land Use, Land-Use Change and Forestry, Intergovernmental Panel on Climate Change, www.ipcc.ch/ipccreports/sres/land_use/index.php?idp=33.

105 "Land-Use Management," Land Use, Land-Use Change, and Forestry, Intergovernmental Panel on Climate Change, www.ipcc.ch/ipccreports/sres/land_use/index.php?idp=34.

106 Kees Jan van Groenigen, Chris van Kessel, and Bruce A. Hungate, "Increased Greenhouse-gas Intensity of Rice Production under Future Atmospheric Conditions," *Nature* 3 (October 2012): 288–291.

107 "Sources and Sinks of Methane," Land Use, Land-Use Change, and Forestry, Intergovernmental Panel on Climate Change, www.ipcc.ch/ipccreports/sres/land_use/index.php?idp=22.

108 Maya Wei-Haas, "Burp by Burp, Fighting Emissions from Cows," *National Geographic*, August 3, 2015, http://news.nationalgeographic.com/2015/08/150803-cows-burp-methane-climate-science/ referencing "Climate Change," Environmental Protection Agency, January 19, 2017 snapshot, http://epa.gov/climatechange/Downloads/ghgemissions/US-GHG-Inventory-2015-Chapter-Executive-Summary.pdf.

109 "Climate Science of Methane," Environmental Change Institute, University of Oxford, www.eci.ox.ac.uk/research/energy/downloads/methaneuk/chapter02.pdf.

110 M. Saunois et al., "The Growing Role of Methane in Anthropogenic Climate Change," *Environmental Research Letters*, 11, no. 12 (December 2016).

111 "Sources and Sinks of Nitrous Oxide," Land Use, Land-Use Change, and Forestry, Intergovernmental Panel on Climate Change, www.ipcc.ch/ipccreports/sres/land_use/index.php?idp=23.

112 Carolien Kroeze, Arvin Mosier, and Lex Bouwman, "Closing the Global N_2O Budget: A Retrospective Analysis 1500–1994," *Global Biogeochemical Cycles* 13, no. 1 (March 1999): 1–8. Quoted in "Land-Use Management," Land Use, Land-Use Change, and Forestry, Intergovernmental Panel on Climate Change, www.ipcc.ch/ipccreports/sres/land_use/index.php?idp=34.

113 Eric A. Davidson, "Representative Concentration Pathways and Mitigation Scenarios for Nitrous Oxide," *Environmental Research Letters* 7 (2012).
   Peter Singer's response in Tim Flannery, *Now or Never: Why We Must Act Now to End Climate Change and Create a Sustainable Future* (New York: Grove Atlantic, 2009).

114 Henning Steinfeld et al., "Livestock's Long Shadow: Environmental Issues and Options," Food and Agriculture Organization of the United Nations, 2006, www.europarl.europa.eu/climatechange/doc/FAO%20report%20executive%20summary.pdf.

115 Anthony J. McMichael, John W. Powles, Colin D. Butler, and Ricardo Uauy, "Food, Livestock Production, Energy, Climate Change, and Health," *The Lancet* 370, no. 9594 (September 2007): 1253–1263.

116 Anthony J. McMichael, John W. Powles, Colin D. Butler, and Ricardo Uauy, "Food, Livestock Production, Energy, Climate Change, and Health," *The Lancet* 370, no. 9594 (September 2007): 1253–1263.

117 Anthony J. McMichael, John W. Powles, Colin D. Butler, and Ricardo Uauy, "Food, Livestock Production, Energy, Climate Change, and Health," *The Lancet* 370, no. 9594 (September 2007): 1253–1263.

118 Ottmar Edenhofer et al., "Summary for Policymakers," in O. Edenhofer et al., eds., *Climate Change 2014: Mitigation of Climate Change. Contribution of Working Group III to the Fifth Assessment Report of the Intergovernmental Panel on Climate Change* (Cambridge: Cambridge University Press, 2014): 24.

119 Pete Smith et al., "Greenhouse Gas Mitigation in Agriculture," *Philosophical Transactions of the Royal Society B* 363, no. 1492 (February 2008): 789–813.

120 Peter Singer's response in Tim Flannery, *Now or Never: Why We Must Act Now to End Climate Change and Create a Sustainable Future* (New York: Grove Atlantic, 2009).

121 Gidon Eshel and Pamela A. Martin, "Diet, Energy, and Global Warming," *Earth Interact* 10 (December 2005): 1–17.
  M. Berners-Lee, C. Hoolohan, H. Cammack, and C.N. Hewitt, "The Relative Greenhouse Gas Impacts of Realistic Dietary Choices," *Energy Policy* 43 (April 2012): 184–190.

122 Peter Scarborough et al., "Dietary Greenhouse Gas Emissions of Meat-eaters, Fish-eaters, Vegetarians and Vegans in the UK," *Climatic Change* 125, no. 2 (July 2014): 179–192.

123 For more on the need to reduce consumption of animal products in order to mitigate greenhouse gas emissions, see:
  Jeff Sebo, "Animals and Climate Change," in Mark Budolfson, Tristram McPherson, and David Plunkett, eds., *Philosophy and Climate Change* (forthcoming).

124 Bojana Bajželj et al., "Importance of Food-demand Management for Climate Mitigation," *Nature Climate Change* 4 (August 2014): 924–929.

125 Nathan Pelletier and Peter Tyedmers, "Forecasting Potential Global Environmental Costs of Livestock Production 2000–2050," Proceedings of the National Academy of Sciences 107, no. 43 (October 2010): 18371–18374.
  They also note that "[s]uch reductions may be particularly feasible and advantageous in developed countries where consumption of meat products is currently twice USDA-recommended levels."

126 "Labour," Food and Agriculture Organization of the United Nations, www.fao.org/docrep/015/i2490e/i2490e01b.pdf.

127 Cheryl Doss, "The Role of Women in Agriculture," The Food and Agriculture Organization of the United Nations, published March 2011, www.fao.org/docrep/013/am307e/am307e00.pdf.
  "The Female Face of Farming," Farming First, https://farmingfirst.org/women_infographic/.

128 "Livestock in a Changing Landscape," United Nations Educational, Scientific, and Cultural Organization, Scientific Committee on Problems of the Environment, United Nations Environment Programme, April 2008, http://unesdoc.unesco.org/images/0015/001591/159194e.pdf.

129 "Wage and Hour Division," United States Department of Labor, last updated July 2008, www.dol.gov/whd/regs/compliance/whdfs12.htm.

130 Patrick Gerland et al., "World Population Stabilization Unlikely This Century," *Science* 346, no. 6206 (October 2014): 234–237.

131 Eileen Crist, Camilo Mora, and Robert Engelman, "The Interaction of Human Population, Food Production, and Biodiversity Protection," *Science* 356, no. 6335 (April 2017): 260–264.

132 Henning Steinfeld et al., "Livestock's Long Shadow: Environmental Issues and Options," Food and Agriculture Organization of the United Nations, 2006,

www.europarl.europa.eu/climatechange/doc/FAO%20report%20executive%20 summary.pdf.

133 Eric Holt-Gimenez, "Food Security, Food Justice, or Food Sovereignty? Crises, Food Movements, and Regime Change," in Alison Hope Alkon and Julian Agyeman, eds., *Cultivating Food Justice: Race, Class, and Sustainability* (Cambridge: MIT Press, 2011): 309–330.

134 "The State of the World's Land and Water Resources for Food and Agriculture," Food and Agriculture Organization of the United Nations, 2011, www.fao.org/docrep/015/ i1688e/i1688e00.pdf.

135 "The State of the World's Land and Water Resources for Food and Agriculture," Food and Agriculture Organization of the United Nations, 2011, www.fao.org/docrep/015/ i1688e/i1688e00.pdf.

136 The San Joaquin Valley in California is sinking due to the overuse of water.
       Joseph Serna, "San Joaquin Valley Continues to Sink because of Groundwater Pumping, NASA Says," *The Los Angeles Times*, February 9, 2017, www.latimes.com/ local/lanow/la-me-ln-central-valley-subsidence-20170209-story.html.

137 For a history of the use of the Colorado River and its subsequent drying out, see:
       Marc Reisner, *Cadillac Desert* (New York: Penguin Random House, 1993).

138 For instance, nitrogen pollution of water impacts young humans.
       Jan Willem Erisman et al., "Consequences of Human Modification of the Global Nitrogen Cycle," *Philosophical Transactions of the Royal Society B* 368, no. 1621 (May 2013).
       Irena Buka, Samuel Koranteng, and Alvaro R Osornio-Vargas, "The Effects of Air Pollution on the Health of Children," *Paediatrics Child Health* 11, no. 8 (October 2006): 513–516.

139 For a case study in North Carolina, see:
       "A Guide to Health, Environmental Justice and Civic Action around Industrial Hog Operations," Rachel Carson Council, https://rachelcarsoncouncil.org/take-action/pork-and-pollution/.

140 Sara Mostafalou and Mohammad Abdollahi, "Pesticides and Human Chronic Diseases: Evidences, Mechanisms, and Perspectives," *Toxicology and Applied Pharmacology* 268, no. 2 (April 2013): 157–177.

141 Tesifón Parrón, Mar Requena, Antonio F. Hernández, and Raquel Alarcón, "Environmental Exposure to Pesticides and Cancer Risk in Multiple Human Organ Systems," *Toxicology Letters* 230, no. 2 (October 2014): 157–165.

142 Christopher N. Connolly, "The Risk of Insecticides to Pollinating Insects," *Communicative & Integrative Biology* 6, no. 5 (September 2013).
       Consumers in regulated states seem to not be negatively impacted by pesticide exposure on their food.
       Crystal Smith-Spangler et al., "Are Organic Foods Safer or Healthier Than Conventional Alternatives? A Systematic Review," *Annals of Internal Medicine* 157, no. 5 (September 2012): 348–366.

143 "Agriculture and Food Security," Food and Agriculture Organization of the United Nations, www.fao.org/docrep/x0262e/x0262e05.htm.

144 Daniel W. O'Neill, Andrew L. Fanning, William F. Lamb, and Julia K. Steinberger, "A Good Life For All within Planetary Boundaries," *Nature Sustainability* 1 (February 2018): 88–95.

145 Vicky W.Y. Lam, William W.L. Cheung, Gabriel Reygondeau, and U. Rashid Sumaila, "Projected Change in Global Fisheries Revenues under Climate Change," *Scientific Reports* 6, no. 32607 (September 2016).

146   We estimate the potential to increase food supplies by closing the "diet gap": shifting 16 major crops to 100% human food and away from the current mix of uses could add over a billion tonnes to global food production (a 28% increase

for those 16 crops), the equivalent of ~3 × 10^{15} kilocalories more food to the global diet (a 49% increase in food calories delivered).

Jonathan A. Foley et al., "Solutions for a Cultivated Planet," *Nature* 478 (October 2011): 337–342.

> If the world's top 16 crops were grown only for human food, instead of the current mix that includes animal feed and biofuels, a billion tons more human food would be available—roughly equivalent to three quadrillion kilocalories. Reducing waste is a corollary step: Roughly 30 percent of the food grown worldwide is lost to failed crops, stockpiles ruined by [animals considered to be] pests, food that is never delivered because of bad infrastructure or markets, and food that spoils or is thrown away after purchase.
>
> In this study, the IBIS-THMB nitrogen modeling system is used to demonstrate how a shift away from meat production from Mississippi Basin crops could reduce total land and fertilizer demands by over 50%, without any change in total production of human food protein.

Simon D. Donner, "Surf or Turf: A Shift from Feed to Food Cultivation Could Reduce Nutrient Flux to the Gulf of Mexico," *Global Environmental Change* 17, no. 1 (February 2007): 105–113.

147 Jonathan Foley, "It's Time to Rethink America's Corn System," *Scientific American*, March 5, 2013, www.scientificamerican.com/article/time-to-rethink-corn/.

148 Erik Stokstad, "Could Less Meat Mean More Food?" Science 327, no. 5967 (February 2010): 810–811.

6   Industrial agriculture

6.1 Introduction

This chapter will explore the impacts of industrial agriculture for animals, the environment, and humans. We will begin with a brief history of industrial agriculture, discussing topics including fertilizer synthesizing, food processing technology, and advanced plant breeding. The next section will present information about animal experiences in the industrial agricultural system. While much can be said about farmed animal welfare in industrial agriculture, our coverage here is intended to briefly summarize some of the main points and provide an empirical basis for the next chapters on animal ethics.[1] We will then discuss the environmental impacts of industrial agriculture, focusing on greenhouse gases and the complexity of multifactor environmental assessment. Finally, we will detail the impacts of industrial agriculture on humans.

6.2 The distinction between industrial and non-industrial agriculture

This and the next chapter describe industrial and non-industrial modes of agriculture. While there are some traits unique to each, the distinction is imperfect and complex. Some agricultural practices combine elements of both.

Deforesting the Brazilian rainforest, for example, causes significant environmental harm in the form of greenhouse gas emissions, air pollution, and habitat (and biodiversity) loss. It is estimated that as much as 80% of deforestation in Brazil is the result of cattle ranching.[2] The scale of deforestation would not be possible without certain modern technologies such as inexpensive, long-distance transportation and refrigeration (much of the beef is exported) and tools for cutting down trees. At the same time, slash-and-burn agriculture and methane emissions from ruminants—both of which can cause significant environmental harms at scale—pre-date industrialization.

As we note throughout these middle chapters, all forms of agriculture require the disruption of environments. This means that a purely plant-based agriculture still requires the clearing of land, harvest of plants, addition of nutrients, elimination of "pests," and other interventions. Harvesting wheat fields kills field mice, organic pesticides kill insects, and clearing land destroys or alters habitat. Although there are significant distinctions and values in the myriad forms of agriculture, intervention in environments is unavoidable. Even foods untouched by industrial agricultural practices might have industrial pollutants in them (such as dioxins, PCBs, plastics, mercury, and DDT). This is because these pollutants have already circulated around the globe.

Polyface Farm, run by farmer Joel Salatin and featured in Michael Pollan's *Omnivore's Dilemma*, uses a hybrid of industrial and non-industrial practices. It is largely described as a non-industrial farm—it is small, bucolic, uses local nutrients, and avoids synthetic fertilizers. At the same time, the animals are often the same modern breeds as in industrial settings (which have some of the same welfare issues on industrial and non-industrial farms) and the chickens are fed genetically engineered grain from the Midwest. The farm relies on modern transportation for distribution, and is subject to the same modern regulations on animal slaughter (which has both advantages and disadvantages). It is difficult to categorize this farm simply as industrial or not. Some, like historian James McWilliams, argue for a "golden mean" that integrates industrial and non-industrial practices to develop mid-size farms that provide significant yield without as much environmental impact as large-scale agriculture.[3]

Some traits generally attributed to industrial agriculture can also apply in non-industrial forms of agriculture. This includes intensively managed and high yielding systems, which are common in industrial agriculture but also exist in organic rice farming (one main example is System of Rice Intensification or SRI). Similarly, organic agriculture—which many think of as an alternative to industrial production—can be produced at a large scale, both farmed and processed mechanically, and transported around the world. Some even argue for GM organic crops[4] as a strategy for reducing synthetic pesticide use, although current USDA regulation would disallow GMOs from being labeled as organic.

Just as the industrial/non-industrial distinction imperfectly captures certain attributes such as environmental damage, the animal/plant distinction only partially captures environmental impacts. Generally speaking, foods made from farmed animals have higher environmental impacts than food made from plants, especially in the case of larger ruminants. But some foods made from nonhuman animals carry a lower environmental cost. This includes foods made from oysters and many insects. Additionally, some foods made from plants carry a high environmental cost. Palm oil production, for instance, destroys orangutan habitats and utilizes slash-and-burn techniques (which have high soot and greenhouse gas emissions), and rice production constitutes one tenth of global methane emissions.[5]

We need to assess an agricultural practice in its context, and consider the many nonhuman, environmental, and human dimensions of these practices. For example: fertilizers of industrial and non-industrial kinds contribute to nitrogen pollution, nitrate contamination of groundwater, and runoff. Likewise, pesticides of industrial and non-industrial kinds are toxic to human and nonhuman animals, and using less land more intensively often has a lower environmental impact than using land more extensively.

Industrial agriculture refers broadly to agriculture that uses modern technologies or methods and that operates at an intensive level of output. It can include one or more of the following: synthetic pesticides, fertilizers, herbicides and fungicides, genetically engineered seeds or animals, mechanized tools for changing landscapes (e.g., tillers and combine harvesters), mechanized water distribution, use of antibiotics and modern medicine for farmed animals, and mechanized ventilation and artificial lighting in confined animal feeding operations or greenhouses.

Industrial agriculture is generally characterized as large in scale and producing commodity and monoculture crops. There are many complications to this characterization, however. Genetically engineered plants can be grown according to certain organic standards[6] and can reduce pesticide use,[7] organic crops might benefit from occasional synthetic pesticide use when a specific insect threatens it, and the use of herbicide limits weed growth, which reduces carbon-releasing tilling.

Some argue that industrialization is an accurate proxy for environmental impact.[8] Imagine a monoculture of genetically modified corn in the midwestern U.S., harvested by global positioning system-guided combines, and sprayed with synthetic pesticides. There are indeed environmental impacts to such a practice. However, all agriculture involves some disruption of a natural landscape and, as such, involves environmental impacts. Thus, what matters is the scale of environmental impact and of the output that is made possible by industrial agriculture. An intensive farm might have significant environmental impacts such as erosion, but might also produce a lot of food. Of course, this does not mean that the benefits are proportional to the costs. Instead, all it means is that a complex host of impacts needs to be considered when making a comprehensive assessment.

In this and the coming chapter, we will note what kinds of impacts and practices are unique to industrial agriculture and alternatives to industrial agriculture, respectively (in other words, we will note the impacts that are different in kind, as well as those that differ only in degree). Industrial agriculture can often operate at a larger scale, but can perform more effectively, at least by some measures—such as how much food is produced.

Before we proceed, it is worth noting that some alternatives to our current industrial food system are themselves industrial. For example, as we will see in Chapter 7, highly engineered plant-based meat substitutes (such as the Impossible Burger) and cellular meat substitutes (which produce meat via cell cultures rather than via once-living animals) are both products of industrial techniques. However, given their potential for disrupting aspects of our current industrial food system, we place them in the "Alternatives to industrial agriculture" section in the following chapter.

6.3 A very brief history of agricultural industrialization

Global trade preceded industrialization. Think of Marco Polo's journeys, the Silk Road's spice trade, or travel to South America to mine guano for fertilizer.

With industrialization came the capability to combust fossil fuels and thereby move many times more goods quickly, and with refrigeration. The scale of international trade exploded, and is now taken for granted in many parts of the world.

The starting point of industrial agriculture can be defined in a number of ways, and is marked by a number of novel practices. These include the creation of synthetic fertilizers and pesticides, synthesizing of vitamins A and D, and creation of antibiotics that allow for industrial animal agriculture, large-scale mechanization of agricultural activities, advanced transportation and storage networks, and the use of advanced technology such as sonar, planes, pumps, and refrigeration.

Industrial applications include mechanization of land use change via tractors, water sourcing via pumps, pesticide application via planes, and harvesting via combines. This allows for a scale of land conversion that was previously unprecedented, especially in areas such as the midwestern U.S.[9] More affordable refrigeration, pasteurization, processing, and radiation technologies allow food to be transported and stored with less spoilage and loss as well.

Another dimension of agriculture that shifted along with industrialization is the scientific knowledge of plant and animal genetics and nutrient needs, and the ability to alter genes and plant and animal health. For example, we started giving antibiotics to farmed animals, mixing fertilizers based on precise ratios of nitrogen, phosphorus, and potassium, and altering genes both in labs as well as in traditional forms of breeding.

The rapid increase in industrial practices in agriculture coincides with the military industrial growth of the two world wars. These activities were also intertwined. War planes became crop dusters, neurotoxins developed as nerve gases were adapted as pesticides, and the industrial process of synthesizing nitrogen facilitated chemical warfare. In general, much of the industrial and transportation infrastructure used for military activities was repurposed for agricultural use after World War II.

A combination of industrial practices allowed for an explosion of agricultural production called the **Green Revolution**, which took place in the 1930s–1960s. As a result of mechanization, irrigation technology, synthetic fertilizers and pesticides, and plant breeding techniques targeting drought resistance and yield, yields grew exponentially—as did the human population. Biologist Norman Borlaug, a leading force behind this movement, received the Nobel Prize for this work. The consequences of the Green Revolution are still hotly debated, as many agricultural variables changed dramatically. These changes include a shift to commodity crops such as wheat, increased trade (which in some cases decreased food security), and depletion of certain nutrients in the soil. Crop diversity decreased, and yield increased. Food production—measured in per capita net production—has increased in almost all parts of the world.[10] Many of the technologies and practices arising from industrialization allowed for the massive increase in the scale of agricultural activities, along with its centralization into fewer but more concentrated areas, **intensification** (increase in yield), and the rise of commodity crops, which are standardized and traded globally.

There are costs and benefits of intensification via minimized land-use change. Since deforestation is such a significant contributor to climate change and other environmental harms, efficient and more intensive land use has the environmental benefit of using less land. If this intensification results in depletion of soil or a net increase in nitrous oxide pollution in the air and water, this might be a net environmental harm. By some estimates, the intensification of agriculture similar to and in the Green Revolution led to a significant amount of land *not* entering agricultural production, which has climate benefits:[11] "The tendency to locate high-input agriculture on the most suitable lands for cropping relieves pressure on land expansion and limits encroachment on forests and other land uses."[12] At the same time, intensive agriculture can deplete the soil of nutrients, cause erosion, or deplete aquifers and other sources of water.[13] Since the Green Revolution produced so many additional calories, we need to use a "per capita fed" figure to understand its proportional environmental impact. Few shifts in the history of agriculture have been so radical (the Haber-Bosch process being the other modern "game changer"): "Although populations had more than doubled, the production of cereal crops tripled during this period, with only a 30% increase in land area cultivated."[14]

One example of the multidimensional implications of agricultural activity is the Dust Bowl, an area (and, eventually, the name of a set of agricultural and social consequences) in the 1930s in the U.S. Many people displaced by the Depression moved west and attempted to farm in the grasslands of Oklahoma, Texas, and the Great Plains area. Partly enabled by industrial tools such as tractors and combines, and a lack of understanding of grassland ecology (and partly out of economic necessity), many people farmed the land in a way that resulted in significant amounts of erosion and dust storms.

The hardship of this period in time was documented by photographer Dorothea Lange and musician Woody Guthrie, and is a lasting example of both the misuse of agricultural land and the suffering experienced by many at this time. Public service announcements from the Dust Bowl era show depleted and dry agricultural landscapes ("starved by lack of plant food") next to fertilized ones. At the time, farmers were desperate to use industrially produced fertilizers (fertilized land was advertised as "nourished on phosphate and lime") to increase yield.[15]

6.4 Animals

Industrialization fundamentally changed the practice of animal agriculture. Starting in the late 1800s, the raising and slaughtering of nonhuman animals for meat, eggs, and milk has grown exponentially in industrialized animal agriculture, and has radically changed in form. It has expanded at different rates across the globe depending on demand, government and industry support, and cultural appropriateness. While the consumption of animal products in many of the richest and most industrialized countries has plateaued in recent years, it is rising rapidly among the "global middle class" in China, South America, Eastern Europe, and other parts of the world where increased disposable income and decreased cost of animal products result in increased animal product consumption.

Each year, humans kill over 70 billion terrestrial animals and hundreds of billions of aquatic animals globally. With respect to terrestrial animals, chickens make up the largest portion of this number, alone numbering 50 billion. Such a scale is unprecedented, and was not possible with pre-industrial technologies. Technologies such as inexpensive refrigeration contributed to this scaling, as larger volumes of animals could be slaughtered in one location, then stored for longer periods of time and transported longer distances. This trend has continued to the present, when a small number of large slaughterhouses slaughter thousands of animals per hour.

Precise numbers on animal slaughter are difficult to calculate due to the large scale, lack of transparency in the slaughtering process, and the fact that fishes are measured in tonnage rather than as individuals. According to one calculation that includes "feed fish," animals killed in crop fields, and animals who die in factory farms before slaughter, "a vegetarian saves between 371 and 582 animals per year."[16]

A number of economic, scientific, and technological shifts contributed to the exponential increase in animal agriculture, as well as to radical changes to animal welfare in agriculture. These changes included:

➜ Animal agriculture shifted indoors, as vitamin D could be added to food to substitute for sunlight
➜ Mechanical ventilation allowed more animals to be packed into smaller spaces
➜ Antibiotics and vaccines improved disease management, once again allowing more animals to be packed into smaller spaces
➜ Growth hormones and antibiotics sped up growth, allowing animals to be slaughtered and sold sooner
➜ The industrialization of crop agriculture created inexpensive and plentiful feed
➜ Advanced feed additives led to faster growth, different muscle characteristics, and different taste
➜ Mechanized milking devices, conveyor belts, and sorting machines increased the scale and speed of production
➜ Electrical lighting allowed farmers to force chickens to stay awake, grow more quickly, mature earlier, convert feed more efficiently, and allowed year-round production of animal products such as meat and eggs.

These shifts together gave rise to concentrated chicken sheds, egg-laying operations, cow-feeding operations, cow-milking operations, intensive pig farming, and more. In these confined spaces animals are often unable to move at all. Additionally, such tight confines and harsh environments result in maladaptive behaviors such as biting metal and pecking or biting other animals.

Breeding also shifted dramatically with industrialization. Our understanding of genetics, and the market demands for certain attributes such as fat, flavors, and muscle tissue, led to breeding of farmed animals primarily for those traits. This resulted in radically faster growth rates, higher proportions of breast tissue in chickens, and higher milk production in cows—all of which leads to an increase in suffering. Modern breeding also results in the reduction in variety of breeds, which leaves populations vulnerable to diseases. (The breeding of older genetic types is called "heirloom" production, and is discussed further in the following chapter.) Unlike aquatic animals used for food, many of whom are still wild (though aquaculture might soon change that fact), almost all terrestrial animals used for food are domesticated.

These shifts changed agricultural practices. Animal agriculture became more consolidated, with operations shifting from smaller, low-density, and often family-run operations to ones where tens or hundreds of thousands of farmed animals are raised and slaughtered. This consolidation and increase in density results in concentrated waste (including manure lagoons), an increased incidence and likelihood of zoonotic and animal diseases, increased animal suffering due to constrained movement, and larger companies controlling fewer operations. The latter is partially caused by concentrated political power—such as in the U.S. where large animal agriculture corporations have powerful lobbyists and minimal oversight.

The result of all these economic, scientific, and technological developments is modern industrial animal agriculture, characterized by high density of animals and mechanized ventilation and slaughtering. Most of these operations are called CAFOs, or "factory farms."[17] The concentration of animals in this setting results in serious environmental and welfare issues. These include:

→ Ear notching, tattooing, and branding animals (to mark and/or track them)
→ Docking pigs' tails without anesthesia (since distressed and confined pigs will bite one another's tails)
→ Debeaking chickens without anesthesia (since distressed and confined chickens will peck at each other)
→ Castrating animals without anesthesia (to increase their growth, alter their behavior, and/or change the flavor of their flesh)
→ Artificially inseminating and continuously impregnating animals, for breeding and/or milk production
→ Forcibly separating animals (including separating very young animals from their parents)
→ Constraining the movement of pigs and cows (in crates) and chickens (in cages), which contributes to the inability to move and to the maladaptive behaviors described previously
→ Creating a high concentration of animal waste, thereby contributing to rise of diseases (in both farmed animals and laborers), increased use of antibiotics, and increased risk of antibiotic-resistant pathogens.

These conditions result in significantly compromised welfare, and increased mortality rates on farms. In industrial operations, mortality has been estimated to be around 5% for chickens and cows, 12% for turkeys, and 16% for pigs.[18] Depending on the operation, these animals live short lives in conditions that deprive them of health, freedom of movement, and control over their bodies. People have been documenting these issues for decades.[19]

Even when they survive to slaughter, animals in CAFOs have a significantly shorter lifespan than animals in other environments such as low-density farms. Chickens live for a few weeks in a CAFO setting,[20] a few months in a low-density setting, and eight or more years in non-agricultural settings. (Male chickens in the egg industry live only one day, and are then macerated—ground up alive in high-speed grinders.[21]) Cows live 12–18 months in CAFO settings,[22] 22–30 months in low-density settings, and around 20 years in non-agricultural settings. Pigs live six months or more[23] in CAFO settings, twice as long in low-density settings, and around 15 years[24] in non-agricultural settings.[25]

The slaughtering process has also industrialized. Mechanized control of animal movement, sterilization chemicals and techniques, electrical shock systems for stunning animals (often unsuccessfully), bolt guns for killing animals (often unsuccessfully), and disassembly lines with highly specialized divisions of labor all yielded an increased rate of slaughter. The animal welfare impacts of these practices are complex, as some industrial techniques such as stunning might reduce suffering, while others, such as the errors resulting from such rapid and repetitive slaughter, might increase suffering.

With that said, industrialized slaughterhouses kill animals at high volumes and high speeds. In some U.S. slaughterhouses, a cow is killed approximately once every 12 seconds.[26] Chickens and pigs are scalded to remove feathers and hair. Chickens are run through electrified baths and cows and pigs are stunned with bolt guns. In some instances, this does not succeed, and the animal is alive and conscious when their throat is slit. As a result, the aggregate animal welfare impacts of industrial slaughter are devastating.

Moreover, although industrialized slaughterhouses have become increasingly mechanized, they still require human labor. Workers who slaughter animals (on the "kill floor") are exposed to blood, brain tissue,[27] and the kicking of animals trying to escape. These workers must also have speed, strength, and dexterity, as much of the slaughtering and butchering occurs on conveyor belts. This results not only in stresses due to repetitive movement for the workers, but also leads to errors, including incomplete stunning or physical injury to workers.

Finally, industrial slaughterhouses, like factory farms, allow infections and diseases to spread to workers and animals much more easily than less dense settings do. And, since workers typically make very little money and have very little job security, illness or injury could be personally ruinous. The possibility of infection and disease in slaughterhouses is one of the reasons why industrial animal agriculture uses high quantities of antibiotics, which increases the risk of the development of antibiotic-resistant pathogens, as we will discuss later.

Part of what facilitates industrial animal agriculture is the fact that nonhuman animals are legally considered to be objects rather than subjects. Laws very often fail to protect nonhuman animals at the federal level (e.g., because of loopholes in the Humane Slaughter Act), and at the state level (e.g., because "humane" is often defined in terms of standard industry practice). For instance, even though they make up the bulk of terrestrial animals slaughtered, chickens are exempt from the Humane Slaughter Act, and so are not subject to certain humane treatment regulations.[28] Furthermore, the U.S. Animal Enterprise Terrorism Act and state-based "ag-gag" laws make whistleblowing and undercover investigations difficult and often illegal.[29] We will discuss some of these topics further in Chapter 11.

6.4.1 Aquatic animals: oceans, rivers, and aquaculture

We use industrial methods to extract a very high number of fishes and other animals from the ocean each year, as industrialization has allowed for an increase in the scale and efficiency of fish "harvests." We use internal combustion engines for fishing fleets, sonar for locating fishes, massive fishing nets for catching fishes, and electrical lighting for night fishing and to allow ships to stay off shore longer (allowing access to more distant locations). As a result, industrial fishing uses an area that covers more than 50% of the oceans—four times the area that land agriculture uses.[30]

How many aquatic animals do we extract from the ocean each year? Nobody knows exactly, since, as mentioned earlier, fish catches are measured in tonnage, not numbers. This practice, which does not occur in terrestrial animal agriculture, illustrates how language can inhibit seeing nonhuman animals as individuals.[31] In particular, we currently remove an estimated 109 million metric tons of aquatic animals from the ocean per year.[32] This translates to hundreds of billions of—and possibly even over one trillion—individuals per year.

Our removal of fishes and other aquatic animals from the ocean is happening so rapidly that some experts predict that we will have empty oceans by the year 2048.[33] The environmental impact is significant as well, including species collapse and ecosystem destruction. Indeed, deep sea bottom trawling is responsible for destroying entire ecosystems[34] as well as for greatly increasing greenhouse gas emissions relative to non-trawling methods of fishing.[35]

A high percentage of aquatic animals caught by industrial fishing methods are "bycatch"—fishes, turtles, sharks, dolphins, and other animals who are not eaten, but are rather thrown back to the sea, often dead, because they are not the target species. Most bycatch is "generated by industrial (i.e., large-scale) fisheries."[36] The average amount of bycatch is 10% and trending downwards industry-wide. However, in some cases, for example shrimp fishing, bycatch can be as high as 97%.[37] This means that for every pound of shrimps purchased by consumers, 32 pounds of aquatic animals were caught and discarded, often dying in the process. Bottom trawling produces an especially high rate of bycatch.[38]

In addition to developing and expanding industrial fishing practices, we are also developing and expanding aquaculture, an aquatic agricultural system modeled on terrestrial animal agriculture. As discussed in the last chapter, aquaculture makes use of controlled settings such as tanks, inland ponds, and large netted enclosures in the open sea (mariculture). Aquaculture at the industrial scale is a rapidly growing part of the production of "seafood," and is already raising and killing billions of aquatic animals each year. This is in part to displace industrial fishing, which is starting to level out due to overfishing and an increased cost of sophisticated equipment and the need to travel greater distances.[39]

Aquaculture interacts with terrestrial industrial agriculture, as we use products from terrestrial industrial agriculture as feed for farmed fishes. This means that the environmental impact of growing feed can be calculated as part of the impact of aquaculture.[40] The conversion efficiencies discussed in Chapter 5 apply here as well—if we grow soy to feed to farmed fishes, a percentage of the calories in the soy will be converted into the fishes eaten by humans, and a large percentage will be lost. Aquaculture interacts with industrial fishing in the same kind of way, as we use products from industrial fishing as feed for farmed fishes as well.

The scale of the industrial production of "fish meal," that is, ground up fishes used as feed for aquatic and terrestrial farmed animals, is incredible as well. By one estimate, "[b]etween 144 and 293 wild sea animals are captured and killed annually to feed the aquacultured fish[es] and shrimp[s] eaten by the average American consumer."[41] This includes a large percentage of fishes:[42] "farmed fish[es], pigs, and chickens consume the equivalent amount of wild seafood as industrialized countries combined."[43]

This use of aquatic animals for fish meal is one of the biggest stressors on marine ecosystems.[44] For example, forage fishes (fishes who are preyed on by other fishes) are typically targeted for fish meal,[45] and removing them from the oceans results in less food for the fishes who would normally eat them. As a result, if aquaculture is to be considered a viable environmental alternative to fishing, it would have to drastically reduce the amount of fish meal used. At a minimum, this would entail greatly reducing the farming of carnivorous fishes such as salmons and tunas.

The industrial removal of shrimps from the oceans and the farming of shrimps in aquaculture are environmentally destructive. Deforestation for aquaculture (in the conversion of mangroves to shrimp fisheries, for example) has climate impacts that compare to car travel,[46] destroys the mangrove habitat, and destroys its ecological function of breaking up waves.

Fish farms and pens can also pollute the local environments with pathogens, antibiotics, herbicides, parasites, fish waste, pigments used to color fish flesh, and escaped fishes. Additionally, fish farms and pens are confined areas, so water pollution, disease, increased mortality, and fish lice are prevalent. Jellyfish attacks can occur as well,[47] as open ocean pens are accessible to other animals but keep farmed fishes mostly contained. Some fish farms, like terrestrial farms, also face problems such as pollution and bioamplification of pesticides and medicine.

Some key features distinguish fishing and aquaculture from terrestrial animal agriculture. One is the history of domestication. While terrestrial animals were domesticated thousands of years ago, the domestication of aquatic animals is more recent.[48] At the same time, a much larger percentage of aquatic animals have been domesticated relative to terrestrial animals.[49] As such, aquaculture has been described as "emerging as a revolution in agriculture of global importance to humankind."[50]

Another difference between these practices is that many people still deny that aquatic animals are sentient beings capable of experiencing pleasure, pain, desire-satisfaction, and desire-frustration. This makes it easier for humans to rationalize harming aquatic animals for food than to rationalize harming terrestrial animals for food. Fortunately, there is now a significant amount of research on fish and shellfish sentience,[51] but this is a recent development within animal ethology and welfare circles.[52]

What does this research show? Fishes, like all vertebrates, have physiological characteristics consistent with the ability to experience pain. This includes having brains, nociceptors, opioid receptors, and responsiveness to analgesics. Fishes also exhibit behaviors consistent with experiencing pain. This includes avoiding noxious stimuli and eating less if doing so allows them to avoid such stimuli. Different fishes and shellfish have different physiologies and behaviors, and so are presumed to have correspondingly different degrees of sentience.[53]

Insofar as aquatic animals are sentient (or insofar as we have reason to treat them as sentient in cases of uncertainty, as discussed in Chapter 4), we should expect that our treatment of them causes substantial pain, in captivity as well as in the wild. Fishes are hooked, suffocated, cut open while alive, and penned in confined, disease-ridden conditions. Sharks have their fins cut off and are then thrown back into the ocean where they suffocate and drown. Lobsters, who are highly sensitive to temperature fluctuations, are steamed or thrown into boiling water. Some of these ethical considerations are amplified in industrial settings where confinement and disease is the norm. However, industrial settings can also mitigate harm to a degree. For example, fishes can be electroshocked to reduce pain during slaughter.

6.5 Environment

Industrialization fundamentally changed the environmental impacts of agriculture, as well as facilitating the exponential expansion of the world's population. The scale, intensity, and scope of environmental impacts shifted from (mostly) localized to both localized and globalized, and food production increased dramatically.

6.5.1 Land, water, and resource use

As we detailed in Chapter 5, clearing land for pasture, grazing, or feed crops releases carbon dioxide into the atmosphere and often increases soil erosion. In cases where land is cleared by fire, additional greenhouse gases and particulate matter are emitted. Brazil (which burns rainforest for pasture and soybeans) and Indonesia (which burns rainforest for palm trees) are both high greenhouse gas emitters.

Land-use change (for instance, the clearing of forest and vegetation, and the tilling of soil) is often the most significant contributor to climate change of any agricultural activity—more than farm machinery, fertilizer production, processing, transportation, or waste. A small fraction of farmland in the U.S. is used for fruits and vegetables,[54] and a percentage is used to grow crops such as cotton, wheat, and others. The remainder, however, is used to grow crops that we feed to farmed animals. Global numbers also show a large proportion of total cropland being used for feed, and another large proportion for grazing.[55]

Crops that we grow to feed farmed animals use about one third of global land, making feed crops the second largest user of land.[56] Corn occupies 30% of U.S. farmland[57] and is a major user of nitrogen fertilizers (65% of U.S. nitrogen-based synthetic fertilizer).[58] Corn and soybeans are used for farmed animal feed[59] and both have significant environmental impacts—including the use of pesticides and herbicides.[60] Overall, 70–80% of U.S. grain production is for farmed animal feed.[61] China directs 70% of its domestic corn toward farmed animal feed, Brazil directs 85%, and the U.S. directs 40%.[62]

We also use about one quarter to one half of global landmass for grazing animals.[63] If we combine the land used for feed and grazing, we see that "[t]he livestock sector is by far the single largest anthropogenic user of land."[64] In particular, 70% of all agricultural land is occupied by farmed animals or feed being grown for farmed animals.[65] Some of this land cannot be used for traditional crops not fed to animals (such land is sometimes called "marginal land"), but much of it can be. These land-use statistics apply to both industrial and non-industrial agriculture.

CAFOs and feedlots have other environmental impacts as well. **Feedlots** are concentrated areas where farmed animals such as cows and pigs are housed and fed, sometimes for the few weeks between grazing and slaughter, and sometimes for most of their lives. In addition to the *volume* of pollutants produced in CAFOs, the *concentration* of pollutants causes different environmental and human health problems. While cow manure distributed across a large area decomposes and adds nutrients to the soil without significant environmental harm, the same manure concentrated in lagoons and combined with urea creates chemical and anaerobic conditions that release methane, carbon dioxide, hydrogen sulfide, and ammonia. The very high concentrations of waste also lead to nitrate leaching, and any spillage from the lagoons leads to nutrient overload problems including dead zones and algal blooms.[66] The concentration of waste includes other harmful pollutants such as antibiotics, heavy metals, pesticides, and bacteria. Waste lagoons are regulated in the U.S. but not as much as human sewage is—despite producing over one hundred times as much waste, at approximately 2 billion tons per year.[67]

6.5.2 Climate

The percentage of greenhouse gases attributable to animal agriculture varies depending on the assumptions and criteria used. The UN FAO estimated in 2006 that animal agriculture contributes about 18% of global anthropogenic emissions,[68] and more recently updated this estimate to 14.5%.[69] A study for the World Resources Institute by World Bank consultants estimates that animal agriculture contributes about 51% of global emissions.[70] However, this study includes animal respiration, and uses a shorter timeline for calculating global warming potential. This amplifies the role of methane and nitrous oxide, since methane and nitrous oxide remain in the atmosphere for less time than carbon, but they also trap heat more effectively while in the atmosphere. (We discussed this in more depth in Chapter 5.)[71]

Industrial agriculture contributes to CO_2 emissions (through land clearing and fossil fuel combustion), methane emissions (from industrial animal agriculture), and nitrous oxide emissions (through synthetic fertilizers and animal manure). Industrialization created some of these sources, for example synthetic fertilizer, and increased the scale and intensity of others, such as land clearing and animal agriculture. These changes resulted in increased climate impacts.

Agriculture is the largest source of nitrous oxide globally, emitting 60% of anthropogenic nitrous oxide annually.[72] Animal agriculture itself produces 53% of anthropogenic nitrous oxide.[73] Industrial agriculture, especially industrial animal agriculture, exacerbates this problem by operating at a more intensive level and larger scale, and by making inexpensive synthetic nitrogen fertilizer readily available. Nitrous oxide in industrial agriculture is produced by fertilizer offgassing, waste lagoons, and farm equipment.

Some nitrous oxide pollution is preventable through efficiency measures, for instance using fertilizer that releases slowly, or fertilizing in the spring. Some pollution is inevitable, however. By some estimates, more than half of the green-house gas footprint of a loaf of bread is due to the nitrogen fertilizer used to grow the wheat.[74] The relative contribution of nitrous oxide pollution is largely a function of how much fertilizer is used on each crop, how much nitrogen the plant needs, and how much of a crop is grown. Since corn and soy are significant commodity crops in the U.S., they have large nitrogen "footprints."

6.5.3 Fertilizers

Nitrogen has been described as "the most commonly yield-limiting nutrient in all pre-industrial agricultures."[75] One of the most significant technological advances of the last few centuries is the **Haber-Bosch process**, the industrial process of synthesizing nitrogen at scale. This has allowed cheap and plentiful fertilizer, which has resulted in rapid intensification of crop yields, providing more food for a rising human population. According to environmental scientist Vaclav Smil:

> [T]he Haber-Bosch synthesis now provides the very means of survival for about 40% of humanity; that only half of today's population could be supplied by pre-fertilizer farming with overwhelmingly vegetarian diets; and that traditional cropping could provide today's average diets to only about 40% of the existing population.[76]

The importance of synthesizing nitrogen is difficult to overstate. Norman Borlaug (the biologist who was a driving force behind the Green Revolution) said that "[i]f the high yielding dwarf wheat and rice varieties are the catalysts that have ignited the Green Revolution, then chemical fertilizer is the fuel that has powered its forward thrust"[77] About half of nitrogen supplied to global agriculture is synthetic.[78] Researchers at the UN Environmental Program estimate that "more than half of the synthetic nitrogen fertilizer ever produced was used in just the past 25 years or less."[79] The scale of synthetic nitrogen is large: "[t]he reactive nitrogen in synthetic fertilizers is now perhaps equal to half of the total fixed by all bacteria in all natural terrestrial ecosystems."[80]

Changes to the nitrogen cycle as a result of synthetic nitrogen fixation have far-reaching environmental and social consequences. According to leading nitrogen researchers, "[h]uman alterations of the nitrogen cycle have:

1) approximately doubled the rate of nitrogen input into the terrestrial nitrogen cycle, with these rates still increasing;
2) increased concentrations of the potent greenhouse gas N_2O globally, and increased concentrations of other oxides of nitrogen that drive the formation of photochemical smog over large regions of Earth;
3) caused losses of soil nutrients, such as calcium and potassium, that are essential for the long-term maintenance of soil fertility;
4) contributed substantially to the acidification of soils, streams, and lakes in several regions; and
5) greatly increased the transfer of nitrogen through rivers to estuaries and coastal oceans.

In addition, based on our review of available scientific evidence, we are confident that human alterations of the nitrogen cycle have:

6) increased the quantity of organic carbon stored within terrestrial ecosystems;
7) accelerated losses of biological diversity, especially losses of plants adapted to efficient use of nitrogen, and losses of the animals and microorganisms that depend on them; and
8) caused changes in the composition and functioning of estuarine and nearshore ecosystems, and contributed to long-term declines in coastal marine fisheries."[81]

While fertilizer is essential, there are also areas for improvement. Environmental physicist Mark A. Sutton points out that most fertilizer use is inefficient:[82]

> The efficiency of nutrient use is very low: considering the full chain, on average over 80% of N and 25–75% of P consumed (where not temporarily stored in agricultural soils) end up lost to the environment, wasting the energy used to prepare them, and causing pollution through emissions of the greenhouse gas nitrous oxide (N_2O) and ammonia (NH_3) to the atmosphere, plus losses of nitrate (NO_3^-), phosphate (PO_4^{3-}) and organic N [and] P compounds to water."[83]

The production of fertilizers also uses energy, which itself has environmental impacts.[84] Up to 5% of all natural gas is used to produce synthetic nitrogen fertilizer,[85] and its production emits a fair amount of greenhouse gases.[86] Synthetic fertilizers are a "key stressor on marine ecosystems"[87] because they create dead zones. Many of the environmental harms created by nitrogen use are exacerbated by industrial monocultures, which often require more fertilizer.[88]

6.5.4 Pesticides

Industrial pesticide use is one of the better known environmental impacts of modern agriculture, in large part thanks to Rachel Carson's canonical book *Silent Spring*. Carson, a U.S. Fish and Wildlife Service scientist with training in marine biology, serialized *Silent Spring* in the *New Yorker* in the early 1960s, engaging a host of environmental and social topics. She told the story of pesticide accumulation, biological magnification (when a toxin increases in concentration in a biological system), and wildlife loss due to pesticide use. The pesticide DDT, for instance, was sprayed on leaves which were eaten by worms (increasing the concentration of DDT), which were eaten by birds, which in turn produced weaker shells, endangering their offspring. It also causes cancer as well as other health problems in humans.

Carson wove a rich picture of the interconnected dimensions of ecological systems. *Silent Spring* also challenges us to think critically about the role of human intervention in natural systems, criticizing the appropriateness of large-scale, industrial intervention in nature. The book is credited with launching the modern environmental movement as well as eventually leading to the restriction of the use of DDT[89] in the early 1970s. Pesticides were not always seen as harmful, however—the earliest form of pesticide regulation was to ensure a sufficient level of purity in the product. We used DDT indoors to kill insects and sprayed it on children for the same purpose (before we understood many of the human and environmental harms caused by pesticide usage above a certain dosage).

Another historical event in industrial pesticide use is the Bhopal disaster of 1984, in which an Indian pesticide factory owned by Union Carbide (now a subsidiary of Dow Chemical) leaked tons of toxic gases, killing thousands of people and seriously harming thousands more. This incident highlights the accountability of foreign companies as well as the potential harm of pesticides.

While many of the earlier industrial pesticides with high human toxicity have been banned or greatly restricted (with some notable exceptions like chlorpyrifos),[90] some newer industrial pesticides do not have readily available alternatives. Further, pesticides impact nonhuman animal life in many forms. Biologist Tyrone Hayes has discovered that atrazine changes the sex of frogs, for instance, and others have noted the risk to pollinators[91] and stream invertebrates.[92] The pesticide family of neonicotinoids has been suspected in recent bee colony collapses, and is strictly regulated in the European Union.

Monocultures require even more pesticides because a continuous area planted with one genetically identical crop will be highly vulnerable to destruction by an insect who is particularly interested in that crop. Because of the scale, monocultures are more likely to be managed through mechanical means (such as tractors and combines), and so the pesticide application is likely with crop dusters or sprayers attached to tractors. This means that pesticides are sprayed broadly with only a small percentage reaching target insects[93]—instead, much of it enters surface waterways, drifting to nearby fields and entering the water table.

Even though the U.S. uses more pesticides than 80 years ago, the loss of crops to insects is increasing. This is largely a function of the increase in monocultures and the increased proportion of insects who have gained resistance to pesticides. In the U.S., the majority of pesticides are used on corn and soy.[94]

Because pesticides are toxic, human and nonhuman animal exposure must be carefully managed to minimize harm. Farm workers and those living near farms are impacted most severely. In less industrialized agriculture settings, pesticide application is often done without proper protection, resulting in significant human health harms. Pesticides can cause various illnesses including leukemia, and are linked to birth defects, cancers, fertility disorders, and neurological disorders. Those most often harmed are handling the pesticide or near the site of application, not the end consumer.

In addition, pesticides can kill non-target animals, such as insects and birds near the agricultural setting.[95] For this reason, they are a significant contributor to biodiversity loss. Because insects have such short reproductive cycles, they can adapt to pesticides quickly—evolving to gain resistance and making the pesticide ineffective against the target organism. This means that a pesticide generally loses effectiveness after extensive use.

6.6 Humans

The human impacts of industrial food are vast, diverse, and complex, and we can only cover a modest number of important points here. Industrial and non-industrial systems involve different numbers of workers and different kinds of demanding work, which we discuss here and in the following chapter.

6.6.1 Labor

Industrialized agricultural practices are less labor intensive; that is, they require less labor to produce the same amount of food. This exposes fewer workers to risk, but it also increases the repetitiveness and potential harm of harvesting and other work. Field workers are exposed to sun, pesticides, fertilizer offgassing, and labor violations. Mechanized planting, harvesting, and factory tasks might reduce some labor harms and increase others, such as being injured by machinery.

The slaughtering and processing industry is more dangerous than most other manufacturing jobs in the U.S.[96] CAFO and slaughterhouse workers are subject to intensive working environments and the psychological stress of killing animals.[97] Similarly, the pressures to extract more aquatic animals from the ocean create risks for people who make a living by fishing, which is already a dangerous job.[98] Even more severely, the combination of these pressures and activity in secluded, extra-governmental areas has resulted in harassment and murder of observers[99] as well as slavery.[100]

The limited legal and political visibility of many farm, factory, slaughterhouse, and fisheries workers serves to exacerbate these risks and leave these workers less visible to a broader community.

6.6.2 Public health

Antibiotic use in farmed animals is estimated to be up to three to four times higher than in human populations,[101] contributing to antibiotic-resistant bacteria. Other antibiotics and antimicrobials, for example arsenic, can accumulate in animals such as chickens and pigs (and eventually make their way into plants like rice). Since bacteria gain resistance to antibiotics, previously effective antibiotics no longer work and need to be replaced. Bacteria with resistance to antibiotics are referred to as "superbugs," as they are very difficult to treat with existing medicine. In some cases, we are already using antibiotics "of last resort" in the farming of chickens—meaning that these antibiotics are likely to be ineffective for human health treatment in the near future.[102]

In addition to superbugs and pollution described earlier in this chapter, industrial agriculture also contributes to zoonotic diseases like avian flu, bovine spongiform encephalopathy, *E. coli*, *Salmonella*, trichinosis, and anisakiasis. CAFO operations and globalized distribution systems both greatly exacerbate the development and transmission of zoonotic diseases. Zoonotic diseases are responsible for "over 2.5 billion cases of human illness and 2.7 million human deaths worldwide each year, with most of the burden in low-income countries and among poor livestock keepers."[103]

The types of foods we increasingly produce often fail to meet some nutritional needs of humans. Malnutrition, starvation, and nutrition-related diseases are prevalent. Even in affluent, industrialized countries, diet-related diseases such as obesity, heart disease, and diabetes are at high levels. This is partly due to the increase in processed, minimally nutritious foods, as well as lifestyle behaviors unrelated to diet, such as exercise.

Historically, there has been a tension between providing affordable calories within current production systems in the short term and developing environmentally sound production systems in the long run. The debate over intensification started with the Green Revolution and continues today.[104] We now produce more food than ever before, yet many world residents are still in need of calories and nutrients. This is a function of what we grow, whether or not we eat it directly, how we distribute it, how we use it, how we price it, and how we dispose of it. We use food for farmed animals and products such as ethanol, waste it in supermarkets and kitchens, and otherwise make it unavailable to those who need it most.

Intensifying agricultural production can lead to increased local environmental impacts, but can also lead to reduced environmental impacts by using less land. The balance between intensive and extensive is actively debated for this reason.

On one hand, we grow enough food for everyone. On the other hand, we do not make food available to everyone, and our population is rapidly increasing—leading to the need for increased production and better distribution.

This leads to conflicts in values. For instance, the UN FAO's 2006 study on the environmental and social impacts of animal agriculture[105] discusses the significant climate impacts of this practice, but also proposes a shift toward more intensive (often CAFO) animal agriculture, using pigs and other non-ruminant animals. Since land use and land-use change are such significant contributors to climate change, and grazing often requires more resources than consolidated CAFOs, the report argues that intensification of pig production has both environmental and food security benefits.

6.7 Conclusion

Industrial agriculture often functions at a more intensive and larger scale than non-industrial agriculture, with the attendant animal, environmental, and human impacts. The nonhuman impacts are almost always significantly worse in industrialized systems. The human and environmental impacts are more complex, as growing more food on less land has costs and benefits, and the increase in food production due to industrialized agriculture provides nutrients for billions of humans. In the next chapter, we describe a set of alternatives to mainstream industrialized agricultural practices.

Notes

1 Further reading on this topic includes Upton Sinclair's *The Jungle* (Doubleday, Jabber & Company, 1906), Ruth Harrison's *Animal Machines* (Ballantine Books, 1964), Peter Singer's *Animal Liberation* (New York Review, distributed by Random House, 1975), Timothy Pachirat's *Every Twelve Seconds* (Yale University Press, 2013), Eric Schlosser's *Fastfood Nation* (Houghton Mifflin Harcourt, 2001), Michael Pollan's *Omnivore's Dilemma* (The Penguin Press, 2006), and Daniel Imhoff's *The CAFO Reader: The Tragedy of Industrial Animal Factories* (Watershed Media, 2010).

2 "Amazon Cattle Footprint," Greenpeace, www.greenpeace.org/international/Global/international/planet-2/report/2009/1/amazon-cattle-footprint-mato.pdf.

3 James McWilliams, *Just Food: Where Locavores Get it Wrong and How We Can Truly Eat Responsibly* (Boston: Little, Brown and Company, 2009): 213–222.

4 Pamela C. Ronald and Raoul W. Adamchak, *Tomorrow's Table: Organic Farming, Genetics, and the Future of Food* (New York: Oxford University Press, 2008).

5 Harvey Augenbraun, Elaine Matthews, and David Sarma, "The Global Methane Cycle," GISS Institute on Climate and Planets, https://icp.giss.nasa.gov/education/methane/intro/cycle.html.

6 For one argument in favor of this, see:
   Pamela C. Ronald and Raoul W. Adamchak, *Tomorrow's Table: Organic Farming, Genetics, and the Future of Food* (New York: Oxford University Press, 2008).

7 Genetically engineered crops such as Bt cotton are designed to resist certain species considered to be "pests"—thereby reducing the need to spray pesticides.

8 For example, see the chapter entitled "Big Organic" in Michael Pollan, *The Omnivore's Dilemma* (New York: Penguin, 2006).

9 "[C]omparable grassland conversion rates have not been seen in the Corn Belt since the 1920s and 1930s . . . the era of rapid mechanization of US agriculture."

   Christopher K. Wright and Michael C. Wimberly, "Recent Land Use Change in the Western Corn Belt Threatens Grasslands and Wetlands," *Proceedings of the National Academy of Sciences* 110, no. 10 (March 2013): 4134–4139.

10 Data available at "Production Indices," Food and Agriculture Organization of the United Nations, http://faostat3.fao.org/browse/Q/QI/E.

11 James R. Stevenson et al., "Green Revolution Research Saved an Estimated 18 to 27 Million Hectares from Being Brought into Agricultural Production," *Proceedings of the National Academy of Sciences* 110, no. 21 (May 2013): 8363–8368.

12 "The State of the World's Land and Water Resources for Food and Agriculture," Food and Agriculture Organization of the United Nations, 2011, www.fao.org/docrep/015/i1688e/i1688e00.pdf.

13 "[A]chievements in production have been associated with management practices that have degraded the land and water systems upon which the production depends."

   "The State of the World's Land and Water Resources for Food and Agriculture," Food and Agriculture Organization of the United Nations, 2011, www.fao.org/docrep/015/i1688e/i1688e00.pdf.

14 Prabhu L. Pingali, "Green Revolution: Impacts, Limits, and the Path Ahead," *Proceedings of the National Academy of Sciences* 109, no. 31 (July 2012): 12302–12308.

15 For the 1942 Tennessee Valley Authority PSA, see:

   "FDR's New Deal Photo: Tennessee Valley Agriculture," Shmoop, www.shmoop.com/fdr-new-deal/photo-tenn-valley-ag.html.

16 Harish Sethu, "How Many Animals Does a Vegetarian Save?" Counting Animals, last updated March 16, 2015, www.countinganimals.com/how-many-animals-does-a-vegetarian-save/.

17 There are hybrid models that include some less confined conditions—such as feedlots that cows are on for only part of their lives, or "free-range" chicken farms that allow the possibility of leaving the confined area at times.

18 Claudia Bono, Cécile Cornou, Søren Lundbye-Christensen, and Anders Ringgaard Kristensen, "Dynamic Production Monitoring in Pig Herds III. Modeling and Monitoring Mortality Rate at Herd Level," *Livestock Science* 168 (October 2014): 128–138.

   Harish Sethu, "How Many Animals Does a Vegetarian Save?" Counting Animals, last updated March 16, 2015, www.countinganimals.com/how-many-animals-does-a-vegetarian-save/ using:

   "Poultry Slaughter: 2013 Summary," National Agricultural Statistics Service, United States Department of Agriculture, February 2014, http://usda.mannlib.cornell.edu/usda/nass/PoulSlauSu//2010s/2014/PoulSlauSu-02-25-2014.pdf.

   "Livestock Slaughter: 2013 Summary," National Agricultural Statistics Service, United States Department of Agriculture, April 2014, http://usda.mannlib.cornell.edu/usda/nass/LiveSlauSu//2010s/2014/LiveSlauSu-04-21-2014.pdf.

19 Upton Sinclair's *The Jungle* (1906), Ruth Harrison's *Animal Machines* (1964), and Peter Singer's *Animal Liberation* (1975) are canonical examples. More recently, dozens of books on the topic have been published.

   Further reading on this topic includes Timothy Pachirat's *Every Twelve Seconds* (2013), Eric Schlosser's *Fastfood Nation* (2001), Michael Pollan's *Omnivore's Dilemma* (2006), and Daniel Imhoff's *The CAFO Reader: The Tragedy of Industrial Animal Factories* (2010).

20 "U.S. Broiler Performance," National Chicken Council, September 26, 2017, www.nationalchickencouncil.org/about-the-industry/statistics/u-s-broiler-performance/.

21 "[M]odern egg production . . . depends on the procedure of 'chick culling'—the maceration or suffocation of hundreds of millions of live male chicks per year just days after they hatch because they have no economic value to the industry."

Matthew C. Halteman, "Varieties of Harm to Animals in Industrial Farming," *Journal of Animal Ethics* 1, no. 2 (2011): 122–131.

22 "By the Second World War, cows only ranged for 1–2 years."
Carol Adams, *Burger* (New York: Bloomsbury Academic, 2018): 40.

23 Pigs are slaughtered at different ages. Generally they can be divided into piglets, which are 1.5 to 3 months old; the fattening pigs, intended for pork and bacon, which are 4 months to one year old; and finally the older pigs, such as sows (female pigs) and boars (uncastrated male pigs).

"Pig Slaughter," Wikipedia, last updated January 22, 2018, https://en.wikipedia.org/wiki/Pig_slaughter.

24 "Domestic Pig," Wikipedia, last updated March 17, 2018, https://en.wikipedia.org/wiki/Domestic_pig.

25 Thank you to Dan Honig for providing some of the data on this topic, including the following resources:

"Quick Stats," National Agricultural Statistics Service, United States Department of Agriculture, https://quickstats.nass.usda.gov/?source_desc=CENSUS#FD6BC30E-D326-3FCA-BFB2-65AF94CDD104.

"Census of Agriculture," United States Department of Agriculture, www.agcensus.usda.gov/.

"Agricultural Statistics 2017," National Agricultural Statistics Service, United States Department of Agriculture, 2017, www.nass.usda.gov/Publications/Ag_Statistics/2017/Complete%20Ag%20Stats%202017.pdf.

"Sector at a Glance," Economic Research Service, United States Department of Agriculture, www.ers.usda.gov/topics/animal-products/cattle-beef/sector-at-a-glance/.

"U.S. Broiler and Egg Production Cycles," National Agricultural Statistics Service, Agricultural Statistics Board, U.S. Department of Agriculture, September 16, 2015, http://usda.mannlib.cornell.edu/usda/current/usbepc/usbepc-09-16-2005.pdf.

Renee Cheung and Paul McMahon, "Back to Grass: The U.S. Market Potential for Grassfed Beef," Stone Barns Center for Food and Agriculture, April 2017, www.stonebarnscenter.org/wp-content/uploads/2017/10/Grassfed_Full_v2.pdf.

26 Timothy Pachirat, *Every Twelve Seconds* (New Haven: Yale University Press, 2011).

27 Brandon Keim, "'Pig Brain Mist' Disease Mystery Concludes," *Wired*, February 24, 2009, www.wired.com/2009/02/pigbrainmystery/.

28 David Wolfson and Mariann Sullivan, "Foxes in the Hen House: Animals, Agribusiness and the Law: A Modern American Fable," in Cass Sunstein and Martha Nussbaum, eds., *Animal Rights* (New York: Oxford University Press, 2005): 205–233.

29 David Wolfson and Mariann Sullivan, "Foxes in the Hen House: Animals, Agribusiness and the Law: A Modern American Fable," in Cass Sunstein and Martha Nussbaum, *Animal Rights* (New York: Oxford University Press, 2005): 205–233.

30 David A. Kroodsma et al., "Tracking the Global Footprint of Fisheries," *Science* 359, no. 6378 (February 2018): 904–908.

31 This concept provoked the title of the conference "Seeing Seafood as Animals," which was held at New York University in April 2016.

32 Daniel Pauly and Dirk Zeller, "Catch Reconstructions Reveal that Global Marine Fisheries Catches Are Higher than Reported and Declining," *Nature Communications* 7, no. 10244 (January 2016).

33 Boris Worm et al., "Impacts of Biodiversity Loss on Ocean Ecosystem Services," *Science* 314, no. 5800 (November 2006): 787–790.

34 "The Impacts of Fishing on Vulnerable Marine Ecosystems," Report of the Secretary-General, United Nations, 2006, www.un.org/Depts/los/general_assembly/documents/impact_of_fishing.pdf.

35 Michael Clark and David Tilman, "Comparative Analysis of Environmental Impacts of Agricultural Production Systems, Agricultural Input Efficiency, and Food Choice," *Environmental Research Letters* 12, no. 6 (June 2017).

36 Dirk Zeller, Tim Cashion, Maria Palomares, and Daniel Pauly, "Global Marine Fisheries Discards: A Synthesis of Reconstructed Data," *Fish and Fisheries* 19, no. 1 (January 2018): 30–39.

37 "Discards and Bycatch in Shrimp Trawl Fisheries," Food and Agriculture Organization of the United Nations, www.fao.org/docrep/W6602E/w6602E09.htm.

38 Dayton L. Alverson, Mark H. Freeberg, Steven A. Murawski, and J.G. Pope, "A Global Assessment of Fisheries Bycatch and Discards," Food and Agriculture Organization of the United Nations, 1996, www.fao.org/docrep/003/T4890E/T4890E00.HTM.

39 "Capture Fisheries vs. Aquaculture (Farmed Fish) Production, World," Our World in Data, https://ourworldindata.org/grapher/capture-fisheries-vs-aquaculture-farmed-fish-production?tab=sources.

40 Jillian P. Fry, "Environmental Health Impacts of Feeding Crops to Farmed Fish," *Environment International* 91 (May 2016): 201–214.

41 Harish Sethu, "The Fish We Kill to Feed the Fish We Eat," Counting Animals, published March 16, 2015, www.countinganimals.com/the-fish-we-kill-to-feed-the-fish-we-eat/.

42 Jacqueline Alder et al., "Forage Fish: From Ecosystems to Markets," *Annual Review of Environment and Resources* 33 (November 2008): 153–166.

> At present, small pelagic forage fish species (includes anchovies, herring, mackerel, sardines, etc.) represent the largest landed species group in capture fisheries (27.3 million t or 29.7% of total capture fisheries landings in 2006). They also currently constitute the major species group actively fished and targeted for nonfood uses, including reduction into fishmeal and fish oil for use within compound animal feeds, or for direct animal feeding; the aquaculture sector alone consumed the equivalent of about 23.8 million tons of fish[es] (live weight equivalent) or 87% in the form of feed inputs in 2006. This article attempts to make a global analysis of the competition for small pelagic forage fish[es] for direct human consumption and nonfood uses, particularly concerning the important and growing role played by small pelagic forage fish[es] in the diet and food security of the poor and needy, especially within the developing countries of Africa and the Sub-Saharan region.

Albert G.J. Tacon and Marc Metian, "Fishing for Feed or Fishing for Food: Increasing Global Competition for Small Pelagic Forage Fish," *AMBIO: A Journal of the Human Environment* 38, no. 6 (September 2009): 294–302.

43 Jennifer Jacquet, David Frank, and Chris Schlottmann, "Asymmetrical Contributions to the Tragedy of the Commons and Some Implications for Conservation," *Sustainability* 5, no. 3 (March 2013): 1036–1048.

44 James S. Diana, "Aquaculture Production and Biodiversity Conservation," *BioScience* 59, no. 1 (January 2009): 27–38.

> The wild captured fish[es] and crustaceans used for "non-food purposes" are low trophic-level species groups such as sardines, anchovies, and herrings, and krill, which are classified as forage fish[es] because they are essential to the diets of larger fish[es], marine mammals and seabirds. Scientists have recently called for a reduction of fishing pressure on forage fish[es] due to their important role in the marine food web, and a more precautionary approach to fishing where information is less reliable. At the same time, scientists have recognized the paradox that aquaculture, as it currently exists (farming primarily carnivorous species),

actually puts additional pressure on wild fish stocks, rather than relieves it, by increasing demand for forage fish[es] for feed.

Jennifer Jacquet, David Frank, and Chris Schlottmann, "Asymmetrical Contributions to the Tragedy of the Commons and Some Implications for Conservation," *Sustainability* 5, no. 3 (March 2013): 1036–1048.
45 Ellen Pikitch et al., "Little Fish, Big Impact: Managing a Crucial Link in Ocean Food Webs," Lenfest Ocean Program, www.oceanconservationscience.org/foragefish/.
    "The State of World Fisheries and Aquaculture 2012," Food and Agriculture Organization of the United Nations, 2012, www.fao.org/docrep/016/i2727e/i2727e.pdf.
    Jennifer Jacquet, David Frank, and Chris Schlottmann, "Asymmetrical Contributions to the Tragedy of the Commons and Some Implications for Conservation," *Sustainability* 5, no. 3 (March 2013): 1036–1048.
    Jacqueline Alder et al., "Forage Fish: From Ecosystems to Markets," *Annual Review of Environment and Resources* 33 (November 2008): 153–166.
    Jennifer Jacquet, John Hocevar, Sherman Lai, and Patricia Majluf, "Conserving Wild Fish in a Sea of Market-based Efforts," *Oryx* 41, no. 1 (January 2010): 45–56.
46   There is a land-use carbon footprint of 1440 kg CO_2e for every kilogram of beef and 1603 kg CO_2e for every kilogram of shrimps produced on lands formerly occupied by mangroves. A typical steak and shrimp cocktail dinner would burden the atmosphere with 816 kg CO_2e. This is approximately the same quantity of GHGs produced by driving a fuel-efficient automobile from Los Angeles to New York City. Failure to include deforestation in life-cycle assessments greatly underestimates the GHG emissions from food production.

J. Boone Kauffman et al., "The Jumbo Carbon Footprint of a Shrimp: Carbon Losses from Mangrove Deforestation," *Frontiers in Ecology and the Environment* 15, no. 4 (April 2017): 183–188.
47 Rebecca Helm, "What You Need to Know about Jellyfish Attacks on Salmon Farms," *The Conversation*, October 24, 2013, https://theconversation.com/what-you-need-to-know-about-jellyfish-attacks-on-salmon-farms-19493.
48 Carlos M. Duarte, Nùria Marbá, and Marianne Holmer, "Rapid Domestication of Marine Species," *Science* 316, no. 5823 (April 2007): 382–383.
49 Approximately 0.13% vs. 0.0002%, or 650 times more marine animals. Numbers from:
    Carlos M. Duarte, Nùria Marbá, and Marianne Holmer, "Rapid Domestication of Marine Species," *Science* 316, no. 5823 (April 2007): 382–383.
50 Carlos M. Duarte, Nùria Marbá, and Marianne Holmer, "Rapid Domestication of Marine Species," *Science* 316, no. 5823 (April 2007): 382–383.
51 Victoria Braithwaite, *Do Fish Feel Pain?* (New York: Oxford University Press, 2010).
    Peter Godfrey-Smith, *Other Minds: The Octopus and the Evolution of Intelligent Life* (New York: Farrar, Straus and Giroux, 2016).
52 For example, see PETA's "Sea kittens" campaign, which attempts to invoke empathy for fishes.
53 Victoria Braithwaite, *Do Fish Feel Pain?* (New York: Oxford University Press, 2010).
54 ~4% of U.S. corn is used for high fructose corn syrup, ~1–2% of U.S. cropland is devoted to vegetables, and ~1–2% of U.S. cropland is devoted to fruit orchards. Numbers synthesized from data tables at:
    "Major Land Uses," Economic Research Service, United States Department of Agriculture, last updated February 5, 2018, www.ers.usda.gov/data-products/major-land-uses.aspx.
    Alicia Harvie and Timothy A. Wise, "Sweetening the Pot: Implicit Subsidies to Corn Sweeteners and the U.S. Obesity Epidemic," Global Development and Environment Institute, Tufts University, February 2009, www.ase.tufts.edu/gdae/Pubs/rp/PB09-01SweeteningPotFeb09.pdf.

55 Jonathan A. Foley et al., "Global Consequences of Land Use," *Science* 309, no. 5734 (July 2005): 570–574.

56 Henning Steinfeld et al., "Livestock's Long Shadow: Environmental Issues and Options," Food and Agriculture Organization of the United Nations, 2006, www.europarl. europa.eu/climatechange/doc/FAO%20report%20executive%20summary.pdf. xx.

57 Marc Ribaudo, "Reducing Agriculture's Nitrogen Footprint: Are New Policy Approaches Needed?" United States Department of Agriculture, www.ers.usda.gov/ amber-waves/2011/september/nitrogen-footprint/.

58 Marc Ribaudo, "Reducing Agriculture's Nitrogen Footprint: Are New Policy Approaches Needed?" United States Department of Agriculture, www.ers.usda.gov/ amber-waves/2011/september/nitrogen-footprint/.

59 "75% of [global] soybean is used for animal feed."
"Soy Facts & Data," World Wildlife Fund Global, http://wwf.panda.org/what_we_do/footprint/agriculture/soy/facts/.
"Just over 70 percent of the soybeans grown in the United States are used for animal feed."
"Soybeans," USDA Coexistence Fact Sheets, United States Department of Agriculture, February 2015, www.usda.gov/sites/default/files/documents/coexistence-soybeans-factsheet.pdf.
"[M]ore than 67 percent of crops—particularly all the soy grown in the Midwest—goes to animal feed."
Brad Plumer, "How Much of the World's Cropland Is Actually Used to Grow Food?" *Vox*, December 16, 2014, www.vox.com/2014/8/21/6053187/cropland-map-food-fuel-animal-feed.

From the 41 crops analyzed in this study, 9.46 × 10^15 calories available in plant form are produced by crops globally, of which 55% directly feed humans. However, 36% of these produced calories go to animal feed, of which 89% is lost, such that only 4% of crop-produced calories are available to humans in the form of animal products.

Emily S. Cassidy, Paul C. West, James S. Gerber, and Jonathan A. Foley, "Redefining Agricultural Yields: From Tonnes to People Nourished Per Hectare," *Environmental Research Letters* 8 (August 2013).

60 Jonathan A. Foley, "It's Time to Rethink America's Corn System," *Scientific American*, March 5, 2013, www.scientificamerican.com/article/time-to-rethink-corn/.

61 James McWilliams, *Just Food: Where Locavores Get It Wrong and How We Can Truly Eat Responsibly* (Boston: Little, Brown and Company, 2009): 127 referencing:
Henning Steinfeld et al., "Livestock's Long Shadow: Environmental Issues and Options," Food and Agriculture Organization of the United Nations, 2006, www.europarl.europa.eu/climatechange/doc/FAO%20report%20executive%20summary.pdf.
M.J. Chrispeels and D.E. Sadava, "Farming Systems: Development, Productivity, and Sustainability," in *Plants, Genes, and Agriculture* (Boston: Jones and Bartlett, 1994): 25–57.

62 "Custom Query," Production, Supply and Distribution, United States Department of Agriculture, Foreign Agricultural Service, www.fas.usda.gov/psdonline/psd query.aspx.

63 The 26% estimate is from:
Henning Steinfeld et al., "Livestock's Long Shadow: Environmental Issues and Options," Food and Agriculture Organization of the United Nations, 2006, www.europarl.europa.eu/climatechange/doc/FAO%20report%20executive%20summary.pdf. xx.
The 45% estimate is from:

Philip Thornton, Mario Herrero, and Polly Ericksen, "Livestock and Climate Change," International Livestock Research Institute, November 2011, http://mahider.ilri.org/bitstream/handle/10568/10601/IssueBrief3.pdf.

64 "Livestock a Major Threat to Environment," Food and Agriculture Organization of the United Nations Newsroom, November 29, 2006, www.fao.org/newsroom/en/news/2006/1000448/index.html.

65 Henning Steinfeld et al., "Livestock's Long Shadow: Environmental Issues and Options," Food and Agriculture Organization of the United Nations, 2006, www.europarl.europa.eu/climatechange/doc/FAO%20report%20executive%20summary.pdf: xxi and Chapter 2.

66 Adam S. Davis et al., "Increasing Cropping System Diversity Balances Productivity, Profitability and Environmental Health," *PLOS ONE* 7, no. 10 (October 2012).
    J. Blesh and L.E. Drinkwater, "The Impact of Nitrogen Source and Crop Rotation on Nitrogen Mass Balances in the Mississippi River Basin," *Ecological Applications* 23, no. 5 (July 2013): 1017–1035.

67 James R. Gillespie and Frank Flanders, *Modern Livestock and Poultry Production* (Boston: Cengage Learning, 2009).
    Jonathan Safran Foer, *Eating Animals* (New York: Hachette Book Group, 2010): 174.
    Carrie Hribar, "Understanding Concentrated Animal Feeding Operations and Their Impact on Communities," National Association of Local Boards of Health, Centers for Disease Control and Prevention, www.cdc.gov/nceh/ehs/docs/understanding_cafos_nalboh.pdf.

68 Henning Steinfeld et al., "Livestock's Long Shadow: Environmental Issues and Options," Food and Agriculture Organization of the United Nations, 2006, www.europarl.europa.eu/climatechange/doc/FAO%20report%20executive%20summary.pdf.

69 "Key Facts and Findings," Food and Agriculture Organization of the United Nations, www.fao.org/news/story/en/item/197623/icode/.

70 Robert Goodland and Jeff Anhang, "Livestock and Climate Change," Worldwatch Institute, November/December 2009, www.worldwatch.org/files/pdf/Livestock%20and%20Climate%20Change.pdf.

71 Peter Singer's response in Tim Flannery, *Now or Never: Why We Must Act Now to End Climate Change and Create a Sustainable Future* (New York: Grove Atlantic, 2009).

72 Dave S. Reay et al., "Global Agriculture and Nitrous Oxide Emissions," *Nature Climate Change* 2 (May 2012): 410–416.

73 "Key Facts and Findings," Food and Agriculture Organization of the United Nations, www.fao.org/news/story/en/item/197623/icode/.

74 Liam Goucher et al., "Environmental Impact of Fertiliser Embodied in a Wheat-to-Bread Supply Chain," *Nature Plants* 3, no. 3 (March 2017).

75 Vaclav Smil, "Nitrogen and Food Production: Proteins for Human Diets," *AMBIO: A Journal of the Human Environment* 31, no. 2 (March 2002): 126–131.

76 Vaclav Smil, "Nitrogen and Food Production: Proteins for Human Diets," *AMBIO: A Journal of the Human Environment* 31, no. 2 (March 2002): 126–131.

77 Norman Borlaug, "The Green Revolution: Peace and Humanity" (speech), Norman Borlaug—Nobel Lecture, December 11, 1970, www.nobelprize.org/nobel_prizes/peace/laureates/1970/borlaug-lecture.html.

78 Vaclav Smil, "Nitrogen and Food Production: Proteins for Human Diets," *AMBIO: A Journal of the Human Environment* 31, no. 2 (March 2002): 126–131.

79 "Assessing Global Land Use: Balancing Consumption with Sustainable Supply—Summary," United Nations Environment Programme, May 27, 2014, https://issuu.com/unep/docs/summary-english.

80 Vaclav Smil, *Enriching the Earth: Fritz Haber, Carl Bosch, and the Transformation of World Food Production* (Cambridge: MIT Press, 2004): xvi.

81 Peter M. Vitousek et al., "Human Alteration of the Global Nitrogen Cycle: Sources and Consequences," *Ecological Applications* 7, no. 3 (August 1997): 737–750.

82 M.A. Sutton et al., "Our Nutrient World: The Challenge to Produce More Food and Energy with Less Pollution," Global Partnership on Nutrient Management and the International Nitrogen Initiative, 2013, http://library.wur.nl/WebQuery/wurpubs/fulltext/249094.

83 M.A. Sutton et al., "Our Nutrient World: The Challenge to Produce More Food and Energy with Less Pollution," Global Partnership on Nutrient Management and the International Nitrogen Initiative, 2013, http://library.wur.nl/WebQuery/wurpubs/fulltext/249094. viii.

84 "[T]he fertilizer industry uses about 1.2% of world energy consumption and is responsible for about the same share of global GHG emissions."
    "Fertilizer Manufacture," Climate Change 2007: Working Group III: Mitigation of Climate Change, Intergovernmental Panel on Climate Change Fourth Assessment Report: Climate Change 2007, www.ipcc.ch/publications_and_data/ar4/wg3/en/ch7s7-4-3-2.html.

85 Vaclav Smil, *Enriching the Earth: Fritz Haber, Carl Bosch, and the Transformation of World Food Production* (Cambridge: MIT Press, 2004): xvi.

86 "Fertilizer Manufacture," Climate Change 2007: Working Group III: Mitigation of Climate Change, Intergovernmental Panel on Climate Change Fourth Assessment Report: Climate Change 2007, www.ipcc.ch/publications_and_data/ar4/wg3/en/ch7s7-4-3-2.html.

87 Stephen C. Wagner, "Biological Nitrogen Fixation," *Nature Education Knowledge* 3, no. 10 (2011).

88 Adam S. Davis et al., "Increasing Cropping System Diversity Balances Productivity, Profitability and Environmental Health," *PLOS ONE* (October 2012).
    J. Blesh and L.E. Drinkwater, "The Impact of Nitrogen Source and Crop Rotation on Nitrogen Mass Balances in the Mississippi River Basin," *Ecological Applications* 23, no. 5 (July 2013): 1017–1035.

89 For more on Carson's role as the subject of attacks by the modern contrarianism movement, see:
    Robin McKie, "Merchants of Doubt by Naomi Oreskes and Erik M Conway," *The Guardian*, August 7, 2010, www.theguardian.com/books/2010/aug/08/merchants-of-doubt-oreskes-conway.

90 Ankush L. Rathod and R.K. Garg, "Chlorpyrifos Poisoning and Its Implications in Human Fatal Cases: A Forensic Perspective with Reference to Indian Scenario," *Journal of Forensic and Legal Medicine* 47 (April 2017): 29–34.

91 Maj Rundlöf et al., "Seed Coating with a Neonicotinoid Insecticide Negatively Affects Wild Bees," *Nature* 521 (May 2015): 77–80.

92 Mikhail A. Beketov, Ben J. Kefford, Ralf B. Schäfer, and Matthias Liess, "Pesticides Reduce Regional Biodiversity of Stream Invertebrates," *Proceedings of the National Academy of Sciences* 11, no. 27 (July 2013): 11039–11043.

93 Sometimes the percentage is well under 1%.
    David Pimentel and Michael Burgess, "Small Amounts of Pesticides Reaching Target Insects," *Environment, Development and Sustainability* 14, no. 1 (February 2012): 1–2.

94 Certain genetically engineered crops and the phase out of certain pesticides have resulted in a more recent decline in insecticide (pesticides that target insects instead of weeds) use.
    Jorge Fernandez-Cornejo et al., "Pesticide Use in U.S. Agriculture: 21 Selected Crops, 1960–2008," *Economic Information Bulletin Number 124*, United States Department of Agriculture, May 2014, www.ers.usda.gov/webdocs/publications/43854/46734_eib124.pdf.

95   Nigel Dudley et al., "How Should Conservationists Respond to Pesticides as a Driver of Biodiversity Loss in Agroecosystems?" *Biological Conservation* 209 (May 2017): 449–453.

96   "Additional Data Needed to Address Continued Hazards in the Meat and Poultry Industry," Workplace Safety and Health, United States Government Accountability Office, April 2016, www.gao.gov/assets/680/676796.pdf.

97   Timothy Pachirat, *Every Twelve Seconds* (New Haven: Yale University Press, 2011).

98   "The Deadliest Jobs in America," Bloomberg, May 13, 2015, www.bloomberg.com/graphics/2015-dangerous-jobs/.

99   "Missing at Sea: The Dangers Faced by Fisheries Observers," Fish Wise, May 25, 2017, https://fishwise.org/missing-sea-dangers-faced-fisheries-observers/.

100 Ian Urbina, "'Sea Slaves:' The Human Misery that Feeds Pets and Livestock," *The New York Times*, July 27, 2015, www.nytimes.com/2015/07/27/world/outlaw-ocean-thailand-fishing-sea-slaves-pets.html.

101 Ralph Loglisci, "New FDA Numbers Reveal Food Animals Consume Lion's Share of Antibiotics," Center for a Livable Future, December 23, 2010, http://livablefutureblog.com/2010/12/new-fda-numbers-reveal-food-animals-consume-lion%E2%80%99s-share-of-antibiotics.

Thomas P. Van Boeckel, "Reducing Antimicrobial Use in Food Animals," *Science* 357, no. 6358 (September 2017): 1350–1352.

102 Madlen Davies, "A Game of Chicken: How Indian Poultry Farming Is Creating Global Superbugs," *The Bureau of Investigative Journalism*, March 1, 2018, www.thebureauinvestigates.com/stories/2018-01-30/a-game-of-chicken-how-indian-poultry-farming-is-creating-global-superbugs.

103 Samuel Lee-Gammage, "What Is the Connection between Infectious Diseases in Humans and Livestock?" Food Climate Research Network, https://foodsource.org.uk/printpdf/book/export/html/114.

104 For example, see:

Tara Garnett and H. Charles J. Godfray, "Sustainable Intensification in Agriculture: Navigating a Course through Competing Food System Priorities," Food Climate Research Network and the Oxford Martin Programme on the Future of Food, www.fcrn.org.uk/sites/default/files/SI_report_final.pdf.

105 Henning Steinfeld et al., "Livestock's Long Shadow: Environmental Issues and Options," Food and Agriculture Organization of the United Nations, 2006, www.europarl.europa.eu/climatechange/doc/FAO%20report%20executive%20summary.pdf.

7 Alternatives to industrial agriculture

7.1 Introduction

This chapter will examine alternatives to the industrial agriculture model, organized around major schools of thought and topics. This includes alternative animal agriculture, local agriculture, organic agriculture, and agriculture without animals (including plant-based agriculture, plant-based meat, and cultured meat). We will present the arguments for and against each system in addition to their animal, environmental, and human impacts. For example, we will discuss methane released by pasture-raised cows, land-use change due to lower productivity, the value of counting food miles, the toxicity in organic pesticides, and the possibility of feeding a rising population through non-industrial methods. The aim will be to more closely analyze both the empirical impacts and the values that underlie each alternative agricultural method. We note that, while we will be discussing these categories separately, they can also overlap. Indeed, a local, organic, free-range farm is in fact one of the most common alternatives to industrial agriculture.

Non-industrial agriculture is a broad category of alternatives to industrial agriculture, including (but not limited to) all forms of agriculture practiced before industrialization. In non-industrial agriculture, land clearing is less mechanized, fertilizer comes from nitrogen-fixing plants, compost, or animal manure, and pesticides are avoided or derived from non-synthetic sources. There are many different forms of non-industrial agriculture, and they are often specific to their local ecosystem. These include regenerative agriculture, permaculture, organic agriculture, carbon farming, bioregional farming, and dry farming. Although these forms vary significantly, many emphasize the importance of building soil nutrients, fertility, function (such as water retention), biomass, and biological communities with a minimum of inputs, especially synthetic inputs.

As with the impacts of industrial agriculture, the impacts of non-industrial agriculture vary depending on the inputs used, the land cleared, the soil tilled, and the output produced. Soil organic matter varies greatly across temperate and tropical climates, and so different practices are appropriate for different climates. This makes it difficult to make general statements about the impacts of alternatives to industrial agriculture without also specifying climate, forms of inputs, and other characteristics.

7.2 History

All agriculture before industrialization was non-industrial agriculture. Growing food required finding appropriate land, which often included cutting or burning forests, redirecting water, changing habitat, extracting energy (harvesting food), and sometimes adding nutrients. It also involved a significant amount of human and nonhuman animal labor to till soil, plant and harvest crops, and manage weeds and insects. Agriculture has resulted in significant environmental changes since its inception, as a consequence of methane emissions from rice paddies and farmed animals, carbon emissions from clearing forests, and a range of geopolitical activities from international trade to resource wars to the global search for fertilizers.[1] Both trade and the search for nutrients are significantly less expensive and more efficient in the industrial model. While we traveled to far corners of the Earth for fertilizer in the mid-1800s, we regularly and inexpensively ship food products around the world today.

Contemporary non-industrial agriculture contributes approximately one third of emissions from all agriculture,[2] and almost half of emissions from agriculture in countries without developed industrial economies.[3] While many alternatives to industrial agriculture minimize certain industrial harms (such as the overuse of synthetic fertilizers), almost all agriculture involves land use, land-use change, the altering of carbon and water cycles, and the extraction of energy from systems (in the form of harvesting food). Ancient rice paddy fields might have emitted sufficient methane to change local climates,[4] and ancient cows exhaled the same methane that we now recognize as a potent greenhouse gas. Since all agriculture necessarily involves transforming nature, it is important to understand and assess these transformations and to aim for better transformations—since we cannot achieve no transformation at all.

Even in carefully planned agricultural systems, environmental impacts are unavoidable. This point is well captured by historian James McWilliams:

> Agriculture by its nature demands human interference with nature's rhythms, and these interferences, synthetic or not, are necessarily contrary to what "nature" intends. No matter how sustainable the process, agriculture is designed to transform nature and yield outputs.[5]

Assessing agricultural practices requires us to balance a wide set of concerns—about biodiversity, greenhouse gas emissions, nonhuman interests, and local economies. For example, even though pre-industrial agriculture required the burning of forests and fields (both to clear land and release minerals into the soil), it also involved the recycling of organic materials (adding manure and crop residuals). Moreover, any land-use change impacts nonhuman animal habitats, biodiversity, and water flow, and involves changing the ecosystem by altering energy cycles and insect communities. The alternatives discussed in this chapter attempt to minimize the animal, environmental, and human impacts of agriculture.

People can be motivated to pursue alternatives to industrial agriculture for different reasons, and these different reasons can lead to different alternatives. For example, some people aim to minimize some of the environmental, human, or nonhuman harms occurring in industrial food agriculture. These people often embrace industrial technology as a means to this end (this might imply a focus on highly processed plant-based or cultured meat, discussed later on in this chapter). Meanwhile, other people aim to reduce use of industrial technology for its own sake (this includes bioregional agriculture or avoidance of the use of synthetic chemicals). Many other people pursue middle-ground solutions. For example, some alternatives—such as organic agriculture using modern strains of plants, modern farm equipment for harvest or preservation, and even genetic engineering—integrate industrial and non-industrial techniques. A host of issues and proposals loosely fall in this category, often synthesizing attributes of local, organic, and free range. These include agroecology, permaculture, seed banks, heirloom plants and animals, hydroponics and aeroponics,[6] dry farming, natural farming,[7] entomophagy (eating insects),[8] farming using Indigenous practices, and holistic grazing.

Local and organic agriculture are not always non-industrial—both can be practiced industrially. However, in the spirit of alternative animal agriculture, local and organic agriculture is rooted in a rejection of most forms of industrialization. For example, philosophers G. Owen Schaefer and Julian Savulescu say, "Factory farming violates [an appropriate balance between technological manipulation . . . with the natural world] insofar as it does not recognise any interdependence with the natural, but instead involves dominating nature and bringing it into line with human needs."[9]

We discuss industrial and non-industrial alternatives to mainstream forms of industrial agriculture in this chapter. In what follows, we describe the animal, environmental, and human dimensions of select types of alternative agriculture: alternative animal agriculture, local, organic, and plant-based and cultured animal products. We briefly discuss other alternatives, then summarize some binding themes that define this area.

7.3 Alternative animal agriculture

The arguments for alternative animal agriculture are complex, and involve nonhuman, environmental, and human considerations. In this section, we will review and discuss these considerations.

7.3.1 *Animals*

The animals in alternative animal agriculture can be either conventional, modern breeds or "heirloom" breeds. Heirloom, or heritage, breeds have an older genetic makeup, often from pre-industrial times. The conservation of these animals can be considered part of a broader effort to preserve genetic diversity that exists outside of conventional agriculture. Insofar as modern breeds introduce novel welfare concerns, heirloom breeds might be better for animal welfare. As we have seen, modern farmed animals are bred for traits that increase profit, but also cause major stresses on their bodies—broiler chickens, for example, are often bred to grow so rapidly that their legs cannot hold the weight of their bodies and will break under them if they try to stand.[10] Heirloom breeds rarely have the same concerns to the same degree. However, since they are still bred as agricultural animals, they are selected to develop certain functions such as high levels of milk production. Further, heirloom animals still suffer harms intrinsic to all animal agriculture. For example, cows are artificially inseminated to ensure milk production and are separated from their children shortly after birth, hens are artificially inseminated to ensure egg production, and many animals are pregnant almost constantly throughout their entire lives. In some forms of alternative animal agriculture, such as rotational grazing, there are increased risks of potentially fatal disorders like ruminal tympany, and environmental exposure still needs to be managed.

In an animal agriculture operation, even heirloom, free-range, and/or grass-fed animals must be slaughtered at a relatively early age for the farm to profit. Since animals in these non-industrial settings are not subject to the same conditions as animals in CAFOs, they are less likely to contract diseases and die early as a result. Their lifespan before slaughter might be the same as in an industrial operation, however, as this is dependent on the economic and market considerations of the farmer.[11] In many cases this involves pain and suffering for the animals slaughtered, as well as for their family and friends (since most farmed animals are social animals)—and either way it involves premature death.

Some have argued that backyard animal operations that attempt slaughter might cause more suffering than industrial operations, as those performing the slaughter are not necessarily trained in rendering the animal unconscious first, and might kill them more slowly.[12] On the other hand, they can take more time and exercise more caution with each individual, since they do not have to slaughter animals at the rate of one every 12 seconds, which, as we have seen, inevitably results in mistakes as well.

Low-density animal agriculture allows animals to play, rest, and engage in natural behaviors that are stunted in industrial operations. (Local and organic agriculture can adopt such practices.) Such a life, including the advantages that come from a farmer protecting animals from predators and providing food, might be preferable to other options, including non-existence, life in a factory farm, and life in the wild.[13] However, while many non-industrial settings can give animals more space, that might not make much of a difference if they still use modern breeds or if they still provide animals with short lives. Another concern with low-density animal agriculture is that these practices are unrepresentative of standard animal agriculture. As a result, they might give consumers the illusion that animal products come from these relatively humane settings much more often than they actually do.[14] Even if all of these concerns are addressed, low-density agricultural systems would need to scale considerably to provide substantial amounts of food. Doing so would require clearing more land, which, as we have noted in previous chapters, comes with significant environmental impacts and would require increased farm labor.

7.3.2 Environment

Assessing the environmental impact of alternative animal agriculture is difficult and contextual. Since land use and land-use change often constitute the bulk of greenhouse gas emissions, we first need to know if the pasture was a cleared forest, and how disrupted the soils are by grazing. In some cases, grass-fed cows might have a greater impact on climate because they grow more slowly and therefore live longer. Additionally, by consuming more cellulosic matter such as grasses, the methane produced by their digestion is estimated to be higher than feedlot cows[15]—by some estimates up to four times higher.[16] Recent analyses have concluded that, even in contexts where grazing results in grassland growth, the net greenhouse gas emissions from such animal agriculture practices are high: either similar to grain-fed[17] or higher than grain-fed.[18]

Some pastures have co-evolved with either prior or current animals, such as bison, and so the animals are a part of the ecology. For example, buffalos and elk used to graze the western U.S., eating certain forage and leaving manure to fertilize plants. Some argue that cows can occupy a similar function now, sequestering carbon[19] by promoting growth of grasses, among other functions.[20] Even if well-managed cows can increase carbon sequestration by promoting the growth of grass, however, their methane and nitrous oxide impacts often outweigh such benefits.[21]

This can be the case in grasslands that evolved with wild grazing animals on them, and that now use domesticated grazing animals to take the role of their wild ancestors. It is important to remember that even in cases where free-range grazing yields local environmental benefits such as pasture fertilization or weed removal, it could also have environmental costs such as methane emissions, soil compaction, and watershed pollution.

The ability of intensively managed cows to restore a landscape is a matter of dispute, with some scholars arguing that "[n]o grazing system has yet shown the capacity to overcome the long-term effects of overstocking and/or drought on vegetation productivity."[22] Some scientists also note that evidence supporting the benefits of holistic grazing is lacking,[23] claiming that "[m]anagers have found that rotational grazing systems can work for diverse management purposes, but scientific experiments have demonstrated that they do not necessarily work for specific ecological purposes,"[24] and that "[t]he scientific evidence refuting the ecological benefits of rotational grazing is robust."[25] However, others defend specific forms of rotational grazing (using practices specific to local ecosystems) against these criticisms.[26] Even if there are local ecological benefits to holistic grazing, we would have to include climate impact in order to make a complete assessment of the environmental impact of cow grazing.

According to the Center for Biological Diversity, "the ecological costs of livestock grazing exceed that of any other western land use."[27] Grazing impacts biodiversity differently, depending on variables such as stocking density, rotations, animal breeds, restriction of grazing areas (e.g., keeping animals and manure away from riverbeds), and the conditions of the grasslands ecosystem itself. In the U.S., grazing land is actively managed and heavily subsidized, including low-cost leasing and extermination of animals such as coyotes, horses, and groundhogs. In addition to the biophysical dimensions of agriculture, there are legal, political, and economic drivers that greatly impact the outcomes of agricultural practices.

Some argue that marginal land, which is not appropriate for growing crops,[28] is better used for grazing.[29] This argument points out that the land is otherwise not producing food, and that ruminant animals can convert indigestible grasses into protein. It makes a number of assumptions, however—including that land uses related to agriculture, such as raising animals for food, are better than land uses not related to agriculture, such as preservation of wilderness. Leaving land free of grazing animals has benefits for biodiversity, animal habitats, ecosystem services, and mitigation of climate change, water pollution, and soil erosion.

Animal manure is a rich source of nitrogen and other nutrients like potash and phosphate (depending on the animal), and can contribute to soil functions such as water retention and microbial activity. This is advantageous when bringing nutrients in from industrial settings is cost-prohibitive or otherwise undesirable (such as in a local food setting). Since grazing animals both remove nutrients (the grasses they eat and nutrients lost by erosion) and add nutrients (via manure and urine), energy both enters and leaves the system. In grassland agriculture, where ruminant animals graze, phosphorus is often depleted—so the grasslands require phosphorus fertilizer.[30] Additionally, pasture needs to be managed, as cows need to be rotated in order for pasture to regrow.

As we noted earlier, assessments of the impacts of agriculture depend not only on the type of agriculture but also on the context in which people use it. In the case of alternative animal agriculture, much depends on which parameters are included in the assessment as well as the region. A further consideration is the degree to which such systems can scale: If rotational grazing is proposed as an alternative to industrial meat production, we need to know how much meat can be produced this way and at what animal, environmental, and human cost (given that many concerns with meat production would be applicable no matter what). Currently, only ~3% of U.S. cows are grass-fed.[31]

7.3.3 Humans

Farmed animals are an important source of income, labor, nutrients, and status for many of the most economically disadvantaged people in the world. About 200 million people are pastoralists, deriving their income from raising farmed animals.[32] Certain farmed animals, such as ruminants, can convert inedible plants like grasses and forage into edible nutrients such as protein and fat, and animal products have some micronutrients that are not common in some less industrialized areas. Grazing animals produce a very small percentage of protein for human consumption.[33]

Farmed animals can sometimes function as a form of insurance during droughts, in that they do not die as easily as a crop might in a drought or winter condition.[34] (Farmed animals are more likely to die when certain diseases spread, however.) Especially for subsistence farmers, this is an important buffer. Farmed animals are used for both labor (pulling farm equipment or moving heavy items) and income generation (by the sale of their products or labor). Finally, certain grazing practices can use marginal lands, allowing food production in a setting otherwise inhospitable to it.

7.4 Local food

Local food is food produced and consumed in a specific area, often a bioregion or political region like a state. A locavore, then, is a person who consumes local food. Due to the limitations of what can be grown in certain regions, this kind of diet is both seasonal and restricted. In colder climates, it would likely be limited to stored, preserved, and animal products in the wintertime. As with other categories we will be discussing, the locality of food is often perceived as a proxy or heuristic for environmentally and socially responsible food. Some people also like local food because it travels less and, as a result, can be harvested closer to ripening, which enhances flavor.

Even if the definition of local food focuses on the distance from farm to fork, in practice local food coincides with other values as well, such as the value of supporting more humane standards and less industrial practices. (A factory farm might technically be local to someone, and might even be called a "family farm," but most locavores would not regard such a farm as compatible with the values that underlie their commitment to local food.) Farmers' markets are often an integral part of local food systems, as they offer producers a more direct way to sell food to consumers. They also yield higher profit margins for farmers (thereby supporting local businesses), and allow consumers a closer relationship with the producers of their food (thereby promoting local relationships). In contrast to organic food, which is highly regulated, local food is unregulated or loosely regulated, so interpretations can vary dramatically.[35]

7.4.1 Animals

The impacts of local food on nonhuman animals are often substantially different from the impacts of concentrated operations. Insofar as the animal agriculture in local food is small-scale, uses more humane practices, and involves less transportation (which is a stressor for animals), its welfare impacts are preferable. However, local animal agriculture still treats nonhuman animals as commodities. It controls their reproduction, separates them from their families, keeps them in captivity, and uses their bodies for their flesh, milk, or eggs—often in ways that involve substantial suffering and premature death. Farmed animal lives might be longer on average in local settings, but this is dictated by economic considerations and market forces such as aesthetic preferences.

7.4.2 Environment

The environmental impact of local food depends greatly on how the food was produced. Certain forms of local food can have modest environmental footprints if they use land that has already been cleared: for example, urban and rooftop farming are two instances in which the environmental impact of the land use has already occurred, so the farm is not causing the clearing of new land.

The transportation of food often makes up a relatively small percentage (around 10%) of its climate impact.[36] As a result, many people criticize the local food movement for overemphasizing one dimension of a multidimensional problem.[37] There are several cases in which food produced locally can require more inputs, such as fertilizer and energy (e.g., for heating a tomato greenhouse in a cold environment), thereby increasing their environmental impact relative to the same food grown less intensively elsewhere and then transported. In the case of urban farming, shifting production locally only reduces greenhouse gas impacts by a percent or two.[38]

However, transportation has environmental impacts beyond just the greenhouse gas emissions it causes. Importantly, pollutants are created by the combustion of fossil fuels, and these pollutants increase environmental harms, including but not limited to the acidification of waterways. These impacts would be greater for foods traveling long distances. As mentioned in Chapter 5, since much transportation in the U.S. is fueled by diesel (which is less refined than gasoline) it produces higher particulate matter pollution.

Authors like Michael Pollan see local food as a solution to many environmental and social problems, and see diets restricted to plant products as being at odds with this. Since local production of food requires getting nutrients locally for all 12 months of the year, it is difficult (especially in colder climates) to imagine local food without nonhuman animals. After all, since an animal-free agricultural system would often require importing synthetic nutrients, a fully local food system would seem to require use of animals for their manure, if not also for their flesh, milk, or eggs. This is part of why Sir Albert Howard, among others, claims that "[m]other nature never attempts to farm without livestock."[39]

A radical version of local food would likely require a shift from the current settlement patterns, since most of the humans in the world live in urban areas with insufficient land to grow enough food, and agriculture is broadly distributed across the globe. Even a highly efficient combination of vertical farms, rooftop farms, and cultured meat factories might not be able to provide a large percentage of the calories and nutrients needed for people situated in or near cities. Urban farms can also produce certain foods (such as lettuces and herbs) better than others (such as bushels of wheat).

Eating locally can result in increased environmental impacts, especially if people eat more animal products rather than seasonal plants. In colder climates, plants can be difficult to grow in the winter months, whereas farmed animals can be used to produce milk, eggs, and meat year-round. This might result in a net increase in methane emissions from the cows and carbon dioxide from land clearing for grazing.

Small-scale, localized production allows for a sense of connectedness with history as well as with seasonality. Some people, such as Wendell Berry, worry that this sense of connectedness will be lost with large-scale, globalized production. One can defend such forms of agriculture from a few perspectives. First, since agricultural practices vary significantly with culture, climate, and topography, local agriculture offers a wealth of specialized, context-specific knowledge about agricultural practices. Second, some people claim to value culture and history more strongly than the environment. We examined whether these priorities are justified in earlier chapters, and we will return to this theme in later chapters as well.

7.4.3 Humans

The impact of local food on humans involves multiple considerations. In some forms, local food gives farmers and communities increased agency and control over their food supply and economy. Even by optimistic assessments, however, food grown in urban areas—where most of the people in the world live—could only provide a very small percentage of food overall.[40]

One concern about local food is that excess commitment to localism tends to coincide with regressive social practices, and some people see local food as an instance of, or a gesture in the direction of, such a trend. Negative impacts of this trend include limited social and economic mobility, restricted professional options due to high labor needs (e.g., disallowing family members from leaving a farm to pursue higher education), and fear of those who are outside of the local area (possibly resulting in nativism or nationalism).[41] In one sense, local food is a movement celebrating local practices and traditions and countering global consolidation of agricultural commodities. In another sense, it can be a form of escapism or isolationism. Whether it is one or the other (or something else) depends upon context and the practices in which community members engage.

If one aspires to minimize support for multinational corporations, then supporting local economies and businesses seems like a laudable goal. However, as Peter Singer and Jim Mason note, the choice is not just between nearby small farmers and distant multinational corporations, but also between nearby small farmers and distant small farmers.[42] In many cases, distant small farmers would benefit much more from our consumer support than nearby ones would (this is especially true for consumers who live in nations with developed industrial economies). Moreover, in many cases the social benefit of supporting distant small farmers could outweigh the environmental cost of increasing the distance from farm to fork. In these cases, if a locavore is acting out of some concern for members of their own community, then they might continue to eat locally; if they are acting out of impartial concern for everyone or for the least well off farmers in the world, then they might sometimes eat globally instead.

Local food systems can be used as educational tools to engage and educate people about agricultural systems, culture, economics, ecology, and history. These programs are often experiential and systems-oriented, which are effective modes of educational practice for environmental and animal topics.

However, the overall efficacy of such educational practices requires an analysis of all dimensions of an educational program, including what content is covered and whether harmful implicit messages are present.[43]

7.5 Organic

Organic agriculture is a set of practices developed in response to industrialized agriculture that attempts to keep and create nutrients close to the area being farmed, rather than importing or synthesizing them. This takes a number of forms. One might define organic food production as food production that omits certain synthetic chemicals. However, people tend to instead define it as a more comprehensive process of building soil nutrients and beneficial characteristics with minimal industrial inputs.[44] About 1% of agriculture is organic,[45] but it is a rapidly growing sector in some countries, including the U.S. It is regulated by a range of agencies.[46]

7.5.1 Animals

Organic farming prioritizes the deterrence of insects who eat crops, and so is less likely to use pesticides. As a result, a greater variety of wild animals are often prevalent in organic agriculture: "organic farming often has positive effects on species richness and abundance, but . . . its effects are likely to differ between organism groups and landscapes."[47] **Polycultures** (the cultivation of multiple crops in close proximity) reduce crop loss to insects by including plants that deter insects and by varying plants so that insects only eat some of the crops. It is more common in organic agriculture—as is **integrated pest management** (IPM). IPM reduces unwelcome insects, weeds, and other organisms by making the environment unfavorable to them. Examples of IPM include introducing natural predators for the insect, or mulching to reduce weeds. Since prevention is the aim, pesticides are used as a last resort.

Weeds, insects, and other "pests" in organic agriculture are not sprayed with most synthetic pesticides. Organic farms can use a list of approved pesticides with natural ingredients, or, in some cases where no natural substitute is available, with synthetic ingredients. Weeds are often manually pulled, or the soil is tilled in order to kill and bury weeds. To repel or kill insects, organic farmers can use *Bacillus thuringiensis* (Bt, which is also used in GE crops such as Bt corn and Bt cotton), copper sulfate, pyrethrin (extracted from chrysanthemum), rotenone (extracted from various plants like jicama), and other insecticides. These insecticides have varying degrees of toxicity to humans, rodents, and fishes, and so they can be harmful to farm workers, farmed animals, and local wild animals (in addition to the targeted insects) if used excessively. The benefits to biodiversity of organic agriculture are modest, variable, and often unclear.[48]

Farmed animals in USDA organic farms are fed organic feed and are not given antibiotics as growth enhancers. Regulations state that they must have some access to the outdoors (e.g., a pasture for cows, or a yard for chickens).

However, regulatory requirements are often skirted or interpreted so narrowly that they are rendered ineffective. The requirement of access to the outdoors, for instance, is often implemented as a small door in the corner of a huge CAFO leading to a small patch of dirt, which few chickens can even access. At best, this minimally improves the welfare of chickens living in these conditions.

In optimal organic agricultural settings, the principle is that animals given better environments and feed are less likely to require medical intervention.[49] There is no independent standard for humane handling of animals in USDA organic standards, and farmed fishes are currently not certified by the USDA.[50]

Even with the improvements of organic feed and fewer antibiotics, some concerns remain. Once again, this practice treats nonhuman animals as commodities, causes them to experience pain and suffering, and causes them to die at an early age.

Finally, since the certification focuses on production, this means that organic plants, meat, and dairy can have synthetic pesticides on them (by drift or illegal spraying), that animals can be slaughtered under the same circumstances as more industrially produced animals, and that milk can have dioxins in it.

7.5.2 Environment

The environmental impact of agricultural production models is a result of land use and land-use change and the types of pesticides and fertilizers used, among other factors. Some organic practices, such as tilling, have environmental impacts, and those impacts could be reduced by herbicide use. If it involves clearing land for grazing and organic feed, many environmental impacts of organic food are still substantial—as production and conversion are the biggest drivers of this. This includes releasing carbon into the atmosphere, killing or destroying habitat for wild animals, and changes in water flow.

The amount of land used for organic agriculture compared to non-organic agriculture is variable. Organic crops can use similar or more land than conventional agriculture—anywhere from the same amount to 40% more.[51] Land use and animal products constitute the bulk (up to 75%) of environmental impacts of food, organic or not.[52] If organic food consistently uses more land, then conversion to organic agriculture might not yield a net environmental improvement over conventional agriculture, despite the decreased use of synthetic pesticides and fertilizers. (See our discussion of intensive, extensive, and sustainably intensive agriculture in Chapter 5.) Such an assessment assumes that we grow the same crops as we currently do. However, if we shift production to more first order food (defined in Chapter 5 as food that humans eat directly, rather than food that is fed to nonhuman animals), and decrease the substantial amount of food waste, we can imagine a scenario that is both organic and includes a net decrease in land use. On average, however, organic systems use more land—which offsets the advantages of less energy use.[53]

Organic agriculture also prohibits the use of genetically engineered organisms. The reason for this is a preference for using traditional breeds and techniques, and the association of genetically engineered crops with companies that hinder farmer autonomy. Some argue for a convergence of genetically engineered crops and organic techniques, by highlighting cases where genetically engineered crops can reduce pesticide use and help subsistence farmers.[54]

Polycultures can result in increased biodiversity, natural insect resistance (in the case of companion planting), and slower soil depletion, since different plants need different nutrients. While they do have these advantages, polycultures also require more labor to plant and harvest. In contrast, monocultures are plantings of a single crop over a large area, as is common in industrial farming of commodity crops. Depending on the definition of organic that is used, one can grow organic crops in large monocultures (but without synthetic inputs). This has the advantage of less labor for planting and harvesting, but the disadvantage of less insect resistance, increased pesticide use, and increased soil depletion. Historically, organic agriculture has included a set of land-care practices. The legal definition of organic agriculture is more flexible, however, allowing monocultures that are certified USDA organic to be organic as well. Some criticize monoculture organic crops as "Big Organic," in violation of the spirit of organic farming, which emphasizes a commitment to polyculture and smaller scale agricultural operations.[55]

Nutrient inputs in organic agriculture are sourced on-site as much as possible. Nitrogen in organic agriculture is sourced through compost, composted manure, bone meal, blood meal, feather meal, peat, fishmeal,[56] crop residue, seaweed, biosolids (in some countries), and "green manure" (nitrogen-rich leguminous plants plowed back into the soil). Many sources of nitrogen are from nonhuman animals, either directly (such as from manure) or indirectly (such as from byproducts like feather meal and bone meal).

As with many agricultural assessments, the use of manures has costs and benefits. When the manure used is from an industrial operation, it can accumulate antibiotics in the soil.[57] Manures, since they are concentrated forms of bioavailable nitrogen, still contribute to greenhouse gases,[58] air pollution,[59] and water pollution, according to environmental scientists Xiaobo Xue and Amy E. Landis:

> Results show that using manure fertilizers as opposed to synthetic fertilizers requires less energy, however the use of manure generates significantly more CH_4, N_2O, CO_2, and results in more variable concentrations of nitrogen and phosphorus leaching from farmlands.[60]

Similarly, compost emits greenhouse gases.[61] Phosphorus in organic agriculture is sourced by rock dust, rock phosphate, and bone meal. In grassland agriculture, where ruminant animals graze, phosphorus is often depleted, so the grasslands require (or will require) phosphorus fertilizer.[62] Potassium in organic agriculture is sourced by ashes, manure, and seaweed, which have modest additional environmental impacts—as they are often byproducts rather than the primary end of a production process.

Planting and harvesting crops and raising and slaughtering animals require that energy leave the system, however. Even the "closed loop"[63] systems that Pollan describes as close to a "free lunch"[64] require introducing and then removing animals from the land, as well as fertilizer for grasslands (at least in the long term), and sometimes imported grain for chickens. Land must be cleared, and the cows emit methane. As a result, organic farms have mixed environmental impacts relative to conventional farms, says agricultural scientist Hanna Tuomisto:[65]

> [O]rganic farming practices generally have positive impacts on the environment per unit of area, but not necessarily per product unit. Organic farms tend to have higher soil organic matter content and lower nutrient losses (nitrogen leaching, nitrous oxide emissions and ammonia emissions) per unit of field area. However, ammonia emissions, nitrogen leaching and nitrous oxide emissions per product unit were higher from organic systems. Organic systems had lower energy requirements, but higher land use, eutrophication potential and acidification potential per product unit.[66]

Practices vary, and impacts are relative to particular sites. Given the ecological complexity of agriculture it is difficult to draw a simple conclusion from the literature. Since by eating food we are removing energy from one system, there is no complete "closed loop" option. And since organic production often requires more land,[67] any lower environmental impacts on the organic land need to be weighed against the increase in land use and land-use change.

7.5.3 Humans

Organic pesticides can be harmful, but since organic agriculture is designed to minimize pesticide use, it often uses significantly fewer pesticides than alternatives. Organic agriculture often requires more labor due to a decrease in the use of chemicals for weeding and the mechanization of planting and harvesting. This has consequences for farm workers.[68] If the conditions are suboptimal, it increases the number of suboptimal jobs. Since pesticide and environmental exposure is present in organic agriculture, such harms continue to exist in this agricultural context. If the conditions are desirable, then increased labor and jobs would be welcome. This is the case in smaller scale, low-input agricultural practices with favorable labor practices. There are no separate labor laws governing farm workers in organic settings.

Even if organic agriculture ends up using more land (as it often does), there are benefits to sourcing nutrients and pesticides more locally. (Local and small-scale organic agriculture often overlap, as both aim to minimize transportation and keep nutrients local.) In the case of market disruptions, supply problems, and shortages, organic farmers can still move forward with food production—as they are less reliant on imported resources. For the farmer and their local area, this can result in increased food security, meaning that food is readily available. Whether or not organic produce is more nutritional is contested and unclear.[69]

The use of substantially fewer antibiotics means that organically farmed animals contribute less (if at all) to the problem of antibiotic-resistant bacteria produced in conventional animal agriculture (discussed in Chapter 6).

If organic agriculture is to contribute to solving the problem of hunger, it must produce enough food to feed people, without clearing more land. The **yield** of organic agriculture impacts food security, environmental impact, and land use. It is very context-dependent,[70] so generalizations should be qualified by including what, where, and how a product was grown. Sometimes, crop loss is higher due to loss to insects (as pesticides are used more sparingly), and sometimes less food is grown in the organic soils that have less nitrogen available. On the other hand, organic agriculture is more likely to yield a stable amount of food over a long period of time, avoiding the level of soil depletion that is common in conventional and some pre-industrial farming practices.[71]

While some studies argue that organic agriculture has similar or higher yields than conventional agriculture,[72] most indicate that it is lower by either a modest amount or a significant amount.[73] Some argue that it can mitigate climate change due to improved soil management practices,[74] or that its biodiversity and food security dimensions should offset its lower yield.

While there are certain environment benefits to non-synthetic nitrogen, our current practices rely heavily on synthetic fertilizers, and the ability of an organic system to produce sufficient food is contested. For context, "[w]ithout [synthetic nitrogen fertilizer], about ⅖ of the world's population would not be around."[75] Any set of proposals for mitigating world hunger that includes organic agriculture must account for how such a significant amount of food would be produced (especially since we would like to do so without increased land use). Further, Vaclav Smil shows that the ability of organic agriculture to support nations without developed industrial economies is also in question:

> Rich countries could fertilize much less by cutting their excessive food production in general, and by reducing their high intakes of animal foods in particular—but even the most assiduous recycling of all organic wastes and the widest practical planting of legumes could not supply enough nitrogen for land-scarce, poor, and populous nations.[76]

As is the case with shifting dietary practices, proposals for agricultural improvements might differ greatly between industrialized and non-industrialized settings. And in a world with land constraints and severe food shortages, any drop in yield needs to be closely analyzed. In fact, Smil notes that it is unclear that we can grow enough food with local resources:

> Traditional farming relied on a combination of increasingly intensive recycling of organic wastes and cultivation of leguminous plants, but these inputs were insufficient to sustain high crop yields over large cultivated areas.[77]

As with many agricultural assessments and proposals, the scale of the proposed solution makes a significant difference. If we propose an organic and local operation but do not clear more land, we will produce significantly less food and require significantly more labor.

7.6 Agriculture without animals

The final alternative that we discuss in this chapter is actually a collection of alternatives, including plant-based agriculture (growing plants for first order food) and highly engineered animal product substitutes (such as plant-based or cellular meat, dairy, and eggs).

While we are referring to this set of alternatives as generally operating "without animals," we will note that they do involve at least some interaction with nonhuman animals. For example, plant-based agriculture and substitutes still impact the lives and habitats of liminal and wild animals. Moreover, as we will see, cellular agriculture still involves animal use at this point in its development, although this use is extremely minor (relative to conventional animal agriculture) and likely temporary. Despite these qualifications, these alternatives aspire to reduce the use of nonhuman animals in food production as much as possible, and so we frame them as "agriculture without animals" for the purposes of our present discussion.

We should also note that these alternatives can involve at least some industrial techniques. Plant-based agriculture can be more or less industrial depending on the particular methods used. For example, a global, non-organic plant-based food system will be more industrial than a series of local, organic, plant-based farms. Moreover, highly engineered plant-based and cellular animal product substitutes are necessarily industrial. However, we are including them here anyway because of their potential to displace conventional industrial animal agriculture.

Finally, since the impacts of plant-based and cellular animal product substitutes are both more complex and less well understood than the impacts of plant-based agriculture, we will start with a brief discussion of the latter alternative here, and we will then turn to a more detailed discussion of the former alternatives for the remainder of this section.

Plant-based agriculture, also known as veganic and stock-free agriculture, involves growing plants for food as well as eliminating animal products in the agricultural process. Nutritional "amendments" such as blood, feathers, and bones (all converted to a meal to add specific nutrients) are prohibited—as is the use of nonhuman animals for labor. (It is worth noting that these features can come apart, however. For example, it is possible to imagine a farm that involves certain kinds of animal labor but that neither produces nor consumes animal products as part of the agricultural process. Depending on the details, this kind of farm might be acceptable on some animal ethics views, as we will see in Chapter 8.)

Assessing the impacts of plant-based agriculture is complex. Some impacts involve trade-offs. For example, if we were to transition to a plant-based food system, we would produce fewer animal products (which many humans desire) but we would also produce more plant products (which can provide people with a nutritionally complete diet in an efficient manner). Similarly, we would allow fewer farmed animals to live, but we would also require fewer farmed animals to suffer and die for food. We will discuss some of the ethical questions raised by these trade-offs (especially the question of whether creating animals to kill for food is better than not creating them at all) in Chapter 8.

However, other impacts of plant-based agriculture are straightforwardly positive. For example, a transition to a plant-based food system would reduce total land, water, energy, pesticide, and fertilizer consumption, since it would eliminate the need to use these resources for feed production (though, as we have seen, not all land that can be used for animal agriculture can also be used for plant agriculture). It would also substantially reduce greenhouse gas emissions, especially methane and nitrous oxide. In particular, some experts estimate that a plant-based agricultural system would result in a 28% decrease in agricultural greenhouse gas emissions and a 23% increase in food production, albeit with nutritional imbalances.[78] Others estimate that the benefits of a plant-based agricultural system are more substantial.[79]

Of course, different plant-based food systems will have different animal and environmental impacts. For example, relatively industrial plant-based food systems will have many of the costs (energy consumption) and benefits (scale and efficiency) of industrial food systems more generally (without the extra costs associated with animal use). In contrast, relatively non-industrial plant-based food systems will have many of the costs and benefits of non-industrial food systems more generally (again, without the extra costs associated with animal use). Which kind of plant-based system is best will likely be a contextual matter, depending on region, type of food, and more. However, it is reasonable to expect that both kinds of plant-based system will have a role to play in replacing conventional industrial animal agriculture.

Now consider plant-based and cellular substitutes. **Plant-based substitutes** are made primarily from plant proteins processed to simulate the taste and texture of animal products. Examples include almond milk, cashew cheese, and veggie burgers. While some techniques are simple, others are complex. For example, in the case of the Impossible Burger, leghemoglobin—produced by a genetically engineered yeast—is used to provide the flavor of heme, a characteristic part of the flavor of animal muscle. Meanwhile, **cellular substitutes** are made through cell cultures, scaffolding, and growth media in a factory. Examples include not only meat but also milk created with an engineered yeast and leather made without growing skin on a nonhuman animal. This occurs in factories often compared to breweries (though the current scale is smaller). Meat in this category is referred to as "cultured meat," "clean meat," or "in-vitro meat."

7.6.1 Animals

Both plant-based and cellular meat substitutes offer significant animal welfare advantages, in that animals are not being raised for meat, eggs, or milk. No CAFO, slaughterhouse, or transportation welfare concerns arise. The net improvement in animal welfare from cellular agriculture is incredibly significant, although it does not avoid all harm to nonhuman animals (and plant-based agriculture does not either).

The raw products such as peas and coconuts used in highly engineered plant-based meat substitutes require the clearing of land and elimination of animals such as insects who are deemed a threat to the crop, meaning that there is still some harm to nonhuman animals related to these products.

Moreover, cellular agriculture currently uses fetal bovine serum as a growth medium. This entails extracting blood from living cow fetuses. The number of nonhuman animals used and the mistreatment of them would decrease by *almost* 100%, but animal use would still be part of the process. Alternative growth media exist, but are currently either cell-specific (limiting their application), human-based (limiting their marketability), or prohibitively expensive. Additionally, insofar as plant-based or cellular products are tested on nonhuman animals, this raises animal ethics questions as well.[80] In order to assess such a practice, we would have to weigh the animal welfare costs associated with sourcing and testing against the animal welfare benefits associated with a reduction in industrial animal agriculture.

7.6.2 Environment

The environmental impacts of highly engineered plant-based meat substitutes include the energy use of the factory and the growing of crops used for the product. The raw products constituting plant-based animal food alternatives, such as coconuts, peas, soy, wheat, and potato would have to be included in a life cycle assessment. These are highly processed foods, so they require more energy use than other plant-based foods. Since methane emissions are avoided, and land use is minimal relative to pastured animals, the environmental impact is very likely to be substantially lower than meat (pastured or grain-fed).

Assessing the environmental impact of cellular agriculture is more difficult, and few studies have assessed it. The environmental impacts of raising farmed animals are avoided, but are partially displaced by the energy used in the factory. Only a few assessments of cellular agriculture have been published, and they put the environmental impact at about 10% of animal agriculture.[81] Since so much of the environmental impact of food is land use, land-use change, methane, and conversion—all of which are avoided in these alternatives—we have good reason to believe that the footprint will be quite modest relative to conventionally produced animal products.

7.6.3 Humans

In the case of both plant-based and cellular substitutes, slaughterhouse workers and their attendant welfare concerns would be largely avoided. Field and slaughterhouse labor would be mostly replaced with factory workers. The psychological harm of slaughtering would be avoided, yet the tedium of repetitive movements in a specialized factory setting would remain.

The public health consequences of industrialized animal agriculture discussed in Chapter 6, including zoonotic diseases, antibiotic-resistant bacteria, water and air contamination, and climate impact would all be minimized or eliminated.

These products might or might not be healthful. Since they are designed to displace animal products, they might contain comparable amounts of saturated fats. For instance, 85 grams of the Impossible Burger (less than the weight of one burger) contains 55% of the USDA's daily saturated fat recommendation in the form of coconut oil.[82] Similarly, cellular agriculture products are actually meat, so they have the same nutritional profile as meat from a slaughtered animal, although some attributes such as fat content can be controlled for, and other concerns such as bacterial contamination are easier to control in factory settings.

Overall, highly engineered plant-based and cellular animal product substitutes hold significant potential to displace the nonhuman, environmental, and human harms inherent in the industrial animal agriculture sector. Some ethical considerations remain, however. Some animal ethicists would object to these products not only because they harm some nonhuman animals directly, but also because they could harm many nonhuman animals indirectly by normalizing the idea of eating meat. (Of course, they do not do so more than actual animal farming does.)

Moreover, as with any technical solution, the feasibility of plant-based and cellular substitutes requires the possibility of scaling up while keeping prices competitive. The Impossible Burger, for instance, is currently being sold at a loss in order to introduce it to the market. Cellular agriculture is not yet ready for the market, but its cost has come down exponentially in the last few years, from hundreds of thousands to hundreds of dollars per burger, for instance.

Finally, some might worry that if we pursue technical solutions such as plant-based and cellular substitutes, then we will be forgoing analysis of other, simpler solutions, including thousands of other plant-based options that we have not yet fully explored. The idea that we need novel products to solve some of our social problems is controversial. Some would argue that an emphasis on our values and social systems leads to more stable and ethically acceptable social change.

With that said, one concern with consumer-driven solutions to large-scale problems is that it is individual, distracting, and uncoordinated. It is individual in that the burden of an ethical dilemma falls on the end consumer, rather than on the policy-makers or companies regulating and creating the product. It is distracting in that we focus our efforts on researching and navigating complex decisions at the individual level, which distracts us from the institutional and systemic contributors to the problem. It is uncoordinated in that millions of separate people would have to change their behavior in the same form in order to effectively solve the problem. One alternative—which is not exclusive of concern for individual action—is an emphasis on regulation and policy. We discuss these points further in Chapters 9 and 10.

In contrast, plant-based and cellular substitutes do not require significant changes from consumers, and, as a result, they avoid some of the problems that other alternative food products encounter. Even if they are not a full solution, then, they might be an important part of a portfolio of solutions.

7.7 Conclusion

We are now in a position to see why ethical discussions about food, animals, and the environment are so challenging. Industrial animal agriculture causes vast amounts of unnecessary harm for humans, nonhumans, and the environment. Meanwhile, many alternatives cause much less harm overall, but they carry risks and costs as well.

The next four chapters will consider ethical questions that these impacts raise for food production, consumption, activism, and advocacy. If an industry causes unnecessary harm, do we have a moral obligation not to support that industry as producers and consumers? Do we have a moral obligation to resist that industry as activists? How might the answers to these questions be different for different people? Either way, what kinds of food systems should we aim for, and what kinds of paths should we take in order to bring these food systems about?

Notes

1 This includes the search for fertilizer resulting in the Guano Islands Act of 1856. For more information see:
   "The Guano Islands Act of 1856," The National Museum of American History, Smithsonian, http://americanhistory.si.edu/norie-atlas/guano-islands-act.
2 Vaclav Smil estimates that non-industrial fertilizers nourish about half of humanity.
   Vaclav Smil, "Nitrogen and Food Production: Proteins for Human Diets," *AMBIO: A Journal of the Human Environment* 31, no. 2 (March 2002).
3 As a rough and high-end estimate, smallholders in developing countries, defined as those with less than 2 ha of farmland, produce approximately 5% (2.5 $GtCO_2e$) of total global greenhouse gas emissions. This is 31% of the total emissions arising from agriculture and land use change (LUC) including deforestation globally and 47% of those emitted from agriculture in developing countries specifically.

   Sonja Vermeulen and Eva Wollenberg, "A Rough Estimate of the Proportion of Global Emissions from Agriculture Due to Smallholders," Research Program on Climate Change, Agriculture, and Food Security, April 2017, https://cgspace.cgiar.org/bitstream/handle/10568/80745/CCAFS_INsmallholder_emissions.pdf?sequence=1&isAllowed=y.
4 William F. Ruddiman, *Plows, Plagues, and Petroleum: How Humans Took Control of Climate* (Princeton: Princeton University Press, 2010).
5 James E. McWilliams, *Just Food: Where Locavores Get It Wrong and How We Can Truly Eat Responsibly* (New York: Hachette Book Group, 2010): 66.
6 Agricultural practices where plants are grown in nutrient-enriched water (hydro-) or misted air (aero-) media.
7 Masanobu Fukuoka, *The One-Straw Revolution* (New York: New York Review Books, 2010).
8 Afton Halloran et al., "Life Cycle Assessment of Edible Insects for Food Protein: A Review," *Agronomy for Sustainable Development* 36, no. 57 (December 2016).
9 G. Owen Schaefer and Julian Savulescu, "The Ethics of Producing *In Vitro* Meat," *Journal of Applied Philosophy* 31, no. 2 (February 2014): 188–202.
10 Jonathan Safran Foer, *Eating Animals* (New York: Hachette Book Group, 2010): 237.
11 Lifespans in different settings are discussed in more detail in Chapter 6.
12 For more detail, see:
   James McWilliams, "The Omnivore's Contradiction: That Free-range, Organic Meat Was Still an Animal Killed for Your Dinner," *Salon*, January 3, 2016, www.salon.com/2016/01/03/the_omnivores_contradiction_that_free_range_organic_meat_was_still_an_animal_killed_for_your_dinner/.
13 Richard Mervyn Hare, "Why I'm a Demivegetarian," in *Essays on Bioethics* (Oxford: Clarendon Press, 1996).

14 This can be seen in Pollan's argument that eating animals is "wrong in practice, not in principle," in his defense of eating industrially raised animals if "table fellowship" is involved, and in the marketing practice of representing animal products as coming from "happy farms."

15 Judith L. Capper, "Is the Grass Always Greener? Comparing the Environmental Impact of Conventional, Natural and Grass-Fed Beef Production Systems," *Animals* 2, no. 2 (2012): 127–143.

Henning Steinfeld and Pierre Gerber, "Livestock Production and the Global Environment: Consume Less or Produce Better?" *Proceedings of the National Academy of Sciences* 107, no. 43 (October 2010): 18237–18238.

Gidon Eshel, "Grass-fed Beef Packs a Punch to Environment," *Reuters*, April 8, 2010, http://blogs.reuters.com/environment/2010/04/08/grass-fed-beef-packs-a-punch-to-environment/.

16 "These measurements clearly document higher CH_4 production (about four times) for cattle receiving low-quality, high-fiber diets than for cattle fed high-grain diets."

L.A. Harper, O.T. Denmead, J.R. Freney, and F.M. Byers, "Direct Measurements of Methane Emissions from Grazing and Feedlot Cattle," *Journal of Animal Science* 77, no. 6 (June 1999): 1392–1401.

17 Michael Clark and David Tilman, "Comparative Analysis of Environmental Impacts of Agricultural Production Systems, Agricultural Input Efficiency, and Food Choice," *Environmental Research Letters* 12, no. 6 (June 2017).

18 Tara Garnett et al., "Grazed and Confused?" Food Climate Research Network, Oxford Martin Programme on the Future of Food, www.fcrn.org.uk/sites/default/files/project-files/fcrn_gnc_report.pdf.

19 J.D. Derner and G.E. Schuman, "Carbon Sequestration and Rangelands: A Synthesis of Land Management and Precipitation Effects," *Journal of Soil and Water Conservation* 62, no. 2 (April 2007): 77–85.

20 Richard T. Conant, "Challenges and Opportunities for Carbon Sequestration in Grassland Systems," *Integrated Crop Management* 9, Food and Agriculture Organization of the United Nations (2010), www.fao.org/fileadmin/templates/agphome/documents/climate/AGPC_grassland_webversion_19.pdf.

Allan Savory and Nicolette Hahn Niman are two proponents of this view.

Allan Savory, "How to fight desertification ad reverse climate change," www.ted.com/talks/allan_savory_how_to_green_the_world_s_deserts_and_reverse_climate_change.

Nicolette Hahn Niman, *Defending Beef: The Case for Sustainable Meat Production* (Chelsea Green Publishing, 2014).

21 Tara Garnett et al., "Grazed and Confused?" Food Climate Research Network, Oxford Martin Programme on the Future of Food, www.fcrn.org.uk/sites/default/files/project-files/fcrn_gnc_report.pdf.

22 Jamus Joseph et al., "Short Duration Grazing Research in Africa," *Rangelands* 24, no. 4 (August 2002): 9–12.

23 D.D. Briske et al., "Rotational Grazing on Rangelands: Reconciliation of Perception and Experimental Evidence," *Rangeland Ecology & Management* 61, no. 1 (January 2008): 3–17.

24 D.D. Briske et al., "Origin, Persistence, and Resolution of the Rotational Grazing Debate: Integrating Human Dimensions into Rangeland Research," *Rangeland Ecology & Management* 64, no. 4 (July 2011): 325–334.

25 D.D. Briske et al., "Origin, Persistence, and Resolution of the Rotational Grazing Debate: Integrating Human Dimensions into Rangeland Research," *Rangeland Ecology & Management* 64, no. 4 (July 2011): 325–334.

26 Richard Teague, "Deficiencies in the Briske Estimates of Carbon Sequestration on Rangelands" (comment), Real Climate, November 17, 2013, www.realclimate.org/

index.php/archives/2013/11/cows-carbon-and-the-anthropocene-commentary-on-savory-ted-video/comment-page-3/#comment-426736.

27 "Grazing," Center for Biological Diversity, www.biologicaldiversity.org/programs/public_lands/grazing/.
The above also notes that:

> In the arid West, livestock grazing is the most widespread cause of species endangerment. By destroying vegetation, damaging wildlife habitats and disrupting natural processes, livestock grazing wreaks ecological havoc on riparian areas, rivers, deserts, grasslands and forests alike—causing significant harm to species and the ecosystems on which they depend.

28 It is unclear how much land fits into this category.

29 Some proponents of this view include Michael Pollan and the Beef Board.
"Fact Sheet: The Environment and Cattle Production," The Beef Checkoff, last updated October 2007, www.beefboard.org/news/files/factsheets/The-Environment-And-Cattle-Producation.pdf.

30 S.Z. Sattari et al., "Negative Global Phosphorus Budgets Challenge Sustainable Intensification of Grasslands," *Nature Communications* 7, no. 10696 (February 2016).

31 Georgina Gustin, "Demand for Grass-fed Beef is Growing," *The Los Angeles Times*, November 23, 2012, http://articles.latimes.com/2012/nov/23/business/la-fi-grassfed-beef-20121123.

32 Tara Garnett et al., "Grazed and Confused?" Food Climate Research Network, Oxford Martin Programme on the Future of Food, www.fcrn.org.uk/sites/default/files/project-files/fcrn_gnc_report.pdf.

33 Estimated at "1g out of . . . 80g from all sources."
Tara Garnett et al., "Grazed and Confused?" Food Climate Research Network, Oxford Martin Programme on the Future of Food, www.fcrn.org.uk/sites/default/files/project-files/fcrn_gnc_report.pdf.

34 T.F. Randolph et al., "Role of Livestock in Human Nutrition and Health for Poverty Reduction in Developing Countries," *Journal of Animal Science* 85 (2007): 2788–2800.
Thank you to Professor Andrew Bell for conversations and references on this topic.

35 Robert Anglen, "'Buy Local' Food Programs Deceive Consumers and Are Rarely Enforced, a USA TODAY Network Investigation Finds," *AZ Central*, March 13, 2018, www.azcentral.com/story/news/local/arizona-investigations/2018/03/13/buy-local-made-food-labels-programs-deceive-consumers-rarely-enforced-usa-today-network-finds/389155002/.

36 Christopher L. Weber and H. Scott Matthews, "Food-Miles and the Relative Climate Impacts of Food Choices in the United States," *Environmental Science & Technology* 42, no. 10 (April 2008): 3508–3513.

37 Pierre Desrochers and Hiroko Shimizu, *The Locavore's Dilemma: In Praise of the 10,000-mile Diet* (New York: Hachette, 2013).
James E. McWilliams, *Just Food: Where Locavores Get It Wrong and How We Can Truly Eat Responsibly* (New York: Hachette Book Group, 2010): 66.

38 Benjamin P. Goldstein, Michael Z. Hauschild, John E. Fernández, and Morten Birkved, "Contributions of Local Farming to Urban Sustainability in the Northeast United States," *Environmental Science & Technology* 51, no. 13 (June 2017): 7340–7349.
The above study also notes that "the analysis showed that consumers in the northeast who are really determined to lower their food-related carbon footprint should minimize purchases of meat and dairy products."

39 Sir Albert Howard quoted in Michael Pollan, *The Omnivore's Dilemma* (New York: Penguin, 2006): 314.

40 Nicholas Clinton et al., "A Global Geospatial Ecosystem Services Estimate of Urban Agriculture," *Earth's Future* 6, no. 1 (January 2018): 40–60.

41 Vasile Stănescu, "'Green' Eggs and Ham? The Myth of Sustainable Meat and the Danger of the Local," United Poultry Concerns, December 10, 2010, www.upc-online. org/thinking/green_eggs.html.
42 Peter Singer and Jim Mason, *The Ethics of What We Eat: Why Our Food Choices Matter* (New York: Rodale Books, 2007).
43 Lori Marino et al., "Do Zoos and Aquariums Promote Attitude Change in Visitors? A Critical Evaluation of the American Zoo and Aquarium Study," *Society and Animals* 18, no. 2 (2010): 126–138.
44 For details on the many tensions that arise in the development and scaling of organic production, focusing on California, see:
  Julie Guthman, *Agrarian Dreams: The Paradox of Organic Farming in California* (Berkeley: University of California Press, 2014).
45 Helga Willer, Julia Lernoud, and Robert Home, "The World of Organic Agriculture 2013: Summary," Research Institute of Organic Agriculture and the International Federation of Organic Agriculture Movements, 2013, www.organic-world.net/ fileadmin/documents/yearbook/2013/web-fibl-ifoam-2013-25-34.pdf.
46 The federal certification program in the U.S. is administered by the USDA, and there are smaller-scale programs like Oregon Tilth. The International Federation of Organic Agriculture Movements certifies organic in the E.U. and over a hundred countries in total.
47 Janne Bengtsson, Johan Ahnström, and Ann-Christin Weibull, "The Effects of Organic Agriculture on Biodiversity and Abundance: A Meta-analysis," *Journal of Applied Ecology* 42, no. 2 (April 2005): 261–269.
48 Species richness is, on average, 10.5% higher in organic than nonorganic production fields, with highest gains in intensive arable fields (around þ 45%). Gains to species richness are partly caused by higher organism abundance and are common in plants and bees but intermittent in earthworms and spiders. Average gains are marginal þ 4.6% at the farm and þ 3.1% at the regional level, even in intensive arable regions.

  Manuel K. Schneider et al., "Gains to Species Diversity in Organically Farmed Fields Are Not Propagated at the Farm Level," *Nature Communications* 5, no. 4151 (June 2014).
49 A. Kijlstra and A.J.M. Eijck, "Animal Health in Organic Livestock Production Systems: A Review," *NJAS – Wageningen Journal of Life Sciences* 54, no. 1 (March 2006): 77–94.
50 "Organic Aquaculture," United States Department of Agriculture, www.nal.usda.gov/ afsic/organic-aquaculture.
51 Hanna Treu et al., "Carbon Footprints and Land Use of Conventional and Organic Diets in Germany," *Journal of Cleaner Production* 161, no. 10 (September 2017): 127–142.
52 "Animal-based food products dominate the carbon footprints and land use (ca. 70–75%) in both diets."
  Hanna Treu et al., "Carbon Footprints and Land Use of Conventional and Organic Diets in Germany," *Journal of Cleaner Production* 161, no. 10 (September 2017): 127–142.
53 [W]hile production of conventional fertilizer is energy—and GHG-intensive, mismatches between nutrient availability and demand in organic systems dependent on manure increase the portion of reactive nitrogen in organic systems that turns into nitrous oxide, a potent greenhouse gas (Myhre et al. 2013), causing organic and conventional systems to have similar GHG emissions.

Michael Clark and David Tilman, "Comparative Analysis of Environmental Impacts of Agricultural Production Systems, Agricultural Input Efficiency, and Food Choice," *Environmental Research Letters* 12, no. 6 (June 2017).

54 Pamela C. Ronald and Raoul W. Adamchik, *Tomorrow's Table: Organic Farming, Genetics, and the Future of Food*, 2nd edition (New York: Oxford University Press, 2018).
   http://embor.embopress.org/content/2/4/256

55 For example, Michael Pollan dedicates a chapter in *The Omnivore's Dilemma* to this argument.

56 Jacqueline Alder et al., "Forage Fish: From Ecosystems to Markets," *Annual Review of Environment and Resources* 33 (November 2008): 153–166.

57 Dong Hee Kang et al., "Antibiotic Uptake by Vegetable Crops from Manure-Applied Soils," *Journal of Agricultural and Food Chemistry* 61, no. 42 (September 2013): 9992–10001.

58 Xiying Hao and Francis J. Larney, "Greenhouse Gas Emissions during Cattle Feedlot Manure Composting," *Frontiers of Environmental Science & Engineering* 11, no. 15 (June 2017).
   Takashi Osada, Kazutaka Kuroda, and Michihiro Yonaga, "Determination of Nitrous Oxide, Methane, and Ammonia Emissions from Swine Waste Composting Process," *Journal of Material Cycles and Waste Management* 2, no. 1 (April 2000): 51–56.
   S.G. Sommer and H.B. Møller, "Emission of Greenhouse Gases during Composting of Deep Litter from Pig Production: Effect of Straw Content," *The Journal of Agricultural Science* 134, no. 3 (May 2000): 327–335.

59 Xiying Hao, Chi Chang, and Francis J. Larney, "Carbon, Nitrogen Balances and Greenhouse Gas Emission during Cattle Feedlot Manure Composting," *Journal of Environmental Quality* 33 (2004): 37–44.

60 Xiaobo Xue and Amy E. Landis, "Effect of Agricultural Practices on Biofuels' Environmental Footprints," *Sustainable Systems and Technology, IEEE International Symposium on Sustainable Systems and Technology* (2009).

61 H.J. Hellebrand, "Emission of Nitrous Oxide and Other Trace Gases during Composting of Grass and Green Waste," *Journal of Agricultural Engineering Research* 69, no. 4 (April 1998): 365–375.
   Udo Jäckel, Kathrin Thummes, and Peter Kämpfer, "Thermophilic Methane Production and Oxidation in Compost," *FEMS Microbiology Ecology* 52, no. 2 (April 2005): 175–184.
   B. Hellmann, L. Zelles, A. Palojarvi, and Q. Bai, "Emission of Climate-relevant Trace Gases and Succession of Microbial Communities during Open-windrow Composting," *Applied and Environmental Microbiology* 63, no. 3 (March 1997): 1011–1018.

62 S.Z. Sattari et al., "Negative Global Phosphorus Budgets Challenge Sustainable Intensification of Grasslands," *Nature Communications* 7, no. 10696 (February 2016).

63 Where nutrients are mostly created and recycled on a farm, for example by using cow manure as fertilizer.

64 Michael Pollan, *The Omnivore's Dilemma* (New York: Penguin, 2006): 127.

65 H.L. Tuomisto, I.D. Hodge, P. Riordan, and D.W. Macdonald, "Does Organic Farming Reduce Environmental Impacts? A Meta-analysis of European Research," *Journal of Environmental Management* 112 (December 2012): 309–320.

66 H.L. Tuomisto, I.D. Hodge, P. Riordan, and D.W. Macdonald, "Does Organic Farming Reduce Environmental Impacts? A Meta-analysis of European Research," *Journal of Environmental Management* 112 (December 2012): 309–320.

67 H.L. Tuomisto, I.D. Hodge, P. Riordan, and D.W. Macdonald, "Does Organic Farming Reduce Environmental Impacts? A Meta-analysis of European Research," *Journal of Environmental Management* 112 (December 2012): 309–320.

68 Julie Guthman, *Agrarian Dreams: The Paradox of Organic Farming in California* (Berkeley: University of California Press, 2014).

69 Crystal Smith-Spangler et al., "Are Organic Foods Safer or Healthier Than Conventional Alternatives? A Systematic Review," *Annals of Internal Medicine* 157, no. 5 (September 2012): 348–366.

70 Verena Seufert and Navin Ramankutty, "Many Shades of Gray: The Context-dependent Performance of Organic Agriculture," *Science Advances* 3, no. 3 (March 2017).

71 For example, see:

Haitao Liu et al., "Biodiversity Management of Organic Farming Enhances Agricultural Sustainability," *Scientific Reports (Nature)* 6, no. 23816 (April 2016).

72 Catherine Brahic, "Organic Farming Could Feed the World," *New Scientist*, July 12, 2007, www.newscientist.com/article/dn12245-organic-farming-could-feed-the-world.html.

Tom Philpott, "5 Ways the Stanford Study Sells Organics Short," *Mother Jones*, September 5, 2012, www.motherjones.com/tom-philpott/2012/09/five-ways-stanford-study-underestimates-organic-food.

73 Verena Seufert, Navin Ramankutty, and Jonathan A. Foley, "Comparing the Yields of Organic and Conventional Agriculture," *Nature* 485 (May 2012): 229–232.

Mae-Wan Ho, "Organic Agriculture and Localized Food & Energy Systems for Mitigating Climate Change: How the World Can Be Food and Energy Secure Without Fossil Fuels" (lecture), East and Southeast Asian Conference-Workshop on Sustainable Agriculture, Food Security and Climate Change, October 2008, www.twn.my/title2/susagri/susagri058.htm.

74 Mae-Wan Ho and Lim Li Ching, "Mitigating Climate Change through Organic Agriculture and Localized Food Systems," Science in Society Archives, published May 12, 2007, www.i-sis.org.uk/mitigatingClimateChange.php.

75 Vaclav Smil, *Enriching the Earth: Fritz Haber, Carl Bosch, and the Transformation of World Food Production* (Cambridge: MIT Press, 2000): xv.

76 Vaclav Smil, *Enriching the Earth: Fritz Haber, Carl Bosch, and the Transformation of World Food Production* (Cambridge: MIT Press, 2000): xv.

77 Vaclav Smil, *Enriching the Earth: Fritz Haber, Carl Bosch, and the Transformation of World Food Production* (Cambridge: MIT Press, 2000): xiv.

78 Robin R. White and Mary Beth Hall, "Nutritional and Greenhouse Gas Impacts of Removing Animals from US Agriculture," *Proceedings of the National Academy of Sciences* 114, no. 48 (November 2017).

79 Isaac Emery, "Without Animals, U.S. Farmers Would Reduce Feed Crop Production," *Proceedings of the National Academy of Sciences* 115, no. 8 (February 2018).

Marco Springmann, Michael Clark, and Walter Willett, "Feedlot Diet for Americans that Results from a Misspecified Optimization Algorithm," *Proceedings of the National Academy of Sciences* 115, no. 8 (February 2018).

Konrad Van Meerbeek and Jens-Christian Svenning, "Causing Confusion in the Debate about the Transition toward a More Plant-based Diet," *Proceedings of the National Academy of Sciences* 115, no. 8 (February 2018).

80 Bruce Friedrich, "Animal Testing and New Proteins: Time for FDA to Move into 21st Century," The Good Food Institute, published August 29, 2017, www.gfi.org/animal-testing-new-proteins-time-for-fda.

81 Hanna L. Tuomisto and M. Joost Teixeira de Mattos, "Environmental Impacts of Cultured Meat Production," *Environmental Science & Technology* 45, no. 14 (June 2011): 6117–6123.

Hannah L. Tuomisto and Avi Roy, "Could Cultured Meat Reduce Environmental Impact of Agriculture in Europe?" 8th International Conference on Life Cycle Assessments in the Agri-Food Sector, October 2012.

Hanna L. Tuomisto, Marianne J. Ellis, and Palle Haastrup, "Environmental Impacts of Cultured Meat: Alternative Production Scenarios," *Proceedings of the 9th International Conference on Life Cycle Assessment in the Agri-Food Sector*, October 2014, http://lcafood2014.org/papers/132.pdf.

Carolyn S. Mattick, Amy E. Landis, Braden R. Allenby, and Nicholas J. Genovese, "Anticipatory Life Cycle Analysis of In Vitro Biomass Cultivation for Cultured Meat Production in the United States," *Environmental Science & Technology* 49, no. 19 (September 2015): 11941–11949.

"Replacing animal-based ground beef with an equal mass of the plant-based Impossible Foods (IF) ground beef would result in 86–91% less blue water used, 61–94% less green water used, 76–90% less greenhouse gas emissions, and 91–97% less land usage."

82 "Frequently Asked Questions," Impossible Foods, www.impossiblefoods.com/faq/.

8 The ethics of food production

8.1 Introduction

This chapter will examine the ethics of food production. If a particular industry causes unnecessary harm to humans, nonhumans, and the environment, is it morally wrong to work in that industry? And, how much, if at all, does the answer to this question depend on the degree to which we make a contribution to that industry or have other options? We will start by considering ethical questions that arise for people within industrial animal agriculture (corporate executives as well as factory farm and slaughterhouse workers). We will then consider ethical questions that arise for people who pursue alternatives. Here we will focus on local, organic, free-range animal agriculture, but we will consider hunting, plant-based agriculture, and plant-based and cultured meat production as well.

8.2 Industrial animal agriculture

We can start by considering ethical questions that arise for people within industrial animal agriculture, ranging from corporate executives to factory farm and slaughterhouse workers.

Consider first **corporate executives**. As we have seen, our food system has changed dramatically over the past century. It is no longer the case that some people make our food, other people distribute it, other people sell it, and so on. Instead, it is increasingly the case that a small number of multinational corporations control every step of this process. Thus, executives of these corporations (as well as other people in leadership positions) have a lot of power. It is not an exaggeration to say that their decisions over the next decade will affect hundreds of billions of human and nonhuman animals, now and in the future.

How should we ethically evaluate people with leadership positions within industrial animal agriculture? That depends on how we answer several other questions. First, what kinds of priorities should an executive have when it comes to making decisions for the corporation? We can distinguish three views. On the first view, **the economic view**, an executive is morally permitted, if not morally required, to maximize profit by any means necessary. If this means breaking the law, then so be it. If it means harming people, then so be it. In accepting this role they make a commitment to maximize profit by any means necessary, and they have a professional responsibility to live up to that commitment. On the second view, **the legal view**, an executive is morally permitted, if not morally required, to maximize profit by any *legal* means necessary. They have a moral duty to follow the law: That sets a limit on what they can do to make money. But beyond that, they can, and should, take advantage of every legal opportunity they have to make money, even if that means harming people along the way. On the third view, **the moral view**, an executive is *not* morally permitted to maximize profit by any legal means necessary. What, beyond merely following the law, do they have a moral duty to do? That depends on what moral theory we accept. But presumably if an executive is causing widespread and unnecessary harm to humans, nonhumans, and the environment, then they are acting wrongly, even if legally, on this view.[1]

Which of these views should we accept? Many executives apparently accept the first view. For example, as Jonathan Safran Foer reports, in 1997 pork producer Smithfield was penalized for "seven thousand violations of the Clean Water Act," accused by the U.S. government of "dumping illegal levels of waste" into a river and then "falsifying and destroying records to cover up its activities."[2] Why might a company do this? One reason is that many of the laws that regulate industrial animal agriculture have limited enforcement and limited penalties. Thus, it makes sense for a company to engage in illegal behavior for two reasons. First, they know that illegal behavior is unlikely to be discovered, since governmental oversight is limited and "ag-gag" laws ensure that non-governmental oversight, in the form of whistleblowing or undercover investigations, is limited as well.[3] (We will consider political repression of non-governmental oversight in more detail in Chapter 11.) Second, they know that if and when illegal information is discovered, the penalty is limited too. Thus, Foer claims that when Smithfield dumped illegal levels of waste into a river, the $12.6 million they were fined for this activity is roughly equivalent to what they now earn every 10 hours. This makes it easy for executives to see this kind of penalty as the cost of doing business—the corporate equivalent of racking up a few parking tickets because it costs less to pay the occasional fine than to pay the meter every day.[4]

When we consider this kind of case, we might be inclined to accept the legal view instead: Yes, maybe a company can take advantage of every *legal* opportunity to make money, but they should at least follow the law. This would place a moral limit on their activity while still allowing them to be competitive in the market. But once we grant that there should be a moral limit on their activity, why should we think that this moral limit starts and stops with the law? After all, we all know that the law and morality can come apart. Indeed, many of the worst moral crimes that humans have committed were perfectly legal at the time (or at least, they were treated as perfectly legal at the time by those with social, political, and economic power). This includes not only clear examples such as slavery (though the fact of slavery should be enough to remind us that the law and morality can come apart) but also child labor violations, food safety violations, waste disposal violations, discrimination in education and employment, and more.[5]

When these practices are happening here and now, people often feel inclined to defend them by citing legal considerations (these practices are permitted by the state) as well as economic considerations (these practices are profitable, perhaps even central to the economy). However, when these practices are happening in other places and times and we have the benefit of distance and hindsight, most of us are inclined to reject this kind of defense. We might or might not agree about particular cases, but as a general matter we agree that a practice can be immoral despite being legal and profitable at the time.

When we consider this kind of case, we might be inclined to accept the moral view instead: There are moral limits to corporate behavior that extend beyond merely following the law. What, then, are these moral limits, and how if at all do they apply to industrial animal agriculture? That depends on which moral theory we accept. For example, a Kantian would say that a corporate executive should aim to treat everyone as ends, a utilitarian would say that they should aim to maximize utility, and so on. It also depends on our view about collective action problems. Recall that a collective action problem arises when people engage in behavior that seems to have good results individually and bad results collectively. That might seem to be happening here, since executives in industrial animal agriculture might seem to be engaging in behavior that has good results individually (since they are benefiting themselves, their families, their employees, and so on individually) and bad results collectively (since they are harming more than 100+ billion farmed animals per year; consuming more land, water, and energy than most other industries; producing more waste, pollution, and greenhouse gases than most other industries; and so on collectively). So even if we think industrial animal agriculture is bad, what we think about the people in positions of power in this industry will depend in part on what we think about this issue.

With that in mind, recall that in Chapter 4 we discussed three different views that we might have about the ethics of collective action problems. First, we might think that making a difference is what matters, and that individuals do not make a difference in the context of collective action problems. Second, we might think that making a difference is not what matters. Third, we might think that making a difference is what matters, and that individuals do make a difference in the context of collective action problems (at least in expectation). It will be useful to say a bit more about each of these views now, as they apply to this case.

The first response we might have is: Making a difference is what matters, and individuals do not make a difference in the context of collective action problems. This is the kind of view that a utilitarian might accept if they think that individual executives do not actually make a difference when they make decisions for their companies. Why might they think this? They could reason as follows (suppose they are thinking about this issue first-personally):

> Yes, I am participating in a system that causes a great deal of harm. So yes, I am complicit in this harm, and yes, I should support structural changes that address this harm. But in the meantime, I benefit from participating in this system, and my family, friends, and employees benefit from my participating

too. And I am not causing harm by participating, since these harms would be taking place either way. After all, if I were to step down, someone else would take my place and nothing would change. And if this is right, why should I act any differently? Why not just support structural changes and stay the course in the meantime?

Many people accept this line of reasoning. But note that if we accept this line of reasoning here, then we have to accept it elsewhere as well. And when we consider the many past, present, and future activities that this line of reasoning would seem to excuse, we might start to worry about it. In particular, we might think that we should either (a) challenge the idea that making a difference is what matters or (b) challenge the idea that individual executives in this case are not, in fact, making a difference. (We will consider challenges to both of these points below, as well as in Chapter 9.)[6]

The second response we might have to this kind of collective action problem is: We might think that making a difference is not what matters. What matters instead? That depends. But in general, people who deny that making a difference is what matters are more drawn to moral theories that tell us to treat others well and be on the right side of history no matter how much good we do individually as a result.

For example, a Kantian might accept this kind of view. Recall that for a Kantian, we can test the morality of an action by asking two questions: (a) What if everyone did that, and (b) Would I be treating everyone as an end if I did that? And if a Kantian asks these questions in this case, they might decide that playing this role is wrong since (a) if everyone played this role in this situation, then the world would be a very bad place, and (b) each person who plays this role treats many human and nonhuman animals merely as means. Granted, some of the harms that our food system causes—such as harms to animals and the environment that result from clearing and developing land—are *side-effects* of corporate activity rather than *means* to corporate ends. Still, (a) at least some of the harms, such as farmed animal and worker harms, are means to corporate ends, and (b) harms can be side-effects and still be wrong according to Kantianism. In particular, many Kantians think that we can permissibly cause harm as a side-effect *only if* our end is morally important *and* we cannot pursue this end without causing this harm. According to this standard, the practice of clearing and developing land is at least sometimes morally permissible, since this practice is at least sometimes necessary to feed the world. However, this practice is clearly *not* morally permissible in the context of industrial animal agriculture, since the level of clearing and development that occurs in this context is not remotely necessary to feed the world. Thus, a Kantian might say that executives who stay the course are acting wrongly whether or not they make a difference individually.[7]

A virtue, care, or relational theorist might accept this kind of view as well. Recall that these theories tend to be pluralistic and situational: Morality involves cultivating character traits that contribute to flourishing (in the case of virtue theory), cultivating relationships of care with others (in the case of care and relational theory), and keeping in mind all relevant features of our social, political, economic, ecological, and historical contexts (in all cases).[8] What might a proponent of such a theory say in this case? That depends on the details. But we can say this much. Whereas in the past it might have made sense for these theorists to focus primarily on interactions with people in our local community (since in the past we interacted primarily with such people), it now makes sense for these theorists to focus on our interactions with people from all over the world (since we now interact with people everywhere, via our shared entanglement in global social, political, and economic systems, whether we like it or not). Thus, for example, yes, corporate executives might still have duties to their family, friends, and employees. But they also have duties to the many other human and/or nonhuman animals who have a stake in the work that they do. And if so, then their moral task is not simply to benefit their family, friends, and employees by any legal means necessary, but rather to experiment with, and gravitate toward, new methods of food production that allow them to do right by everyone they now interact with. So, if a virtue, care, or relational theorist who accepts this kind of view (or, if a Kantian or utilitarian who appreciates the value of character, emotion, and relationships accepts this kind of view), they might say that executives who stay the course are acting viciously or callously whether or not they make a difference individually.[9]

The third response we might have to a collective action problem is: Making a difference is what matters, and individuals *do* make a difference in the context of collective action problems. This is the kind of view that a utilitarian might accept if they think that individual corporate executives *do* make a difference when they make decisions for their companies. Why might they think this? They could reason as follows (suppose, once again, that they are thinking about this issue first-personally):

> Yes, my actions might not make or break everything, but they do make a difference. For example, if I serve as executive, then I can try to do at least *some* good from within the system, for example by investing in research and development of alternative food products and donating a high percentage of my own income to similar initiatives, whereas if I were to step down, then my replacement would likely not do those things. Similarly, if I step down, then I can try to do at least *some* good from the outside, for example by advocating against industrial animal agriculture and in favor of alternatives, whereas if I were to stay in this role, one fewer person would likely be doing that.

Which path will do the most good? It is impossible to say in the abstract. For each of us, it all depends on our talents, interests, and resources (including our ability to work in an industry that we detest in order to mitigate the harms that it causes), who our replacements in each situation would be and what their comparative strengths and limitations are, and so on. But whatever else we say, we might think that at least this much is clear: We would *not* be doing the most good (or even more good than harm) if we serve as executive and stay the course. Instead, we would at the very least have to take a different, more activist, approach to this role.[10]

It is worth noting that some executives seem to accept this line of reasoning. For example, the leadership at Chipotle and Whole Foods seem to be trying to change the food system from within by aspiring to meet relatively high standards for treatment of animals and the environment, while still remaining competitive with other, comparable chains. In so doing, they cause many suppliers to adopt a higher standard too, and they also cause many consumers to become more aware of the need to produce and consume food in an ethical way. But even here, there are risks. For example, insofar as these corporations present their food to the public as friendly to animals and the environment, they risk **humanewashing** and **greenwashing** industrial animal agriculture, that is, they risk leading people to believe that all we need is a few tweaks to industrial animal agriculture for it to be morally acceptable. But as we have seen, this is not the case. Granted, the aspects of industrial animal agriculture that Chipotle, Whole Foods, and other such corporations are targeting (antibiotics, growth hormones, and more) are bad. But they are not the real problem. The real problem is an industry that attempts to feed the world by harming and killing animals; consuming far too much land, water, and energy; producing far too much waste, pollution, and greenhouse gases; and more. And no matter how much we tweak the details, we will not be able to change this basic fact. So the worry is that insofar as we obscure this basic fact by making (and celebrating) reforms to the current system, we risk doing as much harm as good, if not more harm than good, in the long run. Does this mean that an executive should never try to change the food system from within? Not at all. But it does mean that they need to consider many factors when deciding what to do, including the potential for moderate change to make radical change more likely in some respects (by moving closer to this goal or creating momentum toward this goal) and less likely in other respects (by creating more trust in the current system). We will consider this issue more in Chapter 10.[11]

Now consider **factory farm and slaughterhouse workers**. Of course, other positions exist within industrial animal agriculture as well, many of which call for separate moral analysis. However, we are focusing on corporate executives and workers in factory farms and slaughterhouses here, not only because these positions raise special moral issues but also because they provide a stark illustration of the contextual nature of practical ethics.[12]

Workers in factory farms and slaughterhouses receive a lot of attention within food ethics, and it is easy to see why: They are on the front lines of this industry. They are the people who slaughter animals and dump waste in surrounding land and water. They are the people whose actions are recorded in undercover investigations and posted online for everyone to see and hear. As a result, we can see why critics of the food system would focus on these individuals. After all, nobody should treat animals and the environment that way. Moreover, unlike the violence that workers cause to animals *as part of* the food system (e.g., by castrating, de-beaking, force-feeding, and slaughtering them), the violence that they often cause to animals *over and above* these activities (e.g., by punching and kicking them or swinging them around by their tails) is completely unnecessary to food production—and legally counts as animal abuse. (We will discuss the nature and ethics of violence in detail in Chapter 11.)

However, it is important, when thinking about these issues, to consider the broader social, political, and economic context in which these harms occur, and to distinguish two questions. The first is: Are factory farm and slaughterhouse workers acting wrongly? And the second is: Even if they are acting wrongly, does that mean that food activists should seek to blame or punish them for this behavior?

Consider first the question whether or not workers in factory farms and slaughterhouses are acting wrongly. As we saw above, for Kantians the question translates to: Are they treating others as ends? For utilitarians it translates to: Are they maximizing utility? And for virtue, care, or relational theorists it translates to: Are they cultivating the appropriate character traits (in the case of virtue theory) or relationships of care, locally as well as globally (in the case of care and relational theory)? These questions are harder to answer in the case of workers than in the case of executives. To see why, consider two differences between executives and workers that might seem to mitigate the wrongness of what workers are doing.

First, factory farm and slaughterhouse workers have fewer options for making a difference within industrial animal agriculture than executives do. They are not empowered to make any policy level decisions at all. Instead, they each have a specific task to perform in a vast division of labor with near constant surveillance and control from supervisors.[13] Of course, this is not to say that factory farm and slaughterhouse workers have *no* opportunity to make a difference: For example, they might be able to reduce the harm done in these positions and/or document abuses to share with the public (though, this is risky given how little power they have and how much of a risk whistleblowing is). Still, many people think that degree of contribution to harm matters. If we agree, then we might think that making a relatively small contribution to a violent system is less wrong than making a relatively large contribution to a violent system.[14]

Second, factory farm and slaughterhouse workers have fewer alternative career paths available to them than corporate executives. Simply put, if they do not take these jobs, then they might not be able to support themselves or their families at all. If so, then we might think that the harms they cause as part of their jobs are less wrong than they would otherwise be. Why? Because we might think that (a) factory farm and slaughterhouse workers are socially, politically, or economically coerced into taking these jobs, and (b) harming others when you are coerced into doing so is less wrong than harming others when you are not coerced into doing so. Does coercion *cancel* the wrongness of harming others? Not necessarily. Instead, we might think that degree of coercion matters in the same kind of way that degree of contribution to harm does. For instance, we might think that participating in violence because your survival depends on it is less wrong than participating in violence because your social status depends on it, which, in turn, is less wrong than participating in violence because you feel like it.[15]

Granted, some considerations might push in the other direction as well. For example, in Chapters 3 and 4, we considered the idea that *direct* and *personal* harm is morally worse than *indirect* and *impersonal* harm. In particular, we considered this idea in the context of the trolley problem (as one possible justification for the view that killing one to save five is permissible in some cases but not in others), as well as in the context of international and intergenerational ethics (as one possible justification for the view that we owe more to people in our own community than to people in other communities). If we accept this idea, then we might think that insofar as some workers are contributing to violence more directly and personally than executives, their actions are worse all else equal.

However, two points. First, even if we think that some workers are acting worse than executives *all else equal*, taking into account directness of contribution to harm, we might still think that these executives are acting worse than these workers *all things considered*, since we might think that degree of contribution to harm and degree of coercion carry more weight than directness of contribution to harm in this context. Second, when we consider this kind of case, we might wonder whether we should accept the idea that directness of contribution to harm matters in and of itself at all. We might have found that idea plausible earlier. But if we find it less plausible here, then we need to find a way to reconcile these judgments, and this process of reconciliation might or might not lead us to reevaluate some of our earlier judgments.

This brings us to our second, related question: Even if food workers are acting wrongly, does this mean that activists should seek to blame or punish them, for example by targeting them in campaigns or lawsuits? Not necessarily. Again, food workers are victims of our food system too. Yes, they participate in harmful systems, but they often make a relatively small contribution to these systems and are often coerced into doing so. We might also think that some of the harms that workers cause over and above what the system requires (e.g., punching and kicking animals or swinging them by their tails) are a consequence of the psychological toll that their jobs exact from them. On this view, detachment, compartmentalization, and gallows humor are natural—and in some ways helpful, even if in other ways harmful—coping mechanisms. As Marjorie Spiegel discusses, a tendency to respond to your own experience of domination by dominating other, even more vulnerable individuals can be understood in similar ways.[16]

As Kimberly Smith notes, there is a further, related reason why we should be wary of addressing animal abuse by seeking to blame or punish people who abuse animals: This strategy can easily lead to the expansion of another harmful system, namely "a criminal justice system that is at best seriously compromised, and at worst hopelessly dysfunctional."[17] For example, in the U.S. we already incarcerate far too many people, especially low-income people of color. Yet if we seek to address animal abuse through criminal prosecution, we will likely exacerbate this trend, since "harsher sentences for animal abuse" will "likely fall the hardest on the same low-income minority communities that are currently suffering disproportionate rates of imprisonment."[18] Thus, Smith argues, a strategy of addressing animal abuse through criminal prosecution will likely harm humans and nonhumans alike, in part by creating social divisions that "threaten to weaken the very communal bonds that are the best protection for animal welfare."[19]

If we accept these ideas, then what it means in theory is that whether a person acts rightly or wrongly is a separate matter from whether we should praise, blame, reward, or punish them for what they do. And, what it means in practice, in the kind of case that we are currently discussing, is that even if factory farm and slaughterhouse workers are acting wrongly, we should not necessarily address this problem through blame or punishment, especially criminal prosecution. Instead, we should address this problem by holding workers accountable in other ways, and by focusing our moral attention on the system as a whole and on the executives who make most of a difference, and do so most freely, within it.[20]

8.3 Alternatives to industrial animal agriculture

We can now consider ethical questions that arise for people who pursue alternatives to industrial animal agriculture. We will focus on ethical questions that arise for local, organic, alternative (often "free-range") animal agriculture, and we will briefly consider hunting, plant-based agriculture, and plant-based and cultured meat production as well.

As discussed in Chapter 7, alternatives to industrial animal agriculture can be better than this system in many ways, but they are not without problems. Maybe someday someone will invent a way to feed the world without harming anyone in the process. But in the meantime every alternative causes at least some harm. We therefore need to morally evaluate this harm. Moreover, while some alternatives, such as plant-based agriculture, plant-based meat, and cultured meat, are likely to be scalable (i.e., are likely to be able to provide healthful, affordable food for 7+ billion people, assuming that certain social, political, and economic conditions are in place), other alternatives, such as hunting or free-range animal agriculture, are unlikely to be scalable in the same kind of way. Thus, while we will here be focusing on assessing alternatives at the individual level, we need to keep in mind assessments at the collective level too. Thus, for instance, even if we determine that hunting and free-range farming are morally permissible in particular cases, they will almost certainly not be among the primary alternatives that food producers should be moving toward, for practical reasons alone.

With that in mind, consider first local, organic, free-range animal agriculture. (Our focus will be on the free-range aspect of this kind of agriculture, though the local and organic aspects are related to this.) As discussed in Chapters 4 and 7, many people defend this kind of agriculture on the grounds that it provides farmed animals with relatively pleasant lives and relatively painless deaths. Granted, free-range farmed animals are still used, confined, and, in many cases, killed in the prime of their lives. But consider everything they get in return. First of all, they get to live, and, unlike factory farmed animals, many free-range farmed animals clearly have lives worth living: They have at least some access to nature and at least some access to socialization. They also enjoy many privileges that wild animals do not, such as food security, protection from predation, and protection from weather. Finally, even though most free-range farmed animals die young, they also, as a result, avoid the slow agony of death that many wild animals experience. So, why not think that everybody wins in this kind of system? We get to eat meat, dairy, and eggs (at least, some of us do), and the animals who provide us with these products get to live as well as possible, compatibly with making this sacrifice for us.[21]

This argument seems reasonable. There is no denying that free-range farmed animals lead much better lives than factory farmed animals and many wild animals. But does that mean that we are morally permitted to use, confine, or kill them for food? There are at least five issues that we need to consider before we can answer this question: subjective experiences, use, captivity, killing, and indirect effects.[22] (As in the relevant part of Chapter 4, we will assume for the sake of this discussion that we accept a theory of moral status according to which free-range farmed animals can have moral status, such as wide rationalism, sentientism, biocentrism, or virtue, care, or relational theory.)

The details of this discussion will partly depend on an issue that we have not yet discussed in detail, namely what theory of **well-being** (i.e., what makes a life go well or poorly) we accept. According to **subjective theories** of well-being, how well or poorly your life goes depends entirely on *subjective* facts, that is, facts about your subjective states. For example, **hedonists** think that the quality of your life depends entirely on how much *pleasure* and *pain* your life contains. Similarly, **desire theorists** think that the quality of your life depends entirely on how much *desire-satisfaction* and *desire-frustration* your life contains. What is the difference between these theories? In many cases there is no difference, since in many cases pleasure and desire-satisfaction are aligned: What gives us pleasure satisfies our desires, and what satisfies our desires gives us pleasure. But in at least some cases there can be a difference. For example, suppose that you spend the last few years of your life working on a book, hoping that it will be published after you die. Then, during the last week of your life, your publisher lies to you: They tell you the book will be published, when in fact it will not be. In this case you would have pleasure but not desire-satisfaction (since the world would not, in fact, be how you want it to be), and so your quality of life would increase on hedonism but not on desire theory. Now suppose that the opposite happens: Your publisher tells you that your book will not be published, when in fact it will be. In this case you would have desire-satisfaction but not pleasure (since the world would, in fact, be how you want it to be), and so your quality of life would increase on desire theory but not on hedonism.[23]

In contrast, according to **objective theories** of well-being, how well or poorly your life goes depends at least in part on *objective* facts, that is, facts that are not about your subjective states. What kinds of objective facts might be relevant? We will focus here on one influential answer, developed by Amartya Sen, Martha Nussbaum, and others, called **the capabilities approach**.[24] On this view, the quality of your life depends on whether or not you can do the kinds of things that allow typical members of your species to flourish. Nussbaum claims that for many species, this list will include things like: live a full life, have bodily health, have bodily integrity, have a rich sensory and emotional life, exercise your mental and physical abilities, play with others and have relationships with others, and more.[25] Of course, some items on this list are more important for some species than for others (e.g., play is more important for relatively social animals than for relatively non-social animals). And the details will differ from case to case (e.g., a full life for animals with a long lifespan is different than a full life for animals with a short lifespan). But in each case the basic idea is the same: You have a good life if you can flourish in a species-typical way. What is the difference between this theory and subjective theories? As before, in many cases there is no difference, since we tend to derive pleasure and desire-satisfaction from all the items on this list. But also as before, in some cases there can be a difference. For example, for subjective theories, whether death is bad for you will depend entirely on considerations involving your subjective states. Whereas for the capabilities approach, whether death is bad for you will also depend on other considerations, as we will see.[26]

We can combine theories of well-being with moral theories in different ways. For example, a consequentialist hedonist might think that we should maximize pleasure in the world. A consequentialist desire theorist might think that we should maximize desire-satisfaction in the world. A consequentialist capabilities theorist might think that we should maximize flourishing in the world. And so on. (As we have seen, utilitarians such as Bentham, Mill, and Sidgwick are hedonists.) Similar combinations are possible for other theories, though the details differ. As we will now see, which theory of well-being we accept will often matter in practice, since it will determine which forms of treatment are beneficial or harmful and, as a result, right or wrong on moral theories that link benefits and harms with rightness and wrongness.

With that in mind, consider first how free-range animal agriculture affects the *subjective experiences* of farmed animals. Many people like to say that free-range farmed animals have good lives and then "one bad day." But as we saw in Chapter 7, the reality tends to be more complicated. One problem is that, even if we treat free-range farmed animals better than factory farmed animals in many ways, we still treat them badly in many ways as well. Chickens, cows, pigs, and other animals raised for food are conscious, emotional, intelligent, social beings. Yet we still use them for our own purposes, making them do many things they would otherwise not choose to do. We still keep them in captivity, preventing them from doing many things that they would otherwise choose to do. We still kill many of them in the prime of their lives, which not only causes pain and desire-frustration at present but also forecloses pleasure and desire-satisfaction in the future (a fact that we will return to later). And more. As a result, it would be a mistake to assume that free-range farms treat farmed animals as humanely as many claim to in labels and marketing materials. This is part of why conscientious consumers arguably need to do more than simply read labels and marketing materials and act accordingly, as we will discuss in Chapter 9.

Another, related problem is that many free-range farmed animals are bred to experience a certain amount of pain and desire-frustration no matter how well we treat them. In particular, if a free-range farm purchases animals from the same kind of breeder that a factory farm purchases them from, then these animals will still grow as big as possible as quickly as possible and/or produce as much as possible as quickly as possible, with a variety of predictable impacts on their subjective well-being (though there will of course be variation, since the animals might also be eating less and exercising more). Of course, this is not to dispute the claim that many free-range farmed animals have lives worth living: Even if we treat them badly directly (through use, confinement, and early death) as well as indirectly (through supporting breeding practices that cause a certain amount of pain and desire-frustration no matter what), it might still be true that many free-range farmed animals experience more pleasure than pain or more desire-satisfaction than desire-frustration in life. However, this does complicate the image of a perfectly symbiotic, mutually advantageous agricultural system that we might have in mind when we think about free-range animal agriculture. In short, while most free-range farmed animals experience much less pain and desire-frustration than factory farmed animals do, they still experience enough pain and desire-frustration to raise ethical concerns about this practice.[27]

The second and third questions that we have to ask (which we can ask together, since we can answer them in similar ways) is: Can *use* and *captivity* be harmful or wrong, independently of their implications for subjective states? For example, if we accept the capabilities approach, then we might think that use and captivity can be harmful whether or not they cause pain or desire-frustration, since they can interfere with species-typical capacities for liberty or autonomy. Similarly, if we accept a Kantian, virtue, care, or relational theory, then we might think that use and captivity can be wrong whether or not they cause harm, since they can treat this individual merely as a means or express disrespect toward this individual whether or not they also harm this individual. However, even if use and captivity are *sometimes* harmful or wrong on these views, they might not *always* be. For example, if people provide animals with enough space, and with enough options within that space, for them to exercise their capacity for liberty or autonomy, then using or keeping them in this context might not be harmful or wrong on these views. Many people keep animals in homes in this spirit (which is not to say that we always treat companion animals as we should),[28] and we can at least imagine people keeping animals on farms in this spirit as well, as part of what Sue Donaldson and Will Kymlicka call **intentional communities**, characterized by a sense of belonging, egalitarianism, self-determination, and more.[29] Still, when people use and keep animals on farms in the way that they typically do (treating them as commodities with no rights, rather than as community members with robust rights),[30] then this treatment likely interferes with their flourishing, treats them merely as a means, and expresses disrespect toward them, and therefore is likely harmful and wrong on these views.

Alternatively, if we accept a subjective theory of well-being, then we will think that use and captivity *cannot* be harmful or wrong independently of their implications for subjective states. On this view, the only question that we need to ask is: How do use and captivity affect the subjective well-being of farmed animals? In particular, do farmed animals enjoy or desire things that use and captivity make it easier or harder to get? If so, then use and captivity will be relevant to their subjective well-being. But there is a complication, which is that how good or bad a given state of use or captivity is for farmed animals will depend in part on which alternative possibilities, if any, we are comparing it to in order to assess it. As we have seen, many people assess the animal welfare impacts of free-range farming (on subjective as well as objective theories of well-being) by comparing life on a free-range farm to non-existence, or to life in a factory farm or in the wild. And indeed, if we frame the discussion this way, then we might agree that free-range farming is good for many animals, their current state of use and captivity notwithstanding. However, suppose instead that we assess the animal welfare impacts of free-range farming by comparing life on a free-range farm to life in an intentional community, where humans treat nonhumans as community members with robust rights. If we frame the discussion this way, then we might doubt that free-range farming is good for many animals. So, which framing is best? This is a complicated question that we will not be able to fully answer here. However, we will note that we do not, as a general matter, think that we can treat others however we like as long as at least *some* alternative possibilities are worse. ("Yes, I locked John in a cage. But I could have locked him in an even *smaller* cage. So when you really think about it, this is good for John and the right thing for me to do.")[31]

The fourth question that we have to ask is: Can *death* be harmful or wrong, independently of its implications for subjective states? As before, if we accept the capabilities approach, then we might think that death can be harmful whether or not it causes pain or desire-frustration, since it can interfere with species-typical lifespans. Similarly, if we accept a Kantian, virtue, care, or relational theory, then we might think that killing can be wrong whether or not it causes harm, since it can treat this individual merely as a means and express disrespect toward this individual whether or not it also harms this individual. However, as with use and captivity, even if death is *sometimes* harmful or wrong on these views, it might not *always* be. For example, if people euthanize animals toward the end of their natural lives with the aim of preventing a slow death, then this act of killing might not be harmful or wrong on these views. Many people kill companion animals in this spirit (though as before, they might or might not be right to do so depending on the details), and we can at least imagine people killing free-range farmed animals in this spirit as well. Still, when people kill free-range farmed animals in the way that they typically do (i.e., when people kill free-range farmed animals in the prime of their lives with the aim of profiting from their deaths), this act of killing likely interferes with their species-typical lifespans, treats them merely as a means, and expresses disrespect toward them, and therefore is likely harmful and wrong on these views.[32]

Alternatively, if we accept a subjective theory of well-being, then we will think that death cannot be harmful or wrong independently of its implications for subjective states. On this view, the only question that we have to ask is:

How does death affect the subjective well-being of farmed animals? However, since one cannot directly experience death in the same kind of way that one can directly experience use or captivity (for reasons we will discuss in a moment), we will have to approach this question a bit differently. In particular, we will have to focus even more on which alternative possibilities, if any, we are comparing this state of death to in order to assess it. Does the goodness or badness of your death for you depend only on how it impacts the experiences or desires that you actually have in life, or does it also depend on how it impacts the experiences or desires that you could have had in life, if only you had lived longer? Philosophers disagree about which option we should pick.[33]

On one hand, some philosophers accept the more restrictive view that the goodness or badness of your death for you depends only on how it impacts the experiences or desires that you *actually* have in life. On this view, which we can call **the actual well-being view**, the only question we need to ask is: Will your death give you pleasure, pain, desire-satisfaction, or desire-frustration during your life? How would we go about answering this question? That depends on which subjective theory of well-being we are considering.

For example, suppose that we accept the actual well-being view along with hedonism, that is, the idea that well-being consists in pleasure and the absence of pain. In this case, we should say that your death cannot harm you. Why not? To paraphrase Epicurus: As long as there is a "you" to be harmed (i.e., to be in pain), you cannot be dead, and as soon as you are dead, there is no "you" to be harmed (i.e., to be in pain). So on this view, nobody can be harmed by their own death. This includes humans: us, our parents, our children, our partners, our friends, and everyone else we share our lives with. It includes our companion animals: the cats, dogs, mice, fishes, and everyone else we welcome into our families. And it includes farmed animals: the chickens, cows, pigs, fishes, and everyone else we kill for food. Sure, *dying* can harm us on this view (since we can suffer when dying), and our death can harm *others* on this view (since others can suffer when we are dead). But *our death* cannot harm *us*, since as soon as we are dead, there is no "us" to be harmed, that is, to be in pain or to be deprived of pleasure.[34]

In contrast, suppose that we accept the actual well-being view along with desire theory, that is, the idea that well-being consists in desire-satisfaction and the absence of desire-frustration. In this case, we should say that your death *can* harm you. In particular, your death can harm you by frustrating desires whose satisfaction depends on your survival. For example, if you want to become a lawyer, and if your death prevents you from doing so, then your death harms you on this view (since your death frustrates your current desire to be a lawyer whether or not you are around to realize it). How does this view apply to nonhumans? It depends on the nonhuman in question. We might think that at least some nonhumans, such as bivalves, have no future-related desires at all. If so, then death cannot harm them on this view. However, we might think that other nonhumans, such as chickens, cows, and pigs, do have future-related desires. If so, then death can harm them on this view. For example, if a cow wants to spend time with her friends and family, and if her death prevents her from doing so, then her death harms her on this view (since her death frustrates her desire to spend time with her friends and family whether or not she is around to realize it).[35]

On the other hand, other philosophers accept the more expansive view that the goodness or badness of your death for you depends at least in part on how it impacts the experiences or desires that you *could have* had in life, if only you had lived longer. On this view, which we can call the **possible well-being view**, we need to consider not only whether your death will give you pleasure, pain, desire-satisfaction, or desire-frustration at present but also whether your death will prevent you from having pleasure, pain, desire-satisfaction, or desire-frustration in the future. How would we go about answering this question? As with the actual well-being view, that depends on what theory of well-being we accept. But unlike the actual well-being view, the possible well-being view has roughly the same implications either way.

Why? The possible well-being view implies that your death can harm you by depriving you of a good future, and death can deprive you of a good future by preventing you from experiencing future pleasure as well as by preventing you from forming and satisfying future desires. For example, you might not want to get married now. But if you live another ten years, you might want to get married then, and you might derive both pleasure and desire-satisfaction from marriage at that point. If so, then your death harms you in part by depriving you of these possible future goods. How does this view apply to nonhumans? Well, it depends on what kind of future is possible for them. To the degree that they have the potential for a good long life, their death can harm them on this view (since their death can deprive them of this good long life, whether or not they currently have any future-related desires at all). The upshot is that, on this view, death likely harms many free-range farmed animals, since even if *some* free-ranged farmed animals lack the potential for a good future (e.g., because they are near the end of their natural lives), *most* free-range farmed animals, including chickens, cows, pigs, and fishes, have the potential for a good future.[36]

Granted, one could object to this analysis in at least two ways. First, one could deny that free-range farmed animals have the potential for a good future, and therefore could deny that death is a harm for them. For example, a farmer might claim, "There is no realistic future in which these animals have a good life. If I were to let them live, I would not be able to provide them with a good life. So my killing them when I do is actually good for them." How should we assess this reply? That depends. If these really are the only two options that the farmer has (killing the animals now or giving them a bad future), then we might think that this reply is reasonable. However, if what the farmer is really saying is that these are the only two options that allow the farm to be profitable, then we might think that this reply is less reasonable, since, we might think, these animals do in fact have the potential for a good future. The farmer is simply unwilling to provide it for them.

Second, one could accept that these animals have the potential for a good future, and therefore that death is a harm for them, but argue that killing them is morally permissible anyway. For example, a farmer might claim,

Yes, I harm animals when I kill them. But I compensate for that harm by bringing other animals into existence. Then I give those animals good lives. Then, yes, I harm those animals when I kill them. But I compensate for that harm by bringing other animals into existence. And so on down the line. This is the only way that my business can work. And surely a situation that allows these animals to exist at all is better than a situation that does not.

This argument is worth taking seriously. However, note that it is not an argument about the harm of death. Instead, it is an argument about the ethics of harm, that is, the farmer is now claiming that you can permissibly kill someone as long as you replace them with someone else, since the harm of death will be compensated for by the benefit of life. We will briefly consider this argument, which some philosophers call **the replaceability argument**, below.[37]

The fifth and final question that we have to ask (which will be related to our assessment of this claim about the ethics of harm) is: What are the *indirect effects* of free-range animal agriculture, and how should we morally evaluate these effects? Here we might worry that even if free-range farmed animals have relatively good lives, the practice of buying them, selling them, using them, keeping them, and killing them for food still harms animals *indirectly*, because it still perpetuates the idea that animals are here for us rather than for themselves, and, as a result, it still increases rather than decreases the likelihood that people will continue to harm animals in general. After all, we already live in a society that conditions people to see animals as objects rather than as subjects, and we need to be mindful about how our own actions interact with that narrative about the natural order. Granted, free-range farmers might accept a different, more complicated narrative according to which animals are part objects and part subjects. But if the impact of free-range animal agriculture is that consumers still see eating animals as ethically okay (and, as a result, continue to eat factory farmed animals and free-range farmed animals alike), then free-range farmers might be helping to greenwash and humanewash industrial animal agriculture whether they like it or not.[38]

We can also put this point in terms of the **dignity** of human and nonhuman animals. Following Lori Gruen (though her relational view of dignity is more complex than the simple view that we will be sketching here), we say that we *respect the dignity* of an individual when our treatment of them supports social perceptions of them as worthy of respect and compassion, and we *violate the dignity* of an individual when our treatment of them supports social perceptions of them as not worthy of respect and compassion. On this view, when free-range farming involves excessive use, excessive captivity, and premature death, it supports social perceptions of farmed animals as not worthy of respect and compassion, and so it violates their dignity regardless of how much it harms them individually. This is part of why many people affirm the idea that human life is sacred: we affirm this idea since, even if death is sometimes best, the idea that human life is sacred still enhances our respect and compassion for each other and, consequently, improves our treatment of each other overall. If this is right, we might have reason to affirm the idea that nonhuman life is sacred too, since, once again, even if death is sometimes best, the idea that nonhuman life is sacred might still enhance our respect and compassion for animals and, consequently, improve our treatment of them overall. (We will consider this issue more in the next chapter, as it relates to food consumption.)[39]

So what should we say all things considered about free-range farming? As always, a lot will depend on what moral theory we accept. For example, a Kantian will say that this practice can continue if and only if it treats everyone as an end. They will likely also say that excessive use, excessive captivity, and premature death do not, in fact, treat farmed animals as ends, especially if the farmer has other, less harmful options available to them (most Kantians reject the replaceability argument for this reason). A utilitarian will say that this practice can continue if and only if it maximizes utility. They will likely also say that while this practice might maximize utility in *some* cases, it will likely not maximize utility in *most* cases, since in most cases it involves excessive use, excessive captivity, and premature death and the farmer has other, less harmful options available to them (many utilitarians accept the replaceability argument in principle but are skeptical about it in many cases in practice for this reason). Finally, a virtue, care, or relational theorist might or might not think that this practice has some good features and some bad features. However, a central consideration for these theorists will likely be: When you bring someone into existence or accept them into your care, you take on special obligations to them, special obligations that are typically not compatible with killing them in the prime of their lives for profit (many virtue, care, and relational theorists reject the replaceability argument for this reason).

With that in mind, we will now close by considering three alternatives.[40] First, how does **hunting** compare with free-range animal agriculture? On one hand, hunting is similar to animal agriculture in some ways. For example, it still kills animals for human consumption, and it still perpetuates the idea of animals as here for our consumption. On the other hand, hunting is also different from animal agriculture in some ways. Consider four such ways. First, hunting typically allows animals to live natural lives prior to death, with no use or captivity at all. Second, hunting might not always be bad for the animals killed, since life in the wild often involves terrible pain and suffering as a result of hunger, thirst, disease, weather, predation, and more. In these cases, death might not foreclose a good future (and therefore be bad for the animal on some views), but might rather foreclose a bad future (and therefore be good for the animal on some views). Third, even if hunting *is* bad for the animals killed, it might not be bad for animals or the environment overall. After all, if hunting is necessary for species to maintain stable populations and for ecosystems to remain in balance, then the indirect benefits for animals, plants, species, and ecosystems might outweigh the direct harms for the animals killed (which will matter for utilitarians, if not for others). Finally, even if hunting *sometimes* perpetuates the idea that animals are here for our consumption, it might not *always* do so, since while some people might hunt for self-interested reasons, other people might hunt at least partly for other-interested reasons (e.g., for the sake of animals, plants, species, and ecosystems overall). The upshot is that hunting can sometimes be better than animal agriculture, though a lot depends on which moral theory we accept and on the details of the case. For example, a Kantian would say that hunting is permissible if it treats everyone involved as an end, including the animal killed (though some Kantians might wonder how likely this is to be true in most cases). Similarly, a utilitarian would say that hunting is permissible if it maximizes utility (though some utilitarians might wonder how likely this is to be true in most cases). Finally, a virtue, care, and relational theorist would remind us to consider how hunting shapes our character (does it make us more or less respectful and compassionate?), as well as how it impacts our current relationships with everyone involved (including the animals killed). Still, even if hunting is sometimes permissible on these views, it will not always be, especially in cases where people hunt for food or sport when other, less harmful options are available.[41]

Second, how does plant-based agriculture compare with other alternatives? Recall that plant-based agriculture refers to agriculture that does not produce or consume animal products. On one hand, plant farms do still harm animals and the environment. For example, they still modify land; displace, harm, or kill wild animals; consume land, water, and energy; and produce waste, pollution, and greenhouse gases. On the other hand, plant farms cause these harms in different ways and to different degrees than animal farms do: For example, whereas animal farms harm farmed animals as a means *and* wild animals as a side-effect, plant farms harm only wild animals as a side-effect. Moreover, whereas animal farms often rely on plant farms for animal feed, plant farms do not rely on other farms in the same kind of way. As a result, animal products often require a greater amount of total land use for their creation than plant products do, which is not only less efficient but also more harmful for animals and the environment. (Though, as we saw in Chapter 7, a partial exception is that some animal farms use land that might not be usable for other purposes.) These differences can be morally relevant. For instance, a Kantian might reason as follows: If feeding people is a very important end (as it is), if plant-based agriculture harms animals as a side-effect of pursuing this end rather than as a means to this end (as it does), and if we cannot pursue this end without causing this harm (as we plausibly cannot), then plant-based agriculture is morally permissible even though it harms animals. Similarly, a utilitarian might reason as follows: If plant-based agriculture does more good overall than all available alternatives (as it plausibly does in many cases), then plant-based agriculture is morally permissible even though it harms animals. Finally, a virtue, relational, or care theorist might reason as follows: If plant-based agriculture expresses respect and compassion for others and honors our existing relationships more than available alternatives (as it plausibly does in many cases), then plant-based agriculture is morally permissible even though it harms animals. As we have seen, when we think about these empirical questions, we should make sure to consider all relevant impacts, direct as well as indirect. We should also make sure to correct for bias as much as possible along the way. For example, if you enter the discussion as a supporter of animal farming, you should make an extra effort to seek out, and charitably assess, empirical information and moral arguments that challenge animal farming. And if you enter the discussion as an opponent of animal farming, you should do the reverse.

Finally (though there are of course other alternatives to consider too), how does plant-based and cultured meat (along with other substitutes) compare with other alternatives? Recall that plant-based meat refers to meat that comes from plants whereas cultured meat refers to meat that comes from a cell culture, scaffolding, and growth medium in a factory. On one hand, plant-based and cultured meat often require more processing than simpler plant-based foods, and, as a result, they might cause more harm to animals and the environment in the short term. Moreover, insofar as plant-based and cultured meat resemble conventional meat, they risk reinforcing the idea of animals as commodities in the same kind of way that conventional meat does. On the other hand, many people may experience plant-based and cultured meat as a more desirable alternative to conventional meat than simpler plant-based foods, and, if this is true, then even if these products do more harm than good for animals and the environment in the short term, they might do more good than harm for animals and the environment in the long run, by expanding the consumer base for alternative food products. Moreover, even if plant-based and cultured meat perpetuate the idea of animals as commodities to a degree, they might also disrupt this idea to a degree, by showing people that meat can come from sources other than once-living animals. (Of course, this is assuming that producers can overcome social, political, economic, and technological obstacles, especially in the case of cultured meat.) The upshot is that, as with hunting, a lot will depend on our moral theory as well as on the details of the case. For example, a Kantian might be open to cultured meat production if and only if producers can find a plant-based growth medium, since use of fetal bovine serum treats some animals merely as means. In contrast, a utilitarian might be open to cultured meat production either way, since even if producers do use fetal bovine serum initially, they might still be maximizing utility overall. (With that said, utilitarians will be more excited about this technology if and when producers find a plant-based growth medium.) Finally, a virtue, care, and relational theorist will once again invite us to consider how these production methods interact with our characters, emotions, and relationships, drawing special attention to the ways in which normalizing the idea of meat without animals might affect our conceptions of, perceptions of, and treatment of human and nonhuman animals.[42]

8.4 Conclusion

Ultimately, there are certainly moral concerns to be raised about alternatives to industrial animal agriculture. But we should not lose sight of the bigger picture. Over 99% of the meat, dairy, and eggs that people consume comes from an industrial animal agricultural system that causes massive and unnecessary harm to humans, nonhumans, and the environment. Even if we should worry about alternatives to industrial animal agriculture too—and we certainly should—industrial animal agriculture should remain our focus for the foreseeable future.

Notes

1 For a general discussion of business ethics and corporate responsibility, see:
    Jeffrey Moriarty, "Business Ethics," *The Stanford Encyclopedia of Philosophy*, Edward N. Zalta ed., https://plato.stanford.edu/entries/ethics-business/.
2 Jonathan Safran Foer, *Eating Animals* (New York: Penguin Random House, 2010): 178.
3 For more on state repression of animal and environmental activists, see:
    Will Potter, *Green Is the New Red: An Insider's Account of a Social Movement Under Siege* (New York: City Lights Publishers, 2011).
4 Jonathan Safran Foer, *Eating Animals* (New York: Penguin Random House, 2010): 178–179.
5 For what might be the most famous and influential exposé of food safety violations in modern history, see:
    Upton Sinclair, *The Jungle* (Chicago: University of Illinois Press, 1988).
6 For a defense of this kind of view, see:
    Walter Sinnott-Armstrong, "It's Not My Fault: Global Warming and Individual Moral Obligations," in Walter Sinnott-Armstrong and Richard Howarth, eds., *Perspectives on Climate Change: Science, Economics, Politics, Ethics* (Bingley: Emerald Publishing, 2005): 221–253.
7 The view that we can permissibly cause harm only if this harm is a necessary side-effect of morally important activity is called the doctrine of double effect. For more on the doctrine of double effect, see:
    Philippa Foot, "Morality, Action, and Outcome," in Ted Honderich, ed., *Morality and Objectivity: A Tribute to J.L. Mackie* (New York: Routledge, 1985): 23–38.
    Frances Kamm, "The Doctrine of Double Effect: Reflections on Theoretical and Practical Issues," *Journal of Medicine and Philosophy* 16, no. 5 (1991): 571–585.
    Alison McIntyre, "Doctrine of Double Effect," *The Stanford Encyclopedia of Philosophy*, Edward N. Zalta ed., https://plato.stanford.edu/entries/double-effect/.
8 Since virtue theories, care theories, and relational theories tend to be pluralistic and contextual, we will often consider them together and focus on these features. However, this does not mean that these theories are the same: within and across these categories, there are many relevant differences that affect how we should apply them in practice.
9 For an argument that people in nations with developed industrial economies have a special obligation to people in nations without developed industrial economies in light of our complicity in climate change, see:
    Henry Shue, "Global Environment and International Inequality," *International Affairs* 75, no. 3 (1999): 531–545.
    For related arguments, see:
    Clare Palmer, *Animal Ethics in Context* (New York: Columbia University Press, 2010).
10 For more on the ethics of career choice, taking into account how much good we would likely do in a career relative to our replacements, see:
    William MacAskill, *Doing Good Better: Effective Altruism and a Radical New Way to Make a Difference* (Norwich: Guardian Faber Publishing, 2015): 75–76, 155–156.
11 For different perspectives on whether moderate reforms do more harm than good, see:
    Gary Lawrence Francione and Robert Garner, *The Animal Rights Debate: Abolition or Regulation?* (New York: Columbia University Press, 2010).
12 For more on food workers, see the essays in:
    Anne Barnhill, Mark Budolfson, and Tyler Doggett, *Food, Ethics, and Society: An Introductory Text with Readings* (New York: Oxford University Press, 2017), 519–572.

13 For an ethnographic study of a slaughterhouse, with information about how man-
    agers surveil and control workers and reflections about the psychological toll for
    workers, see:
      Timothy Pachirat, *Every Twelve Seconds: Industrialized Slaughter and the Politics of
    Sight* (New Haven: Yale University Press, 2011).
14 For discussion from a utilitarian perspective, see:
      Alastair Norcross, "The Scalar Approach to Utilitarianism," in Henry West,
    ed., *The Blackwell Guide to Mill's Utilitarianism* (Hoboken: Wiley-Blackwell, 2008):
    217–232.
15 For discussion of the moral relevance of coerced harmful action, see:
      Norvin Richards, "Acting under Duress," *The Philosophical Quarterly* 37, no. 146
    (1987): 21–36.
      For a consequentialist perspective, see:
      Johan E. Gustafsson, "Consequentialism with Wrongness Depending on the
    Difficulty of Doing Better," *Thought* 5, no. 2 (2016): 108–118.
16 Marjorie Spiegel, *The Dreaded Comparison: Human and Animal Slavery*, 3rd edition
    (London: Mirror Books, 1997): 91–104.
17 Kimberly Smith, *Governing Animals: Animal Welfare and the Liberal State* (New York:
    Oxford University Press, 2012): 143.
18 Kimberly Smith, *Governing Animals: Animal Welfare and the Liberal State* (New York:
    Oxford University Press, 2012): 144–145.
19 Kimberly Smith, *Governing Animals: Animal Welfare and the Liberal State* (New York:
    Oxford University Press, 2012): 146.
20 For discussion of alternatives to incarceration, see:
      Angela Davis, *Are Prisons Obsolete?* (London: Seven Stories Press, 2010): Chapter 6.
21 For discussion of this kind of consideration, see:
      Michael Pollan, *The Omnivore's Dilemma* (New York: Penguin, 2006): Chapter 17.
22 For more on the harms of suffering, confinement, and death for nonhuman animals, see:
      David DeGrazia, *Animal Rights: A Very Short Introduction* (New York: Oxford
    University Press, 2002): Chapter 4.
23 For discussion of these theories, see:
      Ben Bradley, *Well-being* (Hoboken: John Wiley & Sons, 2015): 13–46.
24 See, for example:
      Amartya Sen, *Commodities and Capabilities* (Amsterdam: North-Holland, 1985).
      Martha C. Nussbaum, *Frontiers of Justice: Disability, Nationality, Species Membership*
    (Cambridge: Harvard University Press, 2009).
25 Martha Nussbaum, "Beyond Compassion and Humanity: Justice for Nonhuman
    Animals," in Cass R. Sunstein and Martha C. Nussbaum, eds., *Animal Rights: Current
    Debates and New Directions* (New York: Oxford University Press, 2004): 299–320,
    313–317.
26 For further discussion, see:
      Ben Bradley, *Well-being* (Hoboken: John Wiley & Sons, 2015): 47–58.
27 For more, see:
      Jonathan Safran Foer, *Eating Animals* (New York: Penguin Random House, 2010):
    156–159.
      Rockwell Schwartz, "Eggs: The Leading Cause of Chicken Cancer Nobody Talks
    About," *The Huffington Post*, August 28, 2017, www.huffingtonpost.com/entry/eggs-the-
    leading-cause-of-cancer-nobody-talks-about_us_59a0b5c5e4b0d0ef9f1c13df?ncid=
    engmodushpmg00000003.
28 For discussion, see:
      Hilary Bok, "Keeping Pets," in Tom Beauchamp and R.G. Frey, eds., *The Oxford
    Handbook of Animal Ethics* (New York: Oxford University Press, 2011): 769–795.

Alexandra Horowitz, "Canis Familiaris: Companion and Captive," in Lori Gruen, ed., *The Ethics of Captivity* (New York: Oxford University Press, 2014): 7–21.

29 Sue Donaldson and Will Kymlicka, "Farmed Animal Sanctuaries: The Heart of the Movement?" *Politics and Animals* 1, no. 1 (2015): 50–74.
See also:
Sue Donaldson and Will Kymlicka, *Zoopolis* (New York: Oxford University Press, 2011): 90–93, 134–135.

30 Sue Donaldson and Will Kymlicka, "Farmed Animal Sanctuaries: The Heart of the Movement?" *Politics and Animals* 1, no. 1 (2015): 50–74.

31 For general discussion about the ethics of captivity, see:
David DeGrazia, "The Ethics of Confining Animals: From Farms to Zoos to Human Homes," in Tom Beauchamp and R.G. Frey, eds., *The Oxford Handbook of Animal Ethics* (Oxford: Oxford University Press, 2015).
Also see many of the chapters in:
Lori Gruen, ed., *The Ethics of Captivity* (New York: Oxford University Press, 2014).

32 For discussion on this point, see:
Martha Nussbaum, "Beyond Compassion and Humanity: Justice for Nonhuman Animals," in Cass R. Sunstein and Martha C. Nussbaum, eds., *Animal Rights: Current Debates and New Directions* (New York: Oxford University Press, 2004): 299–320, 314–315.

33 For more on the harm of death, see:
Steven Luper, "Death," *The Stanford Encyclopedia of Philosophy*, Edward N. Zalta ed., https://plato.stanford.edu/entries/death/.
For more on the harm of death for animals and the ethics of killing animals, see Tatjana Višak and Robert Garner, eds., *The Ethics of Killing Animals* (New York: Oxford University Press, 2015).

34 Epicurus, "Letter to Menoeceus," The Internet Classics Archive, http://classics.mit.edu/Epicurus/menoec.html.

35 For more, see:
Jeff Sebo, "Agency and Moral Status" and Ben Bradley, "Is Death Bad for a Cow?" in *The Ethics of Killing Animals*, (New York: Oxford University Press, 2015): 51–64.

36 For a modified version of this view, see:
Jeff McMahan, "The Comparative Badness for Animals of Suffering and Death," in Tatjana Višak and Robert Garner, eds., *The Ethics of Killing Animals* (Oxford: Oxford University Press, 2015): 65–85.

37 For more on the replaceability argument, see:
Tatjana Višak, "Do Utilitarians Need to Accept the Replaceability Argument?" in Tatjana Višak and Robert Garner, eds., *The Ethics of Killing Animals* (Oxford: Oxford University Press, 2015): 117–135.
Shelly Kagan, "Singer on Killing Animals," in Tatjana Višak and Robert Garner, eds., *The Ethics of Killing Animals* (New York: Oxford University Press, 2015): 136–154.

38 For more on the idea of how eating animals shapes our perceptions and conceptions of them, see:
Cora Diamond, "Eating Meat and Eating People," *Philosophy* 53, no. 206 (October 1978): 465–479.

39 For a relational account of dignity that inspires the account sketched here, see:
Lori Gruen, "Dignity, Captivity, and an Ethics of Sight," in Lori Gruen, ed., *The Ethics of Captivity* (New York: Oxford University Press, 2014): 231–247.

40 We will focus in these comparisons on free-range animal agriculture that produces animal products. Farms that use animals as part of agriculture, but that do not produce animal products, are closer to what we are calling plant-based agriculture for our purposes here.

41 For more on the ethics of hunting, see:

Gary Comstock, "Subsistence Hunting," in Steve Sapontzis, ed., *Food for Thought: The Debate over Eating Meat* (New York: Prometheus Books, 2004): 359–370.

Gary Varner, "Environmental Ethics, Hunting, and the Place of Animals," in Tom Beauchamp and R.G. Frey, eds., *The Oxford Handbook of Animal Ethics* (Oxford: Oxford University Press, 2015): 855–876.

42 For more on the ethics of plant-based and cultured meat, see:

Brianne Donaldson and Christopher Carter, *The Future of Meat without Animals* (London: Rowman & Littlefield, 2016).

Jeff Sebo, "The Ethics and Politics of Plant-based and Cultured Meat," in *Les Ateliers de l'éthique/The Ethics Forum* (forthcoming).

9   The ethics of food consumption

9.1 Introduction

This chapter will examine the ethics of food consumption. If a particular industry causes unnecessary harm to humans, nonhumans, and the environment, is it morally wrong to support that industry as a consumer? And, how much, if at all, does the answer to this question depend on the degree to which we make a contribution to that system or have other options? We will start by considering arguments for ethical consumption as well as the kinds of ethical diets people take these arguments to support. We will then consider the two main objections to arguments for ethical consumption: the futility objection, according to which ethical consumption does not make a difference, and is therefore not morally required, and the demandingness objection, according to which ethical consumption is very demanding, and is therefore not morally required. Along the way we will consider many costs and benefits of different kinds of ethical consumption.

This topic tends to receive more attention than the ethics of food production. One reason is that everyone is a consumer whereas only some people are producers. Another reason is that food consumption is a central part of life. Eating is an activity around which many of our private relationships, as well as many of our public traditions, are centered. It reflects who we are and who we aspire to be in many ways. So, on one hand, it is easy to see why people would call for dietary change. On the other hand, it is also easy to see why people would resist calls for dietary change. It is therefore important that we take the ethics of food consumption seriously, no matter what our starting point in this discussion happens to be.

9.2 Arguments for ethical consumption

We can start by considering arguments for ethical consumption, as well as the kinds of ethical diets that people take these arguments to support.

First, a Kantian might argue for ethical consumption in the following kind of way:

1   We are morally required not to perform actions that (a) cannot be willed as universal laws or (b) do not treat everyone as an end.

2   Supporting harmful food systems when other, less harmful food systems are available to us (a) cannot be willed as a universal law and (b) does not treat everyone as an end.

3   Therefore, we are morally required not to support harmful food systems when other, less harmful food systems are available to us.[1]

Similarly, a utilitarian might argue for ethical consumption in the following kind of way:

1   We are morally required not to cause unnecessary harm.

2   Supporting harmful food systems when other, less harmful food systems are available to us causes unnecessary harm, all else equal.

3   Therefore, we are morally required not to support harmful food systems when other, less harmful food systems are available to us, all else equal.[2]

These arguments appear to have radical implications for food consumption. In particular, they appear to imply that many people are acting wrongly multiple times per day. Granted, we might think that these arguments allow for exceptions, for example in cases where (a) you can eat a harmful food product without supporting the system that produced it (e.g., if you dumpster dive for meat), (b) you need to eat a harmful food product because you do not have access to other, less harmful options (e.g., if you have health or economic needs that limit your options), or (c) you need to eat a harmful food product for the greater good (e.g., if you are working undercover at a factory farm). We will consider these and other possible exceptions later on. However, even if we grant that these arguments allow for exceptions in many cases, we might still think that they have revisionary implications for many other cases. In particular, we might think that in many ordinary cases, people who eat harmful food products *are* supporting the systems that created them, and are *not* eating these products out of necessity or for the greater good. If so, these Kantian and utilitarian arguments would be calling this behavior into question.

What about virtue, care, or relational theories? This depends on how we interpret these theories. As we discussed in previous chapters, a virtue theorist might think that eating harmful food products can help you to express some virtues (such as gratitude to the host of your meal) but not others (such as respect or compassion for the individuals harmed in this food system). Similarly, a care or relational theorist might think that eating harmful food products makes sense in light of some of your relationships (such as your personal relationships) but not in light of others (such as your broader entanglement with the individuals harmed by the food systems that you participate in). If so, then a virtue, care, or relational ethicist will have to ask which considerations take priority in which situations. For example, if a colleague invites you over for dinner, does it matter more that you express gratitude to your host by eating the food they serve or that you express respect and compassion for the victims of factory farming by refusing to do so? Similarly, if your family is celebrating a cultural holiday, does it matter more that you honor your culture by eating a traditional meal or that you honor the individuals who suffer as a result of this tradition by not doing so?[3]

Moreover, and more importantly, if this kind of conflict occurs regularly, a virtue, care, or relational theorist will step back and ask what, if anything, they can do to reduce the frequency or intensity of this kind of conflict (and, a Kantian or utilitarian who thinks structurally might do the same). In particular, when it comes to practices or traditions that harm others, we can ask if this harm is *essential* or *incidental* to these practices. In cases where harm is essential to these practices, we can ask: How can we *resolve* that conflict? That is, should we *preserve* or *replace* this practice, in light of the harm that it causes? And, in cases where harm is incidental to these practices, we can ask: How can we *dissolve* this conflict? That is, how can we *reform* this practice to make it less harmful? Without attempting to answer these questions here, we can note three things. First, as the history of social progress shows, it often makes more sense to try to reform or replace harmful practices than to try to preserve them. Second, the people who are best positioned to make these changes are typically cultural insiders, not cultural outsiders. Third, the more diverse, equitable, and inclusive the food, animal, environmental movements become, the more capable they will be of supporting people in bringing about meaningful cultural changes. (We will consider the value of diversity, equity, and inclusion for social movements in more detail in Chapter 10.)[4]

There are also many kinds of ethical diets that people take these arguments to support. Here are some examples.

Conscientious omnivorism. On this diet, we consume animal products only if the production methods meet certain strict ethical standards. For example, some conscientious omnivores eat free-range meat but not factory farmed meat, since, they think, free-range meat is better for animals and the environment than factory farmed meat is. As we have seen, conscientious omnivores can debate where to draw the line between "good enough" and "not good enough." But what unites them is the belief that we can produce animal products in an ethical way, and that at least some producers are doing so. We can question these beliefs, however. For example, as we saw in the last chapter, even if many free-range farms harm animals and the environment less than factory farms do, they might still harm animals and the environment more than other types of food production. If so, then support for free-range farms might still stand in need of ethical justification.[5]

Reducetarianism. On this diet, we aim to reduce consumption of animal products rather than completely eliminate them from our diets. For example, some reducetarians allow themselves to eat meat, dairy, or eggs once a day, or week, or month, but no more than that. As with conscientious omnivores, reducetarians can debate how much reduction is enough in particular cases. But what unites them is the belief that ethical consumption is not an all-or-nothing matter, since, they think, reducing our contribution to harm still makes a difference, and many people find reduction easier to commit to than elimination, especially at first. But as with conscientious omnivorism, we can question these beliefs. For example, some critics note that people who consume less of one animal might simply consume more of another animal as a result, thereby causing as much if not more harm than before.[6] Other critics note that most of us would not regard people as morally permitted to reduce rather than eliminate other kinds of unnecessary harm. ("Matt is a reducetarian bully who limits himself to beating up one kid a week. Go Matt!"). If this is right, then, as before, we need to examine what, if anything, might justify different moral stances toward reduction and elimination in different contexts.[7]

Pescetarianism. On this diet, we consume *aquatic* animal products but not *terrestrial* animal products. Some pescetarians are motivated by the idea that, whereas terrestrial animals such as chickens, cows, and pigs are sentient (i.e., capable of feeling pain), aquatic animals such as salmons, lobsters, and shrimps are not. In the case of vertebrates such as salmons, this assumption is now widely discredited.[8] But in the case of invertebrates such as lobsters and shrimps, it is still an open question whether they are sentient, which raises questions about risk and uncertainty that we considered in Chapter 3.[9] Other pescetarians are motivated by the idea that fishes are wild caught, and that wild caught animals have better lives than farmed animals. Yet this assumption is now widely discredited too, given that (a) wild caught fishing causes more harm to wild animals than many think, since modern fishing practices kill hundreds of billions of animals annu-ally, not only as means but also as side-effects, (b) wild caught fishing causes more environmental harm than many think, since modern fishing practices disrupt species and ecosystems on a massive scale, and (c) aquaculture—i.e., fish farm-ing—is rapidly expanding, and is replicating many of the welfare, health, and environmental harms of terrestrial animal agriculture.[10]

Vegetarianism. On this diet, we consume animal byproducts such as dairy and eggs but not animal products such as meat. Some vegetarians are motivated by the idea that we cannot make meat without harming animals, whereas we can make eggs and dairy without harming animals. Others are motivated by the idea that eating meat harms animals more than eating eggs or dairy does, since a given animal can produce less food by way of flesh than by way of eggs or dairy. These ideas might sometimes be true. However, they are not always true. First, as we have seen, industrial egg and milk production does result in unnecessary pain, suffering, and death for the animals involved. Free-range egg and milk production often does too. Second, if our aim is to selectively and strategically consume animal products that limit harm to animals and the environment, there are other and better ways of doing this. For example, a pescetarian, reducetarian, or conscientious omnivorous diet involving bivalves and no other animal products causes less harm overall than a vegetarian diet involving eggs and dairy and no other animal products.

Veganism. On this diet, we do not consume animal products or byproducts at all. As with conscientious omnivores, vegans debate where to draw the line. For exam-ple, they debate whether or not to eat items that contain trace amounts of animal products, or whether or not to eat products that exist at the border of the animal/non-animal divide such as cultured meat. They also debate whether or not vegans can make the kinds of principled exceptions considered above, such as eating meat out of necessity or for the greater good. Finally (though there are other examples as well), they also debate whether veganism is a diet or an ethical practice. That is, should we think of vegan as a diet that one can practice regardless of why? Or should we think of veganism as an aspiration to resist oppression in all forms, not only through our diets but also through other parts of our lives? These issues, along with issues about futility and demandingness that we will consider below, can make veganism difficult to comprehend, let alone live up to.[11]

Fruitarianism. On this diet, we do not harm or kill any living organism for food. For example, on some fruitarian diets, we cannot permissibly pluck fruit from a tree or pull root vegetables from the ground, since doing so harms or kills the relevant living organisms. Some fruitarians are motivated by the idea that all living beings are sentient, and others are motivated by the idea that all living beings have interests whether or not they are sentient, as we saw in Chapter 4. We might disagree with either or both of these claims. But if we do not, then we need to take this position seriously. We might also think that fruitarianism raises concerns about futility and demandingness even more than veganism does. How can we live at all, to say nothing of living in the context of our current social, political, and economic structures, if we allow ourselves so few ways of consuming food? We will consider how compelling this kind of concern is below.[12]

Local food. On this diet, we prioritize local food wherever possible. Some locavores are motivated by a sense of community, which can be good insofar as it supports our own community, but bad insofar as it directs support away from other communities who need it more. Of course, many people do have a preference for helping relatively well off people in their own community instead of relatively badly off people in other communities, which raises questions about the relevance of distance in space and time that we considered in Chapter 4, and that we will consider again later on. Other locavores are motivated by a concern for the health and environmental impacts of conventional food, which can be good insofar as local food is better for health and the environment and bad insofar as it is not (since, as we have seen, transportation accounts for only about 11% of the carbon footprint of the food that we eat[13]).[14]

Organic Food. On this diet, we prioritize organic food whenever possible. Some organic eaters are motivated by a preference for natural food. As we saw in Chapter 2, this raises questions about what counts as natural and why we should think that natural things are better than non-natural things all else equal. It also raises questions about whether, now that we live in the Anthropocene or Capitalocene, there is a meaningful distinction between natural things and non-natural things at all anymore. Other organic eaters are motivated by a concern for the health and environmental impacts of conventional food, which can be good insofar as organic food is better for health and the environment and bad insofar as it is not (since, as we have seen, many organic products are good and many organic products are bad, depending on the product as well as on the context, so we have to consider this issue on a case-by-case basis).[15]

Freeganism. On this diet, we can eat anything we like as long as we do not socially or economically support harmful food systems in the process. Thus, for example, many freegans are opposed to purchasing meat, dairy, and eggs (or making others more likely to do so). But if they can eat these products without purchasing them (and without making others more likely to do so), for example by dumpster diving or eating roadkill, then they are happy to do so. (Before you get too grossed out, keep in mind that freegans generally have high standards regarding food safety and multiple procedures in place to ensure that their food meets those standards.) One question that freegans have to ask is: Are they taking food away from other humans or nonhumans who need it more? Another is: Does eating animals perpetuate the idea of animals as commodities whether or not we purchase them? We will consider these issues in more detail below.[16]

Many of these ethical diets are compatible with each other, and a given person in a given situation might think that they should combine them in various ways. For example, you might think that you should eat local, organic, *and* vegan food. Or you might think that you should *purchase* local, organic, vegan food and adopt a freegan diet otherwise. Or, you might take a reducetarian stance toward some aspects of your diet, for example, by eating local and organic food sometimes but not all the time, and take a strict stance toward other aspects of your diet, for example, by eating vegan food whenever possible. Or you might make up your own, novel diet, whether or not it has a name. As we will discuss below and in the next chapter, you might also make a distinction between the diet you *adopt* and the diet you *advocate*: For example, you might adopt a vegan diet because you see this diet as morally required, but then you might also advocate for other, less demanding diets in certain contexts because you calculate that such advocacy is more likely to be effective in those contexts.

As our brief descriptions of these diets suggest, there is a tension that we all need to grapple with when thinking about ethical consumption. In particular, some of the diets on this list, such as conscientious omnivorism, reducetarianism, and pescetarianism, might seem easy to live up to, but they might also seem to fall short of our general ethical standards (again, most of us reject the idea that we can reduce rather than eliminate other kinds of unnecessary harm). Whereas other diets on this list, such as veganism, fruitarianism, and freeganism, might seem to cohere with our general ethical standards, but they might also seem hard to live up to. Meanwhile, certain other diets on this list, such as vegetarianism, local food, and organic food, might seem to be somewhere in the middle depending on availability, affordability, and other factors, which could mean these diets strike a good balance—or could mean that these diets are a half-measure.

We will now consider the two main objections to arguments for ethical consumption, starting with the futility objection and then turning to the demandingness objection.

9.3 Futility and cluelessness

First, consider the **futility objection** to arguments for ethical consumption, which is related to the cluelessness objection to utilitarianism that we considered in Chapter 3. According to this objection, ethical consumption does not make a difference, and is therefore not morally required. Most food corporations are massive: They produce food for millions of people per year and make billions of dollars per year, and they measure success and failure on a correspondingly large scale. So, while they might be responsive to the consumption patterns of entire populations, they are not responsive to the consumption patterns of particular individuals. Thus, your decision whether to order a hamburger or a veggie burger for lunch today will not make any difference at all as to how many animals are harmed or killed, how many resources are consumed, how much pollution is produced, and so on. So why not just get what you want?

How should we evaluate this objection? We should evaluate it the same way as other collective action problems, that is, cases in which our behavior seems to have good results individually but bad results collectively. First, we might say that eating harmful food products is wrong only if it makes a difference, that it does not make a difference, and therefore that it is not wrong. This is what utilitarians who are pessimistic about our individual impacts might say. Second, we might say that eating harmful food products is wrong *whether or not* it makes a difference. This is what Kantians, virtue theorists, care theorists, and relational theorists might say, at least in some cases. Third, we might say that eating harmful food products is wrong only if it makes a difference, that it does make a difference, and therefore that it is wrong. This is what utilitarians who are optimistic about our impacts as individuals might say. In this section, we will unpack the first and third options by considering the kinds of impacts that ethical food consumption might or might not be having.[17] (Of course, even if you accept the second option, you might still see these impacts as morally relevant whether or not you see them as morally decisive.)

First, consider the **economic impact** of our consumption choices. When we "vote with our wallet," does the market register our vote? Some people think that it does. For example, Shelly Kagan argues that simple cost-benefit analysis shows that we should proceed on the assumption that we make a difference. Kagan admits that it might not be the case that for every chicken you buy, that causes another chicken to be killed. It might instead be the case that for every 50 or 100 chickens people buy, that will cause another 50 or 100 chickens to be killed (since it might be that a farm increases production by 50 or 100 chickens for every 50 or 100 chickens sold, instead of increasing production by one chicken for every chicken sold). But Kagan thinks that this complication is irrelevant. Why? Because recall that when you are unsure if a particular action will cause harm, cost-benefit analysis instructs you to multiply the *probability* that your action will cause harm by the *level* of harm that it would cause if it did, and to treat the product of this equation as the amount of harm that it will actually cause. How does that apply to this case? Well, you know that whenever you buy a chicken, there is a $\frac{1}{n}$ chance that your purchase will cause n chickens to be killed (e.g., a $\frac{1}{50}$ chance that it will cause 50 chickens to be killed or a $\frac{1}{100}$ chance that it will cause 100 chickens to be killed). And of course, for all n, $\frac{1}{n} \times n = 1$.

Thus, Kagan argues, you rationally ought to proceed on the assumption that for every chicken you buy, that will cause another chicken to be killed.[18]

Kagan grants that there can be exceptions to this rule. For example, if you have insider knowledge about how a particular restaurant or supermarket operates, then you might know for a fact whether or not a particular purchase of chicken will cause more chickens to be killed.[19] And, of course, some cases of freegan meat consumption might constitute exceptions as well, for example if you dumpster dive for food, or if you eat food that your roommate left in the fridge before they took a long trip. There are further complications as well. For example, some farmed animals, such as chickens and fishes, are relatively small. Others, such as pigs and cows, are relatively large. This complicates our math because the larger an animal is, the more meals their body will provide. Thus, the expected animal welfare impacts of purchasing a typical chicken or fish meal might be worse than the expected animal welfare impacts of purchasing a typical cow or pig meal, all else equal (though, the expected environmental impacts might be the reverse, given the special role that cows play in climate change). A similar point applies to the purchase of eggs or dairy as opposed to flesh. Still, if Kagan is right, then in all cases the basic math is the same, that is, for every food product you buy, you should expect that your purchase will cause another, similar food product to be created in the future (and, therefore, that it will cause all the impacts that come along with the creation of that food product).

However, not everybody accepts this argument. For example, Mark Budolfson argues that the real world is not as simple as Kagan is imagining. Yes, in an ideal food system, there would be a 1:1 ratio between demand and supply. However, our industrial food system is not anywhere close to ideal. Instead, there is slack at every stage in the process, as a result of waste, imprecise measurement, and other such factors. Also, consumer demand is only one of many inputs that factor into decisions about supply, since producers also consider taxes, subsidies, production costs, and more. As a result, Budolfson argues, the expected harm caused by purchasing a typical factory farmed meal might be lower than Kagan is imagining. In fact, Budolfson argues, the expected harm caused by purchasing a typical factory farmed meal might even be lower than the expected harm caused by purchasing a typical free-range farmed meal. Why? Because, even though *production* of a typical factory farmed meal causes more harm than *production* of a typical free-range farmed meal, the *purchase* of a typical factory farmed meal is less likely to benefit that farm than the *purchase* of a typical free-range farmed meal is. So, when we multiply level of harm and probability of harm on the consumption side, we might discover that we can expect to do less harm by purchasing typical factory farmed products than by purchasing typical free-range farmed products overall, economically speaking.[20]

If Budolfson is right, does this mean that we rationally ought to expect that purchasing typical factory farmed products will have no economic impact at all? Not necessarily. However, it does mean that we need to think about the economic impact of ethical consumption in a nuanced way. On one hand, if we think that we have enough information about probabilities and utilities to do cost-benefit analysis in a reliable way, then we can do that. For example, we might think that instead of simply expecting that for every food product we buy, that will cause another, similar food product to be produced, we should use different ratios for different food products. For instance, maybe we can say that for every *five* free-range farmed products we buy, that will cause another, similar free-range farmed product to be produced, and that for every 50 factory farmed products we buy, that will cause another, similar factory farmed product to be produced. In this case, the question then becomes whether the benefits of five free-range farmed meals or 50 factory farmed meals outweigh the harm of causing one such meal to be produced. (Of course, this is prior to factoring in further effects of consumption, including indirect economic effects.) On the other hand, if we do not think that we have enough information about probabilities and utilities to do cost-benefit analysis in a reliable way, then we can switch to a different decision procedure, such as a precautionary principle that instructs us to err on the side of caution.[21]

Consider next the **social impact** of our consumption choices. We do not purchase and consume food in a social vacuum. At least, we do not always do so. Instead, we often purchase and consume food in the presence of family, friends, neighbors, colleagues, and so on. Thus, if you engage in ethical consumption, this practice will often have social benefits. For example, people in your life might accommodate you by preparing food that you can eat, or by going to restaurants that you can eat at. In some of these cases, they might also eat the same kind of food as you. And in the case of intimate, long-term relationships such as romantic relationships, the cumulative effect of this accommodation might be very big indeed: For instance, if a vegan marries an omnivore, it is likely that the omnivore will eat *many more* vegan meals over the course of their relationship than they would have otherwise, simply as a result of the need for compromise and coordination around food. If so, then even if the *direct* economic impact of our consumer behavior is low, the *indirect* economic impact of our consumer behavior is potentially higher.

A related social benefit of ethical consumption is that we might persuade other people to engage in ethical consumption as well, not only in the spirit of accommodation, but also in the spirit of reducing or eliminating support of harmful food systems. In some cases, this might happen because we actively advocate around our ethical stance (in which case our consumer choices might contribute to this advocacy by signaling how committed we are). But in other cases, it might happen as a result of natural social dynamics. For example, if you make your dietary restrictions clear to people, then some people will ask you about them, thereby providing you with a natural opportunity to share information and arguments with them. And while not everybody will be persuaded by what you say, some people might be. So, suppose that the average vegan creates five vegans over the course of their life (and then these five vegans do the same, and then these 25 vegans do the same, and so on down the line). In this case, even if the direct economic impact of our consumer behavior is low, the indirect economic impact of our consumer behavior is potentially *very* high.

Granted, one might object that many of these social effects result from our *claiming* to adopt a certain diet, not from our *actually* adopting that diet. Thus, for example, you could abstain from animal products around people you know, while still buying the occasional Bic Mac when no one is looking, and you could have about the same social impact as if you abstained entirely. This is true as far as it goes. But note two things. First, you never know when people are looking. (We should take care not to overestimate our social influence, but we should also take care not to underestimate it.) Second, as we will discuss in a moment, sneaking the occasional Big Mac when no one is looking can have harmful psychological impacts: For instance, you might experience anxiety as a result of leading a "double life," and you might find yourself tempted to eat meat more often than you otherwise would. So, while at least some moral theorists, such as utilitarians, are open to the possibility of ethical hypocrisy in principle, they often advise against it in practice.

Of course, there can be social risks to ethical consumption as well. One social risk is that we can alienate or offend people. For example, if someone invites you over for a meal, and then you decline the food they offer you on moral grounds, you risk creating conflict in your relationship. This risk is exacerbated by the fact that many people have negative associations with ethical consumption. For example, many people see vegans as elitist or militant (perceptions which are sometimes but not always earned, as we will discuss later on). However, we can reply to this concern in two ways. First, there are ways to mitigate this risk. For example, if you take a conciliatory rather than confrontational approach to conversation about ethical consumption, you can mitigate risk of alienation or offense, and you might even disrupt some of the negative associations that lead to alienation or offense in the first place. Second, to the degree that ethical consumption carries these risks, the long-term benefits might outweigh the short-term risks. After all, sometimes resisting injustice requires making people feel uncomfortable. When it does, we should perhaps be willing to make people feel uncomfortable.[22] (We will consider conciliatory and confrontational activism further in Chapters 10 and 11.)

Another, related social risk of ethical consumption is that, as we have seen, it can interfere with our cultural or religious identities. For example, if you reject certain kinds of foods on ethical grounds, then many of the people in your life might experience you as rejecting your social identity, and you might experience yourself as doing that too. But as we have discussed, this kind of conflict is an inevitable consequence of any form of social progress. Everyone, in every generation, discovers that their ancestors made moral mistakes that they have a duty not to repeat. The challenge, then, is to find creative ways to evolve: to revise and replace harmful cultural and religious practices in ways that allow us to honor our social identities while at the same time honoring the victims of past interpretations of these social identities. In short, if we care about both the past and the future, then our task is *not* to make the future match the past at all costs, but is *rather* to make the future similar to the past in socially relevant ways and different from the past in morally relevant ways. (We will consider reform and revolution further in Chapters 10 and 11 as well.)

Consider next the **psychological impact** of ethical consumption. As we saw in our discussion of virtue, care, and relational theory in Chapter 3, we are not fully rational agents who always make decisions by deliberating about what we have most reason to believe, desire, and do. Instead, our actions play a role in shaping our habits, and our habits play a role in shaping our actions.[23] So, one reason to engage in ethical consumption (and to take a relatively strict approach to ethical consumption) is that anything less than that makes it difficult to develop the relevant habits, and so to live up to the relevant ideals in the hustle and bustle of everyday life. Some people criticize conscientious omnivorism, reducetarianism, and freeganism for this reason, stating that if we allow ourselves to eat meat at all, then we will likely end up eating meat more often than we should. If this is right, then we might think that we should avoid such diets not because eating meat is always wrong in and of itself, but rather because it prevents us from developing habits that would lead us to act rightly in general.

Cora Diamond, Lori Gruen, and other philosophers make a related point, which is that when we eat animals, we place them in the psychological **category of the edible**.[24] This means that we condition ourselves to perceive them as *to-be-consumed* rather than as *not-to-be-consumed*, with implications for our behavior in a wide range of contexts, including food, research, education, entertainment, and more. As Diamond points out (and as we pointed out in the last chapter, in our discussion of dignity), this is part of why we have a nearly universal taboo against eating human flesh: We refuse to eat each other at least in part because this stance reinforces our perception of each other as *fellow persons*, that is, as individuals with whom we have relationships and to whom we have responsibilities.[25] If this is right, perhaps we should adopt a nearly universal taboo against eating animal flesh for the same kind of reason. Does this extend to plant-based and cultured meat too? As we discussed in the last chapter, that depends in part on what kind of effect, if any, eating such products has on our conceptions, perceptions, and treatment of human and nonhuman animals.

Ethical consumption can have other, related psychological benefits as well. Most of us live in social, political, and economic systems that create psychological distance between consumer behavior and its effects. In the case of industrial animal agriculture, many of the worst harms are either hidden from consumers (both physically, through restricted access to factory farms and slaughterhouses, and psychologically, through language that describes animals as "it" and animal flesh as "meat") or too diffuse and far away for consumers to directly perceive.[26] Yet we evolved to respond to harms that we can directly perceive, not harms that we have to read about in a book.[27] As a result, ethical consumption can be a way to regularly remind ourselves of the reality of harmful systems that stand in need of resistance. A related benefit is that when we participate in harmful systems, we can develop biases in favor of these systems as a result of status quo bias, sunk cost reasoning, a desire to see ourselves as virtuous, and more. Thus, for example, if you eat factory farmed meat, then you might have a tendency to evaluate arguments in favor of factory farming more charitably than arguments against factory farming, in light of your complicity in this system. Given this possibility, ethical consumption can be a way to remove ourselves from harmful systems enough to reliably see them for what they are.

Of course, there can be psychological risks to ethical consumption as well. First, ethical consumption can lead to (or exacerbate) an obsession with personal purity, which can bring about multiple harms. One is that it can contribute to eating disorders such as **orthorexia**, which is an unhealthy obsession with healthful diets.[28] Another is that it can contribute to burnout, with the result that we backslide into standard consumer behavior.[29] Another is that, even if we manage to avoid burnout, we might still find ourselves spending so much time and energy on consumer activism that we have nothing left over for other kinds of activism.[30] Does this mean that we should all keep eating factory farmed meat? Not at all. But it does mean that we should keep perspective. What matters is that we do the best we can in general, not that we do the best we can as consumers in particular. So, if we do engage in ethical consumption, we should make sure that we do so in a healthy and sustainable way, and in a way that supports rather than undermines our other, more general efforts to make the world a better place. We will examine this point further later on.

Second, and relatedly, ethical consumption can lead to bias in the same kind of way that standard diets can. For example, ethical consumption can lead to a **moral licensing effect**, which is the tendency to see what one is currently doing as all one needs to be doing in order to be a good person.[31] Relatedly, it can lead us to see people who engage in consumer activism (but not other kinds of activism) as more virtuous than people who engage in other kinds of activism (but not consumer activism), all else equal. As before, does this mean that we should all keep eating factory farmed meat? Not at all. But also as before, it does mean that we need to keep perspective. We can all do better in many respects, and many kinds of activism are compatible with each other. So, we should try to make our moral assessments more consistent than they sometimes are. In particular, we should try to either (a) be less patient with ourselves for the ways in which we fall short, (b) be more patient with others for the ways in which they fall short, or, more plausibly, (c) strike a balance between these extremes (keeping in mind contextual factors that make every choice situation different, of course).[32] We will examine this point further later on as well.

When you add up all these possible impacts, what follows? That depends on which moral theory we accept, as well as on what your life is like in general. All we can say in the abstract is that, as we each ask this question of ourselves, it is important that we think about these economic, social, and psychological impacts holistically, since they can interact in ways that make the whole greater than the sum of its parts. Thus, for example, if all you think about is the direct economic impact of what you buy for lunch today, you might feel the force of the futility objection a bit more. But if you think about how many different kinds of impacts might be interacting with each other within and across contexts, you might start to feel the force of this objection a bit less.

9.4 Partiality and demandingness

Second, consider the **demandingness objection** to arguments for ethical consumption. According to this objection, ethical consumption is very demanding, and is therefore not morally required. There are several related concerns here, about the *possibility* of boycotting harmful food systems, the *personal cost* involved in doing so, and the *political cost* involved in doing so. We will consider each in turn.

First, consider worries about the *possibility* of boycotting harmful food systems. In particular, we might worry that relatively few people in the world have the social, political, and economic privilege necessary to spend time, energy, and money researching, and then purchasing, only ethical products (or retreating from consumer society entirely without causing harm along the way). For example, the World Bank reports that, as of 2013, about 1 in 10 people still live under the international extreme poverty line of $1.90 per day.[33] Even in nations with developed industrial economies, many people live in food deserts, defined as areas with little access to healthful, affordable food, as well as in food swamps, defined as areas with a lot of access to unhealthful, affordable food. Many of these individuals also have other issues to contend with, including racism, sexism, ableism, classism, and a lack of educational and occupational opportunities that would allow them to easily change their situation. Moreover, even many of the people who are fortunate enough to be in the global 1 percent—estimated by World Bank economist Branko Milanovic as anyone with a salary of $34,000 or higher per year—might not be able to fully live up to this standard, especially if they have extra expenses and/or health problems that place additional constraints on their diet.[34] In light of these considerations, many people have, not unreasonably, expressed the concern that the ideal of ethical consumption is elitist, since it assumes a kind of privilege that very few people have, and then it holds everybody up to that standard.

If we share this worry, does that mean that we should reject ethical consumption as an ideal? Not necessarily. Instead, it might simply mean that we should conceptualize ethical consumption in an aspirational and contextual way. Lori Gruen and Robert Jones express this idea with what they call **aspirational veganism**. On this view, veganism is not a "universal norm to be imposed as a moral imperative" but rather a "process of doing the best one can to minimize violence, domination, and exploitation."[35] And, since the best one can do is a contextual matter, the demands of aspirational veganism are a contextual matter too. For example, in the same kind of way that we might think a food executive should do more than a food worker on the production side (since they have more power within the system and more options outside of the system), we might also think that a food executive should do more than a food worker on the consumption side (for the same reasons). Does this mean that, say, rich people have a moral obligation to boycott harmful products whereas poor people do not? Again, not necessarily. But it does mean that ethical consumption can and should mean different things for different people, and can only ever be an aspiration for any of us. As Gruen and Jones write:

> Vegans need to remain realistic about the ethical entanglements that accompany life in consumer culture . . . In contexts like ours, veganism can only be an aspiration. But even as an aspiration, veganism can make a difference in changing systematic cruelty and domination.[36]

We will return to this issue, and especially to the relationship between food activism and social justice, in the next chapter.

Second, consider worries about the *personal cost* involved in boycotting harmful food systems. Suppose that we *are* capable of boycotting harmful food systems. Is it really plausible that morality could require us to do this, given the personal cost involved for us? As we saw in Chapter 3, this is a controversial question. Many philosophers, especially Kantians and other deontologists, will say that there is a limit to how demanding morality can be. On this view, we might think that if we were to sacrifice all our interests for the sake of others, then we would be treating *ourselves* merely as means, and therefore we would be wronging ourselves. If so, then our task on this view is not to do as much good as possible, but rather to live and let live—to pursue our own ends in a way that allows others to do the same. What does this mean in practice? This is hard to say. On one hand, we might not be morally required to try to *prevent* as much unnecessary harm as possible (since these efforts could easily take over our entire lives). On the other hand, we might still be morally required to try to *cause* as little unnecessary harm as possible (since these efforts can still leave room for our own projects and relationships). For example, most of us would agree that you are not pursuing your ends in a way that allows others to do the same if you spend every weekend attending cock fights (after all, think about how many other, less harmful hobbies you could be pursuing!). Similarly, we might think, you are not pursuing your ends in a way that allows others to do the same if you spend every night eating chicken (after all, think about how many other, less harmful meals you could be eating!). Thus, even if Kantianism places limits on how demanding morality can be, we have at least some reason to think that these limits are compatible with the idea that many of us should be consuming much more ethically than we are.[37]

Meanwhile, many other philosophers, especially utilitarians and other consequentialists, will say that there is *not* a limit to how demanding morality can be. On this view, we have a moral obligation to maximize utility, and if we have to sacrifice our own interests in order to accomplish that aim, then so be it. However, as we discussed in Chapter 3, utilitarians are also quick to point out that, in practice, most of us do *not* have to sacrifice our own interests, at least not fully, in order to maximize utility. After all, we are not utility-maximizing machines. We are living, breathing human beings, with complicated social and psychological lives. So, if we really want to make a difference in the world, then we need to strike a balance between caring for ourselves and caring for others, so that we can do our work effectively and sustainably. What does this mean in practice? That will differ from person to person. But generally speaking, it means that we have to be realistic about social and psychological facts when thinking about how to structure our lives. For example, if you need to spend a certain amount of time each week cultivating personal and professional relationships so that you can be an effective advocate, then you should do so. Likewise, if you need to spend a certain amount of time each week having fun so that you can find the motivation and inspiration necessary for effective advocacy, then you should do so. (Though on this view, you should also resist the temptation to use the value of self-care as an excuse for indulging more than you need to.) Thus, even if utilitarianism does not place limits on what morality can require in theory, it does place limits on what morality can require in practice—though, as with Kantianism, we should expect that these limits are compatible with the idea that many of us should be consuming much more ethically than we are.[38]

Meanwhile, still other philosophers, especially virtue, care, and relational theorists (but also some Kantians and utilitarians) will say that it depends on the context.[39] They will also, as we indicated above, distinguish questions about how to *resolve* conflicts of value from questions about how to *dissolve* conflicts of value. First, when it comes to resolving conflicts of value, we will often be able to resolve them in ways that do not involve much personal sacrifice: For example, when your family is celebrating a holiday that involves eating animals, you can agree to attend, remind your family members about your veganism, and offer to bring a dish that you can eat. In many cases this will be enough to make everyone happy. However, we might not always be able to resolve conflicts this way. For example, in some cases (hopefully not many), you might find that some of your family members are resistant to any attempt to supplement or selectively participate in the planned meal. In this case you might need to be willing to allow a certain amount of tension into your relationships as you try to work through this issue (though you can still take a caring approach to these interactions, as we will see in the next chapter). Second, when it comes to dissolving conflicts of value, we can experiment with, and gravitate toward, new forms of life for which conflicts arise less often. As Richard Twine writes regarding so-called vegan killjoys:

> In performing a practice that attempts to *re*-construct happiness, pleasure and politics the vegan killjoy does what all politically willful killjoys attempt to do: create new meanings and practices that underline the shared joy in living outside and beyond social norms once thought fixed.[40]

It can feel liberating to do this work, but it can also involve personal sacrifice. After all, if dissolving conflicts in value requires bringing about social change, and if bringing about social change sometimes requires personal sacrifice, then dissolving conflicts in value sometimes requires personal sacrifice too.[41] We will consider this issue more in the next chapter.

Finally, consider worries about the *political cost* involved in boycotting harmful food systems. In particular, we might worry that consumer activism will distract us from other, more impactful kinds of activism. Partly for this reason,

Michael Maniates argues that individual consumer action is not only ineffective but counterproductive—ineffective because it does not make a difference and counterproductive because it takes time, energy, and money away from other, collective and political approaches that do make a difference. Why does Maniates make this claim? Part of the reason is that individual consumer action operates within the confines of our current economic system and the options currently available to us within that system. Thus, when we vote with our wallets, we send the wrong message to producers, that is, we send the message that we want *this* currently available option rather than *that* currently available option, instead of the message that we want different options or a different economic system altogether. As a result, Maniates argues against individual consumer action not because he thinks that we can permissibly do whatever we like with our time, energy, and money but, rather, because he thinks that we should be focusing on other kinds of activism instead. As he writes:

> Given our deepening alienation from traditional understandings of active citizenship, together with the growing allure of consumption-as-social-action, it is little wonder that at a time when our capacity to imagine an array of ways to build a just and ecologically resilient future must expand, it is in fact narrowing.[42]

What should we think about this political critique? First of all, what should we think about the critique that consumer activism is ineffective and counterproductive? As we saw above, this critique has merit in some cases. In particular, insofar as people take an unhealthy, unsustainable, or apolitical approach to consumer activism, this practice might indeed be taking resources away from other, more effective kinds of activism. However, insofar as people take a healthy, sustainable, and political approach to consumer activism, the opposite might be true: In these latter cases this practice might enhance rather than detract from other kinds of activism, for all the reasons we considered above. Second, and relatedly, what should we think about the critique that consumer activism sends the wrong message to producers? Depending on what our broader social, political, and economic analysis is, we might think that this critique has merit too. But even if we do, the upshot is not that consumer activism is ineffective and counterproductive all things considered. Instead, and at most, the upshot is that consumer activism has benefits as well as risks, and so if we do take this approach, we should make sure to do so in a way that maximizes the benefits and minimizes the risks, for example, by combining boycotts that seek to reduce harm within our current economic system with protests that seek to challenge the options currently available within this system and/or the system as a whole.[43] (Since this point raises broader questions about what kind of food system we should be aiming for and what kind of path we should take toward this goal, we will discuss it in more detail in the next chapter.)

Part of what this discussion reveals is that, if we frame these issues as a choice between individual consumer action and collective political action, we risk distorting the relevant issues. After all, not only is consumer activism compatible with other kinds of activism, but it is also relevantly similar to other kinds of activism, since they can all be done in more or less effective ways and they all raise questions about futility and demandingness. For example, yes, we can boycott harmful systems individually, but we can also boycott them collectively. Likewise, yes, we can protest harmful systems collectively, but we can also protest them individually. Moreover, no matter which of these activities we engage in, we still face questions about whether or not our individual participation in collective actions is too futile or demanding to be morally required. For instance, in the same kind of way that you can ask, "Does my participation in this boycott really make a difference?", you can also ask, "Does my participation in this protest really make a difference?" If this is right, then what we should take away from discussion of individual and collective action is *not* that we should engage in, say, boycotts instead of protests or protests instead of boycotts, but *rather* that we should try to engage in boycotts, protests, and everything else (a) collectively rather than individually wherever possible, and (b) in ways that enhance, rather than detract from, our efforts in other areas wherever possible.

With that said, even if consumer activism and other kinds of activism are *often* compatible, they are not necessarily *always* compatible. Even people with a lot of privilege in life have a limited amount of time, energy, and money, and we have a lot of worthwhile things we could be doing with these resources. In many cases consumer activism will be compatible with other good things we can be doing (especially if we resolve and dissolve conflicts in value in the ways discussed above), but in some cases it might not be (especially if we need to consume harmful food products for health or economic reasons, or if we need to consume harmful food products for the greater good). We will consider other kinds of activism that might or might not compete with consumer activism in particular cases in the next chapter. For now, we can simply make two points. First, to the degree that we face these trade-offs, they are not a reason to reject ethical consumption as an ideal. Instead, they are a reason to interpret this ideal aspirationally and contextually. Second, we should all be mindful of the possibility of bias. In particular, people who engage in consumer activism can sometimes see consumer activism as a more central part of making the world a better place than it is. And, people who consume harmful products can sometimes have the opposite bias.

Do arguments for ethical consumption extend beyond food, to other areas of life? If so, then that raises the stakes for the demandingness objection. In particular, it implies that we should be asking ethical questions regarding not only our food but also our clothes, phones, computers, transportation systems, home energy systems, and much more (since, after all, all of these areas of life provide us with opportunities to participate in more or less harmful industries or practices). Thus, one might pose the following challenge: If we accept that we have a moral obligation not to support harmful food systems when other, less harmful food systems are available, does that mean that we have similar moral obligations in these other areas of life too? If so, then morality is very demanding indeed, and moral trade-offs are everywhere.

We can respond to this attempt to extend arguments for ethical consumption in either of two ways. First, we can deny that arguments for ethical consumption extend to all other areas of life with the same force. Yes, there are many harmful systems in the world, and yes, we have a moral obligation not to support them all wherever possible. However, our moral obligation not to support harmful food systems is stronger than our moral obligation not to support many other harmful systems, since (a) harmful food systems cause more harm for humans, nonhumans, and the environment than many other harmful systems do, and (b) many people can reduce or eliminate support of harmful food systems more easily than they can with many other harmful systems (which is not to say that ethical food consumption is easy).

A second, compatible response is to accept that, to the degree that arguments for ethical consumption *do* extend to other areas of life with the same force, we should accept these arguments in these areas of life as well. Yes, there are many harmful systems in the world, and yes, it would be demanding for us to reduce or eliminate support of them wherever possible. It might even, as we saw above, require radical reimaginings of how we structure our individual and shared lives. However, none of this constitutes an objection to the idea that we have a moral obligation to aspire to do this work. Instead, it simply serves as a reminder that we should view ethical consumption aspirationally and contextually, and as part of a broader approach to making the world a better place.

This is why the claim that there is no ethical consumption under capitalism is potentially misleading. Yes, we might not be able to *eliminate* the harm that we cause through consumption in the modern world, but if we can at least *reduce* this harm (while also seeking to address it in other ways), that can still be ethically significant. Recall our discussion of tough choices in Chapter 3. If you have no choice but to cause either one death or five, is there a right thing for you to do? The idea that there is (you should do the lesser of these evils) has plausible implications in many cases. But if we accept it, then it implies that, even if every consumer option is at least somewhat harmful, if some consumer options are less harmful than others, then those are the options that we ought to select, all else equal.

Finally, and relatedly, one might attempt to cope with the demanding nature of ethical consumption through **moral offsetting**. This is the practice of compensating for bad things that we do with good things that we do. For example, you might offset your consumption of factory farmed meat, dairy, and eggs by donating to organizations that seek to abolish industrial animal agriculture. Or, you might offset your consumption of water and energy by donating to organizations that seek to conserve scarce natural resources. Or, you might offset your greenhouse gas emissions by donating to organizations that seek to mitigate or adapt to climate change. In each case, the rationale behind this practice is that, if you donate even a small amount of money each month to the relevant organization, then the good that you do through your philanthropy will compensate for the harm that you cause through your own consumption.

However, other people feel uncomfortable with moral offsetting. Yes, there are cases where moral offsetting seems appropriate, and where the rationale for offsetting seems to make sense. But there are also cases where moral offsetting seems inappropriate, and where the rationale for offsetting seems more like a rationalization. To return to our example above (regarding reducetarianism), it would not be appropriate for you to bully people at school, and then offset that behavior by donating to organizations that address bullying at schools. Instead, you have a moral obligation to avoid bullying people at school *whether or not* you donate to such organizations. So if moral offsetting is inappropriate in some cases, what makes it appropriate in others? And, if the answer is that moral offsetting is appropriate if and when harm is unavoidable, that raises the question whether all the harm we cause through our consumption is truly unavoidable.[44]

In light of all the issues that we have discussed throughout this chapter, some people might find it tempting to reject arguments for ethical consumption altogether, so that they can avoid having to deal with these issues and avoid feeling like hypocrites insofar as they fall short of living up to a demanding ideal. But as we have seen, this would be a mistake. An argument should stand or fall on its merits, not on what we have to gain or lose from its being true. Moreover, we should not make the perfect the enemy of the good. Whether or not we fully live up to our ideals, it is better to be inconsistently good than consistently bad.

9.5 Conclusion

No matter which moral theory we accept, there is no simple, universal conclusion to draw from our discussion in this chapter. Whether or not we have a moral obligation to avoid certain kinds of food depends on many factors, including individual resources and opportunities. But for many of us, given the harms that industrial animal agriculture causes and the opportunities that we have to be happy and healthy in life without supporting this food system, it is plausible to say that we have a moral obligation to avoid supporting this food system (and maybe to do much more than that). We will consider further questions about food activism in the next two chapters. As we do, we should keep in mind how our discussion of consumer activism here interacts with our discussion of other kinds of activism there.

Notes

1   For arguments along these lines, see:
    Tom Regan, *The Case for Animal Rights* (Berkeley: University of California Press, 2004).
    Christine Korsgaard, "A Kantian Case for Animal Rights," in Tatjana Višak and Robert Garner, eds., *The Ethics of Killing Animals* (Oxford: Oxford University Press, 2015): 154–177.
2   For an argument along these lines, see:
    Peter Singer, *Animal Liberation* (New York: Random House, 1975).
3   For more on the relationship between ethics, culture, and food, see:
    Christopher Ciocchetti, "Veganism and Living Well," *Journal of Agricultural and Environmental Ethics* 25, no. 3 (2012): 405–417.
    Alasdair Cochrane, *Animal Rights Without Liberation: Applied Ethics and Human Obligations* (New York: Columbia University Press, 2012): 181–202.

4 For a wonderful example of this kind of cultural analysis of veganism/vegan analysis of culture, see:

Margaret Robinson, "Intersectionality in Mi'kmaw and Settler Vegan Values," in Julia Feliz Brueck, ed., *Veganism in an Oppressive World: A Vegans of Color Community Project* (Sanctuary Publishers, 2017): 71–88.

V. "Winnie" Kaur, "Sikhi, Ecofeminism, and Technology: Rambling Reflections of an Intersectional Punjabi Vegan Feminist," in Julia Feliz Brueck, ed., *Veganism in an Oppressive World: A Vegans of Color Community Project* (Sanctuary Publishers, 2017): 105–120.

5 For more on conscientious omnivorism, see:

Peter Singer and Jim Mason, *The Ethics of What We Eat* (New York: Rodale Books, 2007): 83–186.

6 For more on the idea that reduction in consumption does not always lead to reduction in harm, see:

C.L. Wrenn and R. Johnson, "A Critique of Single-issue Campaigning and the Importance of Comprehensive Abolitionist Vegan Advocacy," *Food, Culture, and Society* 16, no. 4 (2013): 651–668.

7 For more on reducetarianism, see Brian Kateman, *The Reducetarian Solution* (New York: TarcherPerigee, 2017).

8 For more on pain in fishes, see:

Victoria Braithwaite, *Do Fish Feel Pain?* (Oxford: Oxford University Press, 2010).

9 For more on how to act in cases of uncertainty about whether or not animals feel pain, see:

Jeff Sebo, "The Moral Problem of Other Minds," *The Harvard Review of Philosophy*. Published online May 23, 2018. DOI: 10.5840/harvardreview20185913.

10 For more on the ethics of aquaculture, see:

Jennifer Jacquet, Jeff Sebo, and Max Elder, "Seafood in the Future: Bivalves Are Better," *Solutions* 8, no. 1 (2017): 27–32.

11 For an argument for aspirational veganism, see:

Lori Gruen and Robert Jones, "Veganism as an Aspiration," in Ben Bramble and Bob Fischer, eds., *The Moral Complexities of Eating Meat* (Oxford: Oxford University Press, 2015): 153–171.

For an argument for political veganism, see Julia Feliz Brueck, "Introduction," in Julia Feliz Brueck, ed., *Veganism in an Oppressive World: A Vegans of Color Community Project* (Sanctuary Publishers, 2017): 1–33.

12 For more on fruitarianism, see:

Essie Honiball and T.C. Fry, *I Live on Fruit* (Health Excellence Systems, 1990).

13 Christopher L. Weber and H. Scott Matthews, "Food-Miles and the Relative Climate Impacts of Food Choices in the United States," *Environmental Science & Technology* 42, no. 10 (2008): 3508–3513.

14 For more on local food, see:

James E. McWilliams, *Just Food: Where Locavores Get It Wrong and How We Can Truly Eat Responsibly* (New York: Little, Brown, and Co., 2009): 17–52.

Helena de Bres, "Local Food: The Moral Case," in Anne Barnhill, Mark Budolfson, and Tyler Doggett, eds., *Food, Ethics, and Society: An Introductory Text with Readings* (New York: Oxford University Press, 2017): 495–509.

15 For more on organic food, see:

James E. McWilliams, *Just Food: Where Locavores Get It Wrong and How We Can Truly Eat Responsibly* (New York: Little, Brown, and Co., 2009): 53–80.

Michael Pollan, *The Omnivore's Dilemma* (New York: Penguin, 2006): 134–184.

16 For more on the ethics of freeganism, see:

Donald Bruckner, "Strict Vegetarianism Is Immoral," in Ben Bramble and Bob Fischer, eds., *The Moral Complexities of Eating Meat* (Oxford: Oxford University Press, 2015).

Andy Lamey, "Review of the Moral Complexities of Eating Meat," *Between the Species* 20, no. 1 (2016): 133–146.

Thank you to Josh Milburn and Andy Lamey for these references.

17 For more on the ethics of futility from a Kantian perspective, see:

Eliot Michaelson, "A Kantian Response to Futility Worries?" in Anne Barnhill, Mark Budolfson, and Tyler Doggett, eds., *Food, Ethics, and Society: An Introductory Text with Readings* (New York: Oxford University Press, 2017): 215–218.

18 Shelly Kagan, "Do I Make a Difference?" *Philosophy & Public Affairs* 39, no. 2 (2011): 105–141, 121–127.

19 Shelly Kagan, "Do I Make a Difference?" *Philosophy & Public Affairs* 39, no. 2 (2011): 105–141, 127–128.

20 Mark Budolfson, "Is it Wrong to Eat Meat from Factory Farms? If So, Why?" in Ben Bramble and Bob Fischer, eds., *The Moral Complexities of Eating Meat* (Oxford: Oxford University Press, 2015): 80–98.

21 For a reply to Budolfson, see:

Eliot Michaelson, "Act Consequentialism and Inefficacy," in Anne Barnhill, Mark Budolfson, and Tyler Doggett, eds., *Food, Ethics, and Society: An Introductory Text with Readings* (New York: Oxford University Press, 2017): 210–215.

22 Thank you to Lauren Gazzola for helpful discussion on this point.

23 For more on the limits of human rationality, see:

Jeff Sebo, "Agency and Moral Status," *Journal of Moral Philosophy* 14, no. 1 (2017): 1–22.

24 For more on the idea of the category of the edible, see:

Cora Diamond, "Eating Meat and Eating People," *Philosophy* 53, no. 206 (1978): 465–479.

Lori Gruen, *Ethics and Animals: An Introduction* (New York: Cambridge University Press): 101–104.

25 Cora Diamond, "Eating Meat and Eating People," *Philosophy* 53, no. 206 (1978): 467–471.

26 For more on the concealing function of language, see:

Carol Adams, *The Sexual Politics of Meat: A Feminist-vegetarian Critical Theory* (London: Bloomsbury Publishing, 2015).

For more on distancing, see:

Thomas Princen, Michael Maniates, and Ken Conca, eds., *Confronting Consumption* (Cambridge: MIT Press, 2002).

27 For more on the evolution of morality, see:

Dale Jamieson, *Reason in a Dark Time* (New York: Oxford University Press, 2014): Chapter 5.

28 For more on orthorexia, see:

Christina Van Dyke, "Eat Y'self Fitter: Orthorexia, Health, and Gender," in Anne Barnhill, Mark Budolfson, and Tyler Doggett, eds., *The Oxford Handbook of Food Ethics* (New York: Oxford University Press, 2018): 553–571.

29 For more on burnout, see pattrice jones, *Aftershock: Confronting Trauma in a Violent World: A Guide for Activists and Their Allies* (New York: Lantern Books, 2007).

30 For more on possible conflicts between consumer activism and political activism, see:

Michael Maniates, "Individualization: Plant a Tree, Buy a Bike, Save the World?" in Thomas Princen, Michael Maniates, and Ken Conca, eds., *Confronting Consumption* (Cambridge: MIT Press, 2002): 43–66.

31 For more on moral licensing effects, see:

Uzma Khan and Ravi Dhar, "Licensing Effect in Consumer Choice," *Journal of Marketing Research* 43, no. 2 (2006): 259–266.

32 For more on the need for consistency in our moral evaluations, see:

Jeff Sebo, "Multi-issue Food Activism," in Anne Barnhill, Mark Budolfson, and Tyler Doggett, eds., *The Oxford Handbook of Food Ethics* (Oxford: Oxford University Press, 2018): 399–423.

33 "Understanding Poverty," The World Bank, www.worldbank.org/en/understanding-poverty.

34 Branko Milanovic, *The Haves and the Have-Nots: A Brief and Idiosyncratic History of Global Inequality* (New York: Basic Books, 2010): 169.

35 Lori Gruen and Robert C. Jones, "Veganism as an Aspiration," in Ben Bramble and Bob Fischer, eds., *The Moral Complexities of Eating Meat* (Oxford: Oxford University Press, 2015): 156.
    See also:
    Marti Kheel, "Vegetarianism and Ecofeminism: Toppling Patriarchy with a Fork," in Steve Sapontzis, ed., *Food for Thought: The Debate over Eating Meat* (Prometheus Books, 2004): 327–341.

36 Lori Gruen and Robert C. Jones, "Veganism as an Aspiration," in Ben Bramble and Bob Fischer, eds., *The Moral Complexities of Eating Meat* (Oxford: Oxford University Press, 2015): 168.

37 For a defense of the idea that there are limits on how demanding morality can be, see:
    Samuel Scheffler, *The Rejection of Consequentialism: A Philosophical Investigation of the Considerations Underlying Rival Moral Conceptions* (Oxford: Clarendon Press, 1994).

38 For a defense of the idea that there are no (or at least not many) limits on how demanding morality can be, see:
    Shelly Kagan, *The Limits of Morality* (Oxford: Clarendon Press, 1991).
    See also:
    Iason Gabriel, "The Problem with Yuppie Ethics," *Utilitas* 30, no. 1 (2018): 32–53.

39 For discussion from a feminist ethic of care perspective, see:
    Deane Curtin, "Toward an Ecological Ethic of Care," in Josephine Donovan and Carol Adams, eds., *The Feminist Care Tradition in Animal Ethics* (New York: Columbia University Press, 2007): 87–100.

40 Richard Twine, "Vegan Killjoys at the Table: Contesting Happiness and Negotiating Relationships with Food Practices," *Societies* 4, no. 4 (2014): 623–639, 638.
    Richard Twine, "A Practice Theory Framework for Understanding Vegan Transition," *Animal Studies Journal* 6, no. 2 (2017): 192–224.
    Richard Twine, "Materially Constituting a Sustainable Food Transition: The Case of Vegan Eating Practice," *Sociology* 52, no. 1 (2017): 166–181.

41 For more on virtue theory and consumer activism, see:
    Rosalind Hursthouse, "Applying Virtue Ethics to Our Treatment of the Other Animals," in Jennifer Welchman, ed., *The Practice of Virtue: Classic and Contemporary Readings in Virtue Ethics* (Indianapolis: Hackett Publishing, 2006): 136–155.

42 Michael Maniates, "Individualization: Plant a Tree, Buy a Bike, Save the World?" *Global Environmental Politics* 1, no. 3 (August 2001): 31–52, 51.

43 For more on the relationship between consumer activism and political activism, see:
    Kelly Witwicki, "Social Movement Lessons from the British Antislavery Movement: Focused on Applications to the Movement Against Animal Farming," Sentience Institute, www.sentienceinstitute.org/british-antislavery.

44 For more on moral offsetting, see:
    Amanda Askell and Tyler John, "Moral Offsetting," unpublished manuscript.

10 The ethics of legal food activism

10.1 Introduction

This chapter will examine the ethics of legal food activism. If a particular industry causes unnecessary harm to humans, nonhumans, and the environment, do we have a moral obligation to resist that industry through activism? We will start by discussing whether or not we have a moral obligation to engage in food activism. We will then discuss ethical questions that arise for food activists. For example, should we aspire to abolish or regulate industrial animal agriculture? And regardless of which goal we select, should we pursue this goal through characteristically radical activism (e.g., revolutionary and confrontational approaches) or through characteristically moderate activism (e.g., reformist and conciliatory approaches)?

Like the ethics of food production, the ethics of food activism does not receive as much attention as the ethics of food consumption. As before, one reason is that everyone is a consumer whereas only some people identify as activists. Another reason is that people already find the idea that we have a moral obligation not to support harmful industries unthinkable. Thus, the idea that we might have a moral obligation to *resist* harmful industries never even occurs to many people. Yet as we have seen, boycotts are only one possible response to harmful industries. And, many people reasonably worry that boycotts are not, in themselves, enough to bring about real change. If this is right, then questions about food ethics should not stop and start with (and perhaps should not even centrally concern) boycotts. Instead, they should cover a wide range of approaches, as well as a wide range of arguments for and against each approach.

Before we begin, two caveats. First, we will be using **food activism** in a wide sense that refers to any effort to bring about social, political, and economic change in our food system. This includes activities traditionally understood as activism (such as protest), advocacy (such as public speaking), philanthropy (such as donating money to nonprofit organizations), and none of the above (such as dinner conversation with family and friends).

Second, it is common for people to frame many of the debates that we will be discussing in binary, mutually exclusive terms (should we be abolitionists *or* regulationists, should we be revolutionaries *or* reformists, and so on). For the sake of clarity and simplicity, we will follow this convention when introducing some of the relevant issues. But one of the messages that we hope to convey is that reality is almost never this simple. We almost always have more than two options to choose from, and we might often find that seemingly incompatible approaches are compatible after all.

10.2 Cause selection

We can start by asking whether or not we have a moral obligation to engage in food activism that extends beyond ethical consumption. This breaks down into two related questions. Do we have a moral obligation to engage in activism in general? And, if so, do we have a moral obligation to engage in food activism in particular?

It might seem clear that the answer to these questions is no. As we said a moment ago, for many people the idea that we might have a moral obligation to eat local, organic, and/or vegan food if possible is unthinkable, to say nothing of the idea that we might have a moral obligation to do much more than that. So, with respect to activism in general many people think: Sure, it might be nice if we participated in a protest every now and then, but we are not morally required to do so. And with respect to food activism in particular many people think: If and when we do participate in a protest, we can advocate for any (just) cause we like, rather than having to advocate for a particular (just) cause, such as food justice.

However, we have reason to challenge both of these assumptions. First, we have reason to challenge the assumption that we are not morally required to participate in activism in general. To see why, consider a modified version of the argument that Peter Singer develops in his famous article "Famine, Affluence, and Morality."[1] Singer argues that, if we accept two plausible and widely accepted premises, then it follows that we have a moral obligation to spend much more time, energy, and money helping others than we currently do.

The first premise is that suffering and death are very bad. (Singer focuses on suffering and death that result from starvation, but we can expand this premise to include suffering and death in general.)

The second premise is that, if we can prevent very bad things from happening without sacrificing anything comparably morally significant (e.g., without causing very bad things to happen as a means or side-effect), then we are morally required to do so.

If we accept both of these premises (as, Singer thinks, most of us do and all of us should), then it follows that, if we can prevent suffering and death without sacrificing anything morally significant, then we are morally required to do so.

We considered two applications of this idea in Chapter 4, framed as rescue cases. As a reminder, the first case that we considered was: Suppose that you walk by a pond wearing a brand new $50 outfit, and you see a puppy drowning. If you do nothing, the puppy will drown. Are you morally required to save the puppy, even if doing so will ruin your brand new outfit? Many people think that the answer is yes, and Singer would say that his argument explains why this is correct. In particular, he would say, our intuition in this case is correctly responding to the fact that we morally ought to prevent very bad things from happening when we can do so without sacrificing anything comparably morally significant.

The second case that we considered in this section was: Suppose that you come home from school, and you find a letter informing you that if you send $50 to an effective animal advocacy organization, you can save or spare more than *100 animals* from suffering and dying. Do you have a moral duty to send them $50? Here many people think that the answer is no, and Singer would say that his argument explains why this is *incorrect*. In particular, he would say, our intuition in this case is incorrectly responding to the fact that (a) these animals are very far away from you and (b) you are not the only person who can help them (among other things).

Why does Singer advocate against considering distance or the number of other people who can help? First, he thinks, these considerations do not affect what kind of claim to assistance people have, all else equal. If you can save someone from suffering or death without sacrificing anything morally significant, then why should the fact that they live *here* instead of *there* or *then* instead of *now* affect your obligation to help? Likewise, why should the fact that others are capable of helping them too, but are clearly not interested in doing so, affect your obligation to help? The fact remains that you can help this individual without sacrificing anything of significance, and that if you decide not to help, everyone else will decide not to help too. This is what matters morally, according to Singer.[2]

Granted, we sometimes have reason to consider distance and the number of other people who can help in practice. For example, in cases where you can help people far away less effectively than you can help people nearby, you should help people nearby, all else equal. Similarly, in cases where you expect others to help people far away but not to help people nearby, you should help people nearby, all else equal. However, two points. First, this is not that kind of case. In this case, you can help people more effectively far away, and if you do not, no one else will. Second, even if we did have reason to consider distance and other helpers in this case, the implication would not be that you can do whatever you like. The implication would instead be that you should take a different approach to helping others.

As with arguments for ethical consumption in the last chapter, we might feel a certain kind of tension here, since we might find this argument plausible, yet we might also find the conclusion very demanding. However, note that Singer intentionally limits how demanding his conclusion is in two ways. First, this argument does not imply that we have a moral obligation to *maximize happiness*. Instead, it implies only that we have a moral obligation to *minimize suffering*. Second, this argument does not imply that we have a moral obligation to minimize suffering *by any means necessary*. Instead, it implies only that we have a moral obligation to minimize suffering *if we can do so without sacrificing anything comparably morally significant*.

Thus, for example, this argument implies that, if 100 puppies are suffering and you can reduce their suffering substantially with a $50 donation, then you should do so all else equal. But it does not imply that, if 100 puppies are happy and you can increase their happiness substantially with a $50 donation, then you should do so all else equal. Nor does it imply that, if 100 puppies are suffering and you can reduce their suffering substantially by torturing a puppy as a means to this end, then you should do so all else equal. Of course, if you are a utilitarian, then you might accept these further ideas too, at least in theory. But nothing about the argument that Singer is defending here requires you to do so. As a result, Singer hopes that his argument will be convincing to people no matter which moral theory they accept (though of course, different moral theorists will interpret this argument in different, more or less demanding ways).

What does this have to do with activism? The answer is simple: This argument has implications for much more than how we spend our money. It also has implications for how we spend our time and energy. In short, it implies that if we can prevent suffering and death without sacrificing anything comparably morally significant by engaging in activism, then we are morally required to engage in activism. And of course, most if not all of us (or at least, those of us with at least some discretionary time, energy, and money) likely *can* prevent suffering and death without sacrificing anything comparably morally significant by engaging in activism. Thus, this argument implies that most if not all of us (or at least, those of us with at least some discretionary time, energy, and money) are morally required to engage in activism.

This leads us to the second assumption that we can challenge, which is that we do not have a moral obligation to engage in food activism in particular. To see how we can challenge this assumption, consider debates about **cause selection** in activism. The question here is: Do we have a moral obligation to favor some just causes over others? Why or why not?

Many people think that the answer is yes. For example, **effective altruists** believe that we morally ought to use evidence and reason to prevent the most suffering we can. (Effective altruism is both an ethical framework and a social movement that applies this ethical framework to a wide range of issues.[3]) As William MacAskill puts the point, everyday life is like a state of emergency, and we should respond accordingly. For example, consider how a doctor should act in the aftermath of a hurricane. Many more people need treatment than she has the ability to treat. So how should she prioritize? She should triage, that is, she should prioritize cases where she can help people as effectively and efficiently as possible. So if she has to choose between someone with a serious injury and someone with a mild injury, she should prioritize the former individual all else equal. And if she has to choose between someone with a serious injury that she can easily treat and someone with a serious injury that she cannot easily treat, she should prioritize the former individual all else equal. This approach to priority setting will allow her to do much more good overall than she could otherwise do.[4]

Why does MacAskill think that everyday life is like a state of emergency? Because everyday life is a situation in which many individuals will suffer and die without our assistance—many more, in fact, than we will be able to assist. Thus, MacAskill believes that we, like the doctor, should prioritize cases where we can help people as effectively and efficiently as possible. In particular, we should decide which problems to focus on by asking three questions:

1 *Scale*: How bad is the problem?
2 *Neglectedness*: How neglected is the problem?
3 *Tractability*: How easily can we make progress on this problem?

For example, if you have to choose between donating to an organization that effectively and efficiently prevents children from suffering for years, on one hand, and an organization that ineffectively and inefficiently allows children to be happy for a day, on the other hand, then an effective altruist would say that you morally ought to support the former organization over the latter, for the same reason that the doctor morally ought to favor some patients over others.[5]

How does this framework apply to food ethics? Many effective altruists, including Singer and MacAskill, agree that industrial animal agriculture is a high priority cause area. After all, as we have seen, industrial animal agriculture causes suffering and death for 100+ billion nonhuman animals per year; consumes vast amounts of land, water, and natural resources; and produces vast amounts of waste, pollution, and greenhouse gases. It also increases risk of antimicrobial resistance, thereby increasing risk of global pandemic. Thus, industrial animal agriculture is one of the worst problems we face in terms of scale. Moreover, very few people are focusing on this problem, and we can make progress on this problem very effectively and efficiently, which makes it neglected and tractable as well. As a result, many effective altruist organizations list farmed animal welfare as a high priority cause area, alongside other high priority cause areas such as global health and development, biosecurity and pandemic preparedness, and other global catastrophic risks.[6]

Other people, however, deny that we have a moral obligation to favor some just causes over others. There are at least two sources of skepticism. First, some people reject the impartial moral standpoint that leads effective altruists to accept this conclusion. They think that if you care about some issues more than others, then you can permissibly focus on the former instead of the latter. So, on this view, if you *want* to focus on industrial animal agriculture (e.g., because you want to do the most good you can or because you care about animals and the environment), then you can do that. But if you instead want to focus on a different issue (e.g., if you want to focus on a particular illness because you know people who suffer from that illness), then you can do that too. Many people find it plausible that we should have this kind of moral freedom. However, note that in order to accept this idea, one must accept that either (a) we do not have a moral obligation to triage in states of emergency, or (b) our present situation is not a state of emergency (even though many individuals are suffering and dying, and we can prevent this suffering or death much more effectively and efficiently if we take some approaches instead of others).[7]

Second, some people accept the impartial moral standpoint that leads effective altruists to accept this conclusion, yet they worry that the effective altruist framework risks creating a bias in favor of some approaches and against others. For example, we might worry that using evidence and reason to prevent the most suffering we can will favor approaches with proven track records over other, more creative or experimental approaches—despite the fact that creativity and experimentation have an important role to play in bringing about change.[8] Similarly, we might worry that this framework will favor short-term, individual approaches over long-term, structural approaches (since the impacts of the former are easier to measure than the impacts of the latter)—despite the fact that long-term, structural approaches have an important role to play in bringing about change as well. If this critique is correct, then the implication is not that we should reject effective altruism as an ideal, but rather that we should make sure to correct for status quo bias, measurability bias, and other such biases in our pursuit of this ideal.[9]

Another, related question concerns what kind of stance we should take to other just causes, once we have selected the just causes that we intend to focus on. Should we aspire to do our work in a way that establishes links with other just causes? Or should we aspire to do our own work independently of other just causes?

Some people think that we should engage in **multi-issue activism**, that is, that we should aspire to do our work in a way that establishes links with other just causes.[10] Why should we do this? Part of the reason is that the issues that we care about are linked. First, there are *parallels* across many issues, that is, there are respects in which different oppressive systems function in similar ways. For example, Iris Marion Young argues that many oppressions share features such as violence, exploitation, marginalization, powerlessness, and cultural imperialism.[11] And, Aph Ko and Syl Ko argue that many oppressions are more than similar: they are in fact parts of the same oppressive system, which targets anyone who deviates from a narrow (white, western European, colonial) conception of what it means to be fully human.[12]

Second, there are *interactions* across many issues; that is, there are respects in which, when a person is subject to multiple oppressions, these oppressions interact in a way that makes the whole different from the sum of its parts. For example, Kimberlé Crenshaw argues that if we want to understand the challenges that Black women face in the workplace, we need to do more than simply think about the challenges that Black people and women face in the workplace and add these thoughts together (especially if we have a tendency to think of Black people as male by default or to think of women as white by default, as many people do). We also need to examine the respects in which racism and sexism conspire to create new, distinctive challenges for individuals who hold both marginalized identities in this context.[13]

Third, there are *shared causes* of many issues; that is, there are certain practices, traditions, and institutions that are responsible for many of the harms that people experience. For instance, many people in the food movement believe that modern industries are responsible for many of the problems that people face, and that human nature and neoliberalism are responsible for many modern industries. On this view, we have a tendency to divide the world into "self" and "other" categories and to favor those in the "self" category over those in the "other" category. Moreover, when we pursue our individual self-interest through the free market, or when we pursue our collective self-interest through democratic procedures, these activities will inevitably result in distributions that benefit the powerful over everybody else.[14]

Proponents of multi-issue activism believe that if the issues that we care about are linked, then the movements that address these issues should be linked as well. Theoretically, we should recognize that our reasons for caring about some issues extend to others, and so we should aspire to do our work in a way that helps rather than harms other movements. And practically, we should resist the kind of competitive, zero sum thinking that pits movements against each other, and instead embrace a kind of cooperative, positive sum thinking that puts movements in alliance with each other. Why? Because when we pursue unity, solidarity, and mutual understanding across movements, we can help each other more, harm each other less, and identify and address the shared causes of the problems that we all face. Consider each of these points in turn.

First, we can build **unity** across movements by working together, for example by working in multi-issue groups or on multi-group projects. This kind of collaboration is often useful since different groups have different strengths, for example different resources and constituencies, they can bring to the table. Thus, for example, if your goal is to address the harmful impacts of industrial animal agriculture for people in food deserts, and if you do this work without partnering with members of the relevant communities (and ensuring that they can take the lead in these efforts), then people in your intended audience will likely experience your work as racist, hypocritical, and paternalistic, and they might be right.[15] Similarly, if your goal is to address the harmful impacts of industrial animal agriculture in countries without developed industrial economies, and if you do this work without partnering with members of the relevant communities (and ensuring that they can take the lead in these efforts), then your work will likely have a similar effect. Thus, proponents of multi-issue activism argue, it is important not only to build unity across groups but to expand our sense of unity beyond traditional alliances, and to center the voices of people traditionally marginalized within particular groups.[16]

Second, we can build **solidarity** across movements by helping or at least not harming other movements through our work. It is common for activist groups to harm each other in relatively avoidable ways and/or fail to help each other in relatively costless ways. For example, many food, animal, and environmental groups use racism, sexism, ableism, and so on to sell their moral and political messaging, and they attempt to persuade people to care about animals by comparing animal rights to human rights in simplistic, reductive, and appropriative ways. Meanwhile, many human rights groups use speciesism, packaged as humanism, to sell their moral and political messaging, and they attempt to persuade people to care about humans by distinguishing them from animals. Proponents of multi-issue activism believe that these tactics can often be harmful and wrong, and they advocate for working in harmony across movements by finding ways to promote each issue that help rather than harm other movements. They also advocate for working in other areas where possible, for example by taking time to do anti-racist, anti-sexist, anti-ableist, or anti-speciesist advocacy whether or not these are the main issues that you work on.[17]

Third, and relatedly, we can build **mutual understanding** across movements by sharing information and arguments about links across issues, including about parallels, interactions, and shared causes. This can be a good way of inviting people to expand their compassion, as well as to see what expanded compassion requires. However, as mentioned a moment ago, while many people explore these links in nuanced, respectful ways, many other people do not. For example, while a book-length discussion of the similarities and differences between animal agriculture and slavery or the Holocaust can be useful and important, a simple, pithy ad campaign that compares these atrocities without context or qualification can easily do more harm than good.[18] Does that mean that one can never make these comparisons in these contexts? Not necessarily. But it does mean that one needs to be exceedingly careful. In particular, as Christopher-Sebastian McJetters writes, one should—especially if one is not a member of the communities being discussed[19]—(a) "employ sensitivity and discernment when approaching these discussions," (b) "amplify the voices of marginalized people who talk about these issues," and (c) "make an attempt to understand how layered oppressions impact different groups to maximize our impact and build a broader, more inclusive community."[20]

Other people think that we should engage in **single-issue activism**; that is, we should aspire to do our work independently of other just causes. How do proponents of single-issue activism respond to arguments in favor of multi-issue activism? They grant that we should build unity, solidarity, and mutual understanding with other movements insofar as doing so benefits our own movement. However, they also claim that this is not always the case in practice, for at least three reasons.

First, single-issue activists worry that multi-issue activism is too *restrictive*. If we were to aspire to full unity, solidarity, and mutual understanding with all relevant movements and approaches, this would rule out many, if not most, of the things that we can do to effectively advance our own movement. For example, it would rule out serving meat at environmental fundraisers. It would rule out favoring conventionally attractive models in ad campaigns. It would rule out appealing to racialized or gendered stereotypes in ad campaigns. It would rule out using hierarchical structures in nonprofit organizations. It would rule out working with business leaders who make use of bad labor practices. And so on. In short, proponents of single-issue activism worry that a full commitment to multi-issue activism would make it difficult for us to do the work that we need to do to bring about real change for our cause.

Second, proponents of single-issue activism worry that multi-issue activism is too *demanding*. If we were to aspire to full unity, solidarity, and mutual understanding with all relevant movements and approaches, this work would become all-consuming. Importantly, this is true not only when it comes to helping other movements, for example when we participate in their protests or rallies, but also when it comes to avoiding harm to other movements, for example when we attempt to avoid perpetuating racism, sexism, ableism, speciesism, and so on in our work. After all, it takes active work to identify and address our own personal and institutional biases.[21] We have to research other movements, participate in other movements, participate in trainings and facilitated discussions, and more.[22] Thus, proponents of single-issue activism worry, a full commitment to multi-issue activism is an unattainable ideal, and it would take too much time, energy, and money away from work in our cause area trying and failing to live up to this ideal in practice.

Finally, proponents of single-issue activism argue that some issues are simply more important than others from an impartial perspective. If we are advocating for abolition of industrial animal agriculture, an issue that affects billions of humans, tens of billions of terrestrial animals, and hundreds of billions of aquatic animals every year (to say nothing of the further impacts of waste, pollution, and climate change for humans and nonhumans all over the world), we might think that we can do more good overall if we focus exclusively on this issue than if we try to extend our focus to every other important issue as well.

Suppose that we find some or all of these claims compelling. Does it follow that we should take a single-issue approach to activism? Not necessarily. Instead, what follows is that we should try to strike an ethical and effective balance between multi-issue and single-issue activism in practice. How can we strike this balance? As always, that depends on which moral theory we accept and on the details of the case. However, we can say at least this much in the abstract: As we discussed in the last chapter, many people tend to have a double standard regarding political activism; that is, we tend to demand more from people in other movements and approaches than we demand from ourselves. So, as we think about what kind of balance between multi-issue and single-issue activism is appropriate in particular cases, we should attempt to correct for this bias by (a) demanding the same efforts at unity, solidarity, and mutual understanding from ourselves that we demand from others and (b) extending others the same patience and compassion that we extend ourselves.

So, do we have a moral obligation to engage in food activism? We have not shown that the answer is yes. However, we have discussed several reasons why it might be. First, if we accept that we have a moral obligation to prevent suffering and death if we can do so without sacrificing anything comparably morally significant, then we should also accept that many of us have a moral obligation to engage in activism, since many of us can prevent suffering and death without sacrificing anything comparably morally significant by engaging in activism. Second, if we accept an impartial approach to cause selection, then it follows that many of us should regard industrial animal agriculture as a top priority cause area, since industrial animal agriculture causes massive, neglected, and tractable harm in the world. Third, if we accept that we should take a multi-issue approach to activism, then it follows that many of us should engage in at least some food activism whether or not this is our main cause area, since we should be aspiring to build links with other just cause areas wherever possible. (And of course, the same is true for food activists with respect to other just movements.)[23]

10.3 Ends and means

If we do choose to engage in food activism, either because we want to or because we think that we ought to, the next question to ask is: What should the goal of food activism be?

Some people think that we should aim for **abolition** of our current food system, or certain aspects of it. For example, Gary Francione argues that we should aim to abolish animal agriculture, since he thinks that animal agriculture is fundamentally wrong. On this view, the goal should be empty cages and animal rights. In contrast, other people think that we should aim for **regulation** of our current food system, or certain aspects of it. For example, Robert Garner argues that we should aim to regulate animal agriculture so that we make sure that animals have relatively happy lives and relatively painless deaths. On this view, then, the goal should be bigger cages and animal welfare.[24]

Which of these views should we accept? As always, this depends in part on what our broader moral theory is. For example, there is a tendency for Kantians to be abolitionists, since Kantians are drawn to the absolutist, animal rights spirit of abolition, and vice versa. There is also a tendency for utilitarians to be regulationists, since utilitarians are drawn to the pragmatic, animal welfare spirit of regulation, and vice versa. But these views can come apart. For example, depending on how we interpret these theories, it is possible for Kantians to be regulationists (if they see regulation as strict enough to ensure that animals are being treated as ends) as well as for utilitarians to be abolitionists (if they see abolition as doing more good than regulation overall).

In order to decide which goal is best, one question that we have to ask is: How idealistic should we allow ourselves to be? Do we really think that we can achieve our ideal food system, and if we can achieve it, do we really think that we can sustain it? These kinds of questions motivate pragmatic critiques of abolition and regulation as goals. For example, one critique of abolition is that we could never achieve it in practice. For better or worse, our current system is here to stay, so even if we would ideally like to replace it, the best we can realistically hope to do is regulate it as well as possible. On this view, then, we should aim for regulation *not* because we prefer regulation to abolition in principle (though we might), but *rather* because we think that we can achieve regulation but not abolition in practice. Conversely, one critique of regulation is that we could never *sustain* it in practice. No matter how much we try to regulate animal agriculture, if we allow this practice at all, then we will inevitably slide back into a practice of harming humans, nonhumans, and the environment a great deal. On this view, we should aim for abolition *not* because we prefer abolition to regulation in principle (though we might), but *rather* because we think that abolition is sustainable whereas regulation is not.

Which option should we accept? We will not try to say here. However, we will note that these are not necessarily binary, mutually exclusive options. First, there are different kinds and degrees of both. For example, abolitionists can aim for different kinds of alternatives (e.g., capitalist or anti-capitalist alternatives), and regulationists can aim for different kinds of reforms (e.g., different standards for treatment of humans, nonhumans, and the environment). In fact, it might even be that some "abolitionists" and "regulationists" think that we should aim for roughly the same kind of system—for example, a mostly vegan food system that includes exceedingly small amounts of locally, organically, humanely, and sustainably sourced animal products—but that the former identify as abolitionist in light of the discontinuities with our current food system, and the latter identify as regulationist in light of the continuities with our current food system. Of course, this is not true of many abolitionists and regulationists: In many cases they do disagree about what kind of food system we should aim for. Still, if this point is correct, then the relevant question is not whether we should aim for abolition or regulation full stop, but rather what point on the spectrum between strict abolition and lax regulation we should aim for and why—with respect to animal use as well as other harmful aspects of our food system.

While we will not attempt to say exactly what kind of food system we should aim for here, we will say at least this much: Whatever kind of system we aim for, and however we choose to describe this aim (abolition, regulation, or, in a certain sense, both), we should not aim for anything that remotely resembles our current food system. Given the amount of unnecessary harm that industrial animal agriculture causes for humans, nonhumans, and the environment, there is no reasonable moral perspective from which industrial animal agriculture should continue. Thus, when it comes to whether or not we should aim for a food system that includes animal use, the range of reasonable answers is: yes, we should aim for a food system that includes exceedingly minimal, respectful, and compassionate animal use, or no, we should not aim for a food system that includes any animal use at all. With that said, even if some aspects of our current food system are in need of dramatic change, other aspects of our food system might not be. For example, we might, following James McWilliams, think that we should aim for a food system that differs dramatically from our current food system when it comes to animal use, but not when it comes to industrial technology use (or at least not as much).[25]

In any case, no matter what goal we select, we also face many questions about what path we should take toward that goal, and why. We will here briefly consider four such questions (though there are many more).

One question is whether we should pursue our goal by means of **revolution**, that is, by taking apart our current food system and building a new food system in its place (e.g., aiming for empty cages by seeking to create an alternative without cages now), or pursue our goal by means of **reform**, that is, by making a series of incremental changes to our current food system so that it eventually becomes what we want it to be (e.g., aiming for empty cages by seeking to make cages bigger now, with the hope that each time we make them bigger, we make incremental progress toward making them empty).

Which of these views should we accept? As before, it depends in part on what our broader moral theory is. There is a tendency for Kantians to be revolutionaries, since Kantians think that if we advocate for bigger cages now as a means to bringing about empty cages later, then we are treating current animals merely as means to the liberation of future animals. There is also a tendency for utilitarians to be reformists, since utilitarians are drawn to the pragmatic spirit of this approach. But as before, these views can sometimes come apart. It might or might not be possible for a Kantian to accept reform as a means, or to combine regulation as an end with revolution as a means, but it is certainly possible for a utilitarian to accept revolution as a means, or to combine abolition as an end with reform as a means.

What are the pragmatic costs and benefits of each approach? Here both sides argue that the other is ineffective and counterproductive. For example, Robert Garner argues that revolution is *ineffective* because it will not take us anywhere at all. Instead, the best and only way to make progress is to advocate for a compromise between the real and the ideal, so that we can persuade people to care about the human, nonhuman, and environmental impacts of our food system and steadily increase minimally acceptable standards for treatment of humans, nonhumans, and the environment. Garner also worries that revolution is *counterproductive*, since it foregoes real benefits for everyone here and now for the sake of this unattainable revolutionary ideal. In particular, if we resist reforms to the current system on the grounds that we want people to oppose the current system entirely, then we are guaranteeing that the current food system will continue to cause exactly the harms that it currently does. Moreover, if we accept this revolutionary logic, why not take it one step further and endorse **accelerationism**, which holds that we should actively make the current system *worse* so that we can speed up the collapse that we hope will eventually occur? Garner thinks that accelerationism is clearly bad. Yet he also thinks that there is no real difference between the case for revolution and the case for accelerationism. Thus, Garner claims, we should reject both.[26]

In contrast, Gary Francione argues that reform is *ineffective* because it will not take us where we want to go. Yes, activists have achieved modest reforms in the food system. But how did they achieve these reforms? For the most part, by persuading food producers that these reforms were both ethically and economically beneficial. Yet at a certain point—a point that we will reach well before any food activist is satisfied with the state of our food system—ethics and economics will start to come apart, and this strategy will no longer work. Revolutionaries also worry that reform is *counterproductive*, since any time we argue for reform of the current food system, we greenwash and humanewash our current food system, reinforcing its apparent ethical legitimacy. For example, when animal and environmental organizations persuade food producers to reform their practices and then celebrate them for doing so, they reinforce the idea that these practices are fundamentally okay. This can make it easier for people to think that supporting these practices is, itself, a form of consumer activism. Yet if our strategy for bringing about our ideal food system makes people feel ethically *better* rather than ethically *worse* about supporting a fundamentally unjust system, then we are doing more than not moving forward: We are moving backward.[27]

Which if either argument is correct? We will not try to say. However, we will note that, as with abolition and regulation, revolution and reform are not necessarily binary, mutually exclusive options. There are different kinds and degrees of both (e.g., you can seek to bring about more or less radical alternatives to, or revisions to, current practices here and now), and we might think that a balance of approaches is best.[28] For example, we might think that revolution and reform are mutually reinforcing, since advocacy for revolution can shift the center of debate and pave the way for reform,[29] and reform can shift the goalposts and pave the way for revolution.[30] On this view, it might be that some people (e.g., some grassroots nonprofit leaders) should take a revolutionary approach, other people (e.g., some mainstream nonprofit leaders) should take a reformist approach, and still other people should take a mixed approach, for instance by advocating for abolition of some parts of the current food system and regulation of others.[31] Or it might be that people should take a revolutionary approach in some contexts (e.g., around strangers), a reformist approach in others (e.g., around friends and family), and a mixed approach in others. If this is right, then the relevant question is not: Which approach should we all take all the time? But rather: What kind of balance do we need to strike collectively in order to achieve our goal, and what can I do individually to help us strike that balance in practice?[32]

Another question is whether we should advocate for **structural change**, for example by advocating for social, political, economic, or technological changes that result in different patterns of production and behavior, or advocate for **individual change**, for example by advocating for individuals to make different production or consumption decisions within our current social, political, economic, and technological context.[33]

Is there a relationship between this issue and the above issues? There is a tendency for revolutionaries to be structuralists, since revolutionaries and structuralists tend to share a focus on how the system as a whole shapes what happens within it. There is also a tendency for reformists to be individualists, since reformists and individualists tend to share a focus on how small changes can eventually add up to large changes. But as with the previous divisions, these views can come apart. For example, you might pursue revolution by means of vegan education and outreach (since, you might think, we need to change a certain number of hearts and minds before we can realistically expect to bring about revolutionary change in the food system). If so, then you would be taking an individualist revolutionary path to your goal. Alternatively, you might pursue reform by means of ballot initiatives in your state (since, you might think, we need to bring about incremental reforms to the system as a whole before we can expect to bring about radical changes to the system as a whole). If so, then you would be taking a structuralist reformist path to your goal.

So what are the costs and benefits of structural change and individual change? Some people think that individual change is necessary for structural change. We cannot create social, political, economic, or technological changes out of thin air. Instead, we can create these changes only through a critical mass of individual changes. So if we want to expand social awareness of animal and environmental issues, expand legal and political standing for animals and the environment, shift taxes and subsidies away from industrial animal agriculture and toward alternatives to industrial animal agriculture, and/or develop new alternative food products such as vegan foods, plant-based meat, or cultured meat, then we will first have to persuade individual producers and consumers to accept these ideas and make dietary changes. (This approach will also make it easier for individuals to be committed to the cause, since when they make dietary changes themselves, they will be more motivated to advocate for further individual and structural changes.) These producers and consumers can then persuade other people to do the same, these people can then persuade other people to do the same, and so on. Eventually these individual changes will be substantial enough to allow for the broader social, political, economic, and technological changes that we are seeking. If this is right, then, we might think, we should try to change the choices that individuals are making within the current system rather than try to change the system itself.

Meanwhile, some people think that structural change is necessary for individual change. We cannot persuade individuals to make choices that deviate from the status quo in a context that motivates everybody to maintain the status quo. Instead, we can create these changes only through the creation of new incentive structures. So, if we want to persuade individual producers and consumers to accept our ideas and make our desired changes, then we will first have to expand social awareness of animal and environmental issues, expand legal and political standing for animals and the environment, shift taxes and subsidies away from industrial animal agriculture and toward alternatives to industrial animal agriculture, and develop new alternative food products such as vegan food, plant-based meat, and cultured meat. (This approach will also make it easier to build popular support for the cause, since more people will be willing to participate if dietary change is not a prerequisite for participation.[34]) Eventually these structural changes will be substantial enough to motivate individuals to see healthy, ethical food as desirable, and to start producing and consuming this food naturally. If this is right, then, we might think, we should try to change the system in which individuals are making choices rather than try to change the choices that individuals are making within the system.

Which, if either, argument is correct? As with these other divisions, we will note that these are not necessarily binary, mutually exclusive options. There are different kinds and degrees of both (e.g., you can aim to reach a larger or smaller population of individuals or aim to bring about policy change that impacts a larger or smaller population of individuals), and we might think that a balance of approaches is best. For example, we might think that persuading people to eat alternative foods will help bring the prices down *and* that bringing the prices down will help persuade people to eat alternative foods. If so, then it might be that some people (e.g., some humane educators) should take an individual approach, other people (e.g., some lawyers and policy makers) should take a structural approach, and still other people should take a mixed approach. Or, it might be that some people should take an individual approach in some contexts, a structural approach in others, and a mixed approach in others. If so, then once again, the question is not: Which approach should we all take all the time? But rather: What kind of balance do we need to strike collectively in order to achieve our goal, and what can I do individually to help us strike that balance in practice? In this case, it seems plausible to say that the animal and environmental movements should shift at least somewhat in the direction of structural change, as a way of correcting for the strong emphasis that these movements have placed on individual change in the past.

Finally, no matter what path to our goal we select, we also face many questions about how to ethically and effectively persuade people to accept our point of view. We will here briefly consider two such questions (though, once again, there are many more).

One question is whether we should always use **rational** means of persuasion, such as providing people with information or arguments concerning the human, nonhuman, and environmental impacts of industrial animal agriculture, or whether we should sometimes use **nonrational** means of persuasion as well, such as presenting people with product placements, celebrity endorsements, or shocking images set to stirring music.

One can argue for rational persuasion in different ways. One argument is *principled*: If, like Kantians, you think that you have a moral obligation to treat people as ends, then you might also think that you have a moral obligation not to manipulate people, since doing so undermines rather than affirms their ability to pursue their own goals in life. Granted, maybe you can make an exception in certain situations, for example if you have my prior or tacit consent to manipulate me so that I can more effectively pursue my own ends in life. But if you do not have my prior or tacit consent, then we might think that when you manipulate me, you undermine rather than affirm my ability to pursue my own goals in life.[35] Another argument for rational persuasion is *pragmatic*. Paulo Freire argues that if we manipulate people into accepting our views, then we might get them to accept the right views in the short term, but we will be getting them to accept these views for the wrong reasons, and that will make it hard for us to translate these short-term gains into long-term gains. For example, yes, we might be able to get people to eat alternative foods through product placements and celebrity endorsements, but if we get people to adopt these diets only as a fad, then they will not stay committed when the next fad comes along. Thus, Freire argues, the only path to real change is through education: In particular, privileged people must provide oppressed people with the opportunity to educate themselves (as well as their oppressors) so that they can liberate themselves (as well as their oppressors) in a way that will stick.[36]

How might a proponent of nonrational persuasion reply? With respect to the principled argument: Some people, such as utilitarians, think that you are morally permitted to manipulate people for the greater good whether or not you undermine their capacity for autonomy in the process. Other people, such as some Kantians, think that you are morally permitted to manipulate people for the greater good if and when doing so does not, in fact, undermine their capacity for autonomy. Sure, you might treat me merely as a means if you manipulate me into, say, giving you money because you want me to do so (despite believing that I would permissibly choose to keep my money if I was fully informed and ideally rational). But what if you manipulate me into, say, eating healthy, ethical food because you think that my own beliefs and values entail that I should do so, and/or because you think that I am morally obligated to do so? This case is less clear. And, with respect to the pragmatic argument, some people think that we need to use every tool in our toolkit. If manipulation helps more people to take the idea of food activism seriously, with the result that they spend more time considering information and arguments in support of alternative foods, then we should take advantage of that. Granted, if we persuade people to accept the right view for the wrong reasons, then some of these people might backslide. But others— once they start taking this point of view seriously—might learn more about the relevant issues and come to accept it for the right reasons. And if at the end of the day a partly rational/partly nonrational approach results in more progress than a fully rational approach would, then we will have done the right thing.[37]

Whether we think we should take a fully rational approach or a mixed approach (few if any people think that we should take a fully manipulative approach), it is worth emphasizing how interconnected these approaches are, in theory as well as in practice. First, as with other divisions, there are different kinds and degrees of both (e.g., you can relay information more or less dispassionately or appeal to emotion more or less deceptively), and we might think that a balance is sometimes best. Second, we might also think that rational and nonrational persuasion are, at least in many cases, not only mutually reinforcing but mutually constituting. After all, as we have seen throughout this book, especially in our discussion of virtue, care, and relational theories in Chapter 3, rationality and emotionality are much more intertwined than many people like to think: Our emotional faculties are at least partly rational, and our rational faculties are at least partly emotional.[38] Moreover, we are not talking about these issues in a contextual vacuum. Instead, we are talking about them in the context of a society that conditions us to care about certain issues and not others, and to think about these issues in certain ways and not others. So even if certain emotional appeals are manipulative, they might also be necessary for counteracting manipulative forces pushing in the opposite direction, such that people are better able to look at the relevant issues rationally overall. If so, then, as always, the relevant question is not (indeed, cannot possibly be) which approach should we all take all the time, but rather what kind of balance do we need to strike collectively in order to achieve our goal, and what can I do individually to help us strike that balance in practice?

The final question that we will consider here is whether we should always use **conciliatory** means of persuasion, such as praising people for participating in Meatless Mondays, or whether we should sometimes use **confrontational** means of persuasion as well, for example by admonishing people for consuming animal flesh at all.

Is there a relationship between this issue and the above issues? Some people see a relationship between rational and conciliatory approaches, because they see conciliation as creating space for rational discussion. Likewise, some people see a relationship between nonrational and confrontational approaches, because they see confrontation as creating social pressure through coercion or manipulation. But this might or might not always be right, and even if it is, there can be exceptions. For example, if you think that you should flatter people in your activism because "you catch more flies with honey than with vinegar" (or a non-speciesist equivalent), then you would be taking a nonrational conciliatory approach. Similarly, if you think that you should disrupt the status quo in your activism because doing so is necessary for drawing attention to a particular issue or view at all, then you would be taking a rational confrontational approach.

One can argue for conciliation in different ways. First, one can offer the same kinds of principled arguments that one can offer for rational approaches: Treating people with kindness is more respectful all else equal. One can also offer the same kinds of pragmatic arguments that one can offer for rational approaches: If you treat people with kindness, then not only will you be more likely to make incremental progress in the short term, but you will also be more likely to build momentum toward radical change in the long run. Thus, for example, if you approach restaurants, supermarkets, and so on and demand that they serve fewer "bodies," they might write you off as militant. But if you ask them to serve less "meat" (carefully explaining the reasons why, and then praising them if they do), they might be more open to that. Similarly, if you approach consumers and demand that they eat fewer "bodies," they might write you off as militant. But if you ask them to eat less "meat" (carefully explaining the reasons why, and then praising them if they do), then they might be more open to that as well. And, in both cases, once you persuade people to make one change for ethical reasons, it will be easier to persuade them to make other changes for ethical reasons later on.[39]

How might a proponent of confrontational activism reply? As before, they will say that treating people with kindness is not always more respectful, especially if this kindness is dishonest. They will also say that treating people with kindness is not always more pragmatic. Why not? Because, as Iris Marion Young argues, if you are doing activism in a context that marginalizes your voice, your cause, or your perspective, then confrontation is often necessary for making your voice heard at all.[40] For example, if you ask people to eat less "meat," then yes, you might reach more people in the short term. But you will also be supporting rather than disrupting the idea that veganism is a dietary choice rather than a social justice issue, thereby potentially doing more harm than good for your cause in the long run. In contrast, if you demand that people eat fewer "bodies," then yes, you might alienate some people in the short term. But you will also be disrupting rather than supporting this narrative about food choice, thereby potentially doing more good than harm for your cause in the long run. Of course, this does not mean that confrontation is always best. But it does mean that, as with the other divisions considered here, we should take care not to allow status quo bias, measurability bias, and so on to make us more supportive of approaches that aim for short-term, individual benefits and less supportive of approaches that aim for long-term, structural benefits than we should be.[41]

As with the other divisions we have considered here, it is worth noting how interconnected these approaches are, in theory as well as in practice. There are different kinds and degrees of both (e.g., there are a variety of more or less blunt replies available to the objection, "but bacon!"), and we might think that a balance is sometimes appropriate. And as with structural change/individual change in particular, in this case it seems plausible that a balanced or mixed approach will be best much more often than not. That is, if we want to communicate our message effectively, then it seems plausible that we should often attempt to strike a balance between confrontation and conciliation by, for example, (a) stating our views clearly and directly (thereby preserving an element of confrontation) while at the same time (b) expressing humility, compassion, and understanding to our audience (thereby preserving an element of conciliation). Of course, as we saw in our discussion of virtue, care, and relational theories in Chapter 3, what that means in practice will vary from person to person based on who we are, who our audience is, and what our context is. We each need to find this balance for ourselves through practice and experimentation. Still, it does seem plausible that most people in most situations should be taking a balanced or mixed approach rather than a fully confrontational or fully conciliatory approach—especially when mainstream culture marginalizes food activists, the issues we care about, and the perspectives we have about these issues, and so we need to be at least somewhat confrontational in order to be heard at all.

We can here emphasize a point that we made concerning actual and apparent values in Chapter 2. In a social context that frames some views as standard and others as deviant, even moderate activism can sometimes appear radical. For instance, you might see the practice of describing meat as "bodies" as rational and conciliatory, since you see this term as accurate. However, others might see this practice as manipulative and confrontational, since this term deviates from standard practice and implies that many people are complicit in violence. People of color, women, LGBTQ+ people, disabled people, and other marginalized people are especially at risk of being seen as manipulative or confrontational when they challenge oppression in this kind of way, not only because they are challenging structures that many people take for granted, but also because, as we saw in previous chapters, marginalized people are often labeled as "emotional" and "irrational" whether or not they are, and are often denied epistemic authority as a result of this and other factors.[42] This adds a layer of complication to our analyses here: It means we have to ask not only how radical an activist should *actually* be but also how radical they should be willing to *appear* to be in a particular context.

In this way, activists are often placed in a difficult double bind, since, on one hand, if we allow ourselves to be labeled as manipulative or irrational, we will alienate people as a result. Yet if we take care to avoid these labels, we will allow the opposition to set the terms of debate, and we will risk closing the door on essential strategies for change (even moderate ones!) as a result.

We can also emphasize a related point that will appear in the next chapter. Suppose that we agree that we should take at least a partly multi-issue approach to food activism and seek to build at least some unity, solidarity, and mutual understanding across movements. This will mean seeking to build alliances in spite of disagreement about many issues, including many of the issues discussed here. This raises the question how to draw the line between tolerable and intolerable disagreement in particular cases. For example, we might think that we should tolerate many but not all perspectives about what goals we should aim for; for instance we might think that we should tolerate abolitionist as well as strict regulationist perspectives, but not lax regulationist perspectives. Similarly, we might think that we should tolerate many but not all perspectives about what paths we should take toward our goals; for instance we might think that we should tolerate radical as well as moderate approaches, but not the use of junk science or of racism, sexism, or ableism in political messaging. In some cases, it can be hard to know how to strike a balance between building a broad, pluralistic movement in which activists can agree to disagree, on one hand, and building a narrow, united movement in which activists can uphold certain core values, on the other hand. For example, there are many kinds of bad science, and there are many kinds of racism, sexism, and ableism. Which kinds are grounds for education and which kinds are grounds for exclusion? As with everything else, this is likely to be a contextual matter. For example, activists might have stronger reason to insist on certain shared values in relatively formal alliances than in relatively informal alliances. Still, these questions will arise to a degree for all alliances, and in many cases the relevant considerations will be similar.[43]

10.4 Conclusion

Throughout this chapter, we have emphasized that while people tend to frame questions about food activism in binary, mutually exclusive terms (e.g., abolition vs. regulation and revolution vs. reform), reality is almost always more complex. We also emphasized that while people tend to accept certain combinations of these approaches, other combinations are possible too. For example, even if people tend to see revolution and confrontation as a natural pair, it might sometimes be best to pair revolution with conciliation instead, since making a radical ask in a friendly manner can sometimes make the ask appear to be more relatable. Similarly, even if people tend to see reform and conciliation as a natural pair, it might sometimes be best to pair reform with confrontation instead, since making a moderate ask in an adversarial manner can sometimes create extra incentives in favor of compliance.[44]

This discussion illustrates a point we have been emphasizing throughout this book, which is that no matter which moral theory we accept, we can enrich our interpretation of this theory by taking seriously the insights of other theories. In this case, many moral theories are useful to keep in mind. For example, abstract, general moral theories such as Kantianism and utilitarianism are useful for thinking about what our goal should be. (Though as we have seen, this is not an entirely abstract question, since practical concerns such as achievability and sustainability should inform our thinking about what our goal should be.) And concrete, situational moral frameworks such as virtue, care, and relational theory are useful for thinking about how we should pursue our goal. (Though as we have seen, this is not entirely a concrete question, since our goal will affect our thinking about what paths we should take, and there might be further ethical limits on which paths we should take as well.) In short, then, which approaches are best for a particular person in a particular situation is not a matter that we can reason about entirely abstractly or entirely concretely: Instead, we each have to ask and answer this question for ourselves, through careful consideration of everything we know about the issues in general and about our particular talents, interests, relationships, and more. As always, moral theory is a messy, complex, and holistic enterprise.

Notes

1 Peter Singer, "Famine, Affluence, and Morality," *Philosophy and Public Affairs* 1, no. 1 (1972): 229–243.
2 Peter Singer, "Famine, Affluence, and Morality," *Philosophy and Public Affairs* 1, no. 1 (Spring 1972): 232–235.
3 For more on effective altruism as a moral framework and as a social movement, see:
    William MacAskill, *Doing Good Better* (New York: Avery, 2016).
    Larissa MacFarquhar, *Strangers Drowning: Impossible Idealism, Drastic Choices, and the Urge to Help* (New York: Penguin, 2016).
    Peter Singer, *The Most Good You Can Do: How Effective Altruism Is Changing Ideas About Living Ethically* (New Haven: Yale University Press, 2015).
4 William MacAskill, *Doing Good Better* (New York: Avery, 2016): 29–42.
5 William MacAskill, *Doing Good Better* (New York: Avery, 2016): 179–195.
6 For discussion of these and other high priority cause areas, see:
    Open Philanthropy Project, www.openphilanthropy.org/focus.
    For further discussion, see:
    William MacAskill, *Doing Good Better* (New York: Avery, 2016): 189–190.
7 For more on the idea that we should be free to do what we like within certain limits, see:
    Samuel Scheffler, *The Rejection of Consequentialism: A Philosophical Investigation of the Considerations Underlying Rival Moral Conceptions* (Oxford: Clarendon Press, 1994).
    Susan Wolf, "Moral Saints," *The Journal of Philosophy* 79, no. 8 (August 1982): 419–439.
8 For more on the value of creativity and experimentation in animal activism, see:
    Jasmin Singer and Mariann Sullivan, "Effective Altruism as It Relates to Animal Rights: An Open Ended Approach to Advocacy," Our Hen House, October 28, 2015.
9 For more on the value of long-term, structural approaches to animal activism, see:
    Jeff Sebo and Peter Singer, "Activism," in Lori Gruen, ed., *Critical Terms for Animal Studies* (forthcoming).

10 For more on the ethics of multi-issue food activism and single-issue food activism, see:
  Jeff Sebo, "Multi-issue Food Activism," in Anne Barnhill, Mark Budolfson, and Tyler Doggett, eds., *The Oxford Handbook of Food Ethics* (Oxford: Oxford University Press, 2018): 399–423.
  The rest of this section will draw heavily from material discussed in more detail there.

11 Iris Marion Young, *Justice and the Politics of Difference* (Princeton: Princeton University Press, 1990): 39–65.

12 For more on the idea that oppression targets anyone who deviates from a narrow conception of humanity, see:
  Aph Ko and Syl Ko, *Aphro-ism: Essays on Pop Culture, Feminism, and Black Veganism from Two Sisters* (New York: Lantern Books, 2017): 20–27.

13 For more on intersectionality, see:
  Kimberlé Williams Crenshaw, "Demarginalizing the Intersection of Race and Sex: A Black Feminist Critique of Antidiscrimination Doctrine, Feminist Theory and Antiracist Politics," University of Chicago Legal Forum, 1989: 139–167.
  Kimberlé Williams Crenshaw, "Mapping the Margins: Intersectionality, Identity Politics, and Violence against Women of Color," *Stanford Law Review* 43, no. 6 (1991): 1241–1299.
  Patricia Hill Collins and Sirma Bilge, *Intersectionality* (Hoboken: John Wiley & Sons, 2016).

14 For more on the idea that many problems that people face have shared or root causes, see:
  Bob Torres, *Making a Killing: The Political Economy of Animal Rights* (Oakland: AK Press, 2007).
  For related discussion, see:
  Carole Counihan and Valeria Siniscalchi, *Food Activism: Agency, Democracy and Economy* (New York: Bloomsbury, 2014).
  William Schanbacher, *The Politics of Food: The Global Conflict between Food Security and Food Sovereignty* (Santa Barbara: Praeger Security International, 2010).

15 For more on paternalism in food advocacy, see:
  Anne Barnhill, Katherine King, Nancy Kass, and Ruth Faden, "The Value of Unhealthy Eating and the Ethics of Healthy Eating Policies," *Kennedy Institute of Ethics Journal* 24, no. 3 (2014): 187–217.

16 For more on unity across food movements, see:
  Eric Holt-Giménez, ed., *Food Movements Unite!* (Oakland: Food First Books, 2011).
  Alison Hope Alkon and Julian Agyeman, *Cultivating Food Justice: Race, Class, and Sustainability* (Cambridge: The MIT Press, 2011).

17 For discussion of racism in the animal rights movement, see:
  A. Breeze Harper, ed., *Sistah Vegan: Black Female Vegans Speak on Food, Identity, Health, and Society* (New York: Lantern Books, 2010).
  For discussion of sexism in the animal rights movement, see:
  Emily Gaarder, *Women and the Animal Rights Movement* (New Brunswick: Rutgers University Press, 2011).
  For discussion of ableism in the animal rights movement, see:
  Sunaura Taylor, *Beasts of Burden: Animal and Disability Liberation* (New York: New Press, 2017).
  For discussion of the value of solidarity, see:
  Julia Feliz Brueck, ed., *Veganism in an Oppressive World: A Vegans of Color Community Project* (Sanctuary Publishers, 2017).
  Will Tuttle, ed., *Circles of Compassion: Essays Connecting Issues of Justice* (Danvers: Vegan Publishers, 2014).

18 For detailed, thoughtful discussion about similarities and differences between animal use and slavery, see:
  Marjorie Spiegel, *The Dreaded Comparison* (New York: Mirror Books, 1977).

For detailed, thoughtful discussion about similarities and differences between animal use and the Holocaust, see:

Charles Patterson, *Eternal Treblinka: Our Treatment of Animals and the Holocaust* (New York: Lantern Books, 2002).

19 Julia Feliz Brueck takes a stronger stance, claiming that "linking animal suffering to African slavery or the Holocaust is unacceptable unless you are from the affected community."

Julia Feliz Brueck, "Introduction," in Julia Feliz Brueck, ed. *Veganism in an Oppressive World: A Vegans of Color Community Project* (Sanctuary Publishers, 2017): 6–7.

20 Christopher-Sebastian McJetters, "Animal Rights and the Language of Slavery," Striving with Systems, December 27, 2015, http://strivingwithsystems.com/2015/12/27/animal-rights-and-the-language-of-slavery/.

21 For more on the kind of active work that ethical solidarity takes, see:

Anthony J. Nocella III, "Building an Animal Advocacy Movement for Racial and Disability Justice," in Will Tuttle, ed., *Circles of Compassion: Essays Connecting Issues of Justice* (Danvers: Vegan Publishers, 2014): 159–170.

SONG (Southerners on New Ground), "Being an Ally/Building Solidarity," http://southernersonnewground.org/wp-content/uploads/2012/12/SONG-Being-An-Ally-Building-Solidarity.pdf.

22 For examples of diversity, equity, and inclusion consultants in the animal protection movement, see:

Critical Diversity Solutions, https://criticaldiversitysolutions.com/ and Encompass, http://encompassmovement.org/.

23 For discussion of many of the issues that food ethics interacts with, see:

Anne Barnhill, Mark Budolfson, and Tyler Doggett, eds., *Food, Ethics, and Society: An Introductory Text with Readings* (New York: Oxford University Press, 2017).

24 For more on abolition and regulation, see:

Gary Francione and Robert Garner, *The Animal Rights Debate* (New York: Columbia University Press, 2010).

Tom Regan, *Empty Cages: Facing the Challenge of Animal Rights* (New York: Rowman & Littlefield, 2004).

25 James E. McWilliams, *Just Food: Where Locavores Get It Wrong and How We Can Truly Eat Responsibly* (New York: Little, Brown, and Co., 2009).

26 Robert Garner, "A Defense of Broad Animal Protectionism," in Gary Francione and Robert Garner, eds., *The Animal Rights Debate* (New York: Columbia University Press, 2010): 103–174.

Garner does not discuss accelerationism in particular in this piece, but he does discuss the similar idea that activists should "stand back and let the position of . . . animals deteriorate" to make "their ultimate liberation . . . more likely" (124).

27 Gary Francione, "The Abolition of Animal Exploitation," in Gary Francione and Robert Garner, eds., *The Animal Rights Debate* (New York: Columbia University Press, 2010): 1–102.

For a similar critique, see:

Julia Feliz Brueck, "Introduction," in Julia Feliz Brueck, ed., *Veganism in an Oppressive World: A Vegans of Color Community Project* (Sanctuary Publishers, 2017): 6–7.

28 For more on the meaning of revolution in the modern world, see:

Grace Lee Boggs, *The Next American Revolution: Sustainable Activism for the Twenty-First Century* (Berkeley: University of California Press, 2011).

29 For further discussion of the idea that radical activism can make moderate activism seem more relatable in comparison, see:

Erica Chenoweth and Maria J. Stephan, *Why Civil Resistance Works* (New York: Columbia University Press, 2011): 43.

(They discuss this phenomenon in the context of violent and non-violent activism, but the point applies here as well.)

30 Sentience Politics discusses the idea that moderate reforms can build momentum toward radical changes in "Our Support for the Massachusetts 'Minimum Size Requirements for Farm Animal Containment' Initiative": https://sentience-politics.org/support-massachusetts-minimum-size-requirements-farm-animal-containment-initiative/.

31 For an influential guide to activism written for "Have Nots," see:
Saul Alinsky, *Rules for Radicals: A Pragmatic Primer for Realistic Radicals* (New York: Knopf Doubleday, 2010).

32 For critiques of regulationist, reformist approaches within mainstream philanthropy, see:
INCITE! *The Revolution Will Not Be Funded: Beyond the Non-Profit Industrial Complex* (Durham: Duke University Press, 2017).

33 For more on individual and structural change (among other issues discussed and not discussed in this chapter), see:
Sentience Institute, "Summary of Evidence for Foundational Questions in Effective Animal Advocacy:" www.sentienceinstitute.org/foundational-questions-summaries.

34 "Survey of US Attitudes towards Animal Farming and Animal-free Food October 2017," Sentience Institute, November 20, 2017, www.sentienceinstitute.org/animal-farming-attitudes-survey-2017.

35 For more on freedom and paternalism, see:
Gerald Dworkin, "Paternalism," *The Stanford Encyclopedia of Philosophy*, Edward N. Zalta ed., https://plato.stanford.edu/entries/ethics-business/.
Also see the essays in:
Anne Barnhill, Mark Budolfson, and Tyler Doggett, eds., *Food, Ethics, and Society: An Introductory Text with Readings* (New York: Oxford University Press, 2017): 623–664.

36 Paulo Freire, *Pedagogy of the Oppressed* (trans. Myra Bergman Ramos) (New York: Continuum, 1970): 147–152.

37 For discussion of the value of shame in activism, see:
Jennifer Jacquet, *Is Shame Necessary? New Uses for an Old Tool* (New York: Pantheon Books, 2015).

38 For more on the connection between rationality and emotionality, see:
Martha Nussbaum, *Upheavals of Thought: The Intelligence of Emotions* (New York: Cambridge University Press, 2001).

39 For more on the value of conciliation, see:
Tobias Leenaert, *How to Create a Vegan World: A Pragmatic Approach* (New York: Lantern Books, 2017).

40 Iris Marion Young, "Activist Challenges to Deliberative Democracy," *Political Theory* 29, no. 5 (2001).

41 For more on the value of confrontation, see:
Casey Taft, *Motivational Methods for Vegan Advocacy: A Clinical Psychology Perspective* (Boston: Vegan Publishers, 2016).

42 For more on epistemic injustice, see:
Miranda Fricker, *Epistemic Injustice: Power and the Ethics of Knowing* (Oxford: Clarendon Press, 2007).
Kristie Dotson, "Tracking Epistemic Violence, Tracking Practices of Silencing," *Hypatia* 26, no. 2 (2011): 236–257.
And, for more on the value of anger and other emotions in activism, see:
Marilyn Frye, "A Note on Anger," in *The Politics of Reality: Essays in Feminist Theory* (Berkeley, Crossing Press, 1983): 84–94.
Audre Lorde, "The Uses of Anger: Women Responding to Racism," in *Audre Lorde, Sister Outsider* (Berkeley, Crossing Press, 1984): 124–133.
Maria Lugones, "Hard-to-Handle Anger," in *Maria Lugones, Pilgrimages: Theorizing Coalition against Multiple Oppressions* (New York: Rowman & Littlefield Publishers, 2003): 103–121.

43 This paragraph draws from a paragraph in:
     Jeff Sebo, "Multi-issue Food Activism," in Anne Barnhill, Mark Budolfson, and Tyler Doggett, eds., *The Oxford Handbook of Food Ethics* (Oxford: Oxford University Press, 2018).
     For more on this topic, see:
     "Summary of Evidence for Foundational Questions in Effective Animal Advocacy," Sentience Institute, February 6, 2018, www.sentienceinstitute.org/foundational-questions-summaries#left-wing-vs.-nonpartisan-focus.
44 Thank you to Jay Shooster for discussion on this point.

11 The ethics of illegal food activism

11.1 Introduction

This chapter will close our discussion of the ethics of food, animals, and the environment by examining the ethics of illegal food activism. If a particular industry causes unnecessary harm to humans, nonhumans, and the environment, are we ever morally permitted or required to break the law in the course of resisting this industry? We will start by discussing whether we have a moral obligation to obey the law at all, and whether we can ever be morally permitted or required to break it. We will then consider the nature and ethics of different kinds of illegal activism, including civil disobedience, property destruction, violence, and terrorism. Finally, we will consider the relevance of social labels. In particular, in a society that labels many non-violent, non-terrorist activities as violent terrorism, what kind of stance should activists take toward such activities? These questions are difficult to answer, in part because they raise questions about the nature of violence and terrorism, and in part because they raise questions about actual and apparent values.

11.2 Civil disobedience

Consider first whether we have a moral obligation to obey the law at all. Note that we considered the flip side of this question in Chapter 8. In that earlier discussion, our question was whether an action can be morally wrong despite being legal. In this discussion, our question is whether an action can be morally right despite being illegal. We need to start here because our answer to this question will affect our assessment of different kinds of illegal activism later on.

Some people think that we do have a moral obligation to obey the law. Where does this moral obligation come from? We will consider three possible answers, adapting a framework from A. John Simmons.[1]

First, according to **the justice view**, we have a moral obligation to obey the law because of the *consequences* of doing so. In particular, the state provides us with many benefits, for example it protects us from a stateless society in which life would be, as Thomas Hobbes writes, "solitary, poor, nasty, brutish, and short."[2] And the state can play this role only if citizens play our part; that is, only if we uphold the rule of law and the broader social, political, and economic systems on which the rule of law depends. Thus, we might think that we have a moral obligation to obey the law because (a) we have a moral obligation to uphold justice, and (b) typically, we are more likely to uphold justice if we obey the law than if we do not.

Second, according to **the transaction view**, we have a moral obligation to obey the law because of a certain *transaction* we make with the state, or with our fellow citizens. In particular, the state provides us with many benefits, and these benefits place us in a relationship with the state that calls for certain actions on our part as well. Thus, for example, we might think that we have a moral obligation to obey the law as a matter of (a) *reciprocity* (the state helped me, so I should follow its rules as a way of *repaying* it), (b) *gratitude* (the state helped me, so I should follow its rules as a way of *thanking* it), or (c) *promise-keeping* (the state helped me, and in accepting its help I agreed to follow its rules, so I should do that).

Third, according to **the association view**, we have a moral obligation to obey the law because of a certain *association* that we have with our fellow citizens. In particular, we have relationships of care and interdependence with our fellow citizens, and these relationships are mediated and made possible by the state. Thus, we might think that we have a moral obligation to obey the law because (a) we identify with and care about our fellow citizens, (b) we have a moral obligation to uphold the social, political, and economic systems that make our identities and associations possible, and (c) typically, we are more likely to uphold these social, political, and economic systems if we obey the law than if we do not.

These views are not mutually exclusive. If we accept more than one of these ideas, then we might think that we have a moral obligation to obey the law for more than one of these reasons. Still, *even if* we accept all of these ideas (which, of course, not everybody does), it does not follow that *we all* have a moral obligation to obey *all* laws *all* the time. Instead, it might simply follow that *some of us* have a moral obligation to obey *some* laws *some* of the time. In particular, there are at least two reasons why people might sometimes be morally permitted or required to break the law on these views.

First, we might think that there can be *exceptions* to our obligation to obey the law, that is, cases where we do not have a moral obligation to obey the law at all. For example, we might think that we do not have a moral obligation to obey laws that are clearly unjust; for instance, if a law prohibits same-sex relationships, we might think that we do not have a moral obligation to obey this law, all else equal. Similarly, we might think that we do not have a moral obligation to obey laws in situations for which the laws are clearly not intended; for instance, if a law prohibits driving through red lights, we might think that we do not have a moral obligation to obey this law when we are on a desert road with nobody around for miles. In both kinds of case, the general idea is that we can be morally permitted to break the law because doing so is compatible with the deeper obligations that normally generate a moral obligation to obey; that is, in both kinds of case, breaking the law is compatible with upholding justice; repaying, thanking, or keeping our promises to the state; and/or maintaining the systems on which our relationships depend.

Second, we might think that there can be *obligations that override* our obligation to obey the law, that is, obligations to *break* the law that take priority over our obligation to obey the law. In some cases, we might have a moral obligation to break the law that comes from a different source than our moral obligation to obey the law. For example, if you need to drive over the speed limit in order to take a dying child to the hospital, you might think that you should do so because, in this case, your obligation of assistance to the child is stronger than your obligations of justice, transaction, or association to the state or your fellow citizens. In other cases, we might have a moral obligation to break the law that comes from the same source as our moral obligation to obey the law. For example, if you need to trespass on private property in order to collect information regarding a grave injustice, you might think that you should do so because, in this case, you can uphold justice; repay, thank, or keep your promises to the state; and/or maintain the systems on which your relationships depend more effectively if you break the law than if you follow it.

In part for these reasons, some philosophers are skeptical that many people have a general moral obligation to obey the law at all. For example, Tommie Shelby argues that many people in the U.S. are morally permitted to break the law (assuming that they can do so without violating any independent moral obligations they have), since the state treats them unjustly, and therefore the considerations in favor of obedience do not apply to them.[3] After all, why should you have a general moral obligation to uphold a system that oppresses you? Indeed, we might wonder, why should anyone have a general moral obligation to uphold a system that oppresses anyone?

Similarly, **anarchists** argue that everyone is morally permitted to break the law (assuming that we can do so without violating any independent moral obligations we have), since the state has a monopoly on power, and therefore the considerations in favor of obedience do not apply to anyone. Yes, some of us might receive benefits from the state and make promises to the state. But if we did not ask for those benefits, and if we did not make those promises of our own free will (which we might not have, if we think that promises made in the context of great power differentials are coerced and therefore invalid), then these interactions do not generate an actual moral obligation to obey the law.[4]

If we deny that we have a moral obligation to obey the law for one or more of these reasons, does that mean that we should go around breaking the law all the time? Not necessarily. Even if we deny that we have a moral obligation to obey the law *as such*, we might still think that we should follow the law for other reasons. For example, the state has a lot of power over us, and it often matters more that we avoid punishment than that we break the law. Also, many of the things that the state tells us to do are independently good; for example, if the state tells us not to murder people, we should follow this law because murder is independently wrong. Finally, many of the things that the state tells us to do are solutions to coordination problems; for example if the state tells us to drive on the right side of the road, we should do that because we can expect that other people will be doing it too, and we should do what other people are doing in this kind of case.

Suppose, then, that we accept that there are at least *some* cases in which we are morally permitted or required to break the law, for one or more of these reasons. This raises the further question: When and how should we go about breaking the law in practice? This question is especially pressing for activists, since they might often encounter situations in which there seems to be a conflict between, on one hand, their reasons for obeying the law and, on the other hand, their reasons for breaking it. So, what kind of disobedience, if any, is ethically ideal, and why?

Many people answer this question by invoking the idea of **civil disobedience**. Civil disobedience has a storied history. We associate it with people like Mahatma Gandhi and Martin Luther King Jr., as well as with historical events including the Boston Tea Party, the U.K. and U.S. suffrage movements, and the Vietnam war protests.[5] Thinking about many of the people who have engaged in civil disobedience throughout history, we admire their bravery and appreciate their role in bringing about a more just society. But what is civil disobedience, and does it really merit the special moral status that many people take it to have?[6]

Different people offer different, if overlapping, answers to these questions. We can start by considering the aspects of civil disobedience that many people agree about. In particular, political philosopher Kimberley Brownlee offers a starting definition of civil disobedience that many people seem to agree about: "Civil disobedience involves a conscientious . . . breach of law designed to demonstrate condemnation of a law or policy and to contribute to a change in that law or policy."[7] Consider each of the main parts of this starting definition in turn.

First, according to this starting definition, civil disobedience involves a *conscientious breach of law*. This means that you have to be breaking the law *deliberately* and for *moral reasons*. For example, you might think that the tax code is unjust. But if your reason for not paying your taxes is simply that you forgot about the deadline, or that you want to keep your money, then your action does not count as conscientious, and therefore does not count as civil disobedience on this view.

Second, according to this starting definition, civil disobedience must *aim to demonstrate condemnation of a law or policy*. This means that your action must have an *expressive* aim: It must aim at communicating disapproval of a particular law. Thus, for example, if you refuse to pay your taxes on the grounds that you think that the tax code is unjust, but you have no expectation that anyone will notice your action or interpret it as expressing this moral judgment, then your action does not count as civil disobedience on this view.

Third, according to this starting conception, civil disobedience must *aim to contribute to a change in that law or policy*. This means that your action must have a *practical* aim: It must aim at bringing about a change in the relevant law. Thus, for example, if you refuse to pay your taxes on the grounds that the tax code is unjust, but you have no expectation that your action will make a difference regarding the tax code, then your action does not count as civil disobedience on this view either (instead your action is more like conscientious objection).

Some people also think (unsurprisingly, given the name) that *civility* is an important part of civil disobedience. What does civility mean in the context of illegal activism? Here, briefly, are seven answers people have offered to this question. Your illegal activism counts as civil to the degree that you (1) break the law only as a last resort, (2) break only laws that you are attempting to change, (3) break the law with regulatory/reformist aspirations, (4) break the law in a conciliatory manner rather than in a confrontational manner, (5) break the law openly rather than secretly, (6) accept punishment for your crime, and/or (7) break the law in a non-violent manner rather than in a violent manner.[8]

Why do people think that breaking the law civilly is ethically ideal? The answer is that civility can help to balance out the inherently uncivil nature of breaking the law. This can make for a powerful combination of messages: When we engage in illegal activism civilly, we show that we care about a particular cause enough to break the law, as well as that we care about the law enough to break it respectfully. Thus, some people think, civil disobedience is ethically better than other kinds of disobedience in principle as well as in practice: better in principle because it causes less disruption and violates fewer obligations, and better in practice because it sends a more relatable message to the public, and therefore allows us to communicate our ideas and contribute to a change in law more effectively.

However, not everybody believes that we should always restrict ourselves to civil disobedience, so understood. In particular, many people think that activists should take in whatever kind of approach will be most effective, and that while civil disobedience might *sometimes* be most effective, it might not *always* be. Instead, if activists want to communicate our ideas and contribute to a change in law most effectively in practice, we might sometimes need to (1) break the law as a first resort (or at least not as a last resort), (2) break laws other than those we are attempting to change, (3) break laws with abolitionist/revolutionary aspirations, (4) break laws in a confrontational manner, (5) break laws secretly, and/or (6) evade punishment for our crimes. (Some people are also open to (7) breaking the law violently in cases of self- or other-defense, though this point is more controversial for reasons we will discuss below.)

Why do people think that breaking the law uncivilly is sometimes best? The answer is that, as we discussed in the previous chapter, civil/conciliatory approaches can sometimes end up supporting the status quo more than they disrupt it, thereby doing more harm than good in the long run. (When it comes to openness and acceptance of punishment, civil disobedience can also increase the personal risk involved with illegal activism.) As a result, uncivil/confrontational approaches might sometimes be necessary for disrupting the status quo enough to shift the center of debate and pave the way for real change. (When it comes to secrecy and evasion of punishment, uncivil disobedience can also decrease the personal risk involved in illegal activism.) Thus, some people think, we should be open to incivility in the context of legal as well as illegal activism (even if not as much in the latter context since illegality is already, to a degree, uncivil).[9]

Which if either argument is correct? As with other divisions in the ethics of activism, civil and uncivil disobedience are not necessarily binary or mutually exclusive options. There are different kinds and degrees of each (e.g., you can satisfy more or fewer criteria for civility, and you can satisfy them to greater or lesser degrees), and we might think that a balance of approaches is best. In particular, when disobedience is called for at all, we might think that civility is sometimes best, that incivility is sometimes best, and that a mixed approach is sometimes best. However, we should emphasize that incivility carries risks. In particular, once an activist starts breaking the law uncivilly, they make it easier for people to label them as "militant" or "violent" whether or not they are.[10] As a result, while non-violent uncivil disobedience is certainly possible, it can be hard to reliably come across this way in practice. This underscores the strategic value of civil disobedience, and it also raises questions about actual and apparent values that we will consider in the next section.

With that in mind, we can now consider a few examples of disobedience in the food movement that aspire to a relatively high degree of civility, and consider the strengths and limitations of these approaches. We will then, in the next section, consider less civil approaches.

First, consider **open rescues**. In an open rescue, an activist illegally enters a facility that harms or kills animals and removes one or more of the animals there. They then arrange for these animals to receive medical attention and place them in homes or sanctuaries. Open rescues are clearly illegal: The activist is not only trespassing on property but also stealing property (since animals have the legal status of property[11]). In some jurisdictions they might be breaking other laws as well, as we will discuss below. However, activists engaging in open rescues try to be as civil as possible beyond that. They do not destroy property unless, for example, they need to break a lock. They also do not wear masks and, in fact, often record the entire act (this is why activists describe open rescues as *open*). And in these recordings, they explain their reasons for liberating these animals in a reasonable and relatable manner.[12]

The thinking behind open rescue is that it not only saves a small number of animals in the short term (similar to breaking the law to save the dying child above) but also raises awareness about animal agriculture in the long run (similar to breaking the law to protest an unjust law above). Meanwhile, the *open* part of open rescue underscores how seriously activists take animal liberation (since they are risking their own freedom by rescuing animals openly) and ensures that their actions will be more relatable. And while openness does increase risk of prosecution, many people have been reluctant to press charges, since a public trial could do them more harm than good. However, recently some people have become more willing to press charges in cases involving open rescue. As a result, activists now face a tougher choice between, on one hand, performing rescues fully openly so that they can be as relatable as possible, and, on the other hand, performing rescues at least partly secretly so that they can remain free and active in resistance.[13]

Second, consider **undercover investigations**. In an undercover investigation, an activist works undercover in a facility that harms or kills animals so that they can collect evidence about what happens there, and then bring this evidence to the media or law enforcement. Undercover investigations might or might not always be illegal (since higher courts might or might not always see them as illegal), but local legislatures, local law enforcement, and lower courts often treat them as illegal, which carries many of the same risks. For example, in the U.S., the federal Animal Enterprise Terrorism Act makes it illegal to engage in many activities that interfere with animal enterprise, and many state-based "ag-gag" laws make it illegal to secretly document abuse in the agricultural industry.[14] However, as with open rescues, activists engaging in undercover investigations often try to be as civil as possible beyond that. For example, they carry out this activity with the aim of collecting legally and politically useful information, they treat everyone with respect throughout the investigation, and they often reveal their identities when the investigation is complete.[15]

For many, the thinking behind undercover investigations is that sunlight is the best disinfectant: If people see what happens in the agricultural industry, they will be more likely to want change.[16] And if activists take a civil approach to collecting and sharing this information, then their actions will once again be more relatable. However, as with open rescues, undercover investigations can place activists at risk of prosecution, which raises questions about whether or not people should always engage in them openly. Undercover investigations also raise ethical questions, since investigators often have to participate in harmful behavior in order to maintain cover. Thus we have to ask difficult questions about complicity, harming the few to help the many, and the demandingness of morality in order to evaluate this practice. But generally speaking, if we think that undercover investigations are necessary for social change and that the ends can sometimes justify the means, then we should think that undercover investigations can sometimes be morally permissible even if activists have to cause harm in order to maintain cover.

Third, consider **disruption**. Disruption can include many different kinds of activity, ranging from chanting inside a restaurant or supermarket to sitting in a tree designated for clearing. As with investigation, disruption might or might not always be illegal, but local legislatures, local police, and lower courts often treat them as illegal in practice, which carries many of the same risks. And, as before, activists engaging in disruption often try to be as civil as possible beyond that. They deliver their message peacefully, they are open about their identities, and they accept the consequences of their actions. Moreover, even if activists engaging in disruption resist arrest, they typically do so passively: For example, an activist chanting in a restaurant or supermarket might refuse to leave when asked and a tree sitter might refuse to come down when asked (since, after all, staying put for as long as possible is part of the idea), but they will typically not fight back when police or security remove them from the space (except perhaps in rare cases involving clear and minor acts of self-defense).[17] With that said, while many people engage in relatively civil disruption, many people engage in relatively uncivil disruption as well, as we will discuss in a moment.

For many, the thinking behind disruption is that it raises awareness about the practice in question and places pressure on those participating in the practice in question. And if activists take a civil approach to disruption, they will be more relatable (though there is a limit to how relatable one can be when one disrupts standard practices with a controversial message). However, disruption does involve risks, including risk of arrest, assault, punishment, and negative publicity. Of course, activists might conclude that the benefits of disruption outweigh these risks in particular cases. But if they want to arrive at this conclusion responsibly, then they have to be thoughtful about many issues, including what kind of public narrative their action might be used to support and what the impacts of this public narrative might be. (We will return to this point later on.) As with investigation, disruption also raises ethical questions, since activists might be disrupting good as well as bad activities; for example if they block traffic, then they might be disrupting access to schools, offices, hospitals, and more. Thus we must ask whether or not activists can be morally permitted or required to disrupt good activities as a means to, or as a side-effect of, protesting bad activities.[18]

These kinds of actions are about as close to paradigmatic cases of civil disobedience as we can find in the food movement. Not only are they principled breaches of the law meant to express condemnation of industrial animal agriculture and contribute to a change in that practice, but they also typically err on the side of conciliation, openness, and acceptance of punishment (with some exceptions, as we have seen). Given the social context in which food activism often occurs, it makes sense that activists often see these kinds of disobedience as striking the right balance between (a) disrupting standard practices enough to raise awareness about industrial animal agriculture and pressure producers and consumers to make changes, and (b) not disrupting standard practices so much that the activists cause unnecessary harm to themselves, others, or the state. But two points. First, even these kinds of actions might involve at least *some* incivility. Second, as we discussed above, even if civility is often pragmatically best, it might not always be.

11.3 Property destruction, violence, and terrorism

We will now consider the ethics of property destruction, violence, and terrorism, with special emphasis on the ethics of non-violent, non-terrorist actions that society labels as violence and terrorism.

Will Potter reports that, in 2005, FBI deputy assistant director John Lewis told a Senate subcommittee that the animal and environmental movements were the "number one domestic terrorism threat" in the United States, and that "there is nothing else going on in this country, over the last several years, that is racking up the high number of violent crimes and terrorist actions."[19] Interestingly, in a nation with regular mass shootings, the animal and environmental movements accomplished this feat without injuring anyone at all. What did they do instead?

Most animal and environmental activists engage in typical legal activism. Relatively few also engage in the kinds of civil disobedience described above. And, relatively very few also engage in less civil disobedience. For example, activists in the Animal Liberation Front (ALF) and Earth Liberation Front (ELF) use what they call non-violent property destruction to prevent harm to animals and the environment. In particular, ALF and ELF activists break into facilities that harm animals and the environment, destroy the equipment that people use to cause harm there, and, in some cases, engage in rescue and investigation too. Through it all, they "take all necessary precautions against harming life."[20]

Do any animal and environmental activists push still further, and injure or kill people as part of their activism? According to Potter, the answer is virtually always no. While a very small number of animal and environmental groups do support such tactics, even these groups do not seem to actually injure people. Indeed, Potter reports that a detailed search of so-called "eco-terrorism" crimes revealed only one clear act of violence: an assault that caused non-lethal injuries to one person in England.[21] This search did not reveal any clear acts of violence in the United States at all (unless you count throwing a banana cream pie at someone as a clear act of violence, in which case there have been a few).[22]

Of course, this is not to say that animal and environmental activists are beyond reproach in these respects. Tactics such as property destruction do occupy an uneasy middle ground between clear violence and clear non-violence. This is especially true of property destruction that involves arson, which might not be *intended* to harm anyone, and which might not *actually* harm anyone, but which still carries more *risk* of harm than other, more surgical methods do. So, to what degree are these middle ground cases morally relevantly similar to clear violence and to what degree are they morally relevantly similar to clear non-violence?

In order to answer these questions, we must clarify a number of conceptual and normative issues.[23]

Start with **property destruction**. This tactic, as employed by groups such as the ALF and the ELF, combines elements from several past movements that many people now value, at least in isolation and in retrospect. For example, the liberation aspect (which shares features with the open rescues considered above) draws inspiration from the Underground Railroad, which facilitated the liberation and relocation of formerly enslaved people in the United States. The documentation aspect (which shares features with the undercover investigations considered above) draws inspiration from early twentieth-century muckrakers such as Upton Sinclair, who first exposed the horrors of industrial food production.[24] And the property destruction aspect (a more extreme kind of disruption, considered above) draws inspiration from many sources, ranging from the Boston Tea Party in the pre-revolutionary United States to the anti-Nazi resistance movement during World War II in Germany.

When animal and environmental activists reference past resistance movements, they are not trying to suggest that these movements are at all the same, or that the issues that they are addressing are at all the same. There are many differences in all cases, and these should always be noted. Instead, animal and environmental activists reference past resistance movements in order to remind us that we are not *always* opposed to tactics such as property destruction. Yes, we are very often skeptical of these tactics not only because they break the law and cause disruption but also because they can cause psychological or economic harm to law-abiding citizens. However, as consideration of past resistance movements shows, we also think that at least *some* practices can be so deeply harmful, and so deeply wrong, that tactics such as property destruction can sometimes be an acceptable means for resisting them. This raises the question: While our food system is very different from the systems that past resistance movements were addressing, is it nevertheless harmful or wrong enough that tactics such as property destruction can sometimes be an acceptable means for resisting it?

When we consider past harmful systems with the benefit of distance and hindsight, it can be easy to think that the answer to this question is yes. However, when we consider present harmful systems without these benefits, it can be harder to draw this conclusion. For example, you might not be sure how helpful or harmful the relevant systems are. Or, you might not be sure how helpful or harmful the relevant tactics are. Or, you might be so deeply entangled in the relevant systems that you have an easier time connecting to the risks of the relevant tactics than to the benefits. Or, you might be so deeply angry with the relevant systems that you have an easier time connecting to the benefits of the relevant tactics than to the risks. In light of all this, you might not know what to think. Of course, this is reasonable. Given that we lack the clarity about present issues that we have about past issues, caution and humility are appropriate. At the same time, one never has complete clarity at the time of action, and caution and humility can sometimes serve as rationalizations for inaction. The challenge, then, is to do the best we can with the information we have available.

With that in mind, what do people say in favor of and against property destruction as a means to resisting industrial animal agriculture? The argument in favor of this tactic is as follows (and is similar in structure to the argument in favor of food activism that we considered in the previous chapter): First, factory farms and slaughterhouses are very bad. They harm and/or kill vast numbers of animals; consume vast amounts of natural resources; and produce vast amounts of pollution. Second, if you can prevent something very bad without sacrificing anything comparably morally significant, then you are morally permitted, if not morally required, to do so. Third, activists can sometimes prevent factory farms and slaughterhouses from operating by engaging in property destruction. Fourth, since property destruction is non-violent (it targets objects, not subjects), activists are not sacrificing anything comparably morally significant when they use this tactic to prevent violence. Thus, activists are sometimes morally permitted, if not morally required, to use property destruction to prevent factory farms and slaughterhouses from operating.

However, there are principled as well as pragmatic objections to this argument. The main principled objection (which we can treat as a response to the claim that property destruction does not sacrifice anything comparably morally significant) is that property destruction is not, as proponents claim, non-violent.

Instead, property destruction is both violent and terrorist. Simply put, when you blow something up, you are perpetrating violence. And, when you blow something up in a way that instills fear in law-abiding citizens, you are perpetrating terrorism. And of course, violence and terrorism are morally wrong independently of how much good the perpetrators might be doing as a result. Thus, property destruction, as a kind of violence and/or terrorism, is morally wrong independently of how much good the activists might be doing as a result. (We will consider whether property destruction really is violence and/or terrorism, as well as whether violence and/or terrorism really are always wrong, below.)

Meanwhile, the main pragmatic objection to this argument in favor of property destruction (which we can treat as a response to the claim that activists can prevent factory farms and slaughterhouses from operating if they engage in property destruction) is that property destruction does more harm than good. First of all, this tactic will not necessarily shut down the targeted corporation. Instead, in many cases the corporation will simply absorb the cost or shift the cost to the public. Moreover, even if property destruction *does* achieve this result, it will still not necessarily prevent harm to animals or the environment. Instead, in many cases a different corporation will simply replace the relevant corporation and cause the same amount of harm.[25] Finally, even if property destruction *does* prevent harm to animals and the environment, it might still cause more harm in the long run than it prevents in the short term. After all, activists who engage in property destruction might inspire other activists to engage in property destruction too, but for worse causes and in worse ways. They might also alienate the public, since the public tends to see property destruction as violence and terrorism whether or not it is, especially if the public is not yet convinced that the relevant cause is just.

One issue that complicates this discussion is that not everybody who engages in property destruction does so in an ideal manner. For example, some activists break equipment aggressively; record grainy, shaky-cam footage of this behavior; set this footage to angry, angsty music; and then publish this footage together with angry, poorly written communiqués. Needless to say, this kind of property destruction is far from ideal. However, the concerns that we have about this kind of property destruction might not fully extend to other, more civil and professional kinds of property destruction. For example, imagine an activist who approaches property destruction in the same kind of way that activists often approach open rescues or undercover investigations. Yes, they break the law, and yes, they destroy property (which, admittedly, is already quite uncivil). But they try to be as civil as possible beyond that. They destroy only items that are used to harm or exploit others, they destroy these items calmly and deliberately, they record high-definition footage of this behavior, and then they publish this footage together with reasonable, well-written explanations and justifications. Would we have the same reservations about this kind of property destruction that we have about other, less ideal kinds?

Another issue that complicates this discussion, however, is that even if we support relatively civil property destruction in theory, we might not have reason to

236 The ethics of illegal food activism

expect that activists will engage in this kind of property destruction in practice. For example, we might worry that if we frame property destruction as acceptable at all, then at least some people will take an uncivil approach to this tactic, and then these will be the cases that receive the most media attention, with negative impacts for the movement. We might also worry that, even if people aspire to take a relatively civil approach to property destruction, this tactic requires too much risk, speed, and secrecy to allow for the kind of civility that open rescues and undercover investigations allow for. (And of course, one might have to aspire to an even higher standard of civility in this case in order to offset a higher baseline level of incivility.) To the degree that these worries are warranted, the implication would be that ideal property destruction is unrealistic, and so the choice that activists face in the real world is between non-ideal property destruction and no property destruction at all. And to the degree that this is the choice that activists face, the pragmatic case against property destruction becomes stronger (without necessarily being decisive).[26]

Of course, a defender of industrial animal agriculture might also take issue with premises 1 and 2 of the argument above; that is, they might also take issue with the idea that factory farms and slaughterhouses are very bad and that if you can prevent something very bad from happening without sacrificing anything comparably morally significant, then you are morally permitted, if not morally required, to do so. We have already considered these issues in previous chapters, and we will consider the latter issue in further detail below, so we can set them aside here.

As we have seen, part of the principled case against property destruction is that property destruction is violence and/or terrorism, and is therefore morally wrong independently of how much good it does. This raises several questions: What are violence and terrorism, and what are the ethics of violence and terrorism, especially in the context of animal and environmental activism? These questions matter not only because they illuminate the nature and ethics of property destruction but also because the nature and ethics of violence and terrorism are independently important topics.

With that in mind, what is **violence**? Here is a somewhat narrow starting definition that many people find plausible: We act violently when we attempt to physically harm others against their will. (For rationalists, "others" might refer to rational beings. For sentientists, it might refer to sentient beings. For biocentrists, it might refer to living beings. And so on.) This conception of violence captures paradigmatic cases well. For example, if I punch you in the face against your will, I act violently against you. However, people disagree about whether we should extend the concept of violence to cover other, less paradigmatic cases as well. Here, for example, are three questions about the scope of violence that are relevant for our purposes.[27]

First, should we restrict violence to *intended* harm, or should we extend it to *foreseeable* harm as well? On one hand, we might think that we should extend the concept at least somewhat, since at least some foreseeable harms are intuitively violent. For example, if you throw your hands up during an argument (not in order to hit anybody, but rather only in order to express anger), and you accidentally hit someone, do we really want to say that your action was non-violent? On the other hand, we might think that we should restrict the concept at least somewhat too, since many foreseeable harms are intuitively non-violent. For example, if you throw your hands up during a dance (not in order to hit anybody, but rather only in order to dance), and you accidentally hit someone, do we really want to say that your action was violent?

Second, should we restrict violence to *physical* harm, or should we extend it to *psychological* harm as well? On one hand, we might think that we should extend the concept at least somewhat, since at least some psychological harms are intuitively violent. For example, if you call someone a racist or sexist slur and threaten to kill them, with the result that they live in constant fear for their physical safety, do we really want to say that your words were non-violent? On the other hand, we might think we should restrict the concept at least somewhat too, since many psychological harms are intuitively non-violent. For example, if you call someone a racist or sexist and threaten to boycott them, with the result that they live in fear for their economic safety, do we really want to say that your words were violent?

Third, should we restrict violence to *harm to subjects*, or should we extend it to *damage to objects* as well? On one hand, we might think that we should extend the concept at least somewhat, since at least some damage to objects are intuitively violent. For example, if you hit the wall with a hammer during an argument (not in order to hit anybody, but rather only in order to express anger), do we really want to say that your action was non-violent? On the other hand, we might think that we should restrict the concept at least somewhat too, since a lot of damage to objects is intuitively non-violent. For example, if you hit the wall with a hammer during a home renovation (not in order to hit anybody, but rather only in order to demolish your wall), do we really want to say that your action was violent?

How should we answer these questions? There are costs and benefits either way. On one hand, if we use "violence" in a narrow sense, it will be more likely to retain its force, but it will also apply to fewer activities. For example, we might be able to say that violence is always wrong but not that property destruction is always violent (since property destruction might intentionally damage objects and foreseeably psychologically harm subjects, but it might not intentionally or physically harm subjects at all). On the other hand, if we use "violence" in a wide sense, it will apply to more activities, but it will be less likely to retain its force. For example, we might be able to say that property destruction is always violent but not that violence is always wrong (since intentionally damaging objects and foreseeably psychologically harming subjects are sometimes but not always wrong). Similar observations apply for other activities that people often label as violent, such as relatively uncivil disruption: Depending on which conception of violence we use, either these actions will count as non-violent or they will count as violent but not necessarily as morally wrong.[28]

In any case, suppose that we select a conception of violence that we think strikes this balance well. It implies that most intuitively violent actions are violent and that most intuitively non-violent actions are non-violent. Should we then say that violence is always wrong? Or should we say that violence is sometimes permissible or required?

As always, the answer to this question depends on which moral theory we accept and the details of the case. For example, many Kantians deny that we can permissibly use violence as a means to maximizing utility. However, this does not necessarily mean that they deny that we can permissibly use violence in activism. Why? Because some Kantians think that violence can be morally permissible in cases of self- or other-defense, and they might think that at least some activists face the choice whether or not to use violence in self- or other-defense. For example, suppose that you see a man attempting to torture a cat in an alley, and the only way you can make him stop is by punching him in the face. At least some Kantians would classify the act of punching this man in the face to save the cat as a morally permissible case of violence in other-defense, rather than as a morally impermissible case of violence for the greater good. Now suppose that you see a man attempting to torture *tens of thousands of cats* in a factory, and the only way you can make him stop is by punching him in the face. What should a Kantian say about this case? Should they classify the act of punching this man in the face as a morally permissible case of violence in other-defense, or should they classify it as a morally impermissible case of violence for the greater good? This is a challenging question, in part because it implicates many other questions as well, for example about how these harms and benefits are related to each other.[29]

In contrast, utilitarians think that if violence will maximize utility, then we are not only morally permitted but also morally required to use violence for the greater good. The question for utilitarians, then, is whether violence will, in fact, maximize utility. Some people think the answer is sometimes yes. For example, Ward Churchill argues that violence is sometimes necessary to bring about change, especially in cases where many people are willing to use violence to prevent change.[30] However, other people think the answer is no. Why? For the same reasons as with property destruction, but even more so. First, violence will not necessarily stop the relevant activity. Second, even if it does, it will not necessarily prevent harm to animals or the environment. Finally, even if it does, it will not necessarily do more good than harm in the long run. After all, as Paulo Freire argues, when activists respond to violence with violence, they perpetuate the cycle of violence and risk influencing others to do the same.[31] They also risk alienating the public, since violence in agriculture is legal and normalized whereas violence in activism is illegal and stigmatized, and so the general public is likely to have selective outrage about violent activism. Thus, when activists engage in violence, they make it easier for people to mistakenly see them as distinctively violent, with lasting consequences for their movements.

What about virtue, care, and relational theorists? What they would say about this question depends a lot on the details of the theory as well as the details of the case. A virtue theorist will ask: Would a virtuous person engage in violence in this case? As part of answering this question, they might consider virtues such as respect (which might guide them in a Kantian direction), sympathy (which might guide them in a utilitarian direction), and many others besides. Similarly, a care theorist or relational theorist will ask: What kind of history or relationship do I have with everyone involved, and what kinds of meanings would violence and non-violence have in this context, in light of these histories and relationships? As part of answering this question, they might consider personal relationships (I care about this person as well as about these animals), political relationships (I am fellow citizens with this person, I am in a position of power or domination over this animal[32]), and many others besides. Without attempting to explore all the details here, we can predict that, as with Kantians and utilitarians, many virtue theorists, care theorists, and relational theorists will likely regard violence as morally permissible in at least some cases (for example, cases that clearly involve self- or other-defense and where we are accountable to those who need protection), but will likely regard violence as morally impermissible in most if not all cases that ordinary activists are likely to encounter (if for no other reason than that violence will rarely if ever clearly do more good for those who need protection).

Regardless of which framework we use to assess the ethics of violence, it is important to keep perspective. Given what the world is like, we will likely not be able to find a conception of violence that vindicates our intuitions about violence *and* our hope that violence is out of the ordinary. As Mark Vorobej writes, "We all live lives that are, to an extraordinary extent, mired in violence."[33] Thus, the ethics of violence is about more than whether or not we should ever engage in violence in self- or other-defense. It is also, more centrally, about how we should cope with the fact that we already participate in violence simply in virtue of being alive. Of course, depending on which moral theory we accept, we might or might not think that there are morally relevant differences between causing and allowing violence, or between doing so directly or indirectly. Still, our complicity in violence matters not only for its own sake, but also as essential context for any conversation about the ethics of violence in activism.

Relatedly, what is **terrorism**? We can ask many of the same questions about terrorism that we asked about violence (but with even higher stakes). With that in mind, here is a somewhat narrow starting definition of terrorism that many people find plausible: Terrorism is the use of violence, or the threat of violence, against innocent individuals as a means of creating fear in the general population, for social, political, or economic purposes.[34] As with our narrow definition of violence, this narrow definition of terrorism captures paradigmatic cases well. For example, if I kill 100 innocent people as a means to creating civic unrest for political purposes, I am engaging in terrorism. However, people disagree about whether we should extend the concept of terrorism to cover other, less paradigmatic cases as well. Here, for example, are three questions about the scope of terrorism that are relevant for our purposes.[35]

First, should we restrict terrorism to violence or threats of violence against *innocent individuals*, or should we extend it to violence or threats of violence against *anybody*? On one hand, we might think that we should extend the concept at least somewhat, since otherwise terrorism will be too subjective. For example, suppose that I attack your group as a means of creating fear for political purposes, and you do the same with my group. In this case we would each be performing the same kind of action, yet we would each see the other group as terrorists and our own group as freedom fighters, since we would each see the other group as guilty and our own group as innocent. This makes the idea of terrorism easy to exploit for political propaganda.[36] On the other hand, we might think that we should restrict the concept at least somewhat too, since otherwise we risk obscuring the distinctive strategic logic of terrorism. There is an important difference between targeting truly guilty individuals and targeting truly innocent individuals, and, we might think, the concept of terrorism is useful in part because it emphasizes that difference.

Second, should we restrict terrorism to actions intended to create fear in *the general population* (i.e., people other than the individuals targeted with violence or threats of violence) or should we extend it to actions intended to create fear only in *the target population* (i.e., the individuals targeted with violence or threats of violence)? As before, on one hand we might think that we should extend the concept at least somewhat, since otherwise we might miss many intuitive cases of terrorism. For example, suppose that I attack you in order to make you fear me, for political purposes. Do we really want to say that this is not a case of terrorism, simply because the person I attacked is the same as the person I was aiming to create fear in? On the other hand, we might think that we should restrict the concept at least somewhat too, since, as before, otherwise we risk obscuring the distinctive strategic logic of terrorism. There is an important difference between aiming to create fear in a single person and aiming to create general civic unrest, and, we might think, the concept of terrorism is useful in part because it emphasizes that difference.

Third, should we restrict terrorism to actions that *intentionally* create fear as a *means* to our ends, or should we extend it to actions that *foreseeably* create fear as a *side-effect* of bringing about our ends? Once again, on one hand we might think that we should extend the concept at least somewhat, since otherwise we might miss many intuitive cases of terrorism. For example, if I kill people for political purposes, with the foreseeable but unintended consequence that I also create civic unrest, do we really want to say that this is not a case of terrorism? On the other hand, we might think that we should restrict the concept at least somewhat too, since otherwise we risk obscuring the distinctive strategic logic of terrorism. There is an important difference between creating fear as a means to bringing about change and creating fear as a side-effect of bringing about change, and, we might think, the concept of terrorism is useful in part because it emphasizes that difference.

How should we answer these questions? As before, there are costs and benefits either way. On one hand, if we use "terrorism" in a narrow sense, it will be more likely to retain its force, but it will also apply to fewer activities.

For example, we might be able to say that terrorism is always wrong but not that property destruction is always terrorism (since property destruction might foreseeably psychologically harm guilty or innocent subjects, yet it might not intentionally or physically harm anyone at all). On the other hand, if we use "terrorism" in a wide sense, it will apply to more activities, but it will be less likely to retain its force. For example, we might be able to say that property destruction is always terrorism (assuming that property destruction always involves violence or the threat of violence, which, as we saw above, it might not) but not that terrorism is always wrong. Similar observations apply for other activities that people often label as terrorism, such as relatively uncivil disruption: Depending on which conception of terrorism we use, either these actions will not count as terrorism or they will count as terrorism (again, assuming that they involve violence or the threat of violence) but not necessarily as morally wrong.

In any case, suppose that, as before, we find a conception of terrorism that we think strikes a good balance. It implies that most intuitively terrorist actions are terrorist and that most intuitively non-terrorist actions are non-terrorist. Should we then say that terrorism is always wrong? Or should we say that terrorism is sometimes permissible or required?

Most moral theorists will evaluate terrorism in the same kind of way as violence, though with a recognition that the stakes are typically much higher for terrorism than for violence (at least on narrow conceptions of these concepts). A lot will depend on whether or not the relevant action involves violence toward, threats of violence toward, or creation of fear in innocent individuals—though, again, which individuals are innocent will likely be a disputed matter. A lot will also depend on whether or not the activist performs the relevant action in self- or other-defense (which is easier to imagine for violence than for terrorism, though not impossible to imagine for terrorism) as well as on whether or not the relevant action will likely do more good than harm overall (which is also easier to imagine for violence than terrorism, though not impossible to imagine for terrorism). If this is right, then in general we can say that terrorism is to violence what violence is to property destruction: *maybe* possible to defend in principle (depending on how we assess the relevant conceptual and normative issues), but *much harder* to defend in practice, since it involves much more potential harm for all involved, including the activists and everyone they represent, the targets and everyone they represent, and many others as well.

However, as with violence, it is important to keep perspective. Industrial animal agriculture inflicts physical and psychological harm on billions of nonhuman animals per year to maximize profit. As we have seen, industry and state actors also threaten activists with criminal prosecution in order to intimidate them into silence. Thus, as with the ethics of violence, the ethics of terrorism is about more than whether we should ever inflict physical and psychological harm on others for our own purposes. It is also, and more centrally, about how we should cope with the fact that we already are. Granted, we might or might not think that creating fear in farmed animals or in animal and environmental activists counts as terrorism (that will depend on our conception of terrorism and the details of the case). Still, as before, the physical and psychological harms that occur within and around industrial animal agriculture are morally important not only for their own sake, but also as essential context for any conversation about the ethics of terrorism in activism.

This point relates to our discussion of actual and apparent values in earlier chapters. In a social context that frames some harms as normal (and, therefore, as non-violence/non-terrorism) and others as deviant (and, therefore, as violence/terrorism), it can be easy for people to see animal and environmental activists as violent terrorists (in spite of the fact that they are not actually injuring or killing anyone) and the people they target as innocent victims (in spite of the fact that they are injuring and killing countless individuals). Moreover, as in previous chapters, this issue interacts with identity, privilege, and oppression in complicated ways. For example, people with privilege will often feel tempted to publicly denounce so-called "militant" activists so that they can work with business and political leaders to bring about reforms. Yet people with privilege will also often be in the best position to support so-called "militant" activists in a way that will be taken seriously and will not be personally risky.

As we discussed in the context of legal activism in the previous chapter, this adds a layer of complication to our analyses here: It means we have to ask not only whether we should engage in or support *actual* violence or terrorism (the answer to this question will almost certainly be no, at least on narrow conceptions of violence and terrorism) but also whether we should engage in or support non-violent, non-terrorist actions that are often *labeled* as violence or terrorism. In this way, activists are once again often placed in a difficult double bind, since, on one hand, if we engage in or support such actions, we will make it easier for others to label us as terrorists or terrorist sympathizers, and we will alienate people as a result. Yet if we refuse to engage in or support such actions, we will allow others to set the terms of debate, and we will risk closing the door on essential strategies for change (even non-violent, non-terrorist ones!) as a result.

Finally, suppose we agree that we should not engage in or support violence or terrorism, on narrow conceptions of violence or terrorism. Should we tolerate people who do in our movements? Fortunately, as we have seen, this is currently a hypothetical question in the animal and environmental movements, since these movements currently have near universal consensus on the impermissibility of violence and terrorism, on narrow conceptions. Here we might have a reason to draw a line and make it clear that violence and terrorism are never acceptable in our movements. As for violence or terrorism on wide conceptions, or non-violent, non-terrorist actions that society labels as violence and terrorism, this is likely to be a contextual matter. But at least in some contexts, as tempting as it might be to insist that these "militant" tactics are unacceptable too, we have at least some reason to resist that temptation and challenge these labels instead, so that we can have a broader conversation about which harms are, and are not, most urgently in need of moral attention in society.

11.4 Conclusion

One might expect that questions about the ethics of legal food activism would be more relevant to the average food activist than questions about the ethics of illegal food activism. In a sense, this is true. After all, even if we think that certain illegal tactics are sometimes permissible, we might also think that most activists should follow the law most of the time. But in another sense, this is false. As we have seen, some of the most pressing ethical issues involving illegal activism concern not whether to engage in it (though some of these questions are pressing as well) but rather what kind of public stance, if any, to take toward it. It can be tempting—and it might often be right—for activists to make ourselves relatable by distancing ourselves not only from violence and terrorism but also from a much wider range of illegal actions, including civil disobedience. But if there are costs and risks associated with this act of distancing, then activists should think carefully about our stance on illegal activism, whether or not we engage in it ourselves.

Notes

1 A. John Simmons, "Civil Disobedience and the Duty to Obey the Law," in R.G. Frey and Christopher Heath Wellman, eds., *Blackwell Companion to Applied Ethics* (Oxford: Blackwell Publishing, 2007): 50–61.
2 Thomas Hobbes, *Hobbes's Leviathan reprinted from the edition of 1651 with an Essay by the Late W.G. Pogson Smith* (Oxford: Clarendon Press, 1909): 97.
3 Tommie Shelby, *Dark Ghettos: Injustice, Dissent, and Reform* (Boston: Harvard University Press, 2016).
4 For more on the position that the state does not have legitimate authority no matter how well it treats people, see:
   Robert Paul Wolff, *In Defense of Anarchism* (Berkeley: University of California Press, 1970).
5 For relevant work by Gandhi and King, see:
   Mahatma Gandhi, "Non-violence," in Jeffrie Murphy, *Civil Disobedience and Violence* (Bellmont: Wadsworth Publishing, 1971): 93–102.
   Martin Luther King Jr., "Letter from the Birmingham Jail," in Martin Luther King Jr., ed., *Why We Can't Wait* (New York: Signet, 2000).
6 For more on the philosophy of civil disobedience, see:
   Kimberley Brownlee, *Conscience and Conviction: The Case for Civil Disobedience* (Oxford: Oxford University Press, 2012).
   Carl Cohen, *Civil Disobedience: Conscience, Tactics, and the Law* (New York: Columbia University Press, 1971).
7 Kimberley Brownlee, "Civil Disobedience," *The Stanford Encyclopedia of Philosophy*, Edward N. Zalta ed., https://plato.stanford.edu/entries/civil-disobedience/.
8 For discussion of the value of civility in civil disobedience, see:
   Kimberley Brownlee, "Civil Disobedience," *The Stanford Encyclopedia of Philosophy*, Edward N. Zalta ed., https://plato.stanford.edu/entries/civil-disobedience/.
   Ned Hettinger, "Environmental Disobedience," in Dale Jamieson, ed., *A Companion to Environmental Philosophy* (Hoboken: Blackwell, 2003): 498–509.

9 Iris Marion Young, "Activist Challenges to Deliberative Democracy," *Political Theory* 29, no. 5 (October 2001): 670–690.
10 For more on attempts to frame non-violent activity as terrorism, see:
  Lauren Gazzola, "Bad Things Happened: Metaphorical Fingerprints, Constellations of Evidence, and 'Guilt *for* Association'," *Vermont Law Review* 40, no. 4 (2015): 813–920.
  Will Potter, *Green Is the New Red* (San Francisco: City Lights Publishers, 2011).
11 For more on the legal status of animals, see:
  Steven Wise, *Rattling the Cage: Towards Legal Rights for Animals* (Cambridge: Da Capo Press, 2000).
  David Wolfson and Mariann Sullivan, "Foxes in the Hen House: Animals, Agribusiness, and the Law: A Modern American Fable," in Cass Sunstein and Martha Nussbaum, eds., *Animal Rights: Current Debates and New Directions* (New York: Oxford University Press, 2004): 205–233.
12 For more on liberations, see:
  Karen Davis, "Open Rescues: Putting a Face on the Rescuers and on the Rescued," in Steven Best and Anthony J. Nocella, eds., *Terrorists or Freedom Fighters? Reflections on the Liberation of Animals* (New York: Lantern Books, 2004): 9–64.
13 For examples of cases in which open rescuers have encountered legal trouble, see:
  Glenn Greenwald, "The FBI's Hunt for Two Missing Piglets Reveals the Federal Cover-Up of Barbaric Factory Farms," *The Intercept*, October 5, 2017, https://theintercept.com/2017/10/05/factory-farms-fbi-missing-piglets-animal-rights-glenn-greenwald/.
  Jesse McKinley, "Two Missing Ducks, a Video and a Felony Charge in an Episode at a Foie Gras Farm," *The New York Times*, February 22, 2015, www.nytimes.com/2015/02/23/nyregion/amid-foie-gras-controversy-an-activist-faces-a-felony-charge-in-poaching-of-ducks.html.
14 For more on the Animal Enterprise Terrorism Act, see:
  Will Potter, *Green Is the New Red* (San Francisco: City Lights Publishers, 2011).
15 For an ethnographic study of a slaughterhouse that resulted from an investigation, see:
  Timothy Pachirat, *Every Twelve Seconds* (New Haven: Yale University Press, 2011).
16 For a defense of the idea that sunlight is the best disinfectant, see:
  Michael Pollan, *The Omnivore's Dilemma* (New York: Penguin Random House, 2006): 226–238.
  For a critique of this idea, see:
  Timothy Pachirat, *Every Twelve Seconds* (New Haven: Yale University Press, 2011): 233–256.
17 For discussion of disruption, both civil and uncivil, see:
  Freeman Wicklund, "Direct Action: Progress, Peril, or Both?" in Steven Best and Anthony J. Nocella, eds., *Terrorists or Freedom Fighters? Reflections on the Liberation of Animals* (New York: Lantern Books, 2004): 237–251.
18 For a defense of blocking traffic in the context of Black Lives Matter, see:
  Jeanne Theoharis, "MLK Would Never Shut Down a Freeway, and 6 Other Myths About the Civil Rights Movement and Black Lives Matter," *The Root*, July 15, 2016, www.theroot.com/mlk-would-never-shut-down-a-freeway-and-6-other-myths-1790856033.
19 Will Potter, *Green Is the New Red* (San Francisco: City Lights Publishers, 2011): 44–45.
20 Will Potter, *Green Is the New Red* (San Francisco: City Lights Publishers, 2011): 47.
  For more on the Animal Liberation Front, see:
  Steven Best and Anthony J. Nocella III, eds., *Terrorists or Freedom Fighters? Reflections on the Liberation of Animals* (New York: Lantern Books, 2004).
  For more on the Earth Liberation Front, see:

Steven Best and Anthony J. Nocella III, eds., *Igniting a Revolution: Voices in Defense of the Earth* (Edinburgh: AK Press, 2006).

Much of the discussion in this section is informed by the helpful introductions to these books.

21 Will Potter, *Green Is the New Red* (San Francisco: City Lights Publishers, 2011): 48.
22 Will Potter, *Green Is the New Red* (San Francisco: City Lights Publishers, 2011): 49.

As Potter discusses, there is one documented case of attempted violence in the United States, but this attempt was not only unsuccessful, but was also later revealed to have been orchestrated by a "counterterrorism" firm called Perceptions International (51).

23 For sociological discussion of property destruction and sabotage, see:
David Naguib Pellow, *Total Liberation: The Power and Promise of Animal Rights and the Radical Earth Movement* (Minneapolis: University of Minnesota Press, 2014).
24 Upton Sinclair, *The Jungle* (New York: Doubleday, 1906).
25 Thank you to Lauren Gazzola for helpful discussion on this point.
26 For a similar real-world critique of property destruction, see:
Kim Stallwood, *Growl: Life Lessons, Hard Truths, and Bold Strategies from an Animal Advocate* (New York: Lantern Books, 2014): 13–170.
27 For more on the philosophy of violence, see:
Hannah Arendt, *On Violence* (London: Penguin, 1970).
C.A.J. Coady, "The Idea of Violence," *Journal of Applied Philosophy* 3, no. 1 (1986): 3–19.
R.G. Frey and Christopher Morris, eds., *Violence, Terrorism, and Justice* (New York: Cambridge University Press, 1991).
John Harris, *Violence and Responsibility* (London: Routledge, 1980).
Gene Sharp, *The Politics of Nonviolent Action* (Boston: Porter Sargeant, 1973).
28 For further discussion of how pragmatic considerations can guide our usage of concepts, see:
Sally Haslanger, "Ontology and Social Construction," *Philosophical Topics* 23, no. 2 (1995): 95–125.
Sally Haslanger, *Resisting Reality: Social Construction and Social Critique* (Oxford: Oxford University Press, 2012): Chapter 6.
29 For more on the ethics of violent animal activism from a deontological perspective, see:
Blake Hereth, "Animal Rights Terrorism and Pacifism" (*unpublished manuscript*).
30 Ward Churchill, *Pacifism as Pathology* (Oakland: PM Press, 2017).
31 Paulo Freire, *Pedagogy of the Oppressed* (trans. Myra Bergman Ramos) (New York: Continuum, 1970): 147–152.
32 For discussion of the difference between power and domination in human–nonhuman relationships, see:
Clare Palmer, "'Taming the Wild Profusion of Existing Things'? A Study of Foucault, Power, and Human/animal Relationships," *Environmental Ethics* 23, no. 4 (2001): 339–358.
33 Mark Vorobej, *The Concept of Violence* (Abingdon: Routledge, 2016) quoted in:
Francesca Raimondi, "The Concept of Violence," *Notre Dame Philosophical Reviews*, October 6, 2016, https://ndpr.nd.edu/news/the-concept-of-violence/.
34 For related discussion of the nature of terrorism, see:
Will Potter, *Green Is the New Red* (San Francisco: City Lights Publishers, 2011): Chapter 3.
35 For more on the philosophy of terrorism, see:
Fritz Allhoff, *Terrorism, Ticking Time-bombs, and Torture: A Philosophical Analysis* (New York: Columbia University Press, 2012).
Francis Kamm, *Ethics for Enemies: Terror, Torture and War* (New York: Oxford University Press, 2013).

Will Potter, *Green Is the New Red* (San Francisco: City Lights Publishers, 2011): 35–61.

Igor Primoratz, "Terrorism," *The Stanford Encyclopedia of Philosophy*, Edward N. Zalta ed., https://plato.stanford.edu/entries/terrorism/.

Anne Schwenkenbecher, *Terrorism: A Philosophical Enquiry* (Basingstoke: Palgrave Macmillan, 2012).

36 For more on the philosophy of propaganda, see:

Jason Stanley, *How Propaganda Works* (Princeton: Princeton University Press, 2015).

12 Conclusion

At this point in our discussion, one can be forgiven for feeling a bit hopeless. We have seen that industrial animal agriculture is responsible for harming 100+ billion animals; consuming vast amounts of land, water, and energy; and producing vast amounts of waste, pollution, and greenhouse gas emissions each year. Alternative food systems are promising but involve trade-offs. Moreover, the questions that these impacts raise for food production, consumption, and activism are daunting. We are dealing with a global collective action problem that makes our individual efforts seem both futile and demanding. In light of all this, is it even worth holding out hope for a solution?

The ethics of hope is an important topic in its own right.[1] Food, animals, and the environment might seem to be one of many areas of life where the attitude that seems theoretically best (i.e., the attitude that seems most supported by our evidence) is different from the attitude that seems practically best (i.e., the attitude that seems most productive given our aims). In this case, for instance, we might think that despair is theoretically best and that hope is practically best. If so, what kind of attitude should we attempt to cultivate all things considered? Should we aim for theoretical rationality at all costs, should we aim for practical rationality at all costs, or should we aim to balance these types of rationality somehow?[2]

A further question is what kind of attitude would, in fact, be practically best. Too much hope and too little hope both carry risks. On one hand, if we have too much hope, then we might not feel the urgency of our present situation. Instead we might find it tempting to make a few modest lifestyle changes and then sit back and wait for the world to improve. On the other hand, if we have too little hope, then we might not see the point of trying to change anything. Instead we might find it tempting to try to enjoy life as much as possible while we sit back and wait for the world to fall apart.

We, the authors of this book, are not sure exactly what kind of response is best, theoretically or practically. However, we would not have written this book if we were tempted toward either of these extremes. Throughout this book, we have examined some of the greatest challenges that our species faces, but we have also examined some of the greatest prospects for change that our species has encountered. For better or worse, the next few decades will be transformative, and we are currently in a position to help shape in what direction the world transforms.

However, if we want to be able to play that role, the crucial first step is seeing the problem for what it is, and seeing pat solutions for what they are— empty gestures whose only function is to make us feel better about ourselves. The situation might not be hopeless, but we will not be warranted in feeling hope until we accept that radical individual, collective, and structural change is required. This is part of why we wrote this book: so we can help people (ourselves included) see the scale, scope, and complexity of the problem clearly enough to push past pat solutions (or fatalistic inaction) and start the more difficult search for real solutions.

How we frame these issues will play an important role in this discussion. Are we focusing on humans, nonhumans, and the environment equally? Are we making sure to consider the costs and benefits of natural and artificial systems evenly? Are we considering not only the local costs and benefits of particular food systems but also the global costs and benefits of combinations of food systems, given the need to feed 7+ billion humans?

How imaginative we allow ourselves to be will play an important role in this discussion too. We are living in a new global epoch, during which old ways of thinking, feeling, and being might no longer be appropriate. Identifying and pursuing new ways of being that fit our new situation will require creativity, experimentation, and a willingness to challenge and disrupt social, political, and economic structures that many people still take for granted.

Interwoven with the need for imagination is the need for better stories about food, animals, and the environment. We know the story of negative impacts all too well. Humans often respond equally well if not better to positive stories of progress and hope—we need to craft motivating stories of food systems that promote justice, celebrate culture, benefit humans and nonhumans, and enhance (or have a light footprint on) the environment.

What might these positive visions look like? Our relationships with each other, nonhumans, and the environment can take many forms. Farm sanctuaries can provide us with a model for how to build new human–nonhuman communities that treat everyone with respect and compassion.[3] Meanwhile, we are only starting to realize the potential of many edible plants, as well as of new products such as plant-based meat and cultured meat.

As we have seen, there will necessarily be conflicts and tensions along the way. For instance, consumer activism can have many individual and collective benefits, since it can support alternative food systems, promote the need for alternative food systems, and reinforce the importance of distant and diffuse problems. At the same time, it can also carry individual and collective costs, since, if not done carefully, it can easily be ineffective, alienating, and unsustainable.

Similar tensions arise for other kinds of activism. Radical and moderate approaches each carry costs and benefits. There are good arguments for some approaches being best across the board, and there are also good arguments for different approaches being best in different contexts. Deciding which approach is best for particular individuals in particular contexts is a difficult and fraught matter. Deciding when to insist on our own preferred approach and when to allow for a plurality of different, seemingly conflicting approaches is a difficult and fraught matter as well.

Fortunately, our understanding of food, animals, and the environment has advanced dramatically in the past few decades. This includes our awareness of both the wonders of the natural world and the harms that we cause within it. This awareness makes it easier to appreciate the need to address these harms and improve the state of the world. We hope that, with the right kind of approach, we can translate this appreciation into large-scale collective action.

Notes

1 For more on the ethics of hope in the context of environmental issues, see:
   Andrew Brei, ed., *Ecology, Ethics, and Hope* (London: Rowman & Littlefield, 2016).
2 For more on these questions about theoretical and practical rationality, see Derek Parfit, *Reasons and Persons* (Oxford: Oxford University Press, 1984), 12–13.
3 Sue Donaldson and Will Kymlicka, "Farmed Animal Sanctuaries: The Heart of the Movement?" *Politics and Animals* 1, no. 1 (Fall 2015): 50–74.

Index

Locators in *italics* refer to figures.

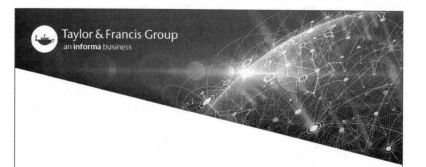